Visions of Jesus

Visions of Jesus

Direct Encounters from the
New Testament to Today

Phillip H. Wiebe

OXFORD UNIVERSITY PRESS

New York   Oxford

Oxford University Press

Oxford   New York

Athens   Auckland   Bangkok   Bogotá   Bombay   Buenos Aires
Calcutta   Cape Town   Dar es Salaam   Delhi   Florence   Hong Kong
Istanbul   Karachi   Kuala Lumpur   Madras   Madrid   Melbourne
Mexico City   Nairobi   Paris   Singapore   Taipei   Tokyo   Toronto

and associated companies in
Berlin   Ibadan

Library of Congress Cataloging-in-Publication Data
Wiebe, Phillip H., 1945–
Visions of Jesus: direct encounters from the
New Testament to today / Phillip H. Wiebe
p. cm.   Includes bibliographical references and index.
ISBN 0-19-512669-6 (Pbk.)
1. Jesus Christ—Apparitions and miracles.   2. Visions.
I. Title.
BT580.A1W54   1997   248.2'9—dc21   96-39445

1 3 5 7 9 8 6 4 2

Printed in the United States of America

Contents

Preface

Vision and apparition experiences in which people believe they encounter Jesus Christ have been reported among Christians for two thousand years. The original Christian belief in the resurrection of Jesus was based primarily upon experiences in which followers thought they had seen him in some posthumous form, for the mere disappearance of his body could hardly have given rise to this belief. Christic visions continue to be experienced by people living today—among laity and clergy, Catholics and Protestants, devout and casual believers, old and young, women and men, well and poorly educated, and among those who "believe in" visions as well as those not predisposed to do so.

The purpose of this book is to examine this phenomenon. I direct much of my attention toward thirty people who described their experiences to me. For some, the experience takes place in an altered state of consciousness as the familiar world of which they are a part suddenly disappears and another "reality" seems to descend upon them. For others, the Christic figure enters their ordinary lives and is superimposed, as it were, on their world. A few even say that this has been witnessed by groups. The information available challenges many stereotypes about the Christic visionary experience, and poses difficult questions about their explanation. It also brings an important perspective into the work of the scholars who have wondered what events, if any, might lie behind the stories found in biblical literature.

The contemporary visionaries who claim to see Jesus attach

no great significance to the places where the experiences occur, unlike those who experience apparitions of the Virgin Mary. Lourdes, Fatima, and now Medjugorje, are legendary because of the Marian apparitions reported there. But there are no shrines of comparable popularity that commemorate apparitions of Jesus. The significance of Christic visions and apparitions seems to be felt primarily in the enriched religious lives of those who experience them.

This study would not have been possible without the cooperation of the persons who allowed me to interview them about their experiences. I gratefully acknowledge their contributions, which are presented in Chapter 2.

I have benefited from the encouragement and critical comments of friends and colleagues in undertaking this study and writing this book. I wish to thank Sarah Coakley, Doug Chaffee, Gary Colwell, Bob Doede, Craig Evans, Philip Gosselin, Irving Hexham, Hugo Meynell, Ron Philipchalk, Karla Poewe, Chris Rowland, Richard Swinburne, Judy Toronchuk, Don Wiebe, and Carol Zaleski. All have read my work at one stage of its development, and have offered helpful comments. I gratefully acknowledge the expert guidance of Cynthia Read, Executive Editor at Oxford University Press, and copyeditor, Norma McLemore.

This project could hardly have been completed without the research grant that I received from my university, as well as the sabbatical leave during 1993. This leave, combined with the hospitality of the University of Oxford, allowed me to write much of this book. I gratefully acknowledge the generosity of my university, the kindness of Sarah Coakley and Richard Swinburne at Oxford, and the opportunity afforded me by Laurie Brown, also at Oxford, to address the Alister Hardy Centre for the Study of Religion about Christic visions.

My family has been patient with me during this research project. I take pleasure in acknowledging the support of my wife, Shirley, and of my children.

Visions of Jesus

Introduction

Jim Link was watching a movie on television one evening in his home in Newmarket, Ontario, when the screen suddenly became invisible. The first thought that occurred to him, which he knew to be absurd, was that maybe he had watched so much television that he had become blind! He next realized that he was unable to hear the television set, and he thought, "Have I been watching so much TV that it is affecting my vision and my hearing?" He stood up to look out of the window next to him just to make sure his eyesight was still intact, but he couldn't see the walls. It seemed as though he was enclosed in a curtain, but he couldn't really see a curtain. A human figure then came into view at the end of the room, starting with an outline that became clearer and clearer, until he could see someone wearing long robes and sandals. He wondered, "What's going on here? Who is this? What is this?" The figure turned to face Jim, extended an arm, and beckoned him three times to come to him. Jim immediately thought to himself, "That is Jesus!" and the lines came to him from the New Testament, "Come to me all you who are weak and heavy laden, and I will give you rest." He thought to himself, "It's real, then, it's real. I have to ask for forgiveness and repent and receive him." At that instant everything in the room returned to normal, and he decided to become a Christian.

The figure that Jim saw was of average height, and seemed to be situated about fifteen to eighteen feet away. The robe that the figure wore was a dark blue or a purplish blue, Jim was not sure. What impressed Jim most was the royalty of the appea-

3

ance and the way the figure welcomed him. The figure wore a hood that prevented its face from being seen, so Jim could not report anything about facial features. Jim had been wondering about the meaning of life, what his purpose in life was, and whether he was just on earth to work and maintain a home and watch television! He had been attending church with his wife, just to please her, but having this experience, at twenty-seven years of age, changed his outlook on life.

Jim had another experience in 1977, some fifteen years later, one evening after a Bible study in the home of his brother-in-law. He was sitting at the kitchen table, just having had coffee and something to eat. He discovered that as he tried to get up he was unable to move. He turned to tell his brother-in-law sitting several feet away about this sudden inability to move, but he could not see him. All he could see was the face of one he took to be Jesus "from sort of three-quarters of the way down his forehead to just below his chin, just as clear as you're sitting there right now." The radiant or glowing figure seen as Jesus had a beard and brown shoulder-length hair, and looked like the popular images of Jesus in pictures. Just to convince himself that he was seeing something genuine, Jim looked away and then looked back again to see if the figure still was there, and he was able to do this several times. Jim was the only one in the room who could see him, however. As he got up a few minutes later to go home, he was flattened by a force that pinned him to the floor. For about three hours he was interrogated by this being about what he valued most—his job, his family, his wife, his possessions, and so on. The others in the group watched in awe but said nothing. They heard Jim's responses, but not the questions that were put to him. His brother-in-law wanted to come over to him to pray with him, Jim reported, but could not do so—it was as if an invisible line had been drawn across the floor that he could not cross. Jim describes the second experience as having confirmed his decision earlier in life to be a Christian. Jim does some oil painting as a hobby, and in the front entrance of his home hangs a painting of a biblical scene in which he tried to capture the likeness as he had seen it.[1]

What are we to make of experiences like these? Do these visions have no more ontological importance than nocturnal dreams? Was Jim only imagining the figure that seemed as real as life? Was he experiencing what

Catholic theology describes as an imaginative vision, produced by an angel or by some similar spiritual being? Was it, alternatively, what Catholic theology describes as a corporeal vision, involving the use of the eyes? Were these "appearances" of Jesus comparable to the appearances described in the New Testament (NT)? Were these experiences similar to the many apparitions reported by psychical researchers during the last one hundred years? Was Jim momentarily insane, as he expected others to think, and experiencing the hallucinations of insanity? Do such experiences suggest a transcendent source of some kind, or can the conceptual resources of the maturing neurosciences be counted on to explain them? These are some of the many questions that such reports evoke.

"Visual encounters" with a being taken to be Jesus have been reported since the earliest days of Christianity. In fact, the Christian belief that Jesus was resurrected seems to have been based largely upon the reports of appearances of him after his apparent death by crucifixion, for the report of an empty tomb by itself would hardly have given rise to the Resurrection belief. Christic visions and apparitions have been reported during the entire history of the Christian church, but little critical study of their characteristics and evidential significance has been undertaken in recent years. The central purpose of this book is to describe and critically reflect on the phenomenon of Christic visions and apparitions, particularly the experiences reported to me by living visionaries.

Reasons for Studying Christic Visions and Apparitions

Karl Rahner remarked several decades ago that a critical examination of apparitions (in general) in Christian history had yet to be undertaken,[2] and this seems to be true with specifically Christic apparitions as well. Although many studies of religious experience have been conducted since William James's seminal work, *The Varieties of Religious Experience*, Christic apparitions have not been the focus of much critical attention. Marian apparitions (apparitions of the Virgin Mary), by contrast, have been well studied, both by those within the Christian church for whom such experiences have spiritual significance and by sociologists interested in religious phenomena.[3] G. Scott Sparrow's recent study of various Christic encounters, including visions and apparitions, is a rare attempt to describe the range of Christic experiences; he also mentions that they have not been extensively studied.[4] It seems clear that certain kinds of visionary experiences have religious significance, although these visions and apparitions need not be interpreted this way. Experiences generally considered to have religious significance are those that give intimations of a transcendent dimension to life, give meaning to life, awaken the moral sense in a person, or evoke a sense of the Infinite.[5] Christic apparitions have obvious religious significance when evaluated in this light, and deserve to be studied along with other kinds of religious experiences.

Deirdre Green argues that theistic mysticism, of which Christic apparitions would be one kind, has been neglected in the Christian church, compared with monistic mysticism.[6] Monistic mysticism, according to Green, sees the ultimate goal of religious life as ascent to the contemplation of the formless Divinity. This kind of contemplation uses no ideas or images, but understands God as different from anything else in our experience (the *via negativa* approach). Theistic mysticism, by contrast, focuses on a personal God known in a loving relationship and conceived in an anthropomorphic form. Green observes that theistic mysticism was largely rejected by Christian mystics such as John of the Cross and Meister Eckhart who knew both forms, although it was of course ardently embraced by such famous visionaries as Teresa of Avila and Julian of Norwich. This study, then, investigates a kind of experience that seems to have been neglected, at least within the Christian church. It should be noted that Jewish mysticism is generally understood to include visionary experiences. One scholar defines mysticism in the Jewish tradition as "diversified forms of direct realizations of divine presences, whether on earth or in heavenly domains."[7] I will not generally describe the experiences under scrutiny in this book as mystical, except where the usage of others requires it. I prefer to use the term *mystical* to refer to experiences without perceptual content, in keeping with a well-established convention in philosophical writing.[8]

A second reason for undertaking this study is to explore the possibility that contemporary phenomena might contribute to the understanding of the NT accounts of the post-Resurrection appearances and visions of Jesus. For well over a century scholars have closely examined these NT accounts, but little attention has been given to the possibility that present-day visionary experience might provide help in understanding them. There are exceptions of course. Michael Perry considers in *The Easter Enigma* the relevance of paranormal phenomena to biblical claims, and Wolfhart Pannenberg mentions in *Jesus—Man and God* the possibility that parapsychological phenomena might shed light on the visionary experience. Carol Zaleski recently made a similar point about the relevance of near-death experiences (NDEs) to theological views. She remarks that for scholars of religion and theologians to refuse to examine the near-death literature "is only to widen the gap between academic theology and popular religious concerns. The result is a loss for both sides; not only does the public lose the benefit of historically informed discussion, but theology is deprived of a potentially revitalizing connection to contemporary experience."[9] Extra-biblical literature that describes Christic visions, such as early gnostic writings and the devotional literature of Christendom, might also be illuminated by the study of contemporary Christic visions.

Another reason for undertaking this kind of study is related to the common belief that religious experience is evidentially relevant to belief in God. One popular argument for the existence of God is the argument from religious experience. This argument in its simplest form contends that the best explanation for certain kinds of experience widely understood to be religious in character is that they are produced by God. Richard Swinburne, perhaps the best-known present-day philosopher defending the rationality of Christian theism, recently endorsed this argument as one among a number of important probabilistic arguments.[10] Caroline Franks Davis has also defended the value of the argument from religious experience, although she is speaking to a general theism, rather than specifically Christian belief.[11] She considers six categories of experience as supportive of theistic belief, including quasi-sensory, visionary, revelatory, interpretive, regenerative, and numinous experience, drawing her examples from Buddhism, Christianity, Hinduism, and Islam.

Caution should be exercised in arguing for an obvious and strong connection between Christic visions and the existence of God. Opponents of theism evidently reject the claim that religious experience provides impressive evidential support for theism; they may grant that such experience occurs but deny its cogency for theism. It is possible that the relation between religious experience and theistic belief has been misconstrued by theists; alternatively, it is possible that the supposed lack of evidential support arises from the fact that not enough evidence has been collected. In that case, this study and others like it could contribute to our knowledge of experiences that have probative force for theism.

Another reason for caution in linking Christic visions and the existence of God is that various theories concerning the relationship between Jesus and God have been propounded by Christians of the first few centuries and by various philosophers and theologians whose views have been considered heretical or marginally tolerable by the Christian communities. One could come to believe, for instance, that Jesus was resurrected and still exists, but not believe that one Supreme Deity exists. In view of the gap between the Resurrection belief and Christian theism, one could take a more modest view of the evidential value of apparition experiences. Janice Connell, writing of the Marian apparitions reported at Medjugorje, says that their significance is broadly metaphysical: "The great illusion that the world of the senses is the only reality is gradually being eroded by the shared testimonies . . . of spiritual realities so powerful that people are willing to give their reputations, their fortunes, even their lives, in defense of a transcendent reality they claim they have experienced."[12] Christic apparitions could be viewed as having similar potential to erode a materialistic world view and to advance a broadly transcendent one. At the very least we can say that Christic visions and apparitions belong to a group of experiences widely considered to have some evidential import for transcendent interpretations of the universe.

Yet another reason for undertaking this study arises from the possibility that all of the experiences to be discussed are wholly subjective (or hallucinatory) and therefore provide information about one important kind of altered state of consciousness. Just what constitutes a hallucination is a matter of considerable dispute, but it is readily conceivable that Christic apparitions, like other apparitions, are best understood using the theoretical constructs of modern psychology. Anthropologist Weston La Barre writes that "there is no 'supernatural' psychic event in tribal life anywhere that may not be better understood as a dissociated state—whether endogenous dream, vision, trance, REM state, sensory deprivation, hysteric 'possession'—or as an hallucinatory activity of the brain, under the influence of exogenous psychotropic substances."[13] If such an appraisal of apparition experiences should turn out to have the greatest plausibility, then detailed descriptions of the experiences themselves would give us important information about one kind of human experience, which the neurosciences would then need to explain.

I have chosen to direct my attention to present-day experiences for two central reasons. The first is that many of the reports that have been advanced in the history of Christianity are essentially devotional literature, and as such generally include neither the attention to detail nor the critical evaluations that characterize studies that attempt to be exact and objective. Though some visionaries, such as Teresa of Avila or Julian of Norwich, do include self-critical remarks and provide a fair amount of detail, they are the exception. A review of the many accounts of Christic visions found in Brewer's *A Dictionary of Miracles*, Walsh's *The Apparitions and Shrines of Heaven's Bright Queen*, or *I Saw the Lord* by the Huyssens provides ample evidence of a general lack of detailed description or criticism. Sparrow provides some detail in his accounts of recent experiences, and thus makes a useful contribution to a description of the phenomenon.

The second reason for directing my attention to current experience is that it *appears* to have an evidential force that older material lacks. I advance this reason with some tentativeness because it touches on controversial and unresolved issues in the assessment of confirming evidence. This can be illustrated by comparing a biblical account of a post-Resurrection appearance with a brief account of another contemporary Christic apparition.

Luke 24:36-43 describes an incident in which Jesus was seen by his disciples soon after his Resurrection. In order to alleviate their doubts and fears that he might be just a spirit, Jesus instructed them to feel his flesh and bones, and he then ate some food. If recent nonliteral interpretations of this story are set aside, and the traditional view that Luke narrates an event is accepted, many questions are still left unanswered. One might wonder about Luke's source for this event, since he himself does not seem to have been present. If Luke's source was the terrified disciples, who apparently believed in ghosts, their reliability as reporters might be suspect. Questions could also be raised about the reliability of memories or oral histories during the thirty- or forty-year lapse between the alleged event and the time Luke wrote it down. Finally, one might wonder about the view of the world that Luke and his contemporaries shared, what criteria for factual correctness they held to, what ontological assumptions they uncritically accepted, and so on. The sheer temporal distance between us and the early Christians who circulated the original stories—more than nineteen hundred years—provides ample opportunity for doubts, many of which can never be allayed.

Compare this event with one described by Christian psychiatrist John White. He says that as he prayed with some friends, he saw the arms and hands of Christ extended toward him. He says that his eyes were open, that he was fully aware of his surroundings, and that his experience was in three dimensions and full color.[14] White and his account are still available for critical scrutiny in a way that Luke and his narrative are not. That White intended his description to be the report of a historical event can be established beyond reasonable doubt, but given the kind of criticism developed with respect to gospel "narratives" in the last century or so, Luke's intentions might not be. We can probably establish White's standards of factual correctness, given his availability for questioning and his training as a doctor and psychiatrist, but we are significantly hampered in trying to determine the standards of "physicians" in Luke's day. Authoritative views can be formed about the kind of world view that White endorses, both by reading his work and talking with him, but comparable information about Luke is a matter of guesswork. The plethora of critical views among biblical scholars demonstrates the caution with which the gospel accounts must be approached.

Even if we should decide that contemporary accounts are inauthentic, more in them can be critically examined than in those ancient accounts that lie beyond our grasp. Philosophers who have studied the nature of confirming evidence generally hold that no difference exists in *evidential* force between descriptions of ancient events and modern ones, and they might well be correct, but there certainly is a difference in *psychological* impact. Whatever the explanation of the difference might be, some greater evidential potency seems to lie in more recent phenomena, and I accordingly direct my attention primarily to them.

Scope of the Present Study

Because of the importance that "visual encounters" with Jesus have had in the Christian faith, both at its inception and in its subsequent history, I have decided to narrow my focus to experiences of primarily a visual kind. The people I have sought out believe (1) that they were awake at the time of their experience, (2) that their eyes were open, and (3) that it was Jesus who appeared to them. Many other kinds of experiences might be considered Christic, both by those undergoing them and by theologians evaluating their significance. Among these are dreams in which people encounter Jesus, out-of-the-body experiences (OBEs) in which people believe they saw Jesus, NDEs in which people believe they met Jesus, experiences in which people sense what they take to be the presence of Jesus but do not see anything, experiences in which statues of Jesus are thought to move, to sweat, or to shed tears,[15] and Christian conversion experiences.[16] I do not include any of these kinds of experience in my study, nor do I include auditory and other nonvisual perceptual experiences, except as they accompany visual ones. This list of exclusions alone gives an indication of how rich and varied such religious experiences are. I am restricting my attention in keeping with a methodological suggestion once made by William James and more recently advocated in a study of psychokinesis by philosopher Stephen Braude, that human qualities are best studied in their extravagant manifestations so that their moderate instances can be seen as instances of the extreme.[17]

A question arises concerning the most appropriate term or terms to describe the phenomena I am examining, if in fact just one or two terms should be used for that purpose. Perhaps these phenomena should not be grouped together, even though they bear more than superficial similarity to one another, because they might belong to different causal orders. Some of the experiences, for instance, took place in what appeared to percipients to be a different physical location from where they thought themselves to be, while other experiences took place in surroundings that were familiar to percipients in every way except for the figure that appeared to them. To use the same term to describe these phenomenologically different experiences is potentially misleading because the explanations for them might ultimately be quite different. I have nevertheless chosen to use the terms *vision* and *apparition* interchangeably, leaving open the possibility of different classifications for the various kinds of phenomena.

The terms I have chosen are not without difficulties, but other possible terms are problematic in their own way. *Hallucination* is generally taken to refer to experiences that are subjective in character, whereas *appearance* carries the connotation that the experience is objective, and I naturally do not wish to prejudge the question of subjectivity or objectivity by my choice of a descriptive term. Moreover, NT critics use *appearance* to refer to those stories in the gospels in which the body of Jesus is experienced as "substantial" or "solid," and *vision* to suggest that the object in the percipient's visual field is ephemeral, rather than real. Ian Stevenson suggests *idiosyncratic perception* and *idiophany* (from the Greek *idios* meaning private, and *phainomai* meaning appear) for apparition experiences of people who are normal,[18] but some of the experiences presented below are alleged to be group experiences.

The advantage to using *vision* and *apparition* is that both terms have been used to refer to the kind of experience under examination, although *apparition* is used mostly by theologians who follow the tradition within Catholic scholarship. It is perhaps of interest to note that *apparition* is not found in the usual Protestant Bible, but is used in two Old Testament (OT) apocryphal books that are part of the Catholic canon, II Maccabees 5:4 and Wisdom 18:17.[19] *Apparition* also implies experiences involving visual perception, for it is derived from the Latin *apparere* meaning "to come or to be in sight."

One more comment about terminology is needed. I will generally use the proper name *Jesus* to refer both to the historical figure described in the NT and to the being whom visionaries think they have encountered, and I will use the adjective *Christic* to modify nouns such as *vision* or *apparition* simply because there is no suitable adjectival form of *Jesus* to perform this function. I will not generally use *Christ* as a proper name. Theologians have long debated Christology and the relationship between the Jesus of history and the Christ of faith, and I do not wish to get entangled in that debate merely by choice of expressions.

Assumptions and Outline

I have made it clear, I trust, that I will present descriptions of phenomena without prejudging whether they have a reality existing apart from and independently of a percipient. I will attempt to approach this question as objectively as I can, although I am haunted by William James's observation that "belief follows psychological and not logical laws. A single veridical hallucination experienced by one's self or by some friend who tells one all the circumstances has more influence over the mind than the largest calculated numerical probability either for or against."[20] While I have not personally had the kind of visionary experience described here, my objectivity could be affected in other ways, not least because of my close contact with a sizable number of people who have had such experiences. Deirdre Green considers mystical experience to be a prerequisite for studying mysticism, in her broad understanding of the term,[21] but I can also see how such experience might affect one's objectivity. I shall indicate in several places below that my limited direct acquaintance with aberrant perceptual experiences has restricted my understanding of the experiences of others.

Addressing the problem of aberrant perceptions is impossible without saying something concerning the problem of skepticism about the external world, bequeathed to modern philosophy by the ancient skeptics and Descartes. The general public may not know very much about philosophy, but one can generally count on members of the public to expect philosophers to be unsure about the reality of ordinary objects that most people unhesitatingly believe in. This expectation has undoubtedly been abetted in this century by metaphysical theories such as idealism and phenomenalism, which consider ideas or sensory perceptions to be the only realities, in terms of which everything else has to be constructed. These theories have been abandoned by many philosophers, and in the last two or three decades philosophers have increasingly sought to integrate scientific findings with the kind of conceptual analysis and the evaluation of foundational beliefs that have been central to philosophy for centuries.

In the current philosophical climate the existence of a world of physical objects requires no defense. But numerous issues remain that need further resolution, including the mechanisms involved in perception, the neurophysiological basis for representation of external objects and their properties, the basis for shared concepts and communication about perceptual experience, and the criteria by which illusory experiences can be identified. I will assume that some form of critical realism gives us an approximation to the truth about the world and about humans as perceivers. I therefore accept that there are physical objects existing apart from us, that the ultimate constituents of them are the complex atomic structures investigated by physicists, that ordinary beliefs about physical objects are subject to error, and that our causal relationships as perceivers to physical objects are discoverable by various sciences, including physics, neurophysiology and the psychology of perception. The phenomena I am dealing with will prove to be sufficiently challenging on their own, even on the assumption that some form of critical realism is correct.

The investigation of the phenomena in question begins at much the same point as do the philosophical disputes over realism, idealism and phenomenalism. In familiar Cartesian fashion we must begin with the perceptual experiences of percipients, as well as the emotions and other introspectible states that they report. Though some skeptics might question whether percipients actually had any experiences at all like those reported below, suggesting that everything was fabricated, I suspect that these would be a very small group. Much larger would be the group who would readily grant them their experiences but reject the probability, maybe even the possibility, of their preferred religious explanation. So, like the philosophical positions that seek to relate the supposed certainties of individual perceptions to claims about the reality and nature of a physical world, the phenomena in question here require relating an individual's reports of perceptions to various ontological claims. The difference is that the existence of a physical world is not usually taken as problematic, though complex issues surround perception, concept formation, representation of objects, and so on.

I wish to say something, finally, about the theoretical stance that I will adopt. Some discussions of apparitions and visions take for granted the existence of certain spiritual realities whose possible explanatory role can therefore be seriously considered. When Catholic theologian Karl Rahner discusses visions, apparitions, locutions, and so on,[22] he assumes the general position of the Christian church, according to which God and other spiritual beings, such as angels, exist. He can therefore go on to present the possibility that angels are the intermediaries between God and humans, responsible for producing the appropriate perceptual experiences in individuals who have visions. But many people living in this age of science, including Christians such as myself, see such a theory of angelic mediation as quite fantastic. For many of us the first touchstone of what is real is what critical common sense and the sciences attest. I take the posits of critical and experimental inquiry to be those with the greatest *prima facie* claim to our rational acceptance. This means that the onus of proof rests upon those who advance religious belief systems and the ontological posits implicit in them. However, I do not regard the existence of suprahuman intelligences or agencies to be beyond the domain of evidence, although I doubt that such evidence is straightforward and unequivocal.

I shall begin my study with the classical Christian view on apparitions and visions that began with Augustine and has been substantially incorporated into Catholic theology. I shall also present representative reports of Christic apparitions that have been advanced since NT times. This material in Chapter 1 will provide a backdrop for the contemporary visions and apparitions. Chapter 2 will consist of descriptions of the apparitions people have told me they experienced, presented in a way that suggests a rough continuum, beginning with experiences that take place in trances and are dreamlike, and ending with those that are similar to normal perceptual experiences. A number of the experiences in Chapter 2 raise important questions about credibility, and I examine them in Chapter 3. I argue that this question is not nearly as easy to settle as defenders of subjectivist interpretations for visionary experiences often suppose. In Chapter 4, I turn my attention to the nature of the NT post-Resurrection appearance accounts. I survey critical positions advanced by selected authors that fall into three broad interpretive groups: traditional, reductionist, and fideist interpretations.

In Chapter 5, I scrutinize various explanatory proposals, either specifically for Christic apparitions or for apparition phenomena in general. This chapter considers explanations suggesting transcendent causes, or what is more commonly called "supernaturalism." I show how recent developments in understanding the structure of scientific theories are relevant to understanding explanations offered by religious belief systems. In Chapter 6, I consider the explanations, ever popular, that propose mental states or processes as the causes of visionary experiences. Chapter 7 is devoted to a consideration of explanations coming from neurophysiology. These are among the most important, culturally speaking, given the widespread suspicion among philosophers and neural scientists about the value of the conceptual resources of mentalism. How well the competing explanations handle the variety of visionary experiences described in Chapter 2 is critically examined. The final chapter, Chapter 8, outlines the conditions under which a theory of transcendence might be considered a tentative explanation for the Christic visionary experience, and offers suggestions for further research.

1 Christic Apparitions in Christian History

The fact that Christic visions and apparitions have been experienced since the earliest days of Christianity is so well accepted that documentation is hardly needed. As in other experiences that are a part of common knowledge, visionary experiences exhibit a variety and complexity that is little understood. I shall introduce the study of Christic visions and apparitions by describing some representative reports offered during the long history of the Christian church. The New Testament literature and apocryphal literature that circulated in the early churches also report encounters with the risen Jesus. Because of the special place of the NT writings in Christian thought, and the critical scrutiny to which they have been subjected, they will receive special attention in a later chapter.

No comprehensive collection of reported Christic visions and apparitions exists, but several sources for ancient and medieval experiences are available, including *A Dictionary of Miracles* by E. C. Brewer,[1] and *The Apparitions and Shrines of Heaven's Bright Queen* by W. J. Walsh.[2] Brewer's title indicates his interest in all of the different kinds of miraculous events documented in the history of the church, not just Christic visions, and the book has thousands of entries. Merely to scan the book's contents begins to give one a sense of how many kinds of unusual phenomena have been claimed. Brewer does offer editorial comment on occasion, but it is really only the most fabulous of accounts on which he casts doubt. Walsh's book too is not primarily concerned with Christic apparitions, but in the course of his discussion of Marian apparitions he refers to several dozen Christic apparitions. He does not exhibit much of a critical attitude toward the material he presents or its sources, saying at one point, "we are not writing for skeptics, but for good Catholics."[3] *I Saw the Lord* by Chester and Lucille Huyssen uncritically documents mostly non-Catholic material, including quite a number of twentieth-century experiences. Allegations of Christic visions have been numerous, and even include the claim that the personage who was worshiped in Mexico as Quetzalcoatl (and by other names in other parts of Latin America) derived from one or more Christic apparitions.[4]

Representative Visions and Apparitions

Tradition has it that Jesus appeared to Mary, his mother, at the time of her death. All the disciples except Thomas were with Mary as they waited for her to die. When that time came the house was filled with mysterious sound and a delicious odor, and "Jesus Himself appeared, accompanied by a brilliant cortege of angels and saints, and the soul of Mary, leaving her mortal tenement, ascended with her son to Heaven." Three days later her body disappeared, giving rise to the belief that it too had been removed into heaven.[5] Another early appearance is ascribed to Martha, the sister of the Lazarus whom Jesus brought back to life.[6] Martha apparently was carried in a boat to Marseilles after being set adrift (without sails or oars) by those who persecuted her for her Christian faith. She introduced the Christian faith to that community, and later moved to Tarascon where she was visited by three bishops. St. Maximin from Aix, Trophimus from Arles, and Eutropius from Orange came to consecrate her house as a Christian church. Since she had no wine for her guests, "Jesus Christ Himself came and changed some water into wine, which the bishops greatly commended."[7] Brewer notes Mgr. Guerin, chamberlain of Pope Leo XIII, as the source of this, and then remarks: "A tale so full of anachronisms can scarcely be matched; but be it remembered that this biography is recorded in the nineteenth century as a history worthy of all men to be received and believed." Though Brewer seldom expresses incredulity about the stories he conveys, this one was evidently too much for him, in spite of its endorsement by a pope's chamberlain.

A number of experiences have been recorded in which people saw scenes of the trial or crucifixion of Jesus. St. Porphory (A.D. 353-420), while in extreme pain, experienced a trance in which he saw Jesus upon the cross along with the penitent thief. Like the thief on the cross, Porphory prayed, "Lord, remember me when Thou comest into Thy kingdom." Jesus then ordered the thief to leave his cross and go to Porphory's assistance. The thief raised Porphory from the ground, brought him to Jesus, who then came down from his own cross to receive him. When Porphory recovered consciousness, his pain was gone.[8] Here we encounter the puzzling phenomenon of events being re-created in the conscious awareness of percipients that are similar to things that occurred many years earlier. St. Rosa of Viterbo (1235-1252) saw Jesus suspended on his cross, nailed by his hands and feet, and crowned with thorns. His body bore many marks of torture and abuse, and at the sight of it Rosa fainted. When she recovered consciousness she is said to have gazed at him and conversed with him, he telling her of his love for the human race.[9] Other saints reported to have seen Jesus crucified include St. Catherine of Siena (1347-1380), St. Columba (1477-1501), St. Bridget of Sweden (c. 1312), and St. Ignatius Loyola (in 1537).

The account that Julian of Norwich has given of her Christic visionary experience (in about 1450) is famous for its detailed description of the sufferings of Jesus. The sixteen "shewings" or revelations took place over several days, as Julian was overcome with an illness that almost took her life. Last rites of the church were administered, and as she fixed her eyes on a crucifix, the shewings began. Julian describes the onset of the visions as follows: "Suddenly I saw the red blood running down from under the garland, hot and fresh, plenteous and life-like, just as it was in the time that the garland of thorns was pressed down on his blessed head."[10] Julian's account of her experiences has become a classic in visionary literature, both because of the nature of the accounts, and Julian's critical reflections. Critics are at odds about their character, and questions have been raised about Julian's own understanding of them, that is, whether they were only vividly imagined pictures or whether they involved the use of her eyes.[11] Equally famous are the Christic visions of Teresa of Avila (1515-1582), nun of the Carmelite order and prioress of the Discalced Carmelites. Teresa's experiences took place over a number of years, according to her account of them in *The Life of the Holy Mother Teresa of Jesus*. She also reports experiences in which diabolical agencies sought her undoing, as well as some apparitions of other heavenly visitors. Her visions culminate in an experience in which an angel took a golden spear with a fiery iron tip and pierced her heart so deeply that it penetrated her entrails. The experiences of Teresa have come under critical scrutiny in recent years, with quite a number of monographs published on her life and the character of her experiences.[12]

A number of accounts describe saints as giving gifts to the poor and finding to their surprise that Jesus was the recipient. One of the earliest such accounts is that of St. Gregory the Great (540-604), who regularly gave to beggars. One night after Gregory had fed the poor, Jesus appeared to him and said, "Ordinarily you receive me in the poor that assemble at your board, but today you received Me personally."[13] Another appearance occurred to a man named Peter, a banker, who first realized the shortcomings of his life as a result of a dream in the year 619. This dream affected him so profoundly that he decided to give away much of his wealth, even to the point of giving his coat to a beggar. Peter was very annoyed when the beggar turned around and sold the coat to someone else, but on his way home that day Peter met Jesus wearing his coat. Jesus commended him for what he had done, and vanished. After this, Peter gave away all his possessions to the poor.[14] In A.D. 714 St. Hubert of Brittany is said to have given a feast to various people of rank and position. The feast was unexpectedly joined by a beggar, and after the beggar was fed, he vanished. The beggar is considered to have been Jesus.[15] A similar account is given concerning St. Julian, bishop of Cuenca, who contributed to the poor every day. One day a guest "clad in mean apparel, but not having a mean demeanour," joined Julian at table, and upon finishing his meal thanked Julian for his hospitality, and vanished.[16] Finally, St. Gregory the Great describes an incident of A.D. 494 in which Jesus is said to have appeared to a priest of Mount Preclaro about to sit down to dinner, instructing him to bring food to St. Benedict.[17]

In several stories Jesus appears angry, or disposed to bring judgment. Jesus appeared to St. Angela of Brescia in 1535, angry because she had neglected the work she was given to do. His manner was menacing, and he bore a whip in his hand. When he granted the pardon she requested, Angela expressed her gratitude by setting up the Ursuline order.[18] St. Dominic saw Jesus angry for the sins of the world and wanting to destroy it. But the Virgin Mary presented St. Dominic and St. Francis to Jesus in order to appease him, predicting that they would effect a great reformation, whereupon Jesus relented.[19] St. Jerome describes having been beaten for his love of Cicero and his neglect of the Scriptures. He was taken to the judgment seat of God and scourged on the orders of Jesus. He remarks: "Let none think this a vision or a dream!! The angels know it was no dream. Christ Himself is my witness it was no dream; yea, my whole body still bears the marks of that terrible flagellation."[20]

This story is interesting because it describes alleged effects that might be seen by any observer, even if the visionary experience involved scenes that were not. Jerome is clearly appealing to the observable effects of flagellation to defend the objectivity of the visionary experience.

Another interesting account is that of Ernest Clifton, a fifteenth-century English monk who left the monastic life to satisfy his immoral desires. One form of depravity led to another, and he finally settled on operating an inn, stealing from and murdering the travelers who lodged with him. One night he entered a room to murder its occupant, but instead of his intended victim, he found himself looking at Jesus full of the wounds of crucifixion. Jesus looked at him in pity and asked: "Do you wish to kill me again? Stretch forth your hand and murder me again." Ernest was so moved by this experience that he confessed all his doings to the authorities, who sentenced him to hang. He somehow managed to avoid being executed, was freed, and returned to monastic life.[21]

Jesus is also said to have been seen at the right hand of God, or as a king reigning in splendor. St. Wulsin, bishop of Sherbourne in Dorsetshire in the tenth century, is said to have seen Jesus at the right hand of God.[22] St. Clara is said to have seen Jesus in 1346, seated on his throne of glory, surrounded by John the Baptist and the apostles. He showed Clara his wound in his side.[23] St. Catherine of Siena, at the age of 6, saw Jesus in pontifical robes above the church of St. Dominic, his face beaming with kindness.[24] St. Alphonsus Rodriquez of Valencia saw Jesus resplendent in glory, along with various saints, including St. Francis.[25] John Massias of Lima, Peru, saw Jesus, Mary, and other saints at the time of his death in 1645.[26] St. Angela of Foligno saw Jesus at her death in 1309. He is said to have shown her the royal robe of light with which a soul is clothed at death.[27] St. Nicholas of Tolentine also saw Jesus at the time of his death in 1310. Jesus appeared to him along with his mother Mary and St. Augustine.[28]

A number of people report having been healed by Jesus when he appeared to them. St. Barbara of Nicomedia was reportedly healed by Jesus when he appeared to her in prison after her father had beaten and imprisoned her for her faith.[29] St. Vincent Ferrier informed Pope Benedict XIII in 1411 that he had been healed when Jesus appeared to him in 1396 and touched his face with his right hand.[30] I shall indicate in the next chapter that this phenomenon continues to be reported.

Christic apparitions have been reported in many other circumstances. St. Gregory the Great, pope of the Roman church, tells of his Aunt Tarsilla's seeing Jesus at the time of her death. As she died, "a refreshing fragrance filled the room, indicating to all the presence of Him as the source of all that is fragrant and refreshing."[31] Forty Christian soldiers imprisoned and awaiting execution for refusing to offer sacrifices to pagan deities are said to have been visited in prison by Jesus in A.D. 320.[32] St. Honore (sixth century) says Jesus came to him and administered the holy elements to him with his own hands.[33] St. Lutgardes is said to have had no true religious feeling until Jesus appeared to her in person in 1246.[34]

Margaret Mary Alacoque of Burgundy (1648-1690), who initiated the devotion to the sacred heart of Jesus[35] and is reported to have had many apparition experiences, had a crown placed on her head by Jesus as he met her going to communion.[36] Emperor St. Henry saw Jesus enter St. Mary Major's church in Rome in 1014 to celebrate mass, accompanied by many saints and angels. One of the angels came up to Henry and touched his thigh, whereupon he became lame and remained so for the rest of his life.[37] St. Hyacinth of Kiev, while saying a mass in 1257, is reported to have seen Jesus crown the Virgin Mary with a crown of flowers and stars, which she promptly gave to Hyacinth.[38] St. Mechtilde of Heldelfs in Germany also saw Jesus with many angels during a mass around 1293, and her sister St. Gertrude saw Jesus around 1334.[39]

Stephana Quinzani of Brescia, Italy, received a marvelous ring from Jesus when he appeared to her and espoused her to himself. This ring is said to have been seen by many people.[40] Robert of Lyons was shown the heavenly city in a vision in 1109, after asking God to show him the path to heaven. He found himself separated from the city by a river, and on the opposite bank were about a dozen poor men washing their clothes. Among them was one in a robe of dazzling whiteness, helping the others. This dazzling figure said to Robert, "I am Jesus Christ, ever ready to help the truly penitent."[41] In 1221 St. Francis of Assisi saw Jesus, Mary his mother, and a multitude of angels, and two years later he saw Jesus again. This time St. Francis was given three white and three red roses of exquisite beauty "as an external ratification of the reality of his vision, it being in the midst of winter, when a rose was nowhere to be found."[42] St. Veronica of Milan is said to have been shown the whole life of Jesus in a series of visions in the fifteenth century.[43]

Various people report seeing Jesus as an infant or a little child, among them Pope Alexander I in A.D. 118, and St. Antony of Padua.[44] Several people are said to have had the infant Jesus placed in their arms, including St. John of the Cross[45] and St. Philomena, the daughter of the governor of Macedonia killed by the Roman emperor Diocletian in 320.[46] Hermann Joseph of Cologne, as a very devout child, is said to have played with the infant Jesus in 1160.[47] St. Rose of Lima, Peru, saw Jesus as a child many times. She also experienced mystic espousal.[48] Osanna of Mantua, Italy, saw Jesus as a lovely child with a crown of thorns on his head and carrying a cross.[49] Benoite Rencural of Laus, France, had numerous apparitions of Mary and the child Jesus, and also saw Jesus in adult form.[50] Anne Catherine Emmerich of Flamske, Germany, saw Jesus offer her a crown of thorns or a crown of flowers. She chose the former in order to identify with him in suffering, and experienced great pain until her death.[51]

Among more recent reports of Christic visions are those experienced by visionaries of the Eastern Orthodox Church as decribed by Brenda Meehan. She writes of Abbess Taisiia (1840-1915), who, at the time of her entry into monastic life, saw Jesus surrounded by angels,[52] and of Mother Angelina (1809-1890), who traced her monastic vocation to a childhood experience in which she saw Jesus.[53] Accounts collected by the Huyssens include the experiences of such well-known figures as William Booth, founder of the Salvation Army, and Sundar Singh, who combined the ideal of self-denial of the Hindu sadhu with the Western Christian ideal of the preaching friar.[54] General Booth reported seeing a myriad of angelic beings as well as patriarchs, apostles, and Christian martyrs. Then he saw Jesus, who rebuked him for his "nominal, useless, lazy, professing Christian life."[55] This experience led to the establishment of the famous mission to the poor more than a century ago.

Sundar Singh's experience took place in 1903, when he was fourteen, after an encounter with Christians who gave him a NT to read. As an expression of contempt for what they believed, he burned the book in public. Three days later he had the vision that changed his life's direction. A bright cloud filled his room, and out of the cloud came the face and figure of Jesus. Jesus spoke to him, and as a consequence Singh converted to Christianity.

The accounts of Christic encounters by psychotherapist Scott Sparrow include meditative states, dreams, near-death experiences, out-of-body experiences, and experiences that would be conventionally described as visions or apparitions. He observes that the common prelude to Jesus's personal manifestation is the appearance of brilliant light.[56] Most of the persons are not specifically named, but they come from various walks of life and religious backgrounds.

The Classical Interpretation

Augustine was the first to give a sustained discussion of apparitions and visions in Christian theological history. In *The Literal Meaning of Genesis* he distinguishes three kinds of vision: corporeal, imaginative, and intellectual. A corporeal (or bodily) vision uses the usual powers of sight; the other two kinds of vision do not. An imaginative (or spiritual) vision is an experience that takes place as a result of the activity of the human imagination, apart from the usual organs of sense. To illustrate imaginative vision Augustine refers to the familiar experience of thinking of our neighbor when that person is absent. An intellectual vision is an experience by means of which we receive understanding "through an intuition of the mind." Augustine gives as an illustration the acquiring of an understanding of love.[57] Evelyn Underhill appropriately remarks that "vision" is barely applicable to this kind of experience.[58] The examples Augustine uses to illustrate imaginative and intellectual visions are drawn from ordinary mental operations, but his larger concern is to elucidate the kind of unusual perceptual experiences that are examined in this study. I shall use Augustine's terminology in this chapter to discuss his and related views of visions and apparitions. The two most important categories here for us are corporeal visions and imaginative visions, because these signify experiences in which vivid perceptual images are before the conscious mind of the percipient.

Augustine's views on corporeal and imaginative visions are complicated slightly by his position on ordinary visual perception, for he did not think it correct to construe our *eyes* as seeing the objects that are presented in normal perception. He maintained, rather, that the *soul* sees these things by means of the eyes. The body, with its organs of sense, is an instrument through which the soul experiences perception. But the distinguishing feature of corporeal visions is that some involvement of the external organs of sense is involved, unlike imaginative visions, in which these organs are bypassed. This implies that in corporeal visions some object outside a percipient is causally responsible for producing a perception, but there is no such implication with imaginative visions. So a clear ontological implication is attached to corporeal vision. Augustine tells the story of a peasant who related his visionary experience but was too simple to determine "whether it was a body or the image of a body" that was before him.[59] Augustine leaves the impression that more discerning individuals could tell the difference, but he does not indicate how.

Whatever the basis for distinguishing one kind of vision from another, this threefold classification passed into the discussion of visions and apparitions in the Christian church and is still used. Commentators disagree, however, about the claim that corporeal vision requires an external object. Paul Molinari argues that "'corporeal vision' by its very definition implies that the *external* senses are stimulated by an external agent,"[60] but Evelyn Underhill contends that corporeal vision "is little more than a more or less uncontrolled externalization of inward memories, thoughts or intuitions—even of some pious picture which has become imprinted on the mind—which may, in some subjects, attain the dimensions of true sensorial hallucination."[61] Underhill *suggests* in these remarks—the only reference to corporeal vision in her long study of mysticism—that corporeal vision does not involve an external agent, but Molinari's view more accurately reflects the position advanced by Augustine.

Augustine accepted many of the accounts of paranormal phenomena that circulated in his day, including apparitions of living and dead people. He describes an incident in which a man "possessed by an unclean spirit . . . would tell when a priest twelve miles away had started to visit him," and could declare where the priest was at each stage in the journey.[62] Augustine evidently believed that corporeal visions could result from spirits of various kinds, including those of either dead or living humans, located (spatially) before the percipients and affecting their organs of sense in the same way that ordinary objects from the mundane world do. But he also allowed that images of bodies might be produced in the spirit (or imagination) of a person by the agency of some other spirit, "just as if bodies were present to the senses of the body."[63] These possibilities are evident in his statement that: "By means of corporeal vision as well as by means of the images of corporeal objects revealed in the spirit, good spirits instruct men and evil spirits deceive them."[64] Augustine probably thought that some imaginative visions had no source outside their percipients, but he obviously thought that external agencies could produce both corporeal and imaginative visions. This means that for Augustine corporeal and imaginative visions do not simply correspond to objective and subjective experience, as conventionally understood. Although intellectual visions are not the focus of attention here, these clearly could have their source outside the persons in whom the intuitive awareness takes place. Augustine thus places the discussion of visions and apparitions in the context of the supernatural agencies or beings that were central to his metaphysical views.

Augustine seems unsure about the mechanisms by which apparitions might be experienced, but he says in *The Care to be Taken for the Dead*: "I might believe that this is done by the working of angels."[65] He relates an incident involving a monk named John (known to Augustine) with whom a woman wished an audience so that she might ask a question. John would not receive her, but told her husband that he would appear to her in a dream to answer her question, which he purportedly did. Augustine says that he would like to ask John: "Did you in person come to that woman in her dreams, that is, was it your spirit in the likeness of your body, just as we dream of ourselves in the likeness of our own body? Or were you doing something else, or, if asleep, were dreaming something else, *or did such a vision appear to the woman in her sleep through an angel*, or even in some other fashion?"[66] Augustine says that he does not know how angels produce such effects,[67] but he advances the theory nevertheless. He elsewhere asserts that all manifestations of God except the Incarnation are mediated by angels,[68] and supplies many OT quotations to support this view. The prominent role played by angels in Augustine's idea of visions is similar to the role of angels in visions of God according to Jewish mystical spirituality. Segal describes this type of Jewish mystical experience as *angelophany*, which is a visionary experience of an angelic mediator who "carries the name of God or somehow participates in God's divinity."[69]

Augustine's idea that angels might be responsible for corporeal or imaginative visions has become embedded in Catholic thought. The *New Catholic Encyclopedia* (1967) puts it thus: "Apparitions of Christ, Mary, and the blessed are to be considered as representations effected through the instrumentality of angels."[70]

Augustine considers intellectual vision superior to the other two kinds of vision, for it is not susceptible to deception, while the other two are. Here, as at many other places, the influence of Plato is evident. Augustine's subsequent influence on this point is also apparent, for much of Christian theology has considered what is known through the intellect as superior to that known through the senses or though the imaginative faculty (so-called). Augustine expected that after the resurrection of all the dead (as taught by Christianity) the things of the intellect would be "far more luminously present to the soul than the corporeal things that now surround us."[71] He deplored the fact that many people were so absorbed in the material forms that they were unaware of the existence of any others. Clearly, conflict between dualistic and materialistic metaphysical systems were a feature of his society, just as it has been in much of subsequent history.

Thomas Aquinas endorsed Augustine's view of the cause of visionary phenomena—a view that accorded with his understanding of a well-ordered world. Angels were seen as occupying a middle position between God and man, so that "the Divine enlightenments and revelations are conveyed from God to men by the angels."[72] His explanation of how this might occur with imaginative visions is in keeping with his Aristotelian outlook:

Both a good and a bad angel by their own natural power can move the human imagination. . . . For corporeal nature obeys the angel as regards local movement, so that whatever can be caused by the local movement of bodies is subject to the natural power of angels. Now it is manifest that imaginative apparitions are sometimes caused in us by the local movement of animal spirits and humours. Hence Aristotle says . . . *when an animal sleeps, the blood descends in abundance to the sensitive principle, and movements descend with it*. . . . Indeed the commotion of the spirits and the humours may be so great that such appearances may even occur to those who are awake, as is seen in mad people, and the like. So, as this happens by a natural disturbance of the humours, and sometimes also by the will of man who voluntarily imagines what he previously experienced, so also the same may be done by the power of a good or a bad angel, sometimes with alienation from the bodily senses, sometimes without such alienation.[73]

Note how Aquinas accords to angels, good or bad, a causal role comparable to that of "animal spirits and humors" in ordinary experience. Aquinas taught that humans can become more susceptible to the influence of angelic ministers by reducing their preoccupation with sensible and corporeal objects.[74] Like Augustine before him, Aquinas was inclined to consider the supernatural truth seen in intellectual vision superior to that found in other kinds of visionary experience. However, reflecting on the Annunciation to the Virgin Mary, in which the angel Gabriel visibly appeared, Aquinas concludes that a combination of corporeal and intellectual vision is more excellent than intellectual alone.[75] When an angel causing a corporeal vision enlightens the intellect at the same time, the percipient is prevented from being deceived.[76]

The Catholic Encyclopedia (1912) develops an even more complex view of how corporeal apparitions or visions, including those of Jesus, might be caused. It says that in a vision,

either a figure really present externally strikes the retina and there determines the physical phenomenon of the vision; or an agent superior to man directly modifies the visual organ and produces in the composite a sensation equivalent to that which an external object would produce. . . . Sometimes the very substance of the being or the person will be presented; sometimes it will be merely an appearance consisting in an arrangement of luminous rays. The first may be true of living persons, and even, it would seem, of the now glorious bodies of Christ and the Blessed Virgin, which by the eminently probable supernatural phenomenon of multilocation may become present to men without leaving the abode of glory.[77]

This account leaves unexplained many details concerning the causal mechanisms of corporeal vision. But it allows for "the substance of the being" of Jesus to be presented to a percipient in such a way that the retina is stimulated, thus producing the vision. It also allows for "an agent superior to man" (such as an angel, presumably) to directly modify the "visual organ," by which the writer seems to mean something other than the eye—for example, the visual cortex—to produce the sensation. This article goes on to define *visions* as those appearances in which the figure seen is connected with a real being, and *apparitions* as appearances in which the figure seen is not connected to such a being. It notes, however, that mystics often use the two terms interchangeably, as I will do.

The *Encyclopedia* article allows for the possibility of simultaneous apparitions of the glorious bodies, without *explicitly* saying that angels might be responsible for producing them, but rather only that such an event would be supernatural. That the article never discusses the mechanism behind such a supernatural phenomenon seems strange. Someone reading it might expect that the article, having allowed for the intermediary role of angels, would conjecture that different angels might produce the simultaneous apparitions. Of course this opens the door to the objection that the resulting experiences are deceptive, for unsuspecting percipients might readily think that what appears to them is actually (spatially) in front of them, producing the sensory perception.

No criterion for the claim that an angel has produced an apparition is offered. This claim resembles the suggestion of some biblical critics that the "appearances" of Jesus after the Resurrection were neither genuine appearances, nor subjective visions, but objective *visions*. In an objective vision one has visual percepts that correspond with a reality existing externally to the percipient, but that external object does not causally produce the percept. For example, if Jesus exists, but a vision of him is produced by an angel rather than by him, that would be an objective vision.

The opinion of the *Catholic Encyclopedia* article that Jesus might appear in substance and thereby affect the senses of the percipient, but do so without "leaving the abode of glory" is *prima facie* self-contradictory. One might wonder how Jesus could appear *in substance* to a person at a given location upon earth without leaving his abode in heaven "at the right hand of the Father," as conventional Christian theology describes the location of Jesus. At issue here is Christian thought concerning the character of the glorified body of Jesus, including the present location of that body. This problem is apt to strike some readers as rather esoteric, for the problem of defending any claim about the existence of spiritual beings seems to be formidable in its own right, without worrying about the suitability of applying spatial predicates to such entities. Some theorists have explored the possibility that the body of Jesus might exist in some space other than the one inhabited by the people and familiar objects in the visible world.[78]

Karl Rahner thinks that apparitions of Jesus or of the saints are probably imaginative visions rather than corporeal ones. He observes, for instance, that in some of the visions, Jesus appears as a child. Because Rahner does not think that Jesus exists in the form of a child, he regards such a vision as imaginative.[79] He also thinks that many visions must be imaginative rather than corporeal because the bodies required for corporeal visions, such as the body of Jesus, are not present on earth:

For what purpose would be served by the "objective" formation of an apparent body, or a miraculous affectation of the visionary's external senses? The presence of Christ's own humanity in such a vision would be no more "objective" than it is in an imaginative vision. In short: most visions are imaginative, above all simply because many visions (including those assumed to be genuine) cannot be corporeal ones: therefore all of them can be at least presumed to be imaginative visions.[80]

He notes Teresa of Avila's opinion that the glorified humanity of Christ has never shown itself on earth since his apparition to St. Paul shortly after his Ascension.[81] John Calvin, too, thought that Jesus was now confined to heaven, far above the world, although this did not prevent Jesus from sending out his power through the world and perhaps sharpening the ability of people to see spiritual realities.[82] As we shall see, the "appearance" experience of Paul complicates issues considerably for NT critics, because it is often considered a real appearance even though it occurs after the Ascension of Jesus into heaven, at a time when all the appearances were supposedly finished. Clearly, the attempt to assign spatial location to the glorified post-Resurrection body of Jesus is significantly influenced by the theological beliefs and assumptions of the Christian church. Also apparent is the fact that some theologians are prepared to allow dogma to supersede empirical evidence on points such as this.

Rahner certainly does not rule out the possibility of corporeal visions, for he accepts the NT "apparitions" of Jesus to the apostles as real appearances. But he thinks that in the absence of conclusive proof, most visions reported in religious experience should be regarded as imaginative ones.[83] He says that an imaginative vision can be "authentic," but he means by this that it was produced by God. He considers a vision to be produced by God if it is accompanied by some objective miracle, such as a cure. Rahner is sensitive to a wide range of possible interpretations of what it means for an event to be produced by God, ranging from the interruption of natural laws to subtle use of natural phenomena to secure spiritual ends. He includes the possibility that natural powers such as telepathy and clairvoyance, if they exist, might be employed to allow people to apprehend religious objects.[84] He also observes that one might have the sense impression of perceiving a corporeal object without there being an object producing that sense impression. He lists factors that might lead one to think that one perceives a corporeal object, including that the object "appears to be integrated in the normal field of perception, is not altered even by deliberate effort, displays the details and materiality of an ordinary object of perception, cannot be produced at will, moves apart from the conscious desire of the subject, speaks, [and] does not accompany movements of the eyes," but he does not consider these to be criteria of objectivity.[85] He also allows that God might make use of the psychic potentialities of people to hallucinate simultaneously. Rahner unfortunately chooses not to enter into the problem of determining the basis for objective perception, saying that for his purposes his reader need only "grasp the simple fact that nothing the visionary is able to communicate to others of the experience and content of his vision will justify them in concluding beyond doubt that the object 'seen' was really present."[86] Whether the situation with all alleged visionary experiences is as straightforward as Rahner says it is will have to await the detailed descriptions in the next chapter.

The Dangers of Apparitions and Visions

The Catholic and Eastern Orthodox churches have exhibited a tolerant attitude toward visions and apparitions, but they have also cautioned people about the inherent danger of deception. The "genuine" visions and apparitions are those that are sent by God, whereas the "non-genuine" ones have a diabolical source. Corporeal visions that are diabolical in origin would not generally be counted "genuine" even though they might be "genuinely corporeal." The Orthodox theologian Vladimir Lossky warns about trying to give images to the Godhead, or wishing to see angels or powers or Christ with the senses "for in the end you will become unbalanced, taking the wolf for the shepherd, and worshipping evil spirits."[87] The recent Catholic *Encyclopedia of Theology,* compiled under Rahner's editorship, describes a "genuine" vision or audition as "a special intervention of God which is outside any normal concrete psychophysical law,"[88] although its effect is conditioned to suit the unique background of the percipient. The author of the article on visions takes considerable care to discuss the circumstances in which visions might be considered genuine. The author rules out the piety, the sincerity, and the good health of the percipient as criteria of genuineness, as well as the good effects that such experiences might have. The criterion that is offered is the presence of a miracle, but because miracles are seldom ascertainable, "one must be satisfied with a greater or lesser probability in distinguishing genuine from psychogenic visions."[89] The author also remarks that they must be measured against the revelation of Christ in the church, and this means, I assume, consistency with established Christian doctrines. Despite the fact that some visions can be diabolical, visions in general are not treated as superfluous but are seen as fulfilling a function both in the church and in the percipient. The value to individual percipients is a more vital experience of the reality of the Christian mystery. The article on visions in *The Catholic Encyclopedia* (1912) describes St. Martin's experience of an allegedly deceptive apparition of Christ. Martin said to the visitor who appeared to him in royal garment and crown that he would not acknowledge him unless he appeared with stigmata and the cross, whereupon the apparition vanished. Luther also uses this experience to illustrate the occurrence of deceptive visions.[90] The *New Catholic Encyclopedia* (1967) specifically speaks of "supernatural visions" in order to distinguish true visions from illusions or hallucinations caused by pathological states or diabolical influences.[91]

As early as the fourth century, Christian leaders offered advice to visionaries to assist them in determining whether their experiences were divine or diabolical. Athanasius, bishop of Alexandria, suggested that an apparition should be asked who it is and where it came from, adding: "And if it should be a vision of holy ones they will assure you, and change your fear into joy. But if the vision should be from the devil, immediately it becomes feeble."[92] He noted that demons greatly feared the sign of the cross and were given to making worldly displays, threatening death, and "capering and changing their forms of appearance,"[93] so that these criteria could also be used in making the appropriate identification. St. Gregory the Great, writing at the turn of the seventh century, said that because many sources of revelation exist, we should not put faith in them. But he thought that saints could distinguish true revelations from "the voices and images of illusion through an inner sensitivity."[94]

John of the Cross, one of the best-known mystical doctors of the Catholic Church, takes a very dim view of corporeal and imaginative visions, and of revelations that involve bodily sensations and feelings. His view is that "between spiritual things and all these bodily things exists no kind of proportion whatever. And thus it may always be supposed that such things as these are more likely to be of the devil than of God; for the devil has more influence in that which is exterior and corporeal, and can deceive a soul more easily thereby than by that which is more interior and spiritual."[95] But he concedes that God uses visions on occasion, for God prepares people in stages to receive the revelations that come through faith alone.[96] His advice was that those who experience such things should not rely on them or accept them, but "always fly away from them, without trying to ascertain whether they be good or evil; for, the more completely exterior and corporeal they are, the less certainly are they of God."[97] His view on some of the NT post-Resurrection appearances of Jesus is interesting, for he thinks that Mary Magdalene's attempt to touch the feet of Jesus, and Thomas's desire to touch Jesus in order to establish for himself that Jesus had really been resurrected, were born out of a seriously deficient approach to spiritual realities.[98] Beginners are apt to use images and forms, he thought, but they need to be led on to surer methods of knowledge.[99] This attitude of John of the Cross toward the physical and corporeal characteristics of the NT appearance accounts is in sharp contrast with that of many current expositors. Many expositors give careful attention to the details of the NT accounts in the hope that these might provide grounds for asserting that the appearances were not hallucinatory, and for defending the claim that the Resurrection of Jesus was a genuine event.

Rahner generally concurs with the attitude toward corporeal and imaginative visions expressed by John of the Cross, writing that "God is always greater than any image of himself and wishes to communicate himself as thus greater, in mystical experience."[100] By "mystical experience" Rahner means a mystical union that is devoid of images. The danger of undue attachment to images, rather than to the reality standing behind images, is the ultimate reason for Rahner's opposition to sensuous experience. By contrast, Deirdre Green believes that the Christian church has exalted the value of nonsensuous forms of religious experience to the neglect of the more sensuous and anthropomorphic experiences, including those that involve Jesus. Green singles out male figures (John of the Cross and Meister Eckhart) in the history of Catholicism as the leading defenders of imageless mystical apprehension, and female figures (Teresa of Avila and Julian of Norwich) for their equally impressive defense of sensuous experience.[101] Recent feminist critiques have suggested that a denigration of the sensuous image, and the approbation of "objective" knowledge, are characteristic of male-dominated epistemology.[102]

Protestant Attitudes

Catholic theologians, generally speaking, have been more sympathetic than Protestant theologians to visions and have discussed them more extensively. I will confine my attention here to some of the early Protestant reformers. Their positions may not be representative of their contemporary descendants, for theological movements often evolve from the original views advanced by their founders, and develop in ways so complex that only those thoroughly immersed in a tradition can describe them authoritatively. *The Encyclopedia of the Lutheran Church* discusses visions mainly in relation to the biblical incidents, noting the possibility of false prophets and impostors, and giving this as the reason visionary phenomena have always been viewed with suspicion. The author asserts: "The Reformation accorded no value to post-biblical visions. . . . It should be noted that the appearances of the Risen Christ are never described in the NT as visions; they are in a class by themselves."[103] This is not Luther's view on the matter, however. Though Luther does speak about having concluded a pact with the Lord that He should not send him any visions, dreams, or angels because he had already been influenced "by that infinite multitude of illusions, deceptions, and impostures by which the world was horribly deceived for a long time through Satan under the papacy," Luther also says that he does not "detract from the gifts of others, if God by chance reveals something to someone beyond Scripture through dreams, through visions, and through angels."[104] For his own part, Luther was content with the knowledge of God derived from the Scriptures.

Luther also makes a threefold distinction between kinds of revelatory experience, but not the three kinds of vision developed by Augustine. Luther's distinction is biblical in origin, deriving from Numbers 12:6-8: "If there is a prophet among you, I the Lord make myself known to him in a vision, I speak with him in a dream. Not so with my servant Moses; he is entrusted with all my house. With him I speak mouth to mouth, clearly, and not in dark speech; and he beholds the form of the Lord." Luther considered dreams to be the lowest form of revelation, but thought that when God appears to people while they are awake, "it is a vision of a form of apparition."[105] Luther acknowledged a third form of revelation far more reliable than dreams or visions; indeed, it is described at one point as completely trustworthy. This is the revelation that occurs "when God speaks face to face and enlightens hearts with the rays of His Spirit."[106] Various prophetic figures in the OT, Moses for example, are described as having had such revelation, but revelations now must be in harmony with Scripture: "If they are not in harmony with the Word or destroy faith, they are of Satan."[107]

Luther offers an intriguing interpretation of Jacob's statement "I have seen God face to face" that bears on the subject of this book. Jacob makes this claim in the context of a narrative that describes how he wrestled all night with a "man," taken to be a divine being, who finally vanquished Jacob by putting his thigh out of joint.[108] Luther says of this divine being: "Without any controversy we shall say that this man was not an angel but our Lord Jesus Christ, eternal God and future man, to be crucified by the Jews. He was very familiar to the holy fathers and often appeared to them and spoke with them. He exhibited himself to the fathers in such a form that he might testify that he would at some time dwell with us in the form of human flesh."[109] Many other interpreters say that Jacob's encounter was with an angel rather than with Jesus Christ, and in understanding Jacob's experience as he does, Luther reverts to the interpretation of the OT theophanies, that is, visible appearances of God, that was almost universally accepted by the church fathers before Augustine.[110] This is a theological issue that I do not wish to argue, and I will not consider OT theophanies as Christic apparitions.

The remarks quoted above from *The Encyclopedia of the Lutheran Church* deserve comment. First, I do not think the evidence supports the position that the NT appearance accounts are *very* different from post-biblical apparition accounts; this will be argued in due course. Second, the statement that the Reformation accorded no value toward post-biblical visions corresponds reasonably well with the attitudes toward visions of reformers other than Luther, and seems to reflect fairly widespread attitudes within Protestant Christianity today. But Luther's own attitude toward visions is quite open.

John Calvin viewed visions with suspicion, observing that Satan often makes use of apparitions "in order to make fools out of those who do not believe. The result is that the bare vision leaves a man's mind in a state of suspense. But the Spirit seals those which truly come from God with a sure mark, so that those whom God wishes to have truly devoted to himself may not waver or hesitate."[111] He says that God illumines the minds of his own so that they are not deceived,[112] and also that God removes every scruple of doubt by clear signs, and provides his servants with a spirit of discernment so "there might be no opportunity for deception."[113] Calvin does not hold out much hope for either oracles or visions to be sent from heaven now, and says that "the Lord Himself does not appear by visions," but he does not rule out the possibility that angels might visit us and confirm the truth.[114] Like Luther, Calvin emphasizes the importance of relying upon the Scriptures for knowledge of spiritual realities, and views with concern the "illusions" that befell the Anabaptists.[115]

Some sense of the theological significance accorded visionary experiences within the early Anabaptist movement can be gleaned from Obbe Philips's *Confession*, written around 1560.[116] Philips says that some Anabaptists had visions that allowed correct predictions of future events, but that false visions and revelations crept in and created great havoc. The recent *Mennonite Encyclopedia* has no article on vision, apparition, or theophany. The article on theology says that Mennonites often view theology with suspicion and distrust, and tend to offer a theology that is "rigorously biblical *rather than* also drawing significantly upon the resources of tradition, experience, and logic as appropriate."[117]

The writings of the early Anglican reformers, the fourth of the large Reformation groups, do not appear to include much commentary on the character or significance of visions. Thomas Cranmer expresses negative sentiments concerning some of the visionary phenomena alleged by clergy of the Catholic Church, and asks: "How shall we then know true visions of angels from false, true apparitions and miracles from counterfeit, but by the scripture of God, which is the rule and true measure wherewith we must try all things?"[118] His guarded acceptance of the possibility of visionary experiences, and his reliance upon the test of Scripture (however this was thought to work), put him in the company of Luther and Calvin.

Much of the tradition bequeathed to subsequent Protestantism has viewed visionary experiences as inconsequential or theologically dangerous. A number of recent Christian theological dictionaries and encyclopedias do not include separate articles on visions or apparitions, including *The Encyclopedia of Southern Baptists*, *The Evangelical Dictionary of Theology*, *The New Dictionary of Theology*, and *The New International Dictionary of the Christian Church*. These topics are mentioned briefly in articles on mysticism or religious experience, but they are not given the kind of extended attention found in Catholic sources.

Competing Christian Theories

The position that can be discerned within the Catholic tradition, sketched above as beginning with Augustine, can be usefully viewed as a *theory* that purports to describe the character of revelatory phenomena and outlines a variety of explanatory possibilities for them. This theory, in what we might describe as its fullest form, has the following elements:

1. A threefold distinction among visions, as described above.

2. A claim that various kinds of spiritual beings exist, including God, Jesus, Satan, angels, demons, and the spirits of living and dead persons.

3. Assumptions about causal powers capable of being exerted by spiritual beings upon humans, thus producing visions and apparitions of various kinds. Spirits of one kind or another are evidently thought to be capable of producing (a) corporeal visions of themselves by causally affecting the external senses, as the spirit of St. Peter could produce a corporeal vision of himself in a human percipient, (b) imaginative visions of themselves by bypassing the external senses and causally affecting the physiological and/or mental functions of percipients, as the spirit of St. Peter could produce an imaginative vision of himself, (c) corporeal visions of beings (or things, presumably) other than themselves, as *an angel* could produce, according to this theory, a corporeal vision of St. Peter by causally affecting the external senses of a human percipient, and (d) imaginative visions of beings or things other than themselves, as an angel could produce an imaginative vision of St. Peter. Other possibilities exist, for presumably a spirit could produce a corporeal or an imaginative vision of something nonexistent. Descartes suggested this when he supposed that an evil spirit might make humans believe that a material world exists when in fact it does not.

4. A distinction between deceptive and nondeceptive visions, accompanied by criteria by means of which these might be identified. The theory allows for various (and different) criteria to be used by percipients and by external observers.

5. Views concerning the physiological mechanisms involved in perception, including the role of external sensory organs such as the eye, the mechanisms involved in forming images without the external senses, and the relationship between the human percipient's mind in perceiving and the relevant physiological mechanisms.

6. Views concerning the psychological powers of human percipients,

such as whether they are capable of clairvoyance and telepathy, along with the usual psychological powers of knowing, believing, doubting, remembering, and so on.

7. Epistemic views concerning knowledge, justified belief, truth, evidence, and so on. Rahner's account allows for miracles and simultaneous hallucinations, for instance, both of which entail significant and controversial epistemic claims.

8. Theological views of various kinds, including those that touch on God's causal role in the world, the Resurrection and Ascension of Jesus, the nature and present location of his glorified body, and Christology. As I observed above, theologians do not agree on whether the glorified body of Jesus can now directly produce a corporeal vision, but for these purposes I shall follow Rahner in interpreting this theory as maintaining that this is not possible. This feature of the theory allows a proponent to speak of *God* as producing revelatory experiences of various kinds, over and above assigning a causal role to spirits thought to be embodied. Theological discourse is often of such a diverse nature that one can speak simultaneously of *an embodied spirit* producing an apparition by appearing to a person, and *God* producing that experience. The usual way of defending this possible duality in causal accounts is to say that God works through the embodied spirit.

A much more truncated theory of visions and apparitions is found among Christians where suspicion of visions dominates, and can be outlined as follows:

1. The appearances of Jesus described in the NT up to his Ascension involved perceptual experiences of an admittedly unusual body, but the perceptual mechanisms involved were no different from those involved in everyday perceptual experience. After the Ascension of Jesus no more appearances took place, for his body was no longer available for appearances. Even the "appearance" to Paul so often mentioned in the writings of Paul and Luke was probably not a real appearance. The problem of where the body of Jesus is now located is not a particularly serious one, for there are no significant apparitions now that might make one wonder if Jesus was directly producing a corporeal vision of himself.

2. The visions that have been reported since the Ascension of Jesus are nothing more than vivid mental images, no doubt having religious significance for those experiencing them.

3. Angels, demons, and the spirits of living and deceased people (including Mary, the apostles, and various departed saints) might exist in disembodied forms, but if they do they no longer appear to people, nor are they involved in producing mental images in percipients.

4. The psychological powers of people do not include clairvoyance

and telepathy, but extend only to a range of powers that would be considered ordinary.

5. A vision—a vivid mental image—is deceptive inasmuch as it produces some false or objectionable effect such as false beliefs, false faith, impious acts, and so forth.

This position insists on subscribing to central tenets of the Christian religion, but takes a very dim view of psychical phenomena and supernatural entities, seeking to minimize their role in an articulated Christian world view as much as possible without abandoning the views considered crucial for Christianity. Many positions fall between the two. Some might consider contemporary Christic apparitions diabolical as far as causal origin is concerned (rather than completely subjective), or as symbols or signs of a transcendent reality that produces them.[119] The antipsychical view just sketched is undoubtedly the kind that prompted Walsh, a Catholic author, to say that Protestants exhibited a rationalistic and materialistic temper, and consequently were not willing to consider seriously the phenomenon of Marian apparitions.[120]

Defenders of competing theories typically advance them in the light of phenomena they believe to be genuine. The second view sketched above considers the events requiring explanation to consist primarily of those described in the NT, and, in keeping with common post-Enlightenment views, considers contemporary stories of psychic phenomena such as apparitions, ghosts, and hauntings to have no basis in fact. The Catholic position considers the relevant phenomena to include the NT accounts, naturally, but to extend far beyond them to allegations of parapsychological phenomena. Some of these claims have been given official endorsement by the Catholic Church.

Evaluating the Angelic Mediation Theory

An immediate conceptual problem arises: Are visions objective or veridical? This distinction comes out in considering the various kinds of causal effects that spirits are said to produce. Suppose an evil spirit were to produce a deceptive vision of Jesus, whether imaginative or corporeal. Should it be counted as objective? As veridical? Or suppose a spirit were to produce a vision, whether imaginative or corporeal, of something that has no instantiation in the history of the universe, such as a centaur. Should this be counted as objective? As veridical? Classifying a vision, whether imaginative or corporeal, apparently is not a problem if a spirit produces an image of *itself* in a percipient. This kind of experience might be described as both objective and veridical: objective because it is produced by an object existing externally to the percipient, and veridical because there is a close (supposed) resemblance between the perceptual experience and the object producing that experience. The notion of veridical experience suggested here is of course problematic, particularly on a critical realist interpretation of the relation between perception and an external object. Critical realists are generally loath to say that perceptions resemble their "corresponding" objects, especially when the objects are understood in the light of physical theories about the composition of things. But even an imprecise conception of veridicality sheds some light on the problem of the objectivity of visionary experience. I note that the notion of an optical illusion, which is featured in any theory of visual perception, presupposes some concept of veridical perception.[121]

The notion of a deceptive vision in the classical Catholic theory trades on the distinction between objective and veridical perception. A deceptive vision is generally construed as produced by a spiritual agency, for example, an evil spirit, that exists apart from the percipient and is thus objective, but the experience somehow fails to reflect the reality it is taken to reflect, and so is not true to its source—it is not veridical. The way in which the apparition experience does not accurately reflect the supposed reality is not always spelled out, and perhaps one cannot assume that a deceptive spirit produces only false "physical" likenesses. Perhaps the deception stems from an inaccurate presentation of moral character, rather than "physical" likeness, but I shall not further complicate the discussion here by introducing a second possibility. It appears, in any case, that an evil spirit might come "as an angel of light"—a biblical phrase from II Corinthians 11:14 often used to give expression to the belief in deceptive powers of diabolical forces—and produce an inaccurate physical likeness of Jesus in a percipient. This vision should then be deemed objective but not veridical.

If we agree that deceptive visions might be described as objective but not veridical, that still leaves the question of how we should describe visions in which spiritual agencies produce images, whether as corporeal visions or imaginative ones, of nonexistent things, such as centaurs. Saying simply that such a vision is objective but not veridical seems inappropriate, for it fails to be veridical not simply because the image ineptly reflects the reality, but because there is no reality at all to be reflected. Though the difference here needs to be registered, I do not think it is significant enough to require another category to classify it.

With this crude distinction between objective and veridical visions in place, I shall consider Rahner's comments about objective visions. He tends to equate corporeal vision with objective experience, and does not distinguish objective from veridical visions as I have done, but his remarks are of considerable interest.

Rahner asserts, as I indicated above, that the objectivity of a visionary experience is not established by the fact that the (humanoid) figure "appears to be integrated in the normal field of perception, is not altered even by deliberate effort, displays the details and materiality of an ordinary object of perception, cannot be produced at will, moves apart from the conscious desire of the subject, speaks, [and] does not accompany movements of the eyes."[122] An experience might indeed have all the characteristics listed above and still have no causal source in an object existing external to a percipient, and therefore not be objective. For example, according to the perceptual release theory (discussed in Chapter 7), which construes apparitions as resulting from memories of earlier perceptions, all of these features could be triggered by events internal to a percipient. Moreover, given the rich conceptual possibilities of the angelic mediation theory, a visionary experience with the characteristics just listed could easily occur without the external senses of a percipient being stimulated. An angel could bypass the external senses and create a vivid, lifelike experience by stimulating something interior to a person's physiological structure, and thus produce an imaginative vision. The characteristics that Rahner lists could evidently be found in a vision that is both nonobjective (subjective) and noncorporeal. So this central assertion on Rahner's part is very reasonable.

He goes on to say, however, that "nothing the visionary is able to communicate to others of the experience and content of his vision will justify them in concluding beyond doubt that the object 'seen' was really present."[123] This is more problematic, for there are several conceivable circumstances in which a visionary might be able to *offer evidence* for the position that the object "seen" is really present. In saying "offer evidence" instead of "conclude beyond doubt" I know I am interpreting Rahner loosely, but it is generally conceded now that no general theories can be established beyond doubt. One circumstance providing evidence of objectivity would be that the spatio-temporal-causal domain was changed—for example, the vision left an image on film. Another would be that several people simultaneously had the same apparition experience. I will discuss a third circumstance momentarily, in connection with a discussion of a criterion for corporeal vision. Christic apparitions satisfying the first two circumstances have been alleged in the history of the Christian church, as I am sure Rahner knew and as I shall report in the next chapter, so his rejection of these as providing evidence for an objective source of the experience is puzzling.

This brings me to Rahner's discussion of group apparitions. Rahner explains group apparitions of Jesus as simultaneous hallucinations, thereby suggesting a subjective source to the experiences (although undoubtedly of religious significance to the percipients). This position is unsatisfactory. That several people might hallucinate much the same object at the same time is of course *conceivable* (allowing for slight perceptual variations to correspond to slight variations in spatial position, as though the experience were not hallucinatory), just as it is *conceivable* that no objects corresponding to perceptions exist at all, and that no minds other than one's own exist. But all these positions strain credulity too much. Simultaneous (and similar) perception constitutes an implicit condition for objective experience, hence experience that is not hallucinatory. If conditions such as these are abandoned, we will find ourselves forced to yield on claims about a world of shared public objects. Rahner's view is strangely controlled by dogmatic theological views on this point. He is so convinced that the risen, ascended, and exalted body of Jesus is in heaven and unavailable for ordinary perception that he is prepared to allow for simultaneous hallucination to explain reports of group apparitions of Jesus. He does not invoke simultaneous hallucination to explain pre-Ascension group appearances alleged in the NT, but any group experience of Jesus afterward is handled that way.

I mentioned a third possible circumstance in which a visionary might offer evidence for an external source of the experience. This is speculative, but it seems to be within the realm of possibility. A technique in microspectrodensitometry allows an experimenter to determine the absorption properties of retinal cells.[124] The experimenter does this by shining a narrow beam of monochromatic light onto the cells of the retina, and then trapping the returning beam and measuring the difference between the two. Other techniques allow the size of retinal images and the varying intensity values across those two-dimensional images to be measured.[125] These kinds of technical tests suggest that some method of determining whether retinal cells are absorbing light during an apparition experience could be developed. Perhaps even an appropriately placed photocell would do so. A positive result would provide evidence for an external source of stimulation. No doubt such technical tests would be difficult to apply in real-life situations outside the laboratory, for they would require predicting the onset of a vision. But we ought to be able to devise such tests to determine the stimulation of the external organs. Perhaps a variety of external tests applicable in complex ways could be devised. In any event, an observer external to a percipient is capable in principle of providing evidence relevant to the claim that there is (or is not) external sensory stimulation. Some people might think that simpler mechanisms exist for determining that external senses are involved, for example, observing whether the pupils of visionaries change size, as psychiatrists have observed with hallucinators.[126] But cortical events could produce these effects.

It *seems* that if a vision is corporeal, then it is objective, but one circumstance is imaginable where this might not be the case. It requires some speculation about imaginative visions, and also about the neurophysiological structures responsible for visual perception (indeed, all sensory perception). If we suppose that an imaginative vision consists wholly of neurophysiological events internal to a percipient, the empirical question that remains is whether the associated electrochemical activity is capable of affecting the external senses, for example the retinal cells. Evidence suggests that electrochemical activity in the visual cortex or in the lateral geniculate nucleus, a subcortical structure between the retina and the visual cortex,[127] can produce activity in retinal cells. The normal path that electrochemical stimulation follows is from the retina to the central nervous system, rather than the other way around. But the feedback loops in human perception might allow for stimulation in the other direction, so that retinal cells are stimulated by cortical events. This possibility that imaginative visions (subjective) might produce retinal activity and thus appear to be corporeal would need to be eliminated to preserve the reasonable view that corporeal vision is objective. Because the nature of the feedback mechanisms and the question of whether the external senses have been stimulated are empirical matters, I conclude that corporeal vision is capable in principle of being detected even in cases where no disturbance of the spatio-temporal-causal domain is detected and where the experience is not a group apparition.

The angelic mediation theory could conceivably be made empirically (more) respectable by linking it with empirical tests suggested in the last few pages. But it is unsatisfactory as a theory if its only grounding is found in a theological tradition. Some empirical basis is needed to allow it to compete in an age where scientific theorizing makes observation and testing central. The angelic mediation theory arose during a time in which the required metaphysical commitments were not problematic, but it would hardly be considered today as the most obvious explanation for apparitions. Contemporary mainline Protestantism is influenced by a theology that takes a dim view of religious experience, and therefore places great emphasis upon the dogmatic content available exclusively from biblical literature, although there is of course some deviation from this strict position.

The classical theory thus can be shown to present various difficulties, and I shall approach the Christic apparition experience in a fresh way.

2 | Contemporary Christic Visions and Apparitions

Introduction

The persons whose experiences form the central material in this study were found mostly through advertisements in newspapers and religious periodicals in Canada, the United States, Great Britain, and Australia. Some were also found through acquaintances who knew about my interest in studying the Christic visionary experience. The advertisement requested that those who had experienced what they took to be a "direct visual encounter with Jesus Christ" write me a letter indicating an interest to speak with me. Subsequent letters or telephone calls were usually sufficient for me to determine if the respondents had experienced the kind of vision I wished to study, although the reticence of percipients to speak about such experiences occasionally prevented me from knowing enough about them until I conducted face-to-face interviews. Several long and arduous trips resulted in accounts of a dream experience, some out-of-body experiences, and an encounter with what the percipient took to be God, not Jesus. I have not included these in my study.

The interviews were conducted between 1988 and 1993. The descriptions that follow are based on transcripts of the conversations I had with percipients. I do not know whether any of them would accept the designation "visionary," for most were quite mystified about having had such an experience, and none is in monastic life, although some are very active in their religious communities. None of them, moreover, seems to have deliberately induced the visionary experience(s), and most appear to think of themselves as quite ordinary. All of them were quite committed in their faith when I spoke to them, although a number indicated that this commitment had fluctuated in their lives, even after the visionary experience(s). Further demographic information about their education, ethnic heritage, religious background, and so on can be found in Appendix I. I recognize that the group of cases I have assembled is neither large nor randomly selected, and a study of this kind should be viewed as only exploratory. Quite a number of the percipients live in my home province of British Columbia, and the fact that I found as many as I did living near to me suggests that many more such experiences have never been documented.

I shall divide the experiences into five groups. These groupings are tentative, for the phenomenological variety (i.e., the variety in the content of the experiences, as experienced by the percipients) makes them difficult to categorize. The first group consists of experiences in which people appear to have fallen into trances, or where the experience began in what seemed to the percipient to be the "normal" world but did not continue there, or where the experience had a dreamlike character. I shall refer to these as "Trance and Dreamlike Experiences." I am not using "trance" in a technical sense, complete with physiological criteria, but only in its ordinary sense, in order to identify experiences that hardly seem to occur in a person's normal waking consciousness.

The second group of experiences consists of those in which percipients were aware of a significant change in the physical environment they knew themselves to be in. Jim Link's first apparition experience, for instance, described in the Introduction, involved a phenomenological change in his physical environment, inasmuch as his surroundings did not appear to be his own living room, where he knew himself to be. I shall identify the broad group of cases to which Jim's belongs as "Experiences in an Altered Environment."

The third group of experiences consists of those in which the physical environment appeared to percipients as they knew it to be, apart from the visionary figure that appeared in it. I shall refer to them as "Private Experiences," because although they may have occurred in public, only a selected percipient experienced the apparition.

The fourth group of experiences applies to those in which several percipients were simultaneously affected, including cases in which two or more percipients apparently saw the same thing, as well as one unusual case in which one percipient only saw that which another person only felt as a tactile sensation. This group will also include cases in which other intersubjectively observable effects or causal concomitants were alleged, for example, a case in which the Christic apparition was allegedly filmed. I add the qualifier "causal concomitant" because it is difficult to differentiate causal effects from concomitants in isolated cases. I shall collect this fourth group under the heading "Experiences with Observable Effects."

A fifth kind of Christic vision was not presented in detail by the percipients, but is well known from the literature surveyed in Chapter 1. I am referring to visions in which some event in the life of Jesus is apparently reenacted, for example, an event of his childhood or his crucifixion. Perhaps this kind of experience could be classified with trance and dreamlike experiences, but I have chosen to classify them separately.

The descriptions that follow do not generally include precise information on where these experiences took place, for that did not appear to be significant to percipients, and in some cases percipients were unsure about the precise locale. Many of these percipients have moved far from the places where their experiences took place, and show no evidence of attaching significance to the physical locations where the apparitions occurred, by, say, erecting statues or shrines. The accounts often make use of descriptive phrases deriving from religious traditions within Christianity that have influenced percipients, as well as some quite explicitly biblical phraseology. I occasionally had difficulty understanding what percipients were talking about, but had the advantage of being able to ask for explanations. Further details of the phenomenological characteristics of the experiences described here can be found in Appendix II.

Group I: Trance and Dreamlike Experiences

Case 1: Joy Kinsey

Joy Kinsey was born in Oakland, California, and has lived in the vicinity of Oakland much of her life. One of her earliest memories is kneeling with her sister at her father's knee, saying prayers just before bed. Joy and her sister went to the Presbyterian church near their home in San Leondro as children, but in 1947, at fourteen Joy began to attend a Pentecostal Holiness church in Oakland, which is where her experience took place some ten years later. Prayer was a central feature in the life of her new church, and people would pray together for hours on end, sometimes all night long. The informal nature of the services allowed people to come to the altar for prayer during the service, and this is what Joy did one evening, along with others, as the service was in progress. Her intention was "just to kneel and pray and just really totally surrender my will to God for whatever purpose." A minister came over to pray with her, and when he touched the back of her head in a gesture of blessing, she fell backward and lost consciousness.

For three hours Joy was unaware of anyone or anything around her. She had the sense of being in a place where a temple was surrounded by a courtyard. The temple had three domed parts to it, attached together so that they formed one continuous building. She began to walk through it, each part beautiful beyond description, but when she came to the threshold of the third part she stopped, for she felt unworthy to enter. As she looked in she saw Jesus sitting on a throne about fifteen feet away, but sitting sideways in relation to her and partially obscured by a lattice. He looked pleased at her having come so far, such as a parent might look upon seeing his or her child take its first steps. He appeared average in size, solid in appearance, much as she had pictured him.

Joy attempted to enter the third part of the temple, but he put out his hand in a gesture that indicated that she could not. He told her from behind the lattice that she was not allowed to approach him. At hearing this she fell to her knees and prostrated herself on the floor, which seemed to be made of marble or alabaster. It was so immaculate that she felt dirty and unworthy. She begged permission to approach him closer, but he would not allow it, and instead instructed her to get up and go to a nearby window. She looked out of the window onto a landscape of fields and trees bent by the wind. He drew her attention in the ensuing conversation to a kite, which was barely flying because its tail was too long. He told her that her life was like the kite, burdened down by sins and encumbrances that impeded its flight. As she looked at the kite again its tail became caught in a tree, whereupon the one flying it yanked on the string and freed it to soar away, leaving half the tail in the tree. Jesus told her that her life could be like that kite. She left the window and fell on her knees again. As she looked in front of her she saw a goblet filled with wine. Jesus then said to her, "I will give you a new anointing.[1] Drink the wine." As she obeyed she could see him smiling at her. He was still seated, but now his hand was on the lattice in a parting gesture of blessing.

Joy regained consciousness and discovered that approximately three hours had elapsed since the vision began. She found that the people around her were distressed because they smelled a strong aroma of sweet wine coming from her mouth. The smell filled the church, and she felt drunk. She was so wobbly that she could not stand on her own but needed two people to hold her up, and when she tried to speak she could not speak English but could speak only a language that she had not learned.[2] Joy had never had an alcoholic drink in her life; moreover, the church of which she was a part practiced total abstinence, even refraining from the use of wine during eucharistic or communion services. Joy says that the experience made her feel greatly loved by Jesus. Her life has been difficult at times, particularly because of the care that her husband, who has Alzheimer's and Parkinson's disease, has required. But she has also sensed the sustaining presence of God. She has two children, and still lives in the Oakland area.

COMMENT   This experience would not have qualified for inclusion in my study, since Joy had her eyes closed, but for the provocative, intersubjectively observable effects that she reported. I haven't verified them however. I place her account first because it is the most dreamlike of the experiences described to me. Readers familiar with the NT will hardly fail to notice the striking similarity between this experience and the one briefly described by Luke in Acts 2 when glossolalia was first experienced in Christian circles, and bystanders thought those speaking were drunk.

Case 2: Robin Wheeler

Robin had very little contact with the church or with Christians for the first thirty-eight years of his life. He occasionally went to a Catholic or an Anglican church when he was young, but he had no interest in religion until neighbors moved in who were quite religious. His wife became a Christian as a result of their influence. This annoyed him greatly, especially when she prayed openly for him. One Saturday night several weeks after her conversion he had what he described as a battle with an evil creature as he was trying to sleep. Its face resembled a human face without skin, and it frightened him. He tried to fight off this creature, but he was not successful. Just off to his right stood a man wearing a brown sackcloth robe with a sash around his waist. Robin never did see above the shoulders of this second figure, but he considers it to have been Jesus. Robin tried to tie up the creature with the sash from Jesus, and as he did so Jesus disappeared. Again and again he would struggle with the monster, and each time Jesus would appear long enough for Robin to grab the sash, and then would disappear.

Robin's wife was with him while this struggle was taking place. She told me that he levitated for long periods of time that coincided with the struggles, and seemed to go in and out of consciousness. She says that Robin floated in midair in a horizontal position about a foot above the bed. His body was in a perfectly rigid position, and all the veins in his body were bulging. His head was bent so far back, she says, that she thought it would break. Although she did not see the figures that appeared to him, she could ask him what was happening, and he would describe the events taking place. She estimates that the various struggles occurred over a six-hour period, but he had no sense of the passing of time. When a fight sequence came to an end, his body would drop back onto the bed, and he would relax until a new struggle began. But Robin was not aware of his levitation. During the fights he could see his wife as well as these two other beings, and they seemed as real as ordinary persons. The place he seemed to be in did not fit with the physical description of the bedroom, however. Jesus would appear with Roman sandals, and he entered the scene with his feet first, as though he descended from above. The struggles finally ended when Robin found that his efforts to tie up the monster did not succeed, and he requested help from Jesus who bound the monster for him. Robin considers this to be symbolic of his own inability to restrain the powers of evil that tried to envelop him. The next day Robin decided to become a Christian. This event took place in Abbotsford, British Columbia, in 1984.

COMMENT   This is one of the few experiences involving a struggle with forces considered to be diabolical. Robin's wife clearly understood the levitation she witnessed to be an intersubjectively observable concomitant, but no one else was there to see it. Their children and pets were elsewhere in the house, and slept through the bizarre events, even though Robin shouted all night long. Robin and his wife said that they interpreted this deep sleep as indicative of unseen forces that were controlling the events of that night. Robin's wife evinced no surprise at the fact that he had levitated, for she said she had witnessed levitation of other people on several occasions. Both said they had been involved in "occult" practices earlier in their lives.

Case 3: Marian Hathaway

Marian was brought up in Swansea, Wales, as an atheist, by parents who were atheists. She said she was really a third-generation atheist, for her paternal grandfather had also been one. She wanted to believe in God when she was young, but could not find any reason to do so. When she was seventeen she had a dream in which a man with dark bushy hair came toward her with his arms open, asking her to love him. She said she knew it was Jesus, even though she did not know much about him. She had heard a story about Jesus born in a manger, who grew up to be a good man, but that was the extent of her knowledge. Her education in a state school included prayers and religious instruction, but these meant nothing to her.

Marian married soon after secondary school and had children, but she was not happy. She gradually became so depressed that it interfered with her ability to work, and she began to contemplate suicide. In her desperation she prayed to God for help. She soon began to sleep better, which she attributed to her prayer. She then went to hospital for a short stint in order to rid her body of toxins that had accumulated from the medications she had been taking. She began to feel better, and she wondered if her prayer for help had worked.

Several days after returning home Marian received a visit from a young couple who belonged to the Jehovah's Witnesses. Marian was very receptive to the things they said, and soon they visited her four times a week to instruct her. But the position of the Jehovah's Witnesses on blood transfusions—that they violate scripture—was a point of contention with her mother, who encouraged an old family friend from a different religious persuasion to visit Marian. Marian now heard a different point of view on a variety of subjects. For the next seven months she studied both points of view. She asked God to show her the truth, particularly about the divinity of Jesus but felt desperate about ever finding it because of her own sense of unworthiness. In Easter week of 1969, as she was riding the bus home from one of these instructional meetings, she heard the words inside her, "I died for you, and I love you just the way you are, with all your sin." Then she heard the words, "I am God." At this she burst into tears of joy. The bus driver asked her if she was all right as she left the bus, and she assured him she was. The question that remained, as a result of this experience, was whether she should attend any conventional Christian churches, since she wondered if God was present in any denominations besides the Jehovah's Witnesses. She decided to attend the Baptist church with the old family friend. She worried greatly about being at the service, however, wondering if it was the right thing to do. She was seated in the balcony of the church, and as she looked toward the large pipe organ she saw shimmering blue and gold colors in front of it. The images reminded her of the jumpy pictures of the earliest silent movies. They gradually became clearer until she found herself looking at a big face with beautiful golden hair and a golden beard. The face was so large it filled the front of the church—some twenty feet high. She thought it must be Jesus, but she was puzzled by the fact that he neither looked Jewish nor resembled the image of the person that appeared in her dream when she was seventeen. She saw him looking at the congregation, with a smile and an expression of love for the people. Then she saw his arms, draped in white, move in an embrace of everyone present at the service. They were large enough to take in several rows at once. To describe his action Marian used a Welsh word meaning to cuddle, to comfort, or to love by touching someone. He loved everyone there, including her. She kissed his cheek in response, and felt his warmth, although not the feel of his skin. Because Marian did not know if this experience was real or imaginary, she closed her eyes, but she could still see him with her eyes closed. When she opened them a moment later he was still there. This went on for some time, and Marian felt assured that she had come to the right place. When she went home that day she prayed, asking God whether it was really Jesus that had appeared to her, and if it was, why he appeared with only his face and arms. She reached for her Bible, which was still quite new to her, and opened it at random. The first thing she saw was the passage in *Ephesians* 1 that speaks of Jesus being the head of the church, and the church being his body. Everything fell into place for her at that moment, and Christian beliefs about him and his death became clear.

This experience took place in Swansea in 1969, when Marian was thirty years of age. She worked as a library assistant when I interviewed her in 1993.

COMMENT This was one of the few experiences in which a percipient described the Christic figure that appeared as much larger than life-size. It was also the only case in which having one's eyes open or closed made no difference. I surmise that this would warrant its being classified as imaginative, rather than corporeal, according to Augustine's traditional classification. The two experiences previously described are clearly trancelike in character, whereas this one is less so, since Marian was awake. Yet it shares a dreamlike quality with them, for it made no difference if her eyes were open or shut. Her experience is illustrative of the difficulty in classifying visions in precise categories.

Case 4: John Vasse

John Vasse was brought up in a devout Catholic home in Fairfield, Connecticut, attended church regularly as a child, and was educated at a Jesuit high school. But something happened halfway through high school—something he did not divulge—that made him turn his back on God and the church. For the next twenty-six years or so he was filled with loathing and contempt for God. He would go into churches to scream at and curse the figure on the crucifix, daring Jesus to come off the cross so he could physically abuse him. Meanwhile, he attended college, graduated with a degree in engineering, married, and entered the U.S. Air Force. Although he held down a number of good engineering jobs, he lived a life that revolved around going to bars and consuming alcohol. He drank so much that by the time he was forty he had damaged his liver and suffered an apparent heart attack. His drinking also affected his marriage, and when he got word of a transfer to St. Louis, where his wife was unwilling to move, he felt as though his life had reached bottom. At this point a friend who had recently become a Christian suggested to John that he should follow his example. John decided that there was nothing to lose by praying, and so he prayed, apologizing to God for the way he had behaved for most of his life. He took the transfer to St. Louis, and after about six months his wife decided to join him there. On Christmas Day that year, 1984, the experience that changed his life occurred.

John and his wife tried to go to church on Christmas Eve, but ice had made the highways treacherous. The roads had not improved much by morning, so they stayed in their apartment and ate a late breakfast. As John sat at the table after breakfast, reading the editorial pages of the local paper, he had the uncomfortable and peculiar feeling that someone was standing behind him. He knew that no one was there, but nevertheless felt a "presence" who wanted "entry." John felt he had the choice of excluding this unidentified presence or inviting it in, and made a split-second decision: "OK, sure, come on in." He was immediately flooded with a weight of despondency or heaviness. But it did not seem to be his own despondency that he was feeling, but that of the presence he had invited in. John began to weep uncontrollably because of it, and not wanting to be seen crying, went to the bathroom to be alone. He locked the door and stood before the mirror as this weight became heavier and heavier. As he stood there he realized that the presence that he was feeling was Jesus. As he reflected on his contemptuous attitude in the past, John was filled with enormous guilt and shame. He fell to his knees and began to weep uncontrollably again, wetting his clothes, his shoes, and the bathroom floor with his tears. He sobbed, "Please forgive me, please forgive me." He wanted to crawl into the tub, pull the shade around himself and hide from this presence, but he was unable to move. As he continued to beg forgiveness he felt as though two plugs at the bottom of his feet popped out, and all the shame and guilt in him drained away as water would drain out of a bathtub. He was still immobilized, but the feelings of guilt and shame disappeared. The presence gradually faded. He returned to the kitchen table but could not talk to his wife about the events that had just happened. He anticipated that something else was going to happen, and in less than a minute the presence he had felt before was back. He did not want to fall onto the floor of the kitchen, so he walked toward the couch in the living room. Halfway there, he collapsed. Again the weight crushed him, but this time it did not last. It lifted, and the whole room was flooded with light, but not from any apparent natural source. He says that the wall of the living room in front of him was lit up as bright as the sun, but he could look into it without hurting his eyes. In the center was an area not illuminated quite as intensely as the rest, and here he could see the outline of a head, neck, and shoulders (a cameo). He was instinctively certain that this was Jesus, from whom came an overpowering sense of love and compassion that extended to John and then returned back as though in circular motion. The intensity of the light surrounding the figure obliterated facial features and other details. Ecstatic joy replaced John's earlier sense of anguish and despondency. As the experience came to an end, Jesus raised his hands in an inviting gesture. The whole experience lasted about thirty minutes—John happened to look at his watch before and after—and he had no control from the moment he made the decision to let the presence in. John was not sure if his eyes were open during the visual part of the experience, and he is uncertain about whether the figure appeared on the wall in front of him or was present only in his own visual space. His wife was in the apartment at the time but saw nothing.

John still lives in St. Louis. When I interviewed him he was working as a computer systems analyst with the U.S. Army. He has since taken early retirement, and works with an organization in St. Louis that seeks to develop lay leadership in the church.

COMMENT   The visual elements of this experience were clearly secondary to the emotional effects of it, and the difficulty that John had in determining whether the figure that appeared was present only in his visual space or might have been visibly present, as this is conventionally understood, induces me to classify it with the trance cases. Though this was not the only experience in which a presence was strongly felt, it is a striking example. Andrew Mackenzie contends that presences should be included as apparitions, "although the experience is not externalized."[3] He remarks that figures can sometimes be described in detail even though they are not seen, and he rejects the common view that things that are only "felt" and not seen are experientially inferior.[4] John's experience seems to have hovered between an altered state of consciousness and ordinary perception.

Group II: Altered Environment Cases

Case 5: Marian Gallife

Marian was devastated by the death of her son, Joe. A week after his funeral she began to lock herself in his room for long periods of time, just to lie on his bed and be alone with his childhood toys and other mementoes of him. Joe, 18, was killed in a traffic accident, the only fatality in a car with four other teenagers. He had been an extraordinarily caring child, and so his death left a great void in the lives of Marian and her husband. One afternoon as she lay on his bed she began to express her anger toward God, demanding an answer to the question how he could have caused or allowed Joe to die. She felt betrayed by God, for she had been devoted to God and had tried to obey him. She fell asleep after this outburst and awakened around nine o'clock that evening. She felt as though someone had awakened her, but no one else was around. As Marian sat up she felt as though she was commanded to go downstairs and gather her family for prayer and a reading from the Bible. She came downstairs to join her family in the living room, but didn't quite know how to convey the command, thinking that her family would think her mad if she spoke about it. She finally told her husband that she wanted to read the Bible and pray, and he consented. As she opened the Bible to a passage in the gospel of John, she sensed a command to stand up. They all stood up as she read, and then joined hands to pray. At that moment the back door flew open from what seemed to be a gust of wind, and a breeze moved through the room. The atmosphere of the room suddenly changed. A painful sensation creased Marian's chest, and she wondered aloud how much more pain she would have to bear. Then a light brighter than anything she had ever seen exploded upon her and filled the room.

The light gradually faded, and a man dressed in white came into view. It was Jesus. He appeared to be transparent rather than solid, and his long hair caught her attention. She first saw his profile, and then he turned to her, stretched out his hand, and commanded her (so it seemed) to look down the length of his arm. As she did so, his body disappeared from view until she could see only his hand. From the end of his hand a hill covered with green grass began to form. As her attention was directed toward the hill she saw Joe running toward her with three other children. Joe was wearing his favorite checkered shirt, blue jeans and jacket, and the belt with the big brass Harley Davidson buckle. She kept saying, "Look at our Joe. Our Joe's coming." But the command came to her, "Look past Joe. Haven't you forgotten them? They are with me." Then she realized who the smaller children were. One was her child from a pregnancy that had been terminated because of fibroids in her womb, and the two other children were twins that she later lost because of the effect of the terminated pregnancy. The twins would have been fourteen if they had lived, and the other child sixteen, and the three children who appeared with Joe seemed to be of these ages. Marian's sorrow turned to joy at the realization of who the children were. In response to encouragement from Joe, she began to sing in praise to God. Marian's husband did not see any of the things that she reported, but he observed that she was in an extraordinary ecstasy as these events unfolded. Her attitude toward the death of her son changed after that, and she now felt like saying to everyone she knew, "Joe is alive, do you realize? I know now that we're all going to meet him." When they went through Joe's room sometime later, she found the clothes she had seen him wear in the vision. Marian lived in London, England, when I interviewed her in 1993, working as a homemaker and dressmaker. The experience had taken place two years earlier.

Case 6: Eve Zelle

Eve was brought up in the eastern United States with a variety of Christian influences. She was born into a Greek Orthodox family and raised in that church, but sometime in her youth her family adopted the beliefs of the Jehovah's Witnesses. By fourteen she had abandoned most of her religious beliefs, apart from the belief that God exists. She occasionally went to a Catholic church with some of her friends, and attended a Catholic college because it was near her home. She took a major in mathematics and a minor in Catholic philosophy, and became a teacher. After she married and had children, she took them to church, and sometime in her thirties she finally felt comfortable calling herself a Christian. She began to go to various churches, both Protestant and Catholic, as well as to Bible studies, in order to learn whatever she could about being a Christian. Eve's first experience took place in 1987 or 1988, when she was about forty-six. By this time she was single, responsible for two teenage daughters, and unemployed.

Eve was desperate about her situation. Not only had she been without work for a long period of time, but her oldest daughter was giving her a hard time. Eve began to feel that God was not aware of her need, and she wondered if he was real, or if she was only fooling herself about his existence. She remembers extending her hand in a moment of desperate prayer and saying to God, "If I could only touch you, if I could only touch your hand." She opened her eyes, and was startled to see Jesus in front of her. Her words were: "He was on his knees holding both my hands with the most compassionate, warm eyes that I had ever seen, with strength behind them." The look on his face extended warmth and compassion toward her and let her know that he understood her desperation. He had large brown eyes and looked Jewish to her. She cannot recall anything else about his appearance, although she thinks he had a short beard. He appeared to be normal in size, although an assessment of this was difficult because he was kneeling. Her impression was that he was wearing white clothing, but she could not say whether it was the kind of robe traditionally associated with him. Though the experience was comforting and reassuring, it also scared her, and she ran from the room. The one odd feature of the experience was that she was kneeling at her bed, facing her bed, when it took place. Eve's words were: "He was where the bed would have been, and there was nothing else." She is at a loss to explain how the perceptual sense of the bed could disappear and how she could see Jesus in its place, for her eyes were open.

Eve had a second experience some two years later, again in response to prayer. Eve describes herself as very pro-life, and she was devastated to learn that a close friend had chosen to have an abortion. She walked "screaming angry" into her bedroom to pray about this, but before her knees hit the floor she saw Jesus standing and holding a baby. He held it in such a way that the baby seemed part of him. She could see the head of a child, but the rest of the child blended in with him. She got the sense that he had received the aborted child, and that he was not bringing condemnation on its mother. He gave the sense of taking care of his own children. Jesus appeared to be about six feet tall, and stood some eight feet away, clothed in robes that Eve described as priestly in color, perhaps blue trimmed with gold. Although Eve was in her bedroom when this took place, all she could see was Jesus. It seemed as though all the normal furniture in the room had disappeared, much as in the first experience in which her bed disappeared. Both of the experiences gave her a sense that God is deeply concerned about her life.

COMMENT These experiences are remarkable because, like some dreams, they exhibit spatio-temporal discontinuities. It goes without saying that different objects do not occupy the same space at the same time in ordinary experience, but some visions evidently violate this principle.

Case 7: Ernie Hollands

Ernie was born in 1930 in the slums of Halifax, Nova Scotia, to what would now be called a dysfunctional family. Alcoholism, as well as physical and emotional abuse, characterize memories of his earliest years, and he has no memory of having been loved or embraced. His "private education" began at eight when his mother took him shopping and taught him how to steal. By the time he was ten he was quite expert at it. Ernie was caught and sent to reform school. The challenge of escape was appealing, and thus began a cycle of crime, arrest, detention, and escape. Numerous Canadian and American prisons were "home" for Ernie during the next twenty-five years or so. The events that changed his life took place when he was incarcerated at Millhaven Penitentiary in Bath, Ontario.

During his prison term in Millhaven, Ernie developed a successful business selling hand-tied fishing flies. One of his business contacts, Grant Bailey from Pembroke, Ontario, urged Ernie to read the Bible and become a Christian. Ernie's initial response was contempt, but the warmth of friendship extended to him by Grant made him reconsider, and so Ernie began to read and reread the Bible. On March 12, 1975, at two o'clock in the morning Ernie awoke with the sense that he should confess his sins to God. He wept as he knelt down by his bed to pray, and felt that his past had been forgiven. When he stood up, his vision, as he calls it, began. He turned to look at the door of his cell, for no particular reason, but what he saw was no longer his cell but the room of a house with a door on the right side of it, positioned where the cell door was located. This door opened up, and Jesus walked through it toward Ernie, stood in front of him, touched him on his left shoulder (which he felt) and said three things. He first said, "I'm so glad you didn't kill that police officer," and then he smiled. Ernie understands this to be a reference to the crime he had committed before being sent to Millhaven. In the course of a robbery of a supermarket in Hollywood, California, he had struggled with a policeman for control of a stolen gun, and in the tussle he accidentally shot the policeman in the leg. Ernie then gave himself up, hoping that the policeman would perhaps shoot him and put him out of misery. Instead, he found himself incarcerated in Los Angeles until he was released to the Canadian authorities for crimes committed in Canada. Then Jesus said, "Your slate is now wiped clean," and here he moved his hands in a way that suggested that something was being erased. The third thing Jesus said was, "Now you can start all over again," making a semicircular motion with his arms, to suggest that Ernie was being sent into a whole new life. Then Jesus disappeared.

He appeared to Ernie much as he is traditionally portrayed, wearing white, and of medium height. Ernie was not able to be more precise about any other physical details, however. Ernie describes the three statements made to him as sounding as though they came from inside himself, and he was not aware of the movement of the lips of Jesus as these things were uttered. He describes the voice as though it was thunder coming from inside of himself. Ernie's story was reported by the Ottawa press, and has become widely known through his own telling of it in person and through a book.[5] In 1983 he opened Hebron Farm near London, Ontario, as a Christian home for ex-offenders, dedicated to helping them obtain employment and readjust to society.

Case 8: Jim Link

See the Introduction for the description of two experiences.

Case 9: Kris Nelson

Kris's experience took place in the context of a long, drawn-out illness. She went into the hospital to have a hysterectomy, thinking she would recuperate in six weeks or so, but the operation was followed by complications, including internal bleeding, thrombosis, and blood infections. Two more operations were required before her health improved, and she found herself incapacitated for six months rather than six weeks. Just before her last operation the doctor came to her home to assess her condition. When she heard that another operation would be required, she was devastated, for she knew that her husband and her children needed her at home. As she lay in bed feeling very sad, a sense of peace unexpectedly came over her. She glanced over to the corner of the room, for no apparent reason, and saw the face of Jesus. She describes his face as having been the mirror image of how she had felt. The hurt and sadness were on his face, and tears streamed down his face, as though he was identifying with her sadness. When Kris saw him she felt that all would be well in just a little while.

Kris saw only his face, which appeared about eight to ten feet away and looked very lifelike in the well-lighted room. She described his appearance as quite ordinary, and not quite like any portrayals that she had seen. His hair was fairly long and brown, and Kris was not sure whether he had a beard. It was his eyes that caught her attention, however, for they seemed to show that he knew her heart and was sympathetic. Some radiance shone around his head, but not so much as to obscure the image itself. Kris does not know how she made the identification of the person as Jesus, but did not hesitate in doing so. The only medication she was on at the time was an antibiotic.

Kris is a secretary as well as a homemaker, and has lived in Melbourne, Australia, all her life. Her experience took place in June 1992, and I interviewed her the following year.

COMMENT This experience is peculiar because it involved the visual perception of only a face. It is not really like the trance experiences described earlier, nor the cases to follow in which the physical environment changed, nor those in which the whole figure was superimposed upon the normal environment.

Group III: Private Experiences

Case 10: Ethel Chilvers

Ethel Chilvers had a visionary experience in her small apartment in Toronto when she was ninety-one years of age. She was in the kitchen washing dishes, and when she looked up in the direction of the table some six to eight feet away, she saw the figure of Jesus in profile above the table. He was not walking or moving, but seemed to be in midstride facing the direction of the city center. She said he appeared much as he does in children's picture books, with brown shoulder-length hair, beard, white skin, and of average size. He wore a cape or cloak similar to that which she had seen worn by a man from Afghanistan who lived in her apartment block. Jesus did not move at all, and his appearance was like that of a statue, but a living statue and solid. As Ethel said: "It was just as though a man stood there. It could have been you." He did not appear happy or pleased, but looked to her as though he wanted to "execute judgment on somebody somewhere or do something. I felt like he was capable of destroying the whole world. I had the sense that he had that much power, that he could stop it [the world] if he wanted to, but he was restrained from doing it." He somehow communicated all this without saying a word. She later reflected on the sense of power that he seemed to her to have, and felt that what was restraining him was his love for humanity.

Ethel had immigrated to Canada from England with her parents when she was six years old. She trained as a nurse in Port Simpson Hospital and Vancouver General Hospital during 1918-1921, and practiced nursing for about sixty years. She was brought up in the Methodist Church and has attended a variety of churches during her lifetime. I spoke to her when she was ninety-three years of age, and although her health was beginning to fail, she was lively in conversation and continued to read and keep up correspondence with friends.

COMMENT Most of the experiences reported to me have had great personal significance for the percipients, and were often related to some difficult or tragic feature of their lives. This one was different, inasmuch as it did not carry any significant personal message for Ethel. The experience did make her regret not having pursued more conscientiously certain plans she had when she was much younger to work as a missionary nurse in China, but the experience was not interpreted by her in a distinctly personal way. The fact that the figure showed no movement at all and was seen only in profile made this experience unusual.

Case 11: Deby Stamm-Loya

Deby Stamm-Loya, now living in Southern California, moved home just before Christmas 1972 to live with her parents in Tucson, Arizona, after her marriage failed. She watched a movie one evening with her parents that awakened a desire to know God better. She went to her bed and began to think about life, and about the desire that the movie had evoked. She lay on her back for some time with her eyes closed, thinking about these things, and when she opened them some minutes later a man she instantly identified as Jesus stood at the end of her bed some five or six feet away. His arms were stretched out as though he was reaching for her. He stood there for a moment, appearing much as he does in traditional portrayals of him, and in a manner similar to that in which any normal person would appear, and then he began to change. A radiance enveloped him in a pure white light that gradually increased in intensity. As this radiance intensified, it extended farther and farther beyond him, so that it finally consisted of a pure white light nearest to him and various shades of yellow, orange, and amber beyond the whiteness. As this transformation took place, Deby became conscious of being drawn into the immense universe of which he seemed a part, and had the sense of being in a place far removed from her parents' home. Then she lost natural consciousness and became aware only of his voice and the things he said to her. In reflecting back on the experience, Deby says that the things that he said had the greatest significance for her. He told her that he had everything in the universe under control, including her life, and that he had many things to teach her. He said that he loved her, and that she should keep her attention fixed on him. How long this experience lasted she does not know, for when she regained natural consciousness she was lying in her bed, and it was morning. She firmly believes that she had not fallen asleep at the time the vision (her term) began, because she does not fall asleep lying on her back. Moreover, the bedroom door was open to the adjacent room where her parents were sitting, and she saw the figure standing at the end of her bed against the background of that room.

Deby had had a difficult childhood and adolescence. Her father had abused her mentally and physically. He was an atheist, her mother a Mormon of sorts, but the dominating influence in their home was anger and depression. By the time she was thirteen she was a thief and a compulsive runaway; by fifteen she was the leader of a girl's gang in Albuquerque. She experimented extensively with drugs, mostly LSD, but eventually tired of drug experiences. One day she decided to do something different, so she went downtown to the public library, stole one of the books on religion, and took it home to read. This book aroused an interest in the Bible, so she acquired one and began to read it several hours each day. One day she became aware of a living presence that seemed to emanate from its pages, and although she neither saw nor heard anything unusual, she surrendered to that presence. This presence felt as though someone she had known long ago had returned. That is how she describes becoming a Christian.

Deby describes her drug experiences as having magnified or distorted her physical perceptions. If she looked at flowers, they would appear to bloom much more than they normally did; if she watched television, the set would appear to melt. The nature of her drug experiences was such that images in her visual field were always of things she knew to be there, never of nonexistent things. She also experienced flashbacks because of the large amount of LSD she had taken, but these experiences filled her with dread, and gave her the sensation of being paralysed from the neck down. She says that the difference between these experiences and the visionary one was like night and day. Deby was not able to describe the figure in her vision in detail, although she says he seemed average in height, and appeared alive and solid. It was not so much his appearance that impressed her, but rather the way he spoke to her and what he said. She was convinced that it was Jesus in part because his appearance conformed to traditional images of him, but also because of the transformation that took place before her eyes. She was not aware of any other person in recent times having had a visionary experience. It confirmed her Christian faith, and prepared her for the death of her parents soon afterward and the challenges of raising a child as a single parent. Deby had completed a first degree in theology when I spoke to her, and was on her way to completing a doctorate in ministry. She has founded a Christian organization that works with prison inmates.

COMMENT This experience was interesting for several reasons. First, it combined an experience that apparently involved ordinary perception with one that sounds like an OBE. A person skeptical of visionary experiences might think that the experience was really a dream, particularly in view of its having occurred at night while lying in bed, and also because Deby did lose consciousness. But Deby is adamant about having been awake when the vision began. The second interesting feature is the change in appearance of the figure in Deby's visual field. I questioned her closely on this matter, and she insisted that the experience definitely did not begin with the radiance that later enveloped the figure. It is also interesting that this transformation contributed to the identification that Deby made. The third element that is of interest is the unique position she was in to compare her drug and flashback experiences with the vision. It is natural to expect that the vision might have been similar to a drug or flashback experience, and perhaps there are cases in which such a favorable comparison might be made, but Deby was quite insistent about the sharp contrast, both phenomenologically and emotionally, between the visionary experience and the others. Though some might think that having taken drugs earlier in life disqualifies percipients from advancing their visionary experiences with authority, it might be noted that only a person who has experienced both can credibly compare their phenomenological character.

Case 12: Maria Elena Martinez

When Maria was young she lived with her mother on weekends, and with her paternal grandparents during the week. Her family was Roman Catholic, and she attended a Catholic school. Maria's experience occurred as she was walking down the street with her mother. They were waiting to cross a busy intersection when she noticed a tree nearby. It had two trunks, either because two trees had grown together or because the main trunk had divided. As she focused her attention on the tree, she saw that a man was framed by the two trunks. He stood about seven feet away, life-size and semitransparent, for she could see the traffic through him. Maria does not believe she would have been able to touch him if she had stood near enough. His robe was white, and a red cape rested on his shoulders. His complexion was fair, and he had a beard. He looked at her with gentleness and grace, but also penetratingly.

Maria felt that she was being invited to gaze upon him, and as she did so, an extraordinary sense of peace came over her. Because Maria's parents had divorced, she felt a lot of rejection. His message to her was, "You will go through life feeling humiliated, embarrassed, and made a fool of. You will be laughed at, you will be ridiculed, you will not be believed. You are going to go basically through a lot of rejection." Then he added, "If you'll just focus on me, I will see you through this. I will make sure that some day you will be believed, you will be respected, you will be lifted. But you must know that I am with you and you must know that you must focus on me and me alone." He somehow communicated this message to her, although his lips did not appear to move. He disappeared just as quickly as he had appeared, but just before doing so he raised his hand in a gesture of blessing. His hand was on his heart, with two of his fingers extended, just as he appears in the picture of the Sacred Heart widely circulated among Catholics. Her explanation of this is that he was giving her a mark by which she could recognize him.

By the time the vision was over her mother was some distance ahead of her, but it seemed to Maria as though time had stood still. She has carried the sense of love he communicated to her since this experience, which took place in Florida in 1964. Maria still lives in Miami, and works as a homemaker as well as for a Messianic Jewish organization.

Case 13: Ron Lindsay

Ron Lindsay spent his early years alternating between an orphanage and the home of his grandparents. The neglect and abuse he experienced as a result of being abandoned as a child left him emotionally scarred. After he fell off a swing at sixteen, he began to have epileptic seizures. These seizures compounded his feelings of rejection, insecurity, and fear. It was about this time that he became a Christian. He had attended a Catholic church when he was growing up, but did not take his faith very seriously until he became involved with the Youth for Christ organization. He then started attending a Pentecostal church near his home, and this is where his vision took place.

By the time Ron was twenty his epileptic seizures caused him to be hospitalized for about nine months. Ron was in and out of a mental hospital. The medications he was on compounded his feelings of disorientation. He wondered if anyone loved him, and consoled himself with the thought that God loved him. As he attended church one Sunday morning he was startled to see Jesus appear at the front of the church. Ron jumped to his feet and exclaimed, "Jesus, you're here! You're here!" Jesus looked at him with eyes that glistened with compassion, held out his hands in a welcoming gesture, and said, "I love you, and I'm going to heal you." Ron responded with, "Oh! Have you come for me?" Jesus replied, "I've come, and I'm going to heal you." He stayed for a few moments, gleaming with radiance, and then disappeared. Ron was able to be specific about some of the details of the vision. He said that Jesus appeared from the waist up, wearing a robe that was off-white in color. He stood some twenty-five to thirty-five feet away, appearing solid and obscuring other objects, with the rest of the room looking normal. His lips moved as he spoke. What made the greatest impression on Ron was the brightness in his eyes, for they spoke of love. The congregation accepted his outburst of surprise without much comment. This took place in the early fall of 1965.

The months that followed were difficult. Ron lived in a dark basement room when he was not in hospital. He would sense what he took to be the presence of God, especially in the mental hospital, but he also sensed evil forces that threatened him with death, particularly in his basement room. The voices would say, "I'm going to kill you. You're finished. Commit suicide. You know you're done with." His only solace at these times would come through prayer.

Ron reports that he was healed nine months after his vision. As he entered his church one night, a voice that he describes as that of the Holy Spirit said to him, "This is your night." As he went for prayer at the end of the service, he had another seizure. The voices said, "I'm going to kill him. He's mine." The people in the church prayed for him for several hours, and conducted what he describes as an exorcism. For the first time in a long time he slept well, and when he got up the next morning he felt different.

He felt peace and joy, and it seemed as though someone with strong arms held him tight and said to him, "I'll be your father, I'll be your mother, I'll be everything you have need of. Go in peace." For a minute or so he was overwhelmed by a presence, and then he yelled, "Oh Jesus, you're here again!" For a moment the outline or shadow of a person's back was visible, and then it vanished. Ron considers this outline and the arms that embraced him to have been those of Jesus.

Ron completed his high school after this experience, and took some Bible college education by correspondence. He eventually became an evangelist, and for many years now has made his living this way, often sharing his experience with his audiences.

Case 14: Rose Fairs

Rose was brought up in a Greek Orthodox home, and because her husband was from another denominational background, they could not agree about religious matters, including where they should go to church. So they didn't attend anywhere.

Rose's first vision occurred in about 1963. She is not sure of the date, because the significance of it did not really dawn on her until some time afterward. She was lying in bed one morning, wide awake, when the Venetian blinds opened up and the head of Jesus appeared. Only his bearded head was visible, but for Rose it was the most beautiful face with the bluest of eyes. The first thought that came to her was that she should pray. She thought it would be selfish to pray for herself, so she prayed, "Would you save thy people." As she said this tears came into his eyes and rolled down his cheeks. Then he vanished. She woke her husband up to tell him what had happened. The Venetian blinds had been closed before this incident took place, but when the head of Jesus appeared they mysteriously opened. The head appeared solid, for the blinds could be seen on either side of it, but not where his head appeared. She estimates that he was some six to eight feet away, and that his size looked normal for that distance. The experience made her feel elated, and as though she were floating. She could hardly contain the news. After this she began to attend church periodically, but no particularly significant change in her religious life occurred as a result of it.

The second Christic apparition took place in Palm Springs, California, on October 29, 1988, early in the morning. Again she was lying in her bed, and again Jesus appeared about six to eight feet away, but on this occasion she saw his whole form standing in the doorway of the bedroom. He wore a robe, off-white in color, loosely tied up by a cord. Again she was attracted to his face, especially his eyes. He had brown curly hair, and a beard to match his hair, and again his eyes were blue. This point puzzled her then and still does, for she doesn't think that a Jewish person would have blue eyes. His facial expression was pleasant, but he was not smiling. He stood there for some seconds and then disappeared. The experience seemed as real to Rose as if a normal person had stood there. No message was communicated on this occasion, and Rose believes its purpose was simply to let her know that he exists. Rose and her husband are retired and live in Langley, British Columbia.

Case 15: Margaret Moyse

Margaret was brought up in a Methodist home in Australia. After completing conventional schooling she took up the study of art, and by the time she was sixteen she had left the religious beliefs of her parents behind her and was an atheist. One evening, at age 26, as she was having a conversation with her husband and a friend, she felt compelled to turn around and look toward the kitchen behind her. There in the doorway some eight feet away was a figure whom she immediately recognized as Jesus. She turned away and then looked back again to discover that he was still standing there. He wore a white garment, was of medium height, and had dark hair and a dark complexion. But it was his eyes that particularly caught her attention, for from them flowed a tremendous stream of love. She believes her attention was drawn to his eyes because of her interest as a painter in the human face. The light from the kitchen illuminated him, and he appeared as real as any person standing there would appear. No radiance accompanied his appearance, nor did he appear to move, and nothing was said. But the absolute stillness of the moment seemed to her like a little bit of eternity. She turned away and looked a third time, but he was gone. Her husband noticed that something had happened, and she told him and her friend what she had seen.

Margaret describes the effect of the experience as having awakened in her the importance of love for others. After this experience she felt as though the love of Jesus entered her and flowed through her to others. She began to attend an Anglican church at that time, and is still active in a church near her home, believing this to be scriptural.

This experience took place in 1952, but it has remained as fresh for her as if it had been recent, she said. Margaret worked for some years as a nurse, raised a family, and has been active in a community-based mental health organization. Her experience took place in Adelaide, Australia, and this is where I interviewed her in 1993.

Case 16: Sheila Dalrymple

Sheila was brought up on Vancouver Island in British Columbia, by a mother who was Presbyterian and a father who was Catholic. Because of these differences, Sheila and the other children were brought up without much direct religious influence. Her parents thought they should receive some religious instruction, so they were sent to the United Church.[6] Sheila was interested in religious matters when she married, but not involved in religious life at all. When she and her husband moved to Nelson, British Columbia, they attended the United Church, and this is where her experience took place. As the congregation prayed during a communion service one morning, she saw Jesus walk out of the door of the minister's office. He went to the center of the podium, looked at her and said, "Live by my commandments." The sandals on his feet made a noise as he walked, just as if he had been an ordinary person walking across the stage. She looked at her friends sitting on either side of her, wondering if they saw what she saw, but they gave no indication that they did. She wondered if she was hallucinating, so she looked again to where she had seen Jesus, and he was still standing there. This time he said to her, "I am here," which convinced her that her experience was real. She did not hesitate in making the identification.

Sheila was sitting about the fifth row from the front, twenty feet or so away from him, and saw his facial features very clearly. He appeared similarly to the image tradition presents him in, but the blue color of the robe that he wore was quite unlike anything she had seen before. He was Mediterranean in appearance, and had dark hair. He was normal in size, and looked solid. The sense of beauty and love that emanated from him was overpowering. Sheila said that something extraordinary was present in the atmosphere of the church that she could not explain. It gave her a sense of "weather," but she was not able to be more specific about what this meant. This "atmospheric effect" made her feel like a grain of sand on the seashore, and also suggested that he had absolute power. She had a sense of foreboding, but was not sure about whether this was communicated via visual effects or whether it was a feeling whose source she could not identify. Sheila also said that she had the sense of being confronted by God.

She is still haunted by not knowing why this event happened to her. She had not given Jesus much thought prior to this event and does not know why he would concern himself with her. A week prior she had conceived a daughter, who died at birth six months later. Sheila wonders if he was there to strengthen her, for she felt a lot of love and comfort coming from him. Sheila says that Jesus became very real to her through this event, and that it solidified her faith. She now lives in Vancouver, and works at home.

Case 17: Chris M.

Chris was born and raised a Catholic, but found religion a source of ambiguity and confusion. The answer that people gave to his many questions always seemed to be, "It's a mystery, so don't worry about it." When Chris was twenty-five he discovered that he had been adopted, and his sense of having been deceived motivated him to move away from home. He was out of work for a while, but finally found a job in a convenience store in a small town in Kentucky. Everyone in the town seemed to take their religion very seriously, and every street seemed to have a church. A Christian television station had recently begun broadcasting in the area, so Chris began to watch some of its programs. These influences resulted in a search for a meaningful relationship with God.

Working in the convenience store was demanding, for Chris was expected to work ten days in a row before getting two days off. He was sometimes also required to work the night shift. The owner would watch Chris like a hawk as he served the customers, and then accuse him of stealing from the till. On top of everything else, the store was a distance away from the rest of the town, and Chris worried about being robbed. It was patronized mostly by blue-collar workers who worked in factories nearby. They would get their morning coffee and doughnuts at the store before going to work. He was serving a long line of customers at five o'clock one morning when he noticed that someone in line was wearing a tie. Chris wondered what he was doing in the store so early in the morning, for he did not seem to be dressed for factory work. Chris did not pay him close attention, as he was preoccupied with pouring coffee and making change. The man was about thirty years old, six feet tall, and had light brown hair and a full beard. He did not fit the stereotype of a community resident, as far as Chris was concerned, because he looked refined, highly intelligent, and very kind and loving. As he stepped up to be served, Chris gave him the customary "Good morning." The customer asked for coffee, and Chris went behind the counter to pour it. When Chris returned with the coffee, the appearance of this mysterious customer suddenly changed before Chris's eyes. He turned into someone slightly shorter in stature, with short, black, curly hair, very dark eyes, a perfectly manicured, thin, black beard and very white skin. Chris set the coffee on the counter and was about to ask him if he needed a paper bag to carry it out, for many of the customers ordered take-out. But he somehow tripped over his words, and instead of asking the stranger if he wanted a paper bag, said, "You carried the cross for me," with an intonation suggesting surprise. The stranger answered in a soft voice with what sounded like "Sure," picked up his coffee and walked out. Chris suddenly lost all sense of heaviness, and felt as though he was floating away into an amber light. The euphoria that accompanied the experience was like being drunk. He took hold of himself in order to do his work, but the experience left him changed. All feelings of guilt and inadequacy mysteriously left him. It was only later in the day, when listening to a Christian program in which the speaker talked about Jesus Christ taking away sin and guilt, that Chris put this interpretation on the event that had transpired. Some years later, after moving to Miami where he met Hasidic Jews, Chris learned that the Hebrew pronunciation of 'Jesus' is something like 'Yeshua,' and he now wonders if the stranger was introducing himself as Yeshua, rather than saying "Sure." This event took place in February 1980, when Chris was twenty-seven years old.

Chris reported that he took hallucinogens when he was in high school, between 1970 and 1973, and said that he experienced a hallucination during that time that was similar to the experience described above. He had not used hallucinogens during the seven years before this event, however. Chris requested anonymity.

Case 18: Erika Sabo

Erika Sabo was brought up in a small Canadian denomination known as the Apostolic Christian Church, which she described as similar to certain Baptist churches. She was fourteen years old when she experienced what she describes as a vision of Jesus. At the time she was thinking a lot about questions of faith. She wondered, for instance, if she believed in God only because her parents had told her to do so. She thought that she ought to have a greater Christian commitment, but could not help wondering if the beliefs she had been taught were somehow dreamed up, rather than founded on fact. She wanted to know for herself that Christ existed.

One evening her youth group at the church had a campfire service. They circled around the large bonfire, and as she looked at it she saw Jesus walking in the fire. She first saw his profile, and then he turned to look at her with a look of sorrow, but also compassion. Erika was both shocked and slightly frightened, for she had never heard of such a thing happening in recent times. He was of average height, and appeared as he does in traditional portrayals, with shoulder-length hair, robe, and so on. She could not see his feet because they were obscured by the fire, but he seemed to be solid, for he obscured the fire behind him. After a short while he disappeared from view. The service ended soon afterward, and a friend who had been sitting on the opposite side came up to her and said, "What just happened to you? I just know that something spiritual just happened to you." Erika did not know how to reply, but it amazed her to think that someone recognized that she had undergone a religious experience. Erika believes that she was the only person who experienced the vision, however.

She describes this experience as having been a turning point in her life as a Christian. She interprets the sorrowful expression as reflecting disappointment over her lack of commitment at the time. Although the experience did not result in her complete commitment to a Christian way of life immediately, she did not doubt the existence of Jesus after that. The experience also proved to be a consolation to her some years later, when her parents were killed in an automobile accident. Erika was married and attended a university when I interviewed her in 1988.

Case 19: Peter Isaac

Peter Isaac is now retired, after teaching English, history and geography in British Columbia high schools for more than thirty years. He reports two experiences in which he was aware of the physical presence of Jesus. The first one took place in a hospital in Kelowna, British Columbia, on March 25, 1964. Peter had been hospitalized twice before because of a bleeding duodenal ulcer, but this time the bleeding was more serious. The doctor who attended him warned him that if he did not have the operation he would die. Peter consented to it, although it required the removal of three-quarters of his stomach. He reported that he had experienced healing in response to prayer on a previous occasion, and as he lay there in his hospital bed he wondered why his requests for healing had not been heard. Two days after the operation his wife, Lena, came to visit him, and as they were talking quietly to each other, he became transfixed by what he saw at the foot of his hospital bed. He says: "It was a man of average height, but what was different about him was that he was not wearing a shirt nor any other clothing above his waist. On his right side, at waist level, was a large, ugly scar, and he was facing me with a broad smile. It was Jesus. Jesus had come to see me. I knew without doubt that it was him, for he appeared as he did so that I would immediately recognize him." Jesus appeared to be of average height and build, had no beard, looked solid, but did not move. The experience was just as real to Peter as if a friend had dropped in to see him, apart from the manner of dress. What especially captured Peter's attention was Jesus's smiling, compassionate face, for the smile told Peter that he was loved and understood. Peter says that this image has not faded with time. The look of compassion that Jesus gave him told him that he did not need to worry about his recovery. Although his wife, Lena, was with him during this experience, she did not see any of what he reported seeing.

The second time Jesus appeared was in an experience on January 10, 1990 that Peter refers to as a vision that began with a dream. He dreamed that he was involved, contrary to his will, in a most brutal and cruel murder. Almost killed by the assassins, he began to flee from the scene, begging to be shot because of his reprehensible involvement. Someone came along with a shotgun and shot him in the chest. Even though parts of his body were blown away, he was still alive, crawling along the ground and sobbing in grief. He then woke up, aware of his wife in the bed beside him, but still sobbing uncontrollably. He tried to bring himself under control so that he would not awaken her, but could not do so. Suddenly Jesus came toward him, from a distance of about twelve feet away, looking as real as life. Peter describes the event as follows: "His form was that of a healthy man dressed in casual clothes, and he had a bit of a brownish complexion. But when he saw me, he was not walking anymore, but was immediately down on the ground beside me and putting his arms around me." Peter describes this experience as one in which the dream changed into a vision, for when he woke up, the images that had formed the content of his dream remained as real and vivid as they had been in the dream. He knew that he was in his own bed, and that his wife was beside him, but he still had the sense of crawling along the ground in an alley after having been wounded by a shotgun blast. It was in that alley that Jesus came to him, to comfort him, to hold him, and to calm his fears. In his words: "In my mind I was crawling along that alley in the city, knowing at the same time that I was lying in bed. I didn't want to cry so loud that Lena would waken. I can't explain." Peter was unable to say if the appearance of Jesus on the second occasion was similar to that on the first.

Peter believes that this vision came to him as an answer to his prayer before retiring for the night. He had been preparing an adult lesson on the deity of Christ, and had asked God to show him why Isaiah refers to Christ as "mighty God." Peter lives in Chilliwack, British Columbia, and is a member of the Chilliwack Central Mennonite Brethren Church.

COMMENT The second of Peter's experiences belongs with the trance and dreamlike experiences forming Group I, but his first experience is similar to the others in Group III.

Case 20: Fran Haskett

Fran's experience took place in conjunction with a serious illness that befell her husband Al, about two years after they married in 1948. An obstruction in his bowel required an operation, and infection in his wounds as well as pneumonia put him on the critical list. Over the next two months Fran divided her time between the hospital and her job checking policies with a life insurance company. Her husband was on her mind day and night, and her waking life consisted of a constant stream of unspoken prayers for his recovery. During this time she began to see her own selfishness—always wanting this or that thing that others around her had—and began to realize that the most important thing a person can have is love for others. A sense of gratitude for what she did have began to develop in her, and it was in this context that her experience took place.

One day after work Fran was sitting in the bedroom of her home in London, Ontario, thinking about the importance of gratitude and love, when her attention was drawn to a patch of white light six to eight inches in height shining in the corner of the room. There were no windows that could explain why that patch of light six feet away appeared, and she found herself staring at it in disbelief. It began to grow in size, and to her amazement it took the form of a person she immediately identified as Jesus. He appeared as tradition portrays him, but Fran was not able to describe further details of his appearance. He was as real as if an ordinary person had been standing there, and she had no doubt about his identity. Although Fran has not shared her experience with many people, she once described it to a Bible teacher whom she greatly respected. He told her that the Holy Spirit, not Jesus, had appeared to her, but she disagrees.

Just as the light had grown to form the image of a grown man, so the image began to dwindle in size until it disappeared, much to Fran's disappointment. But the experience left her convinced that Jesus was alive. She found, moreover, a wave of love coming over her that she could not adequately describe. The hurt and anger she had felt about Al's sickness disappeared, and an understanding about love in life dawned upon her. Fran views the experience as one in which God decided to show her that his love for her is complete, and that she should not worry about the events over which she has no control. To her amazement, and that of the doctors who were attending Al, he began to mend so quickly that his recovery seemed miraculous. Fran was seventy-four years of age when I interviewed her, and lives with her husband in retirement near London, Ontario.

Case 21: Helen Huizinga

Helen's experience occurred in connection with her reflections as a Christian about the significance of baptism. She was brought up in the Christian Reformed Church, and had been baptized as an infant. She had an opportunity to work with children in a Baptist church near her home, and although the church allowed her to do this work because she was a Christian, church leaders really wanted her to be baptized as an adult. This made her read and think about Christian baptism for a period of about three years. Second baptism was a point of contention between her and some members of her family, however, particularly her husband, Joe. She eventually decided that she would like to be baptized, and prayed to God that he would somehow allow this to happen.

Helen went to the Baptist church by herself one Sunday morning, knowing that baptisms would be conducted that day. As the pastor preached she noticed that the front of the church began to be illuminated with light, and that a cloud was forming. In the midst of the light and the cloud, a human figure appeared. Helen stared at it transfixed, and a voice spoke to her saying, "Helen, you can be baptized now." She immediately identified the person as Jesus, and replied (in her mind, not out loud) to him, "Lord, can I really? But what about Joe?" Jesus replied that he would take care of Joe, and then he slowly faded from view. Helen looked around from her seat about five rows from the front to see if anyone gave any indication of having seen what she had seen, but she did not notice anything suggesting that they did. When the pastor completed his preaching, he went to the vestibule to prepare for the baptismal service. Helen followed him, told him what had just happened, and asked him to baptize her there and then. The pastor complied with her request, and when she told her husband later what she had done, he didn't say a word in objection.

Helen said that Jesus appeared to be six to eight feet tall, certainly larger than she expected. He appeared to be solid, not transparent, but Helen could not make out any other details. He seemed to be wearing a long white robe, for instance, but the features of his face were not sharp, and she could not tell whether he had a beard or whether his hair was long. These details were of secondary significance to her, however, for she was overpowered by what was happening. The glory that emanated from and surrounded him captured her attention. Her response was a combination of joy and awe, for she could hardly believe that Jesus would do such a thing for her. The sense of awe evoked by the experience stayed with her for years, and she still feels honored and grateful. Helen was forty years old at the time, and the experience occurred in Richmond, British Columbia.

This was not the first time that Helen sensed the presence of God. When she was thirteen she lived in the Nazi-occupied Netherlands. Her family sheltered Jews in their home, and she was alone when a house-to-house search was conducted in her town. She saw the soldiers coming down her street, and prayed to God for protection. When the soldiers mysteriously passed by her house, she became convinced that God cared for her. Helen is presently employed as a university library technician, has authored a book, and has raised a family.

Case 22: Helen Bezanson

Helen's first experience occurred when she was about twenty-one, living in Southern Ontario. She went to the Anglican church as a child, but by the time she married and began a family she was not interested in religion. Her husband's parents took her to a summer camp meeting sponsored by a Pentecostal church, but she did not really understand what was being preached. It seemed to be coming out of the Bible, so she thought it was acceptable. The service ended with an invitation to pray at the front, and when her mother-in-law suggested that she go, Helen did so to please her. Helen returned on the next three nights, going forward each time for prayer because doing so made her feel better about herself. As she prayed that fourth night she felt a warm presence around her, and thought that someone had touched her. She opened her eyes to see if anyone was nearby, but no one was close enough to be touching her, so she decided to continue praying. She felt a touch again, this time on one of her hands that was raised in prayer. She opened her eyes again to see if anyone was touching her, and again she saw no one, but then she felt that she ought to look up. Her words to me were: "I looked up, my eyes wide open, and I saw Jesus standing just as clear as I can see you sitting there now, and he had both hands out like this [stretched toward her] and he was smiling as though he was accepting me finally." He made a gathering motion with his hands, as though to show her that he was accepting her, and looked so real and alive Helen thought that others must be looking at him too. She looked around to see if others were paying attention to him, but no one else seemed to notice him. She thought to herself, "What's wrong with them? They're not looking at him." She looked back to see if he was still there, and he was.

He stood there some eight to ten feet away, smiling and moving. He looked much as tradition portrays him, although what caught her attention was his eyes and the motion of his hands. Helen also had the sense that she was looking at God, which gave the visual impression a characteristic that she was not able to describe. Another unusual feature of the experience was that Jesus seemed to be standing on a pedestal or pillar, for he was not standing on the floor and he did not appear to be floating. Moreover, it seemed as though he stood in an oval doorway on the pedestal, and that a radiance or glow emanated from the oval doorway and surrounded him. As she gazed on him she began talking in another language that she knew nothing about at the time. He gradually faded from view and was gone. This experience created a desire in her to please Jesus as much as she could, and to study the Bible. It also convinced her that Jesus was real. Her words were: "He's not just something that you learn about in a Bible, in a Sunday school class. Or it isn't just a story. He showed me that he was real, that he's a real person. He's not just an apparition, he's not a figment of our imagination. Nobody has even been able to tell me since that Jesus isn't real and that he can't make himself known to people, because I saw it myself, and that's all the proof I needed."

Helen's second experience took place thirty years later in the church she now attends on Vancouver Island. A group of people were praying for the healing of a woman in the church, and although everyone else had their eyes closed, Helen thought that she should keep her eyes open. Again she felt a warm presence come over her, and as they prayed a figure suddenly appeared on the overhead screen at the front of the church. She blinked her eyes to make sure she was seeing properly, and it was still there. Then she looked around at the others who were praying to see if any of them were looking at the screen, but all of them had their eyes closed. She blinked again and thought to herself, "That's Jesus." He was kneeling on one knee and looking up toward heaven. One of his hands was raised, and blood was running down his back. He again seemed as real as life, even though the image was on the screen. Helen wondered if this was just a picture projected onto the screen, but when she looked to the back of the auditorium, she saw that no one was operating the projector. As she looked back to the screen she saw Jesus drop his head and slump. Meanwhile, blood continued to pour down his back. The woman for whom the church was praying never was healed, and Helen thinks there is some connection between this fact and the last scene she saw. Helen said that these experiences convinced her of the spiritual realities affirmed by the Christian church. She lives in the small community of Black Creek, and is a homemaker.

Case 23: Maureen Hason

Maureen Hason had her first visionary experience (her term) when she was twenty-nine years old. She and her husband were living in Kitchener, Ontario, at the time, but they were not happy. They decided to go to a weekend retreat designed specially for marriage enrichment. The theme on the last day of the retreat was unconditional love, and the advice they were given was to love their spouses unconditionally, as God loves people. This suggestion was not very helpful for Maureen, for she was accustomed to conditional love and did not understand what was meant by unconditional love. She went back to her room to be alone and to think about the meaning of this kind of love, and as she sat there contemplating this question Jesus appeared before her open eyes, extending his hands toward her in a gesture of compassion. His face was sad, and although he did not say anything to her, he communicated with his eyes. She could tell by the look on his face that he knew her through and through, and that he loved her. She saw that she had been living her own life without his help. What his face said was, "I've been here all along. If you would have just come to me I would have been able to help you." At that moment she understood the Christian doctrine of forgiveness, and the meaning of the Christian belief that Jesus is the Lord of everything. She identifies this experience as the turning point in her religious life.

Jesus appeared only from the waist up, but in other respects appeared very much like the traditional images of him, viz., with a white robe, brown hair and beard, pleasing gentle look, and a tanned complexion. But it was the expression on his face that captured her attention, not his physical appearance. This experience took place in March 1982, and by the time I had interviewed her in 1988 she had experienced several other visions. I will describe one more.

Maureen and a friend were having lunch in Dutch Mothers, a popular restaurant in Lynden, Washington, when Jesus appeared. They were sitting at a table for four when he suddenly occupied a vacant chair diagonally opposite Maureen. He looked as though he was eager and excited to be there with them, for they had been talking about their faith. He did not say anything audible to her but somehow communicated the thought found in the biblical text, "When two or three are gathered in my name, I am there also." Maureen describes this as having her mind opened to understand the Scriptures, and compares it to Luke's account of Jesus's opening the minds of his disciples.[7] The experience had an air of reality about it for Maureen because he appeared to be solid, and the back of the chair was obscured in just the way it would have been if an ordinary person had been sitting there. Her friend did not see anything, however. Jesus's appearance on this occasion, as on the others, made Maureen weep. When he disappeared she became a little giddy as she described to her friend what she had just experienced, and somewhat casually said, "You'd think he'd wear normal clothes if he's coming out to lunch." Her friend stared at her in disbelief, because of her impudence, and they both "heard" this remark: "That is how you recognize me." Maureen explained that this simultaneous hearing was not audible.

Maureen has had other experiences of an intense spiritual nature. She described one that she interprets as an encounter with God in his throne room. Although it took place one night while she was asleep, she does not consider it a dream. In the days before it she had been reminiscing about the time when she first heard about God, through a Bible study for children conducted by a woman who lived on her street. She wanted to repay the woman, and was praying to God that she might find her and repay her. That night God said to her, "Your debt is not to Mrs. _____, it's to me." He then instructed her to open up her home to children for a study similar to the one she had attended as a child. Maureen said that this experience was different from those with Jesus, for she felt comfortable with Jesus, but from God there was no escape. Her words were: "There was no reasoning, and he was everywhere. And I remember when he gave me the instruction, I turned, and he was there. And I kept turning, and he was everywhere. It was like he was air. He just enveloped the whole room. It wasn't a human figure, and the thought came to me, 'I can't escape God.'" When she awoke she felt as though she had been somewhere else.

Maureen has wondered why she has been privileged to have visions. After the first one occurred she thought that all Christians experienced them, and said as much to a friend who had been a Christian for a long time. She was surprised to discover that they are not common. She has struggled with "spiritual pride" because she has had these experiences and most other people have not, and told me she believes that she has them because she is a doubter by instinct, and is weak in faith. Maureen now lives in Calgary, Alberta, and is married to an executive of a large food company.

Case 24: Pauline Langlois

Pauline Langlois was twenty-three years of age when she had her first visual encounter. Although she had been brought up as a Catholic, she didn't go to church or practice her faith, apart from saying the occasional "Our Father" before going to bed. She had been through two divorces and various abusive relationships, and she did not want to live. She drank to cope with what was happening in her life, and was becoming the kind of person that she hated. Although she wanted to commit suicide, she hesitated to carry it out because of her daughter, who was five years old at the time. One night as she lay in her bed and thought about killing herself, she became aware of a presence in the room. She wasn't afraid, but she sensed that someone was there even though she could not see anything at first. Then she saw a man standing beside her bed looking at her with compassion. He touched her with his hand to comfort her. She wanted to put out her hand to touch him to see if he was real, but was reluctant to do so for fear that doing so would drive him away. So she just lay there, not daring to move. Then he spoke to her, although his lips did not move. The words she heard in her heart were, "It's OK. I'm going to take care of you. It's all right. I'm taking care of you." She felt great love and joy, and throwing restraint aside, reached out her hand and touched his side. It felt solid to her touch. He stayed there for some time and then just faded from view.

Pauline said that the man who appeared wore conventional clothes and was average in height and build, but she could not describe other features of his appearance. His eyes captured her attention, and nothing else was important at the moment. Pauline did not make an identification at the time about who had appeared to her, but the desire to take her own life disappeared.

Pauline did not believe in a spiritual world to this point in her life, but events involving no visible agents convinced her that an evil spirit, as she called it, was trying to scare her. For the next six months, doors would slam behind her, plants would move across the table, water taps would switch on and off, music would come from the corners of the rooms, and furniture would move across the floor of its own accord. At first she wondered if she had gone crazy, but when members of her extended family witnessed these events as well, she thought there must be some other explanation. She went to several priests for help. One gave her holy water to sprinkle on her home, as well as on her daughter, whose safety she was worried about, but this did not seem to help. Pauline finally traveled halfway across Canada to consult the family priest. When he heard about the troubling events, he instructed her to take "the good spirit" with her to confront them. Thereafter, each time a bizarre event took place, she would say something like, "OK, good spirit, that's what I want you to get rid of," and eventually all of the frightening events disappeared. During these months she also began attending a Bible study near her home.

A short while after the frightening events stopped she had another experience that made her want to commit suicide. She did not describe the nature of it, except to suggest that it involved physical assault. She acquired the pills by which she could take her life, but the thought came to her that she should pray first. She prayed, "God, if there is a God, if you are really there, I need you now." Pauline says that the same presence entered the room that was there at the first experience. He said to her, "I'm so happy to see you," and she felt the same love that she had felt the first time. Although Pauline saw nothing, she is convinced that the presence on this occasion, as well as the first, was Jesus.

In another experience, Jesus appeared in the sky above her head. He appeared from the waist up and was surrounded by a very bright cloud. His form was so large it filled the sky. She describes this second visual experience as a vision, but refused to call the first one a vision. Her words about the first experience were: "It was very different. It was alive. It was like me and you. . . . It was like a real man standing right there. It was a man, not a spirit." These events were life-changing for Pauline, and when I met her about nine years later she, her husband, and four children were operating a small farm near Sudbury, Ontario.

Group IV: Cases with Observable Effects

Case 25: Henry Hinn

Henry Hinn had his encounter when he was nineteen years old. He was brought up in a Greek Orthodox family in Israel, and became committed in his faith soon after immigrating to Canada. The family lived in Scarborough, Ontario, in a new development at the edge of the city. Their house was next to a forest, and Henry often walked in it. He would go there to pray, often grieving over the rebellious things he had done as a teenager. Henry went there one day in January 1976, just after snow had fallen. The accumulated snow was about a foot and a half deep, and as he walked along Jesus suddenly appeared no more than eight feet away.

Henry reported that the snow had mysteriously disappeared at the spot where Jesus stood, and that dead grass was visible in an area about three feet in diameter. No tracks to or from this spot could be seen, however. Jesus looked at Henry, smiled, and said, "You are mine." Henry replied, "I'm yours, and I promise I'll always be yours." Jesus wore a white robe draped with blue, and was of average height. His hair was long and a golden color, and his beard was trimmed. Henry was unsure whether his body was transparent or solid. Henry describes his demeanor as commanding and overwhelming. After Jesus disappeared, Henry went over and stood on the dead grass, just to ponder what he had seen and heard. He felt secure in the thought that his life had been surrendered to the will of God. Henry is now a minister and lives in Vancouver, British Columbia.

Case 26: Barry Dyck

Barry Dyck was eighteen years old when his vision (his term) of Jesus took place. He was attending a Bible college in British Columbia at the time, and had gone to nearby Mt. Baker in Washington state to ski. As he skied that day, his goggles fogged up, and before he knew what was happening he went over a drop-off. When he reached bottom the back of his skis struck his neck, breaking three vertebrae and herniating one disc. The pain was excruciating as he was taken off the mountain by the ski patrol. He was rushed to St. Mary's Hospital in Bellingham, where he was placed in a neck brace and traction, and was kept as immobile as possible. During the next week his ability to see became impaired as the swelling in his head created pressure on his brain. Surgery was planned to relieve the pressure. In the middle of the night eight days after the accident he woke up to find Jesus standing at the end of his bed. Jesus stretched out his arms toward Barry, and Barry immediately sat up. Despite all the equipment that was attached to him and the orders not to move, he grasped the hands of Jesus and begged, "Take me with you." Barry explained that he made this request to die because he was drawn by an indescribable feeling of love. Jesus somehow indicated that satisfying this request was not possible, and that everything would be fine. Barry went back to a fitful sleep, and during the night he took off the neck brace that was limiting his movement. When he woke up the next morning he was disappointed to discover that he was still alive! But he found that he could see perfectly, and that the swelling and pain were gone. He convinced the attending doctor the next day that he was well enough to go home, and the doctor reluctantly agreed. Barry had been expected to be in hospital for three months, and to need a neck brace for an additional eight months. Within three or four days of returning home he resumed his regimen of running, without any ill effects. Barry said that X-rays taken by his family doctor in Seattle several weeks later showed no evidence of fracture in his neck vertebrae, and that the many x-rays taken during the week in the hospital had shown obvious signs of fracture. Barry believes that he was healed by Jesus during that encounter that lasted no more than sixty seconds. Barry's family and the people in the church they attended were as shocked by Barry's healing as he was. Although the church he attended did not deny the possibility of miraculous interventions, it did not encourage people to expect them.

Barry says that Jesus seemed to be about six feet in height, and that his hair extended six inches below his shoulders. Barry says that the overall impression of his face was like Sallman's *Head of Christ*, but Barry could not see any features in detail. Barry could see the hair draped around the face, but it was as if Jesus's face were hollow. Barry does not know how he made the identification of the radiant figure as Jesus, but it came to him immediately and without any question or doubt. The experience convinced him that he was loved, but he thinks the incident may have had another purpose. He has often shared his experience with other people, and influenced them to think about God and the spiritual life generally.

Barry went to a college to study science for three years after completing that year in Bible college, and he pursued further studies in accounting after that. When I met him he was working for a trucking firm in Abbotsford, British Columbia, and has since become a stock market trader.

Case 27: John Occhipinti

John Occhipinti was brought up in a very devout home in Connecticut and New Jersey. His mother went to the Catholic church every day to pray, and also attended the services of the Assemblies of God. John was a special child because of an incident that took place when he was two years of age. He fell into the river just behind their home, and was not recovered for more than half an hour. John was rushed to a hospital, where doctors worked for hours to save his life. His mother was convinced that there was a special reason for his having survived. John became serious about his faith when he was about eighteen years old. The next year he went to Bible college in Texas to prepare for pastoral work, and this was where, in 1958, his experience took place.

John shared a room with Nathan, but could not understand what Nathan was doing in Bible college, for he already seemed to know most of what they had come there to learn. During November of that year Nathan came down with a virus and stayed in bed to recover. Nathan was not particularly perturbed about being sick, but said that he was in bed for a reason. Although this was not a serious illness, John felt sympathy for him, and brought him food from the cafeteria when he could, and prayed with him before retiring for the night. As he was praying for Nathan one night he opened his eyes to look at his friend lying about eight feet away. John was shocked to see someone standing over Nathan's bed, but facing and looking at him. John immediately identified the person as Jesus, in part because of the sense of awe that the appearance of the person evoked. John was about to tell his sick friend what he was seeing when Jesus reached over and placed his hand on Nathan's forehead and disappeared. At that instant Nathan leaped out of bed and ran down the halls of the dormitory shouting, "I've been healed, I've been healed." Nathan later said that although he did not see anyone, he felt something touch his head. John himself intended to go over to touch Jesus in order to establish his reality for himself, but did not get a chance to do so. He muses now on his boldness, but he was only nineteen at the time, and rather new in his faith.

Jesus appeared much as tradition portrays him, with a long white robe, shoulder length hair, and a short beard. He seemed to be just under six feet tall. He exhibited no radiance, and he seemed as solid as any ordinary person. His skin was neither very dark nor very light, but his eyes seemed to be on fire. John preferred the term *encounter* rather than *vision* to describe the experience. It was as real to him as seeing an ordinary person, and he does not think that Nathan would have felt the touch on his head if it had been a vision. Moreover, John does not consider experiences that occur while a percipient's eyes are open to be visions. He was not aware at the time of anyone else in recent times having had such an experience. John considers the experience to have had two purposes: to bring healing to his friend, and to reaffirm John's desire to do evangelistic work.

John now lives in Scranton, Pennsylvania, and is active as an evangelist, a counselor, and a musician.

Case 28: Kenneth Logie/Lakeshore Gospel Chapel

Kenneth Logie's life has been marked by a number of extraordinary experiences. He has been the minister of a Pentecostal Holiness church in Oakland, California, for about forty years,[8] and reports events that rival the NT in kind and number. Among these are various Christic encounters, including several claims of group experiences.

When Kenneth and his wife moved to Oakland the church was not capable of fully supporting them financially, so he sold bread to supplement his income. His work sometimes meant that he was late for the evening service, but the small congregation accepted that. He would begin his preaching a little later than usual when this happened. One Sunday night in April 1954 he again arrived late and, as a result, was still preaching at 9:15, when he saw a shadow on the exterior glass doors, made by someone standing outside. He wondered who might be arriving so late in the evening. He reported that "the door opened up, and Jesus started walking down the aisle just as plain as you are." He turned to the people on one side of the aisle, and then to the people on the other side of the aisle, smiling as he went. He walked up to platform where Kenneth was preaching, but instead of walking around the pulpit, moved right through it. When he placed his left hand on Kenneth's shoulder, Kenneth collapsed to the floor. Jesus then knelt down alongside him and spoke to him in another language. Kenneth responded in English, believing that he was interpreting what was being said to him. He says that this event was witnessed by the congregation of about fifty people present on that occasion.

Kenneth reported another incident that took place in May 1959 in the same church. A woman in the congregation described a vision she said she had when she was in a hospital and was thought dead. Mrs. Lucero reported that Jesus appeared wearing the clerical robe of a Catholic priest. He told her to have faith in God. She explained that because she was of Catholic background, this apparel somehow assisted her in making the identification of the figure as Jesus.

Kenneth says that when Mrs. Lucero got up to tell her story, she was wearing a black raincoat because the weather had been rainy that day. As she spoke she disappeared from view, and in her place stood a figure taken to be Jesus. He wore sandals, a glistening white robe, and had nail prints in his hands—hands that dripped with oil. Kenneth reports that this figure was seen by virtually everyone in the congregation, which he estimated at two hundred people. He also reports that the figure was filmed (in color) by a member of the church with the kind of eight-millimeter movie camera popular at the time. Kenneth says that the photographer was so awestruck that he shook, and placed the camera on top of the organ in order to keep it steady. The appearance was much like Sallman's *Head of Christ*. Kenneth says that the effect upon the people in the church was electrifying. After several minutes Jesus disappeared, and Mrs. Lucero was again visible.

COMMENT These allegations put the Christic apparition experience into the spatio-temporal domain and, if authentic, would challenge the reigning hegemony of physicalism within the scientific community. They would also challenge the religious beliefs of many people, including Christians. I shall elaborate on the second case in some detail because of its significance.

The circumstances surrounding the film were described to me in 1965 by Kenneth Logie and his wife, both in a public meeting in Grenfell, Saskatchewan, and in private conversation. I was a young undergraduate at the time, and was not comfortable with the thought of giving the film or the supposed incident any attention. I did not speak in detail with Kenneth about these events again until 1991, by which time his first wife had died. I visited him and the church that summer, and spoke with four or five persons who were present in his church in 1959 when the incident took place. They supported the account given above. I naturally wanted to see the film again, primarily to refresh my memory concerning what I had seen twenty-six years earlier, and was disappointed to learn that it had been stolen from the apartment in which Kenneth lives. I estimate that there were about two hundred people present in the public meeting in Grenfell when I saw the film. I do not know how often it was shown in public, but my impression is that Kenneth showed it in his church from time to time. The woman involved in the incident, Mrs. Lucero, who was already quite old at the time it took place, died a few years later.

My own memory of the film is that it showed a figure that looked like traditional images of Jesus. The woman in the black raincoat did not appear, to my recollection, evidently because it was not significant enough to attract the attention of the person who held the camera (with whom I have not spoken). My memory of the glistening white robe as well as the outstretched and scarred hands is clear, but I cannot remember any movement of the figure, nor do I remember seeing the full face appear. Kenneth, who naturally saw the film a number of times, says that the face appeared on the film. Joy Kinsey (Case 1), who was a member of the church at the time, concurs with his memory of the content of the film. The memories of others who were present at the public screening in 1965 conflict. One remembers it the way I saw it, another remembers it the way Kenneth describes it, and several others have no memory of having seen the film at all (and I am sure they were present at the public meeting). I cannot explain these discrepancies. The conflicting memories of the public screening in 1965 illustrate how different people's memories can overlap substantially on general matters, yet differ in detail, even on important points. The fact that some have no memory of the film at all is intriguing, for it suggests that the implications of the film for claims about what is real were not noticed, or perhaps were not important to them.

There are competing views, naturally, on how the film was produced or what it represents. Some people of course believe that it recorded a paranormal event. Some who saw it with me are convinced that the whole thing was fraudulent, that an actor was hired to play the part, and that an amateur photographer filmed it. But I am sure they reached this conclusion without investigating the circumstances surrounding it. One person who attended the church regularly at about the time of the alleged event, but was not there for it and saw the film only later, told me that he wondered whether the film might have been a film of a (painted) portrait of Jesus. My own recollection is that there was movement on the film of various members of the congregation that could not be explained by motion of the camera. The suggestion that it was produced by the kinds of sophisticated methods of film enhancement now available seems dubious to me, because its production in 1959 probably predates the easy availability of the required equipment, and it had the amateurish quality that home movies from that era generally display. The conflicting views on events and possible explanations illustrate what typically happens to reports of paranormal events, and this incident shows how paranormal claims often (nearly) evaporate under critical scrutiny.

There is quite a bit more to the Oakland context than so far suggested. It is natural to wonder why someone would have had a movie camera in the services, and the explanation for this lies in the accounts of other strange phenomena alleged to have taken place in the church. Kenneth says that the church went through a period of extraordinary healings, exorcisms, prophetic insights, glossolalia, resuscitations, and so on—he has dozens of fascinating accounts. He reports an experience, for instance, in which the roof of the church was bathed in visible but nonconsuming fire, causing the neighbors to call the fire department. He also reports that images of crosses, hearts, and hands mysteriously appeared on the walls of the church, and from these flowed streams of liquid having the consistency of oil. The appearance of these images coincided with fragrant aromas that seemed to come from them. The person who wondered if the film might have been produced by filming a portrait of Jesus told me (in 1994) that although he was of a skeptical bent, he had witnessed the formation of the images firsthand and was convinced of their authenticity. But he also reported to me that when the church was remodeled some years after these events, his skeptical disposition induced him to examine the structure of the walls on which the images appeared, just to make sure that these images had not been contrived. He said that he found no evidence of tampering, and found himself still pondering these phenomena some thirty-five years later. I suspect that this curious combination of belief and doubt is often felt by those who have encountered (or believe they have encountered) paranormal phenomena. This witness seemed to exhibit the attitude that Aristotle recommended concerning claims that the future could occasionally be divined through the interpretation of dreams, that is, that one should neither summarily dismiss such claims nor uncritically accept them.[9]

In 1991 Kenneth showed me still photographs (black and white) of the images that had appeared on the walls. He also had still photographs of one or two occasions during which stigmata appeared on his hands, and another of an occasion on which a white cross appeared on his forehead. I asked him about the stigmata, and he said that these had occurred perhaps nine or ten times during a period of about three years, and were accompanied by a burning sensation, as if his hands were on fire. He was understandably sympathetic to similar claims that have been made over the centuries by Christians of all persuasions, and he showed me a few newspaper clippings and photographs he had collected that featured similar incidents from various Christian traditions. The subject of stigmata recently received critical attention from Ian Wilson.[10] Wilson's study also includes crosses on foreheads and other strange phenomena reminiscent of the Crucifixion of Jesus.

This was the context in which the Oakland apparition experiences described above supposedly took place. Kenneth said that he did not know what to expect next in the life of his church, and so bought the home movie camera in the hope that he might record any noteworthy incident. The accounts that Kenneth gives of various wonders and miracles that were part of his church for a number of years are reminiscent of NT accounts, for of course the Gospels and Acts are replete with accounts of such phenomena. There is much other Christian literature alleging paranormal phenomena, such as the account of the life and work of St.

Francis of Assisi.[11] Augustine also speaks extensively in *The City of God* about miracles of which he knows either first- or second-hand, and mentions seventy miracles attested during a two-year period at Hippo.[12] Augustine goes on to deplore the fact that the taking of formal depositions was not generally practiced by Christians—a sentiment that is still appropriate today, I regret to say.

The time gap between the alleged event in Oakland and the present time corresponds quite well to the thirty-five years or so that is widely thought to separate the alleged incidents central to the Christian faith and the first gospel narratives of them. I am not aware that any attempt has been made to document the events alleged to have taken place in this small church in Oakland, although people in the church told me in 1991 that they had been visited quite often by reporters and cultural anthropologists. Neither Kenneth nor members of his congregation, to my knowledge, have written anything down, although he spoke to me in 1991 of wanting to do so. One wonders why these experiences have been kept alive only in the oral history of the community and are not documented. Are such experiences considered so holy that they are reserved only for the hushed contexts in which participants speak of them to select audiences? Do the participants expect "unbelievers" to dismiss the allegations with contempt, and expect "believers" not to need the authenticating value of depositions and documents? Do phenomena of this kind (or even the belief that they are taking place) produce such strong apocalyptic expectations that participants think the "end of the world" is imminent—too imminent to make documentation of any use? It is tempting to think that a deeper understanding of the mind-set of those associated with earliest Christianity might be gained by examining contemporary religious communities in which paranormal claims comparable to those found in the NT are made.

A group apparition experience is remarkable in itself, but the photographic images are perhaps more remarkable, for mental or neurophysiological mechanisms internal to percipients cannot be plausibly suggested as an explanation. The suggestion that telepathic powers might somehow account for such images is as challenging to a physicalist understanding of the world as any supernaturalistic explanation. It is curious to note the insistence of some psychical researchers that apparitions are not photographable.[13] This position does not tally with an article titled "Ghosts" in *Man, Myth and Magic: An Illustrated Encyclopedia of the Supernatural*, in which it is asserted that hundreds of still photographs portray what are said to be ghosts.[14] Half a dozen or so are reproduced in the article. They include some amorphous shapes that are in keeping with various popular ideas of how ghosts might appear, but also several semitransparent human shapes, and a photograph of cherubs (with wings) hovering over a child's bed. There evidently is no agreement among those who investigate paranormal phenomena about the susceptibility of such events to being photographed. Perhaps nothing can be established beyond reasonable doubt concerning the Oakland experience, in view of the unavailability of the film for critical scrutiny, but the number of claims emanating from this single locale make it worthy of serious study.

Additional Cases

I will comment briefly on several other people's Christic apparitions. Two accounts derive from percipients with whom I could conduct only brief and incomplete interviews, and two derive from percipients with whom I was unable to make direct contact, but who are well-known to acquaintances of mine. I present these four cases separately from the accounts of the twenty-eight percipients with whom I was able to establish direct and significant contact. The two with whom I conducted brief interviews are well-known public figures and authors.

Hugh Montefiore, now retired, was an instructor in the NT at Cambridge University and later a bishop of the Church of England. He was brought up in the Jewish faith, and as a child never attended Christian worship or read the NT. He credits his conversion to Christianity to a vision he experienced at sixteen years of age. The figure that appeared to him said, "Follow me," and "knowing it to be Jesus" (this is how he described the effect of this experience to me), decided to embrace the Christian faith, although he says he has not ceased to be a Jew. Only later did he discover that the invitation "Follow me" was in the NT. When I spoke to him in 1993 some fifty-seven years had elapsed since the incident, so he was not able to remember many of the details on which I wanted to query him. He said that the import of the experience still had validity for him. "For me it has total reality," he said.

John White, also retired, was associate professor of psychiatry at the University of Manitoba for many years, and is well-known in Canadian Christian circles for the books he has written. I made brief mention of John White's experience in the Introduction, including his account of having seen the arms and hands of Christ extended toward him as he was in prayer with some of his friends. His comments on this experience are significant: "The effect was overwhelming. All strength left me, so that it was with difficulty that I remained kneeling. I began to sweat profusely and to tremble uncontrollably."[15] He goes on to say that he was "fully aware that what I saw was a product of my own brain. I felt that God was, as it were, using my mind as a projectionist uses a projector. The hands I saw were not the real hands of Christ: They were weak and effeminate, whereas I knew that the hands should have shown the evidence of manual toil. They weren't carpenter's hands." He goes on to remark that the wounds of the Crucifixion were in the palms, not the wrists, where they should have been if they had been the hands of Christ, for Romans nailed those they crucified in the wrists, not the hands.

John White spoke to me of another experience that had taken place in Honolulu several weeks before I interviewed him in October 1990. He was sitting on a settee, and was wondering what it would be like to have Jesus sit with him. He says that Jesus was suddenly there, sitting at the other end of the settee, although he could see Jesus only in outline, and could see through him. Jesus sat there for a moment, and then raised his arm and placed his hand on John's left hand that rested on the back of the settee. After a while Jesus stood up to go, and John said, "Please don't go, stay." But this request was not granted. While Jesus sat there on the settee, John was unable to see his eyes, but when Jesus got up to leave, John saw them. He interpreted this as indicative of some unconscious reluctance to get too close to Jesus, and he described this experience as one in which he felt that he was "penetrating into the beyond."

John White's remarks to me about hallucinations were fascinating, for his experience with patients in psychiatric hospitals has given him a perspective on the experiences of hallucinators that those of us who are not in psychiatric services rarely have. He said his impression was that the hallucinations of those in psychiatric hospitals could possibly be their encounters with evil forces, but he did not think that having had such a hallucinatory experience implied that such a person was demonically controlled. He thought that psychoses left the psychotic vulnerable to the "dark world," and that such people might be encountering other realities in visual terms.

White's position on this point is similar to one expressed by Sergius Bulgakov, who was a professor of theology at an Orthodox seminary in the early part of the twentieth century, and a popular exponent of the theology of the Orthodox Church. Bulgakov writes: "It cannot be affirmed that all mental maladies are of a spiritual nature or origin, but neither can it be affirmed that demoniac influences have no connection with mental maladies; what is called hallucination may be considered—at least sometimes—as a vision of the spiritual world, not in its luminous, but in its dark aspect."[16]

John White's impression was that those who had aberrant experiences in two sensory domains at once, visual and haptic (or tactile) domains, for example, were not simply hallucinating—experiencing something whose causal origins lay only within the percipient—but he acknowledged that other psychiatrists would look at this phenomenon differently. He said he regards the hallucination theory as just as much a theory as the theory that there is a spiritual world into which some people are capable of seeing. It is apparent that he is using the concepts coming from various competing explanatory structures, each with its own characteristic ontology.

The two Christic apparitions that came to my attention through acquaintances are people who know the principal persons well. Both experiences involve healings, and have been published. Betty Baxter has very widely recounted her experience of having been healed by Jesus when she was twelve from a condition of being crippled and deformed. Her mother and several other people were present at this event, and reportedly also saw Jesus perform the healing. Betty Baxter describes details of trying to touch him as he stood before her, of a friend reprimanding him for standing too far away, of seeing a vision within this apparition experience, and finally of being healed as he placed his hand upon her severely deformed spine. Her story was written up in *The Fairmont Daily Sentinel* (Fairmont, Minnesota) in 1952, according to the dust jacket of a recording.[17] Her story was available in booklet form for some time, but I have only heard the recording. Gulshan Esther reports having been healed after an apparition of Jesus at a time in her life when she was a devout Muslim and her only knowledge of Christianity was the little information found in the Quran.[18] She was crippled by typhoid when only six months of age. She claims that Jesus and his apostles all appeared to her, and that she was taught the Lord's Prayer during this encounter nineteen years later. It was her knowledge of this prayer that convinced a Christian missionary in Pakistan to risk his right to stay in the country by catechizing her. Esther now lives in Oxford, England, and conducts frequent missions to Pakistan. This case is unusual inasmuch as the knowledge apparently exhibited about Christian beliefs by the percipient seems to have been very minimal. It presents interesting evidence pertaining to the extent to which previous knowledge shapes the phenomenological content of a percipient's experience.

I identified a fifth group of cases in my introductory remarks to this chapter, cases in which percipients see Jesus as a child or as a crucified adult. These are cases in which people seem to "see" events as they happened long ago, or ones in which people somehow have events of the past replicated in their phenomenological experience. Julian of Norwich's experience was of this kind, and some of Teresa of Avila's experiences were as well, and in each of these cases we have some fairly detailed accounts. *Christianity Today* recently conveyed a report of such an event having been collectively observed in China. The account comes from Karen Feaver, legislative assistant for U.S. Congressman Frank Wolf. She reports the following incident as a message was preached to a crowd unfamiliar with

Christianity: "A vision of Jesus walking among them and then suffering on the cross appeared to all gathered. When the teacher told of Jesus rising from the dead, the vision showed Jesus ascending to heaven gloriously."[19] Ted Harrison also gives an account of a twentieth-century stigmatic who saw, among other things, "Christ being whipped, mocked and given the crown of thorns."[20] It is very difficult to understand how one might experience visual reenactments of past events "not as a dream but as real life," as one author has described this phenomenon.[21] The extraordinary character of these claims is far beyond the scope of conceptual resources derived from ordinary experience to handle. These kinds of experiences are reminiscent of time-travel stories found in science fiction, where people are able to experience events of the past.

This completes the cases toward which most of my critical reflection will be directed. I believe it is instructive to compare them with cases of Christic "encounters" that are very clearly experienced as OBEs. One person not included among the percipients already mentioned described an OBE experience to me in which she saw and touched Jesus in so lifelike a form that she was convinced that he somehow presently exists. Ann Bukalski had the sensation of leaving her body and traveling to a place of very bright light, where she saw and embraced him and her deceased parents. She described her OBE experience in the words: "I had physical sensations that felt as physically real to me as strong physical sensations feel when I am awake," adding that she felt that she was fully awake at the time. The figure that appeared to Ann as Jesus was a man wearing a long white gown made of tightly woven, smooth linen. He had long dark brown hair, piercing eyes, but no beard. He seemed to be about thirty years of age and of average height (under six feet). No wounds appeared on his body, but the recognition was instantaneous and unquestioned. Ann said that in her OBEs she would "leave her body" through her head, and would see places from some distance above the earth. On one occasion she saw well-known landmarks in Washington, D.C. When I had driven up to her house a few hours earlier I had noticed two basketball hoops at right-angles to each other, attached to the house and garage. I suppose they caught my attention because few houses have two such hoops. I asked her about her sense of location in her OBEs, and whether she had ever had experienced images of these hoops and the roof of the house from the top. She assured me that she had, and went on to describe an incident in which she had "left her body" and was positioned between two expanses of wood, one of which was moving. This puzzled her greatly, for she did not know where she was. Finally she figured out that she was below the wooden ceiling of the family room, and above the wooden blade of a moving fan. She directed my attention to the exact spot where this had occurred. I find it remarkable that people can provide convincing descriptions of experiences whose phenomenological details do not correspond to positions that their bodies would normally be in. By excluding from my study the OBEs that involve a Christic encounter, I do not mean to imply anything about the relative value of this kind of experience compared to Christic visions and apparitions. I simply think there is value in examining a cluster of similar experiences, all the while retaining awareness of the much broader experiential domain to which this cluster can be considered to belong.

I mentioned above that my interest in Christic apparitions was aroused in 1965 by seeing the film mentioned in connection with Kenneth Logie. But several reports in the seven or eight years after that persuaded me that the phenomenon deserved closer scrutiny. One report was made by a professor of engineering from India in a public meeting in Adelaide, South Australia, during 1970 or 1971. My recollection is that he told of two Christic apparitions, and after the second he converted to Christianity. This experience caught my attention at the time because it seemed that the dominant religious influence in his life had been Hinduism, not Christianity, so the experience did not seem to fit with the common belief that it is only Christians who have visions of Jesus. Of course, Christianity has been in India for a very long time, so the influences upon him might have been subconscious. I did not speak to him about his experiences, and cannot report their details with any confidence.

A second incident is of a more personal kind, inasmuch as it involves a Christic visionary experience reported to my mother by one of her friends. It seems that her friend had such an experience just after Mother had prayed for her, and reported it while it was happening. Mother saw nothing, but was awestruck by the incident. My recollection is that it happened in about 1972, but Mother did not speak of it often, and would only do so if she was fairly sure that it would not be met with ridicule. She died well before the research on this book began, and I do not know the identity of the person involved, so I cannot say much more about it. Lifelong associations with family members produce convictions about their credibility that argument is impotent to alter, so I have no doubt at all about the accuracy of Mother's portion of the report. I cannot comment on her source, however, although I know she believed it was genuine.

Concluding Remarks

There are several features of the foregoing accounts that I find particularly thought provoking. The first is their extraordinary variety, and in saying this I reveal my earlier inclination to think of visionary phenomena in a stereotypical way. A careful scrutiny of the accounts that have come down to us in history would probably have revealed this variety, but only upon being confronted with the contemporary experiences did I come to appreciate their variety and complexity. This point has important implications for any explanations that might be proposed, and might even call into the question the plausibility of grouping together all of the Christic visions and apparitions described above for purposes of explaining them, as though a single kind of explanation could be adequate.

A second interesting feature of the accounts is the complexity of the experiences revealed in them. Visions are much more than vivid mental images produced at will by concentrating on sensory information previously experienced, perhaps aided by closing one's eyes, dimming the lights, or ingesting mind-altering substances. The percipients I met seemed to have little control over the onset, duration, or content of their visions. Moreover, the phenomena were not confined to the visual domain. Philosophers have often isolated momentary perceptions for analysis, such as the circular red sensation. Such an approach to analyzing experience could tempt one to interpret a vision as a series of visual phenomena isolated from sensory phenomena of other sorts, and poorly connected to the physical environment in which visionaries find themselves. Perhaps visions of these kinds occur, but the ones reported to me included a complex interplay of sensations of various kinds and interaction with the immediate environment.

James Gibson is often credited with having shown the complexity of ordinary perception. In *The Senses Considered as Perceptual Systems* he develops the view that the senses are active systems, not passive ones, and that they are interrelated, rather than mutually exclusive.[22] He notes that five systems are typically involved in ordinary perception: (1) the basic orienting system, (2) the visual system, (3) the haptic system (including touch), (4) the auditory, and (5) the system of taste and smell. Although taste and smell were seldom reported to me, most of the other systems were frequently involved. The basic orienting system allows us to determine the position of our own bodies without the use of sight or touch. It very rarely functions independently of other systems, however, and the combined and integrated information they yield allows us to know about the space we are in and changes to the environment. For example, the interaction between the changes in retinal images and the semicircular canals in the inner ear that detect movement allows us to avoid misinterpreting movement of our heads as moving objects. People whose canals do not work properly report the world bobbing up and down as they walk, for the correction of retinal information does not take place as it should.[23] Virtually all of the apparition percipients give silent testimony to the functioning of their basic orienting systems in close cooperation with their visual systems. Even in cases where percipients thought that the environment they were in had changed, the experience did not seem to exhibit any deviance as far as the basic orienting system was concerned, for they knew if they were lying down or standing, moving or stationary, and so on.

A third provocative feature of the accounts was the presence of reports that placed the experience in a group setting or in the intersubjectively observable domain. Though there are not many of these, there are enough to give one pause. Reports of intersubjective experiences naturally call to mind the NT post-Resurrection appearance stories, for that literature describes both private and group experiences, as well as some with intersubjectively observable effects. Of course, the post-biblical literature on Christic visions also makes reference to group experiences and those with intersubjectively observable effects. The arresting quality of the contemporary experience cries out for a reconsideration of the NT appearance stories.

3 | Evaluation of the Evidence

The most obvious questions evoked by contemporary reports of Christic apparitions are whether the reports are credible, how the experiences that have occurred are to be explained, and whether contemporary experiences bear any similarity to those that seem to lie behind NT accounts of post-Resurrection appearances of Jesus. The first question—assessing the credibility of Christic apparition reports—has, moreover, a direct bearing on the other two questions. If, for instance, all of the reports of Group IV apparition experiences—cases with observable effects—are judged as having inadequate epistemic foundations, because so few plausible reports can be found, explanations that have been developed for such experiences can be ignored. Such a negative evaluation on reports about a unique class of experiences might warrant rejection of similar NT accounts as well. If such reports are deemed credible, however, this will have implications for explanations that are proposed, and for various critical views of the NT accounts. This chapter will look at the reports presented in Chapter 2, particularly in the light of various epistemic principles that have been thought of value in evaluating religious experience.

My comments will inevitably (perhaps unconsciously at times) rely on methodological, epistemological, and ontological principles that form part of a world view or *Weltanschauung,* or what Peter Berger calls a plausibility structure.[1] These terms have come to be used to identify the foundational beliefs that undergird views of what things are real, how these things are related to one another, how they can be investigated, and, in

Berger's account, the social structures and organized practices in conjunction with which foundational principles are advanced, for example, the structures and practices of a community of scientists.

Theorists are not united over the fundamental principles that constitute a world view. They disagree, for example, on whether knowledge has foundations and what these might be, whether pluralistic or monistic ontologies provide the most adequate account of our world, what methodological principles characterize scientific investigation, and whether these are applicable in all fields of rational inquiry. The only satisfactory response to the problem of differing intuitions about such principles is to say that these principles are open to challenge and debate in much the same way that the phenomena adduced and theories offered to explain phenomena are open to challenge and debate. There is no vantage point from which the "truth" of a plausibility structure can be decisively determined. Every theorist uses some plausibility structure or other, and although wide agreement on some elements can often be found in cohesive social groups, such as a scientific community, controversy attends them as much as it does the "facts" that are adduced and the explanations that are proffered. It is in a probing and tentative spirit that I wish to approach the foundational issues here.

I will assume that the sciences and critical common sense give us the most plausible initial accounts of what exists and how things are. This means that theories positing irreducible mental entities (e.g., mental states such as desiring, believing, and knowing) or supernatural beings must have their claims to rationality defended. This stance is different from physicalism, the view that all events are capable of being described using the concepts of the physical sciences, for physicalists are generally adamant about the implausibility of descriptions and explanations found in mentalism and supernaturalism. I regard supernaturalism as a kind of theory quite independent of mentalism, although mentalism might have provided useful models for supernaturalism in the past. I have argued elsewhere that in order for the posited entities of supernaturalistic theories to make any plausible ontological claim, they would need to be grounded in unique forms of experience not wholly explicable (evidently) in physicalist terms.[2] I shall assume this position here. At one time the posits of mentalism and supernaturalism did not need defense, but the growing influence of the sciences has changed that.

The Epistemic Potency of Contemporary Experience

A fundamental methodological assumption implicit in this study is that it is appropriate to concentrate attention on contemporary Christic visionary experiences. Some theorists might think otherwise. Some might prefer, for instance, to consider the material available from such writers as Julian of Norwich and Teresa of Avila, given their self-awareness and capacity for self-evaluation. And some theologians might prefer to begin with the NT material, believing this to be as historically reliable as material available from subsequent historical periods, including the contemporary one. But there are good reasons to begin with contemporary claims.

Apparitions in general carry with them the possibility that no physicalist explanations for them will be found, and that some other kind of explanation, such as a supernaturalistic one, will be required. Moreover, the study of apparitions cannot be conducted in accordance with the standards usually set for scientific inquiry, such as the demand for repeatability, control of variables, quantitative measurement, and experiments to test competing theories. Apparitions, then, threaten both the hegemony of physicalism and the supremacy of scientific standards of inquiry. Accounts of apparition experiences from the distant past or antiquity cannot compete in such an intellectual environment; there are too many ways in which they might be found questionable. While we might look sympathetically on reports obtained no more than a century ago, collected by scientists who share many of our standards for data collection, we are apt to be unsure about reports that derive from contexts unknown to us, or from reporters or percipients whose beliefs or world views we question.

Some of the advantages of dealing with reports derived from living subjects, as opposed to ancient documents, can readily be itemized: Living subjects can be scrutinized for signs of sincerity; living subjects can be cross-examined to determine whether language is being used to assert a proposition, rather than being used in some performative sense that excludes assertion;[3] living subjects can be questioned about ontological commitments implicit in their descriptions; living subjects can be quizzed about further details of their experiences; living subjects can be scrutinized for signs of psychopathology in order to satisfy the misgivings of skeptics; living subjects can be scrutinized for deception. These factors give reports from contemporary experience greater epistemic value than those coming from antiquity.

Philosopher Stephen Braude has offered some helpful comments on the problems of research into parapsychological phenomena. He suggests that evidence can be divided into three categories: experimental, semi-experimental, and anecdotal.[4] The distinction between the last two kinds is of interest here. Anecdotal evidence reports phenomena that occur outside a laboratory setting and do not occur repeatedly with respect to a certain person or place. Semi-experimental evidence, while reporting phenomena not obtained in a laboratory setting, reports phenomena that occur repeatedly.[5] The evidence in this study belongs to the semi-experimental kind, for it pertains to one broad class of experiences reported in many circumstances, at many places, by many people, and over a long period of time. This kind of evidence, while not enjoying the prestigious place accorded to experimental evidence, can still be substantial and significant for influencing world views, and commands more respect than anecdotal accounts. Braude considers the non-experimental evidence for parapsychological phenomena in general to be substantial.[6] I suggest that evidence for Christic visions and apparitions is substantial as well, given the reports of the last two thousand years. This does not mean such evidence has no problems. As Braude observes, in the study of paranormal phenomena we have to reckon with the possibility that experiences are reported by persons motivated by reasons other than the desire to report what they consider to be the truth; moreover, some witnesses or investigators eager for publicity or notoriety exhibit self-deception, exaggeration, naivete, misperception, and outright dishonesty.[7] But the existence of such problems does not provide grounds for rejecting all apparition reports completely.

Braude also comments on the likely effect upon a science such as physics, should parapsychological phenomena ever become accepted both within the scientific community and the larger academic community.[8] He notes that physics limits itself in what it can describe and explain; it does not purport to describe, for example, organic activities generally. Moreover, many laws of physics are already thought to have exceptions, so that such laws are considered approximations. Also, many features of persons are not thought to be explicable by the laws of physics alone. Braude suggests that the most that would happen if paranormal phenomena became accepted would be that the belief that everything is reducible to physics would have to be abandoned. The net effect of accepting reports of paranormal phenomena would be that "global physical theories would need to be embedded within a different philosophical nexus."[9] Braude says that the conflict between physical theory and parapsychological claims is not as great as it is often imagined to be.

But in order for paranormal claims to be accepted, a substantial amount of evidence would have to be presented. That is what is widely thought to be lacking. Because the reports from the distant past are generally considered inadequate to support parapsychological claims, evidence for such phenomena has to come from contemporary experience. Of course a critical scrutiny of contemporary experience could have the effect of eroding claims concerning paranormal phenomena in general, including those claims made in the distant past and antiquity. But a scrutiny of contemporary experience could have the opposite effect, namely, showing that reports from the distant past and antiquity, hitherto in doubt, have a significant amount of credibility. This has happened in the last two decades in connection with the near-death experiences, and I shall comment further on this in the next section.

Before I leave the topic of contemporary experiences, I wish to comment on the apparent effects of firsthand testimony. Firsthand testimony demands evaluation by those directly confronted with it. Those who are not directly confronted with testimony are not forced to evaluate its credibility. A person who merely reads about an event can enjoy a state of suspended judgment about the credibility of what is reported, for it is possible to question the reliability of the sources through which transmission occurs. Those confronted with direct testimony are not as insulated from the original events, and generally do not have the luxury of being able to suspend their judgment. This point has nothing to do with reports of paranormal phenomena *per se*. But it is an important one for those not privy to firsthand testimony to reflect on. Some parts of the world views of persons confronted with direct testimony are likely to be developed in unique and *unavoidable* ways, simply because of the witnesses and the testimony that they are forced to assess. Those who ridicule the world views of persons who have been confronted with direct testimony overlook the forced character of the assessments that shape the content (in part) of world views. This point is an important one in connection with studies of paranormal phenomena—a point that critics often overlook. People who are intimately involved with such phenomena often have beliefs produced in them that they are powerless to prevent, even when they know such beliefs to rest on uncertain epistemic foundations. This does not mean, of course, that those beliefs cannot be subjected to critical scrutiny, but the vantage point from which such a person does the scrutinizing will be different from the vantage point of one who does not already have (coerced) beliefs. This is a just an observation I offer about an important psychological process involved in acquiring beliefs.

A Methodological Anomaly Regarding Vision Reports

That Christic visions have occurred and continue to occur is one of the commonplace beliefs about religious experience shared by academics and the general public. The belief is so ubiquitous that no substantiation of it seems needed. The belief is often expressed in some form such as, "Just as Muhammad appears in visions to Muslims, and the Virgin Mary appears in visions to Catholic Christians, so Jesus appears in visions to Christians in general." Implicit, perhaps, is the supposition that the religious belief systems that people already espouse somehow influence the content of their visions. I am only interested now, however, in the fact that people widely accept that visions (or apparitions) of a religious character, including Christic visions, occur. The general public, and, more especially, the academic community, considers it to be so obviously true that it has not been thought worthy of critical attention. Even the Christian community seems to have neglected its investigation, perhaps with the exception of those whose theological traditions give a significant place to ongoing religious experience, such as the Catholic, Orthodox, and Pentecostal churches. But the possibility of deceptive visions has made even these communities chary about Christic visions.

But now an important question arises: Which Christic visions are likely to have occurred as reported (or nearly so)? Visions experienced by groups of people, or those with intersubjectively observable effects? Or those in which percipients were able to look away from the figure that appeared to them, and then look back and find it in their visual field once more? A physicalist might be hard pressed to admit the genuineness of both of these kinds of experiences, which do not appear to be readily explicable using the conceptual resources of existing sciences. To admit the genuineness of such experiences might require an expansion of ontological commitments, perhaps an expansion that takes supernaturalistic beings seriously. By contrast, private apparition experiences that do not affect the causal order in any obvious way seem to be readily amenable to an explanation using the resources of neurophysiology. Here is the methodological anomaly. Certain kinds of reports are apt to be questioned because they challenge the hegemony of a broadly physicalistic explanatory system, and other kinds go unchallenged because they fit into a physicalistic scheme. But this does not appear to comply with the requirements of an "objective" inquiry, for objectivity would appear to require that we establish the "facts" first and then cast about for satisfactory explanations of them, even if it requires introducing new ontological posits.

The methodological problem described here might not be thought unique, for there are many accounts of extraordinary events for which no adequate physicalistic explanations exist. But the problem is remarkable inasmuch as no one doubts that visions, including Christic visions, do take place. This point is acknowledged by everyone, even the most adamant opponents of supernaturalism. Other kinds of extraordinary events—typical paranormal events such as telepathy, clairvoyance, psychokinesis, and ghost sightings—are often not conceded to occur. Having admitted that these visionary experiences occur, it appears excessively "theory serving" to admit only the occurrence of those visions that comply with explanatory systems broadly endorsed by physicalists. We could dub the methodological principle employed here as the *Principle of Conservativism*, for it expresses an unwillingness or conservativism about expanding the conceptual resources to account for these novel allegations. It has some affinity to the familiar principle known as Occam's Razor: "Do not multiply entities beyond necessity," but the Principle of Conservativism concerns both the epistemological issue of assessing reports for credibility and the ontological issue of introducing explanatory schemes that make novel posits. Occam's Razor, in contrast, deals with ontological issues alone.

Richard Schlagel is a physicalist who embraces what I call the Principle of Conservativism with respect to a group of "factual" claims closely related to the phenomena under scrutiny in this book—reports of ghosts.[10] He defends his decision to ignore reports of ghost sightings on the grounds that these reports, if authentic, would require abandoning physicalism and embracing radical views about human nature and human destiny after death. He remarks that he has encountered extremely objective, rational, "tough-minded" people whose judgment he would unhesitatingly accept on other matters, who have conveyed reports to him of ghost sightings, even firsthand experiences, but he continues to consider ghosts to be "unreal" and evidence for their "authenticity" to be questionable. Schlagel defends his position on the grounds that ghosts "do not behave as do the physical objects around us (they cannot be publicly observed, they cannot be photographed, they have an anomalous space-time existence, and so forth), and their presence cannot be experimentally observed, unlike unobservable scientific entities."[11] The ontological framework of physicalism is taken by Schlagel as the touchstone of what is "real," and any other ontological contender is required to satisfy its requirements in order to be accepted. The difference between Schlagel's situation and that of the physicalist confronted with reports of Christic visions is that reports of Christic visions are not generally dismissed *in toto*, as reports of ghosts are dismissed by Schlagel and many other members of the academic community. Virtually everyone admits that there are Christic visions. The physicalist, in granting that at least some occur, is forced into an irrational position on the admission of evidence.

The question when pride of place should be given to evidence, and when it should be given to reigning theories, is as deep-seated and far-reaching as any in epistemology. There is, however, a debate currently in progress with respect to near-death experiences that demonstrates the plausibility of endorsing the Principle of Conservativism. The ancient theory of the disembodied soul is being revived as a possible explanation of the NDE, even among theorists whose scientific background is inimical to such a theory. Of course various theories using the conceptual resources of the existing sciences are serious competitors, but the much older theory (in an entity-positing form) is being mooted. One reason this theory is being considered is that it offers an explanation for a unique group of NDEs—"recalcitrant facts"—for which no other compelling explanation has been found. Raymond Moody, a medical doctor with a doctorate in philosophy, reported incidents in his groundbreaking 1975 work, *Life After Life*, in which people who were revived in hospital rooms said that while "out of the body" they had "traveled" to other rooms and heard conversations that were later verified as having taken place. Patients in other studies reported that during their NDEs they "observed" objects located in places that, from the spatial position of their bodies, they would not have been able to see. One resuscitated patient reported "seeing" a shoe high on a ledge of the hospital, though the shoe could not be seen from inside the building.[12] Some theorists think that this kind of observation, if authentic, would provide some basis for the disembodied soul theory. In an effort to obtain more information on NDEs of this kind, one medical researcher recently installed a mechanism in a hospital room frequently used to resuscitate patients. On the top of a cupboard high above the patients an electronic device spells out a message on a screen that could be seen only by someone located near the ceiling.[13] The Principle of Conservativism is in play here, inasmuch as most theorists are not sufficiently convinced that there are enough "recalcitrant facts" to warrant introducing the disembodied soul theory, although some theorists are sufficiently convinced by the number of reports that have been made to investigate such "recalcitrant facts" in more detail. Moreover, the disembodied soul theory has not been ruled out completely. The use of the Principle of Conservativism in this case seems reasonable.

It is instructive to compare reports of these "recalcitrant facts" with the reports of NDEs in general prior to 1975. The NDE in general was in much the same epistemic position two decades ago that these unique NDEs now are in. Though scattered reports recounted unusual experiences in which individuals thought they had "left their bodies," they were too few or unconvincing to attract serious attention within the scientific community. Medical resuscitation changed all that. Thousands of similar cases quite quickly became widely known, and a "critical mass" was reached so that NDEs, once rejected or marginalized, were taken seriously, even though no single, obvious explanation for them was immediately at hand. Moody reported in 1977, in *Reflections on Life After Life*, that many colleagues had challenged him to supply names and addresses of those he had interviewed in order to give his reports greater credibility. Making such a demand of an NDE researcher is hardly necessary now, for a wealth of similar cases give the experience authenticity, broadly speaking.

These unique NDEs offering evidence for a disembodied soul that can perceive from a position outside the body are now in an epistemic position that the NDE in general was in prior to 1975, for there are not enough such cases at present to warrant acceptance. We seem rationally justified in suspending judgment concerning their authenticity, and in not introducing an explanation for them, especially one that challenges the physicalism that characterizes the sciences. But if they should become as common as NDEs, we would be unreasonably stubborn to deny their occurrence altogether, whatever the explanation for them might turn out to be, even if it should require expanding our physicalistic ontology. Here we have a "limited defense" for the Principle of Conservativism. It is an example of the kind of piecemeal critical reflection on elements of a world view that is increasingly characterizing the discipline of philosophy.

The foregoing discussion suggests that caution should be exercised in accepting reports of Christic apparitions that pose a challenge to a physicalist perspective, such as reports of group experiences, or of apparitions that were photographed or that in other ways affected the causal order. This caution is appropriate in view of the small number of cases forming this unique group of apparition experiences. In this respect they are like the "recalcitrant facts" associated with the NDE. One must note, however, that Christic visions have been reported throughout the long history of Christianity, including those that occurred after the alleged Resurrection of Jesus. The combined number of such experiences might not be sufficiently large to judge them indisputably authentic, but it is enough, in my judgment, to warrant further investigation, just as the small number of "recalcitrant facts" associated with the NDE warrant further investigation.

A second important implication that can be drawn from recent studies of the NDE has to do with the status of reports of extraordinary phenomena. Philosophical circles widely accept that reports of extraordinary phenomena cannot be trusted, because our prior experience of such events is outweighed by experiences in which such events have not occurred, and because people have a penchant for misrepresentation. David Hume is best known for having given expression to such skeptical views. Hume expresses his antagonism toward according any probability to extraordinary claims as follows: "But as finite added to finite never approaches a hair's breadth nearer to infinite; so a fact incredible in itself, acquires not the smallest accession of probability by the accumulation of testimony."[14] If by "a fact incredible in itself" Hume means an alleged fact whose probability of occurring is zero, his point is well taken. But it is more plausible to interpret "an incredible fact" as a certain kind of fact whose probability is just extremely low.

The probability calculus can illuminate what has happened in the last two decades of NDE research. Consider a simple model in which only two evidence reports are available. If two alleged instances of a certain kind of fact are assigned a very low degree of probability of having occurred, the probability that *one or other* of them has occurred increases, rather than remaining the same. If the probability that event A has occurred is 1/1,000 and the probability that (independent) event B has occurred is also 1/1,000, the probability that either one has occurred is 2/1,000. A similar effect is generated by models with many evidence reports. The research into the NDE during the last two decades has shown that (some) reports of extraordinary kinds of phenomena can become acceptable if enough of them exist. We might not be able to point to a specific credible report, but we can say that one or some other is credible. The NDE research has shown up Hume's position for what it is, namely, an *a priori* approach to matters of evidence that actual experience has rendered implausible. It shows that methodological principles are susceptible to possible falsification—certainly to refinement—just as are reports of particular events and the theories conjectured to explain those events.

I suggest that adopting the Principle of Conservativism is reasonable in response to allegations of group Christic apparitions and those that affect the causal order (Group IV visions). Though enough reports of this kind have emerged in contemporary experience and in the history of Christianity to suggest that they should not be summarily dismissed, there might not be enough of them to *insist* upon their occurrence; hence one might not plausibly *insist* upon an explanation that makes use of conceptual resources beyond those available within physicalism.

The Principles of Credulity and Testimony

Two important principles have recently been advanced in connection with theistic arguments. If they have probative force in that context, they should have probative force in other evidential contexts; if they lack probative force in the latter contexts, that reduces their cogency for arguments in favor of theism. Richard Swinburne defines the Principle of Credulity as saying, "If it seems to me that I have a glimpse of Heaven, or a vision of God, that is grounds for me and others to suppose that I do."[15] He grants that special circumstances may limit this principle—for example, if a person's past perception has been unreliable, or if some other cause of the apparent perception can be offered. But Swinburne considers apparent perception to be substantial evidence for belief in the existence of the apparent object.[16] Caroline Davis similarly formulates the Principle of Credulity to say, roughly, that if something seems present to a person then it probably is[17]—a principle that certainly reflects the way in which ordinary perceptual experience is regarded. She takes the Principle of Testimony to assert, "In the absence of good grounds for believing otherwise, subjects' descriptions of their experiences should be taken as probably revealing the way things appeared to them at the time."[18]Davis's study also makes use of the Principle of Cumulative Effect, which asserts that the evidential force of a group of phenomena is greater than the mere sum of their individual effects, but I shall not comment on it.

Davis's impressive survey of religious experiences (from numerous religious traditions) includes the following: quasi-sensory experiences in which people sense a presence or experience visions, such as that of St. Paul; revelatory experiences, such as a sudden flash of insight; regenerative experiences, that is, experiences in which people find their faith is renewed; numinous experiences, such as those documented by Rudolf Otto; and mystical experiences of the extrovertive or introvertive kinds.[19] Christic apparitions are clearly within the scope of the phenomena whose evidential force she is interested in assessing. Let us examine, then, what value, if any, these Principles of Credulity and Testimony might have in assessing the evidential claims of the percipients I interviewed.

The Principle of Credulity in its simple form would allow percipients to affirm that if Jesus (or a figure taken to be Jesus) seemed to be present to them, then he (or such a figure) probably was. The Principle of Testimony would endorse our taking the reports of percipients pretty much at face value, unless we found some reason for setting them aside. These two principles would prompt us to accept not only the reports of percipients who said that the visual domain that they believed themselves to be in had suddenly changed, a report that we might not find that unusual, but also those who said that the Christic figure left a circle of melted snow after he disappeared, and that the Christic figure walked right through objects and was photographed. The last of these are rather extraordinary claims, for they challenge the hegemony of physicalism in a direct way.

Physicalists are sure to insist at this point that at least the Principle of Credulity should be set aside for various reasons—for example, because of flaws in the report (or reporters), or because of the availability of explanations for unusual phenomena that use the conceptual resources of physicalism. The initial plausibility of the Principle of Credulity derives from our extensive use of it in evaluating ordinary perceptual experience; we normally accept that if something appears to be present, then it probably is. But it is questionable that its plausibility can be extended to contexts in which people have perceptions in what would appear to be altered states of consciousness. The testimony that could successfully challenge physicalism would have to be substantial and sustained. I again point to the effects of NDE research over the last twenty years. Reports of events that might be paranormal in character evidently can become accepted in the academic community provided there are enough of them. I think the import of reports of NDEs for theorizing about paranormal phenomena has yet to be fully realized.

The Principle of Testimony looks promising. This principle puts the "onus of proof" on those who would reject the testimony of individuals reporting visionary experiences—and perhaps that is how it should be. Observing that testimony is often neglected by philosophers despite its importance to the question of how knowledge is acquired, C.A.J. Coady has undertaken a careful study of testimony drawn from witnesses. He notes that the English law tradition requires that formal testimony be firsthand rather than hearsay, and that persons who offer testimony have the relevant authority, competence, and credentials to do so.[20] Interestingly, this tradition does not require that testimony be corroborated. Coady observes that the conditions for natural testimony are even less stringent than those for formal testimony. I believe that the important conditions for formal testimony are readily met by most of the firsthand reports I was given.

Coady addresses the reductionist theory of testimony advanced by David Hume and, more recently, John Mackie, according to which knowledge coming from witnesses can be believed only if we check the credibility of the witness for ourselves. Coady objects to this view, noting that "it seems absurd to suggest that, individually, we have done anything like the amount of field-work that [this theory] requires. . . . [M]any of us have never seen a baby born, nor have most of us examined the circulation of the blood."[21] These remarks support the expression and interpretation of the Principle of Testimony found in Davis's discussion. But such a principle should be viewed as only a rough guide to assessing the testimony of visionaries.

I conclude that we cannot plausibly guarantee the authenticity of all the reported visionary experiences by appealing to the Principles of Credulity and Testimony. Perhaps the strongest "evidence" for my position on these principles is the widespread reluctance among educated people, Christian or otherwise, to endorse their value when it comes to evaluating Christic visions.

Principles Used for Biblical Authenticity

There are a number of principles used by conservatives in debates over biblical authenticity that might be of value in attempting to assess contemporary claims of extraordinary events. Defenders of NT authenticity often appeal to various features of the NT documents themselves to defend the general historicity of such extraordinary claims as the virgin birth, miracles, and the Resurrection of Jesus. Among such characteristics are the (near) internal consistency among different texts reporting the same events (for example, healing miracles reported by several synoptic Gospel writers), the Semitic character of the writings, the numerous documents that form the basis of the standard text, and the alleged absence of mythical elements even in the miracle stories.[22] Sometimes conservative defenders appeal to the fact that the ordinary elements in a complex narrative, which also contains extraordinary elements, have been established as accurate. For example, they argue that because Luke's gospel has been found to be accurate concerning ordinary historical claims on which he can be tested, such as the administrative or political offices held by various officials in Roman Palestine, his reports of the virgin birth or the Resurrection of Jesus can also be trusted.[23]

Someone might appeal to the latter principle to render contemporary reports of extraordinary phenomena credible. This principle is implausible, however, because it yields questionable results in questionable domains of inquiry. Endorsing this principle would warrant accepting all those UFO reports in which we found the ordinary facts reported to be correct. A similar result could be advanced with respect to reports of parapsychological phenomena in which we found the ordinary facts that are part of the whole account to be correctly reported. Accuracy on ordinary details might instill *some* confidence in its reporters, but a reporter might be deceived or misled in too many ways to warrant carte blanche approval of the entire report, including the controversial extraordinary details. Reports of UFOs and parapsychological phenomena are not widely accepted by the scientific and academic communities on these insubstantial grounds, and this obvious fact must be considered when developing plausible epistemic principles. This methodological approach to defending the authenticity of contemporary Christic visions, or, for that matter, the authenticity of biblical claims, has very little epistemic value.

The first approach to defending NT authenticity—the appeal to various features of documentary materials such as the number of documents, internal consistency among different documents, the presence of Semitic characteristics, or the absence of mythical elements—provides only a very modest basis for accepting reports of extraordinary events as authentic. The reference to numerous (independent) documents is an appeal to a legitimate principle in the assessment of evidence. The point about internal consistency is also important, although it is difficult to determine how much inconsistency would render a report worthless.

The appeal to Semitic characteristics in defending NT authenticity is a curious one, and I suspect that an equivocation on the use of *authentic* is at work here. The primary sense of *authentic* in the argument over biblical authenticity is the sense of "actually having happened." But it makes no sense to suggest that an alleged event in Roman Palestine might actually have happened because the account exhibits cultural characteristics distinctive of Semitic peoples in its use of language or in cultural allusions. This might be relevant in a dispute about whether an account is *authentic to the time and cultural setting*. A narrative account that purported to be of an event in first century Palestine, but that used linguistic devices of or made cultural allusions unique to Alexandrian Jews of the second century A.D., might be deemed "inauthentic" inasmuch as the purported event did not fit with the appropriate cultural characteristics. But this incongruity does not prove that the purported event did not occur. Nor does authenticity to a cultural setting show that the purported event likely did occur. Any uncertainty about the question of the meaning of authenticity can be settled by asking if an account of a UFO sighting in Great Britain is rendered authentic by its exhibiting typical British characteristics, such as British idioms, spelling, and allusions. It is equally unreasonable to assert that a Christic apparition experience reported by an Anglo-Indian, say, is rendered authentic because its percipient uses linguistic and cultural expressions distinctive to Anglo-Indians.

The appeal to the absence of mythical elements is also problematic, primarily because of the uncertainty of what should count as a myth. An example of important non-biblical Christian literature that includes an obvious myth is the story told by Bishop Clement in the first century of the phoenix that comes back to life from its own decaying flesh.[24] Defenders of NT authenticity sometimes use this kind of illustration in arguing that the NT does not include myths, and so has authenticity. A similar argument could be developed to defend the authenticity of contemporary Christic vision reports. I suppose some people would consider reports of Christic apparitions as mythical, and by such a criterion for authenticity would reject all contemporary, historical, and NT allegations. Such a blanket judgment may be unreasonable, but the difficulty over the meaning of mythical can be readily seen by asking whether some of the remarkable reports of intersubjectively observable features of Christic apparitions count as mythical, for example, the smell of wine reported by Joy Kinsey, or the melted snow reported by Henry Hinn.

The cluster of principles considered here deserve closer scrutiny, but their capacity to lend credibility to reports of extraordinary phenomena is dubious. The one clear exception is the principle that we should give credence to a particular kind of phenomenon if a large number of similar reports are forthcoming. Of course this principle needs to be qualified by, for example, requiring that the reports be independent, defining what constitutes a large number, and so on. The recent research into the NDE again provides the best example of how this epistemic principle can actually work.

Conservative NT critic Craig A. Evans claims that attitudes toward authenticity claims for the NT gospels are now quite different than they characteristically were thirty to forty years ago, when Rudolf Bultmann's call to demythologize the NT was popular. Evans says that the NT gospels are now widely seen as useful historical sources, perhaps even reliable ones, and that research on the life of Jesus is no longer overtly driven by theological-philosophical concerns that make miracle impossible.[25] He observes a distinctly different attitude toward the possibility of miracles, at least among biblical critics.

Such a change might be noticeable among biblical scholars and even in the general population,[26] but I doubt that a similar change is taking place in the rest of academia. Most academics seem impervious to paranormal claims, whether found in ancient literary sources or contemporary culture. This opinion is shared by Carl Becker, professor of comparative thought at Kyoto University, who cites the recent attacks on the work of John Eccles, Raymond Moody, Elisabeth Kübler-Ross, Ian Stevenson, and Wilhelm Reich, all of whom have endorsed controversial paranormal claims of one kind or another.[27] Stephen Braude gives expression to his great disappointment with academic colleagues who refuse to consider the evidence for psychokinesis (causing physical objects to move by mental efforts alone) and reject its claims out of hand.[28] David Griffin remarks that few philosophers and scientists have examined the records of psychical research, adding: "One of the scandals of modern philosophy is the scant amount of attention given to psychical research."[29] The growing influence of and interest in New Age religious beliefs, which include parapsychological claims, suggests that Western culture is moving in the direction that Evans increasingly detects among biblical critics, but academia in general shows little evidence of a similar shift in perspective.

Non-Stereotypical Reports

It might seem plausible to suggest that accounts which break with stereotypical or expected beliefs concerning visionary or apparition experiences should be accorded more credibility than those that conform to stereotypes or expectations. Consider Joy Kinsey's experience, which took place when she was unconscious, but also had an intersubjectively observable effect (her "drunken" state, and the smell of wine coming from her). These are strange properties to juxtapose. She might easily have concealed from me the fact that her experience occurred while she was unconscious, which gives it a subjective character markedly at variance with the intersubjectively observable effects also reported. It might seem plausible to accord the report of this experience a high degree of credibility, simply because of the way it seems to conflict with stereotypes about either trances or experiences involving observable effects. Another experience that violates stereotypes about visions is that in which John Occhipinti allegedly saw (and only saw) what his friend allegedly felt (and only felt). Again, John could have reported an experience in which he both saw *and* felt the figure that only appeared (supposedly) to him. A third example is that of Ethel Chilvers, who said she saw a figure in stride, but motionless and looking away from her, rather than toward her. In the stereotypical visionary experience, the percipient makes eye contact with the figure that appears, and the figure typically moves.

A critic might say that percipients are familiar with stereotypes and tailor their reports to clash with these stereotypes to make them more believable. Such an objection evades the force of evidence too assiduously, however, and attributes to percipients a conniving character that I find difficult to accept, especially in the absence of evidence for connivance.

In responding to this seemingly plausible principle, one must distinguish between the sincerity of a percipient and the authenticity of what a percipient reports. To attribute sincerity to a percipient is to make an evaluation of the relationship between what is reported and the event that the percipient *believes* took place. But to attribute authenticity to a report (as I understand "authenticity") is to evaluate the relationship between the gist of what is reported and the event that actually took place. When I say that I believe the percipients whom I interviewed to have been sincere in what they reported to me, I mean that they believed the events they reported took place pretty much as reported. But to say that these reports were authentic is to suggest that the events occurred somewhat as described, and this is clearly a separate matter.

Many reports could be sincere without being authentic; people might be sincerely mistaken. Apparition percipients might be mistaken about being awake, for instance. It is also possible, I suppose, for images to be remembered with such vividness that the events that gave rise to the memories begin to be interpreted as real events, rather than imagined ones. No doubt there are other circumstances in which a percipient might offer a sincere report of an event that somehow failed to be authentic.

The principle concerning stereotypes can be formulated either with respect to the sincerity of reporters or to the authenticity of reports. I think that if the principle has any plausibility at all, it is an indicator of the sincerity of a reporter, rather than an indicator of the authenticity of a report. The authenticity of a report seems to be dependent upon, among other things, finding enough that are similar to one another.

Educational Background of Percipients

We might expect well-educated people to give the most authoritative accounts of their experience, because of their command of language, their ability to evaluate their own experiences critically, and their probable familiarity with various competing explanations. The two most educated percipients I met were John White and Hugh Montefiore. John White's educational background in medicine and psychiatry, and the fact that he taught at a well-respected Canadian university for many years until his recent retirement, would give his testimony a high degree of credibility in the opinion of many people. Similarly, Hugh Montefiore's education in NT studies at Cambridge, followed by an appointment there, as well as his holding the office of bishop in the Anglican Church, would also give his testimony considerable authority. But critics might argue that these men, as important, public, Christian leaders, could have a vested interest in reporting visionary experiences, even if they had not experienced them. A critic might further suggest that a Christic visionary experience is valued among Christians as a badge of authority, much as St. Paul regarded his own experience.[30] I would say in response to this imagined objection that public figures having the prestige and respect that accompany positions such as professor, psychiatrist, or bishop have a vested interest in *not* revealing their apparition experiences. So much stigma or suspicion attaches to these experiences that one could reasonably expect such public figures to keep them private. The fact that public figures do speak of them at all makes it very likely that they experienced something similar to what they reported. This fact, combined with their educational backgrounds, gives their reports considerable credibility.

Many academics view such experiences with suspicion, apparently because they see such experiences as indicators of psychopathology, or because these experiences are grouped with parapsychological claims. Two decades ago Alister Hardy offered four reasons why scientists are apt to reject parapsychological claims: (1) The experimental results have not been repeated at will, (2) earlier work was fraudulent, and the risk of fraud persists in this kind of empirical inquiry, (3) those who work in this field might want a particular result and so lack objectivity about their experimental work, and (4) they believe that parapsychology is incompatible with the rest of science.[31] I do not think the situation has changed much since then. Even biblical literalists are often suspicious of visionary experiences, perhaps because of their inclination toward fideism (believing without insisting upon evidence and good reasons) and their fear that empirical inquiry will erode the conclusions they have already drawn about religious matters (including empirical matters) on purely textual grounds. Timothy Beardsworth remarks that visions are "out of fashion among the Christian orthodox."[32] This statement appears in a study of visionary and ecstatic experiences based on one thousand contemporary firsthand accounts. Of course many religious people are more open to religious experience in general, and these, not surprisingly, would be apt to view apparitions favorably as possible sources of information. The fact that well-educated people report Christic experiences in a context where they are at risk suggests, at the very least, that their reports are sincere. The fact that people come forward and report visionary experiences despite a general climate of suspicion also suggests that they are sincere. These reports might also be authoritative, if the conditions outlined above are satisfied.

Claiming that only the educated are capable of providing authoritative reports of extraordinary phenomena is probably a myth perpetuated by the educated. Percipients who completed high school should easily have enough education to report on their experiences adequately. Even those with simply the ability to read and write can probably report quite adequately upon the phenomenological characteristics of their perceptual experiences. The reports of those who are well-educated can be plausibly construed as lending credence to the reports of those who are not. When we find highly educated persons, well-versed in the issues surrounding such controversial claims, coming forward to report their own experiences, and even risking their public reputations by doing so, we can legitimately give more credence to the reports from those whose authority is in doubt. We could speak of this as the confirming influence of evidence on other (putative) evidence.

Alister Hardy illustrates the use of a principle very similar to this one in his discussion of two recent examples of apparitions seen by "responsible citizens." The first example is mentioned in the autobiography of Harold Owen, who had an apparition of his brother Wilfred, the poet, who was one of the last casualties of the First World War.[33] Hardy's second example comprises the two apparition experiences that Canon J. B. Phillips had of C. S. Lewis, Christian apologist and professor of English literature. Hardy remarks: "These examples of apparitions, seen by responsible citizens of the present day, show us that we can accept the stories of the appearances of Jesus to those who had been close to him, and felt his love when he was alive, without any damage to our intellectual integrity."[34] We might question Hardy's claim that appearances of Jesus are supported by authoritative reports of apparitions in general, for bibli-

cal commentators have supposed that those appearances were quite different from other apparitions. But Hardy's point about the value of authoritative evidence is plausible. I believe that enough reports of Christic
apparitions come from people with strong educational backgrounds to
warrant giving serious attention to the whole body of evidence, including
that from percipients with weak educational backgrounds.

The Identification of the Apparition as Jesus

One curious feature of Christic visions and apparitions is the confidence
that the percipients generally exhibit about the identity of the figure in the
apparition experience. Although no authoritative account of Jesus's
appearance exists,[35] and the physical appearance reported by percipients
varies, all "know" it is Jesus. In many of the conventional accounts of
other types of apparition experiences, percipients already know the person
who supposedly appears to them, and consequently are well aware of how
the person appears (or appeared) in ordinary life. But the appearance of
Jesus in ordinary life is not known, and so it is curious that the identification is made at all. Also curious is the number of cases in which this identification seems to be instantaneous, with relatively little reference to
physical appearance. The critical debate on the Shroud of Turin during the
last two decades has brought the question of the physical appearance of
Jesus into public discussion, probably enhancing popular beliefs already in
place. The conventional idea about the appearance of Jesus is of a man
with a full beard, moustache, and long hair parted in the center of the
head. The source of this belief is itself mysterious, although several books
published a century or so ago probably contributed to this belief among
people in the English-speaking world.

Thomas Heaphy's study of the likeness of Jesus has had a significant
influence since its publication in 1880. Heaphy refers to five classes of evidence relating to the physical appearance of Jesus: (1) mosaics executed
between the second and seventh centuries, (2) pictures on unprepared
linen from before the third century, (3) pictures in tempera on wood, of
Eastern or Byzantine origin, and traditionally ascribed to Luke, (4) metal-
work from the fifth century, and (5) sculptures, frescoes and designs
worked on glass in the first to fourth centuries, including sketches from
the walls of the Roman catacombs.[36] The engravings on the bottoms of
glass cups (paterae) are particularly interesting, for some of these depict
Jesus without the halo that became a standard element of portrayals quite
early in the Christian era, suggesting that they are very early. Heaphy
remarks: "The hair parted in the middle, flowing to the shoulders, and

beginning to curl or wave from the ear downward—the thin beard, the hair upon the lip, and the oval face—were recognized as the distinguishing characteristic of the true likeness, even at that early period."[37] The work of Heaphy on the likeness of Jesus attracted the interest of Rex Bayliss, president of the Royal Society of British Artists, and he edited Heaphy's work. He also contributed a volume to the subject, approaching it from the standpoint of an artist.[38] Cyril Dobson, writing some fifty years later, says: "A traditional likeness exists. That is too apparent to need demonstration. The age of Constantine flooded the world with reproductions of it. . . . But Constantine did not invent the traditional likeness in his time. He drew it forth from its secret hiding-place in the catacombs."[39] Ian Wilson, however, questions the genuineness of Heaphy's work on several of the "holy faces" on cloth, charging that "Heaphy lied both in word and in paintbrush."[40] Wilson notes, for instance, that Heaphy's copy of the painting that he said he saw has the hair and beard pointing in a direction opposite to that in which they point in the original.[41] Whatever the truth might be about the source of the traditional likeness, it does exist, and evidently influences judgments in visionary experiences down to the present day. Those who have studied mystical experiences in general say that they are mediated by the beliefs of those who have them,[42] and expectations of how Jesus appeared might be expected to influence the content of contemporary Christic visions.

Youthful, beardless images of Jesus also circulated in the ancient world. Bayliss says these might have been a symbol—an idea but not a likeness—adopted by Christians in view of Christian persecution.[43] Franz Wolter argues that the gnostics were responsible for promoting this image in a desire to make Hellenistic culture harmonize with Christian doctrine.[44] Wolter describes an alabaster bust of Jesus (supposedly) found in Jerusalem and brought to Munich around 1905. It features a short, parted beard, and long hair parted in the center. Adolf Furtwängler, described by Wolter as "the most learned expert on antique art,"[45] pronounced the head to be Hellenistic from the first third of the first century. Wolter observes: "Every one, without exception, who has enjoyed the memorable experience of beholding this Jerusalem-Christ, answered the question, whom or what this head represented, with: 'This is Christ!' No matter what degree of education or culture—all were of the same mind."[46] Wolter infers from this that a uniform conception must have prevailed since early Christian times, noting that the fourth-century historian Eusebius referred to images of Jesus.[47] Eusebius says he saw a statue of Jesus at Caesarea Philippi, and also colored portraits,[48] but he does not give a detailed description of what he saw.

This brief discussion of the physical appearance of Jesus suggests that it cannot be established in any satisfactory way. Ian Wilson has considered the appearance of Jesus in a number of his books,[49] and has shown its problematic nature quite convincingly. Several different portrayals of Jesus have been offered by portrait painters who claim to have had visions or dreams of Jesus. These are of particular interest because of portrait painters' special ability to notice details. Warner Sallman's famous 1940 painting depicts the head of Jesus very much in keeping with the traditional likeness: long, dark brown hair parted in the center, fairly long, dark brown beard, blue eyes, and light brown complexion. Sallman is said to have seen this likeness in a dream or vision after much frustration in trying to paint a likeness of Jesus. His words are: "In the early hours of the morning before dawn there emerged, in one illuminous moment, a visual picturization of Jesus, so clear and definite. And it appeared to me that I was seated at the drawing broad with the completed drawing before me."[50] More than six million copies of this painting were distributed during World War II alone, and it is still widely reproduced. Herbert Beecroft's portrayal, by contrast, shows Jesus with ruddy complexion, a short beard, bright blue eyes, and reddish hair. He apparently had long wanted to paint a picture of Jesus, and one day had a vision that lasted long enough to leave an indelible impression upon him.[51] This painting hangs in a church somewhere in London, England, but I have seen only a copy of it and have not been able to discover more details about it. I note that two of the percipients I interviewed, Jim Link and Margaret Moyse, do (or did) painting as a hobby, and paid particular attention to the kinds of details typically noticed by painters.

Two or three other elements of the Christic visionary experience could unconsciously contribute to the identification of the figure as Jesus. The feelings that it typically evokes—majesty, reverence, being loved, joy— could understandably give percipients the sense that this encounter was with someone or something transcendent. The serious character of these experiences might also contribute to such an identification. It is a short step for those who live in a context where Christian beliefs circulate to think, from clusters of images and appropriate feelings, that they have had a Christic encounter. I suspect that emotions evoked by the experience contribute in some subtle way in making the identification. Perhaps the identifications are not always as instantaneous as they seem to be after the event. It is possible that a rapid evaluation of items of evidence also occurs during the experience.

The radiance that occasionally accompanies the experience probably contributes to the identification as well, for there are widely held beliefs about light and radiance signifying objects or experiences having transcendent dimensions. One wonders whether radiance could have been such a frequent feature of Christic visionary experiences in antiquity that including a halo as part of the likeness had as much representational significance as artistic purpose?

Experiences in which healing or some other powerful influence over the natural order was an alleged concomitant might be expected to give the percipient the impression that this was a transcendent encounter. But this feature, like the others mentioned, is capable of being interpreted in a variety of ways, even among those for whom supernaturalistic beliefs are readily accepted. I suggest that the fact that percipients identify the figure in the apparition as Jesus is still curious. The possibility that it is brought about by self-disclosure should not be excluded.

I have already indicated the importance of the earliest Christian traditions with respect to the problem of Christic visions, apparitions, and alleged appearances. I now turn to this important piece of the puzzle.

4 | Christic Appearances and Visions in the New Testament

The New Testament includes numerous accounts of post-Resurrection appearances and visions of Jesus. The Resurrection itself is never described in detail in the canonical writings, but a partial account can be found in the apocryphal *Gospel of Peter*. It tells the story of two men coming down from heaven in great brightness, opening the sepulchre in which Jesus was buried, and helping him to walk out. As they left the sepulchre, a cross inexplicably followed them. But neither classical nor recent theological reflection gives much weight to this story.[1]

Scholars believe that the earliest NT document referring to the Resurrection and various appearances is I Corinthians, where Paul says that the Resurrection was a tradition he received from others, and lists six groups or individuals to whom Jesus appeared: Peter; the Twelve Disciples; more than five hundred brethren at once; James; all the apostles; and Paul himself. This list seems to present the appearances in something like chronological order, identifying Peter as the first to have seen Jesus alive, but providing few other details. As *evidence* for the Resurrection, the information is sparse, but Paul may have assumed that his hearers were familiar with the details of the tradition he had received. This discourse is also significant for its discussion of the nature of the resurrected body of Jesus. Paul says that it was not a natural one, but spiritual, imperishable, glorious, and powerful.[2] Many other brief references to the Resurrection appear in Paul's writings, but this passage from I Corinthians 15 is widely recognized as the most important one. Taken together, these references suggest that some tradition was well-known in the early Christian communities.

Mark is widely considered to be the earliest of the Gospels. Many recent scholars think that the gospel originally ended with the story of the women going to the tomb to anoint the dead body of Jesus, finding the tomb empty, and leaving in amazement and fear.[3] This ending includes no reference to a Christic appearance at all, and thus reflects only the tradition of an empty tomb. The longer, disputed ending includes brief accounts of appearances to Mary Magdalene, to two people walking in the country, and to the eleven disciples. This ending identifies Mary Magdalene as the first to whom Jesus appeared, apparently conflicting with the supposed chronology of appearances given by Paul in I Corinthians. These brief accounts in Mark seem to have more complete counterparts in Matthew and Luke, which are synoptic Gospels widely thought to have been dependent upon Mark.

Matthew reflects both the empty tomb and the appearance traditions. He tells the story of an angel descending from heaven to roll back the stone over the opening to the sepulchre in which the dead body of Jesus had been placed.[4] The angel told Mary Magdalene and another Mary, who had come to see the sepulchre, that Jesus had risen, and instructed them to tell the disciples the news. As the women left the tomb Jesus met them. They responded by taking hold of his feet and worshiping him. His words to them were: "Do not be afraid; go and tell my brethren to go to Galilee, and there they will see me." Matthew concludes his gospel with an account of the eleven disciples going to Galilee as they had been directed. When Jesus met them there, they worshiped him, but some doubted. He then commissioned them in these words: "Go therefore and make disciples of all nations, baptizing them in the name of the Father and of the Son and of the Holy Spirit."[5]

Matthew's account of the two women's taking hold of the feet of Jesus is handled in different ways by biblical critics. Those who endorse the traditional Christian interpretation of the gospel narratives see it as providing convincing evidence that the Resurrection body of Jesus was substantial and real. But critics of a reductionist bent see it as Matthew's reconstruction of an event, not designed to report the facts but to counter the docetic view emerging within Christendom that the resurrected body of Jesus was not real.

Luke also reflects the empty tomb and appearance traditions. The women are mentioned in his account, but their encounter is not with Jesus but with two angels who tell them of the Resurrection. Like Matthew, Luke gives accounts of only two appearances. The first one is experienced by someone named Cleopas and an unidentified man as they walked the seven miles from Jerusalem to Emmaus. Many have thought that the second man was Peter. If it was, Luke's account would be consistent with Paul's statement that Jesus first appeared to Peter. As the three walked along they talked about the Crucifixion, and even the rumor that Jesus had been resurrected. But the two disciples did not recognize their companion until they sat down to eat in Emmaus. Luke describes it thus: "When he was at table with them, he took the bread and blessed, and broke it, and gave it to them. And their eyes were opened and they recognized him; and he vanished out of their sight."[6] Some scholars believe that the longer, disputed ending of Mark preserves this story in a much shorter form, and offers a different explanation for their failure to recognize Jesus. The text in Mark reads: "After this he appeared in a different form to two of them, as they were walking into the country."

Luke then relates how these two disciples returned that same night to Jerusalem to tell the eleven disciples what they had seen. As they told their story "Jesus himself stood among them."[7] This frightened the gathered disciples, for they supposed that they saw a spirit. But Jesus calmed them, inviting them to handle him and convince themselves that he was not a spirit. To give further proof of his materiality, he ate the piece of broiled fish that they gave him. Some scholars see in this a further attempt to combat docetism. Luke concludes his gospel with Jesus's leading his disciples to nearby Bethany, commissioning them to preach, and parting from them. Luke opens Acts with an account of the Ascension from Mount Olivet, slightly more than half a mile from Jerusalem, forty days after the Resurrection. But Matthew clearly puts the Ascension in Galilee, far from Jerusalem.

The non-synoptic Gospel of John also presents both the empty tomb and appearance traditions. An appearance to Mary Magdalene is described, but in John's account she is not allowed to touch him because he has not yet ascended. John implies in this account that the Ascension took place just after the Resurrection, for Jesus does not object to being touched shortly thereafter. John goes on to describe three more appearances, each time to a group of Jesus's disciples. In the first of these doubting Thomas is not present, and when Thomas hears about it he exclaims, "Unless I see in his hands the print of the nails, and place my finger in the mark of the nails, and place my hand in his side, I will not believe."[8] Eight days later Thomas is satisfied, and for the second time Jesus appears in a room whose doors are shut. Jesus' words to Thomas are: "Put your finger here, and see my hands; and put out your hand, and place it in my side; do not be faithless, but believing." Thomas responds with, "My Lord and my God."

The fourth appearance described by John takes place at the Sea of Galilee.[9] Seven disciples are fishing when they see someone on the shore whom they do not recognize. This stranger instructs them to cast their net on the right side of the boat, and when they do they catch so many fish they are hardly able to haul them in. Simon Peter realizes at that moment that it was Jesus who stood on the shore, already having prepared a meal of baked fish and bread. John's account continues with a poignant conversation between Peter and Jesus in which Peter, who had denied knowing Jesus at the trial, expresses his love and devotion.

These seventeen appearance accounts in the canonical writings (including the long ending of Mark) are naturally thought to overlap considerably, although the lack of detail makes it impossible to establish a definitive list of incidents, if these stories are in fact accounts of *events*. The appearance references, so called, are widely considered to present the following challenges: determining their number and order; fixing their locations; establishing their temporal relationship to the Ascension; establishing the nature of Paul's experience, in comparison with the earlier experiences of the disciples; and answering questions concerning the corporeality of the body of Jesus.

A number of incidents in the Gospels are considered by some critics to be "displaced references" to post-Resurrection appearances—references to post-Resurrection appearances that the oral tradition somehow altered so that the stories became told as pre-Crucifixion events. The best-known of these is the transfiguration story, in which Jesus was transformed before three of his disciples so that, as Luke puts it, "The appearance of his countenance was altered, and his raiment become dazzling white."[10] The accounts also say that a cloud then descended upon Jesus and his disciples. The transfiguration story is most interesting, for the references to the cloud and the radiant face of Jesus are similar to visual effects frequently reported in Christic visions. Some scholars also include some or all of the following stories or teachings as displaced: the story of the miraculous catch of fish in Luke 5, the story of Jesus walking on water in Mark 6, the story of Jesus stilling the storm in Mark 4, the story of feeding the multitude in Mark 6, and the speech beginning with "Thou art Peter" in Matthew 16.[11] The status of these possible "displaced references" is a matter of some controversy, and I shall not discuss them further.

Post-Ascension Visions

Several post-Ascension encounters with Jesus are also described in the NT, although most of them are considered visions, not appearances, because they occur after the Ascension as traditionally interpreted, forty days after the Resurrection. The most significant is the experience that took place at Paul's conversion on the way to Damascus. This is generally discussed in connection with the appearance tradition, primarily because it appears in Paul's own list of witnesses to the Resurrection in I Corinthians 15. Three accounts of Paul's experience appear in Acts, one presented directly by Luke and two others included in sermons preached by Paul.[12] All accounts agree that a light shone from heaven, and that someone spoke to Paul identifying himself as Jesus. But the accounts differ on details, including the content of the message, whether Paul was the only one to fall to the ground, and whether Paul's companions also heard the voice and saw the light.[13] Each of the accounts refers to a different effect experienced by everyone present, suggesting that the experience was understood as belonging to the domain of public events, and was not merely subjective.

Several other Christic experiences of a visual character are attributed to Paul. He had a trance (*ekstasei* in Greek) experience just after returning to Jerusalem following his conversion: "I fell into a trance and saw him [Jesus] saying to me."[14] Luke does not give further details about this experience, but places emphasis on the message that was communicated. In Acts 18 Luke makes a reference to an experience in Corinth: "And the Lord said to Paul one night in a vision (*horamatos*)," but he provides no phenomenological detail here either. The account implies that something of a visual nature occurred. In Acts 23 Luke mentions a fourth experience. He says that Jesus stood by Paul in the night to comfort him because of his persecutors in Jerusalem, and to inform him that he would be going to Rome. Although the description is very brief, it presents the encounter as taking place on earth.

Paul may have had a fifth Christic vision. In one of his letters he says: "I will go on to visions (*optasias*) and revelations of the Lord. I know a man in Christ who fourteen years ago was caught up to the third heaven— whether in the body or out of the body I do not know, God knows."[15] Commentators generally agree that this refers to Paul's own experience, despite the indirect way in which he describes it. While the phrase "of the Lord" could be variously interpreted, it may denote a visionary experience of Jesus.[16] The use of *optasias* suggests that Paul saw something, as does the reference to his being caught up into the third heaven. The reason for thinking that this might be a fifth distinct incident is his dating of it. His conversion is widely believed to have occurred in about 35 A.D. (the occasion of his first two experiences), and his visit to Corinth described in Acts 18 is thought to date to about 55 A.D. (the probable date of Paul's third experience). The letter in which this account appears was written about 60 A.D., so the experience in question seems to have occurred around 46 A.D. Because this experience involved being "caught up to the third heaven," it seems to be different from the fourth experience.

Yet another Christic vision is associated with the conversion of Paul.

Luke describes how a disciple named Ananias was instructed by Jesus in a vision to find Paul and lay his hands on him so that he might receive his sight.[17] Jesus also tells Ananias that Paul is waiting for him to come, for "he has seen [in a vision] a man named Ananias come in and lay hands on him so that he might regain his sight."[18]

Another Christic vision is attributed to Stephen as he was being stoned to death. Luke says that Stephen "gazed into heaven and saw the glory of God, and Jesus standing at the right hand of God."[19] No more detail is given about this experience, and Luke does not say whether bystanders could see what Stephen described, but it is generally assumed that he was the only one who could see Jesus.

Revelation is well-known for its dramatic and mysterious visions. It opens with a detailed account of a vision of Jesus, experienced by some-one named John (not, according to recent scholarship, the apostle John). The Greek term used to describe John's experience is *apokalypsis*, which means "revelation or enlightenment," not *horama*, which is translated "vision," so a legitimate question could be raised about how this experi-ence should be classified. But since the whole domain of aberrant visual experiences is so little understood, there seems to be no harm in continu-ing to describe it as a vision, provided this does not prejudice ideas about its significance. John also describes this revelation as coming through an angel, which is an idea we have already encountered in surveying the views of the Christian church on visions and apparitions. One wonders how much this text contributed to the angelic mediation theory in the his-tory of the Christian church.

John's Christic vision is the only one in the NT in which the phenom-enological content is described in any detail at all.[20] Ironically, what is described does not conform at all to the traditional depiction of Jesus. Jesus is seen with hair as white as wool or snow, eyes like a flame of fire, feet like fire, a voice like the sound of many waters, and a face shining like the sun in full strength; moreover, in his right hand he holds seven stars, and a flame issues out of his mouth.[21] This description is altogether different from that thought to have been experienced in the appearances, and it has a symbolic character that the other accounts do not have. Christopher Rowland has discussed the influence of the Jewish visionary tradition upon early Christianity, and points out that John's description at this point owes much to one of Daniel's visions found in the Hebrew scriptures.[22]

This completes the Christic visions mentioned in the NT. Except for Paul's Damascus experience, they are not discussed extensively by biblical critics in evaluating the appearance traditions. In choosing to ignore them and to concentrate on the appearances, commentators have given credence to the sharp distinction traditionally made between appearances and visions. Even critics who espouse a subjectivist interpretation of the appearance accounts generally gloss over the vision accounts, confining their attention to the accounts in I Corinthians, the Gospels, and to Paul's conversion experience. But it is doubtful, as I shall argue below, that a sharp distinction between the appearances and visions can be maintained.

To complete the summary of significant literature I will mention some of the appearance stories found in apocryphal literature.[23] Some of these accounts do more than tell stories, for they suggest mechanisms that are thought to be responsible for visionary experiences. The first part of the *Gospel of Mary* describes a post-Resurrection conversation between Jesus, his disciples, and Mary.[24] In the second part Mary relates a vision in which Jesus informs her that a person's understanding is what sees a vision, not a person's soul or spirit. The understanding is described here as being between the soul and spirit, anticipating a medieval tripartite view of the person.[25] The *Apocryphon of James* describes an appearance of Jesus to the Twelve Disciples 550 days after the Resurrection. In this incident James and Peter are drawn aside for special instruction, and after Jesus leaves them, these two disciples "send their spirits to heaven" to hear and see various sights, including angels in worship.[26]

The *Epistula Apostolorum* describes an appearance to the eleven disciples strikingly similar to accounts found in the Gospels, and having similar apologetical purposes. When Jesus appears to his disciples, they are doubtful about what they see.[27] To reassure them about his identity, Jesus invites Peter to put his finger in the nail print of his hands, Thomas to put his hand in his side, and Andrew to verify that his footstep leaves an imprint in the ground. The text continues: "For it is written in the prophet, 'But a ghost, or demon, leaves no print on the ground.'"[28] This account is reminiscent of the canonical Gospels, where sense experience is used to establish the character of the resurrected body of Jesus. No canonical Gospel includes a "footprint test," however.

The *Acts of Thomas* includes several appearances, including one to Thomas, another to a merchant who buys Thomas as a slave, and an appearance to a bridal couple who are counseled by Jesus to abandon sexual intercourse so that they may become holy and pure temples.[29] The last of these visions obviously reinforced the value placed upon celibacy by the early church. The *Letter of Peter to Philip* refers to a vision of Jesus so bright that a mountain was illuminated by it. The vision was accompanied by a voice that said, "Hear my words, that I may send you! Why do you seek after me? I am Jesus Christ, who is with you forever."[30] Finally, *Acts of Peter* describes various visions of Paul and Peter, including ones in which Jesus instructs Paul to go to Spain, and warns Peter about the coming opposition of Simon the sorcerer.[31] In one of these visions to Peter, Jesus is described as smiling and wearing a robe of splendor.

The experiences described in the apocryphal books have not entered significantly into theological debates over Christic appearances and visions. The frequent expression of Gnostic views in these books made them unacceptable to Christian orthodoxy. Although some circulated quite early in the life of the church, they have not been accorded the authority that is given to canonical writings. Willis Barnstone, editor of a recent collection of ancient books under the title *The Other Bible*, remarks that if the Gnostic Valentinus had been chosen Pope of Rome, the fixing of the NT canon in Carthage in 397 would have looked rather different.[32] Biblical scholars devote most of their attention to the NT writings in interpreting the appearances and visions, although other writings, especially those of Jewish origin, are also given consideration. My remarks in this chapter will be directed to the canonical literature. The main issue I wish to raise is whether contemporary apparitions can illuminate features of the NT texts, or vice versa. This issue is complicated by the diverging interpretations of those texts, as I shall show.

The Traditional Interpretation

One approach to the NT accounts of the Resurrection and the post-Resurrection appearances and visions of Jesus can be described as traditional. Tradition has it that Jesus ascended after appearing to his disciples for forty days, and that he has been seen in visions since that time, not in appearances, apart from a possible exception in the case of Paul. The appearances have been understood as real and substantial, while the visions have been understood as experiences having great religious significance for their subjects, but as subjective in character. These appearances, moreover, have been widely understood to have had a consistent form, and to have exhibited the marks of the Crucifixion. Traditionalists have been inclined to view the Resurrection belief as highly probable on the biblical documentary evidence alone. Moreover, their approach to interpreting these documents has been to harmonize discrepant accounts as much as possible, and to eschew the claim that the accounts show varying degrees of historicity. Positions are sometimes articulated that vary slightly from the one just described.

Merrill Tenney's defense of the historicity of the Resurrection is representative of this position. He considers the NT sources to have complete historical integrity, and regards the Resurrection as not merely possible but highly probable.[33] Tenney grants that the Gospels reflect an elemental faith among Jesus's close followers, but accepts the NT descriptions at face value as reports, without critical evaluation. He rejects the position that the post-Resurrection appearances were hallucinatory, for he notes that Jesus was heard to speak, was visible to many people at once, and had a tangible body.[34] Another expression of substantially the traditional position is found in G. E. Ladd's *I believe in the resurrection of Jesus*. Ladd concedes minor divergences among the synoptic Gospels concerning the events that took place, but he offers an account that harmonizes all of the stories and smooths over discrepancies.[35] He affirms the historicity of the "corporeal accounts" in Luke and John in which Jesus is described as having been touched, and concludes, "Jesus had a real, visible, palpable body, and yet a body which possessed new and marvelous properties," such as the ability to move through solid walls.[36] Ladd defends two ascensions of Jesus. The first Ascension (or exaltation) of Jesus into heaven is considered to have taken place at the time of the Resurrection, as suggested by John. The second Ascension is considered to have taken place forty days later, in keeping with Acts and tradition. Ladd takes the second Ascension to be a signal that the appearances have ended, but he does allow the later appearance to Paul as an exception—Ladd describes it as "an abnormal situation."[37] Ladd is clearly attempting to accord authority to Paul's post-Ascension experience without having to give similar authority to the other NT post-Ascension experiences (such as Stephen's) or to the many subsequent experiences reported throughout the history of Christendom. Ladd's harmonized account gives the material from Paul, the synoptic Gospels, John and Acts an equal reporting function, and is characteristic of the traditional position. William Craig is another recent defender of much the same position,[38] although Craig gives more consideration to the possibility of objective visions (explained in Chapter 1) than is characteristic of the traditional view.

The traditional view dominated the world of Christianity until the end of the eighteenth century, when Reimarius questioned the historicity of the NT accounts.[39] Various nineteenth-century authors began to argue that the documents failed to report authentic events, or that they reported experiences that were only subjective in character. David F. Strauss's *A New Life of Jesus*, published in 1865, set the stage for a critical scrutiny of the life of Jesus that continues to this day. Strauss says his objective is to provide an interpretation of the Gospels such that "in the person and acts of Jesus no supernaturalism shall be suffered to remain; nothing which shall press upon the souls of men with the leaden weight of arbitrary inscrutable authority."[40] He considers the contradictions in the appearance stories in the synoptic Gospels as giving the impression of separate visions that were later colored up and exaggerated in various ways. Strauss suggests that some of these visions were brought on by mental excitement over the death of Jesus, or messianic expectations, or Jesus's own allusions to the Resurrection, or OT stories of prophets such as Enoch and Elijah who did not die.[41] Strauss is now considered unsophisticated about the use of critical methods, but his subjectivist interpretation remains influential.

Since his time serious questions have been raised concerning the nature of the documents themselves, particularly the extent to which the supposed narratives report events, or were even attempts to do so. An illustration of how the reporting function has been challenged can be found in Joseph Grassi's conjecture concerning the story of the resurrected Jesus appearing to two disciples as they walked to Emmaus. He suggests that this story is not an attempt to narrate an event, but only an attempt to teach that Jesus is always present to the Christian at any time through the preaching of the Word and the breaking of bread, especially when these are done by the traveling apostle.[42] Another expression of a reductionist position can be found in Bishop Spong's lively book titled *Resurrection: Myth or Reality?* It offers a nonliteral interpretation of the gospel narratives, reworking them using the method of Jewish midrash,[43] so that they express themes that were important in Jewish life. The Resurrection and post-Resurrection appearance "narratives" are reconstructed by Spong in relation to the Jewish feast of tabernacles.[44] Sebastian Moore notes that the shift in NT criticism has replaced "objective" questions of who moved the stone at the sepulchre or what became of the body of Jesus with more "subjective" questions, such as what was happening in the minds of those who said "The Lord is risen," and whether the appearance stories express the faith of the early community rather than describe an experience that gave rise to that faith.[45] The traditional view is widely seen by recent biblical scholars as giving too little attention to questions about the literary forms of the NT documents, the role that editors (redactors) might have had in piecing together various oral traditions, the sources of the accounts, and the results of historical criticism. The plausibility of the Resurrection of Jesus, as traditionally understood, is widely questioned.

The claim of some traditionalists that the NT documentary evidence is sufficient to render the Resurrection highly probable is suspect. Though the evidential strength of these documents is admittedly difficult to assess, many more people would likely accept the historicity of the Resurrection if the NT writings were as impressive as they are thought to be by those traditionalists who advance this argument. Many people are familiar with the basic story of the NT and sympathetic to the moral ideals of Christianity, but find its metaphysical claims improbable. This fact suggests that the NT evidence does not render the Resurrection belief highly probable.

Moreover, many traditionalists betray their own uncertainties about this epistemic point by insisting that the Resurrection comes down to "faith." An appeal to faith would not be needed if the claim were highly probable on the NT evidence alone. Finally, traditionalists claim that other evidence of the Resurrection is persuasive. Some theologians hold that the very existence of the Christian church is evidence of the Resurrection, for, they argue, if the Resurrection had not occurred, the disciples of Jesus would not have had the courage to preach it and Jesus's deity. William James, F.W.H. Myers, and Michael Perry suggest that apparitions in general provide additional evidence for the Resurrection beyond that provided by the NT accounts,[46] and John Hick considers resurrections from other religious traditions as evidence.[47] The Shroud of Turin is sometimes thought to constitute still more evidence, although its evidential value is controversial. These items of evidence would all have to be counted as neutral, rather than confirmatory, if the probability of the Resurrection were virtually certain on the basis of the NT alone (See Appendix III for further details). As we will see in the discussion that follows, other elements in the traditional position have also been challenged, although not always successfully.

The Form-Critical Views of Bultmann and Dibelius

Rudolf Bultmann and Martin Dibelius are credited with having changed the character of NT studies by the development of form criticism in the early part of the twentieth century. Bultmann charges that the biblical cosmology is no longer tenable, and describes its three-storied universe of heaven, earth, and hell as part of a prescientific mythology derived from Jewish apocalyptic and gnostic redemption myths.[48] He says that this outmoded cosmology needs to be replaced with a world view that is existentialist in character, and therefore one that twentieth-century people can embrace. Bultmann grants that the Bible, as a historical document, could be read merely for the purposes of reconstructing the world view of a past epoch, but he considers the real interest in reading it to be "to hear what is the truth about life and about our soul."[49]

Central to the NT mythology is the event of Jesus Christ, particularly his Crucifixion and Resurrection. While Bultmann grants that Jesus's death by Crucifixion is a historical event, he says that its importance lies in the mythology created around it. The original mythology made use of various juridical and sacrificial analogies that hold no meaning for our generation, but the cross can be reinterpreted as signifying the importance of being released from guilt, from our natural dread of suffering, and from our attachment to the securities of ordinary life. The cross and Resurrection are considered "a single indivisible cosmic event which brings judgement to the world and opens up for men the possibility of authentic life."[50] The historian is not capable of capturing the cosmic meaning of this "event," according to Bultmann, for the Resurrection is not an event in past history. The Resurrection, like the Crucifixion, has its origin in something susceptible to historical analysis, such as a series of subjective visions, but this deflects attention away from its existential—and ultimate—meaning.[51]

Dibelius puts a slightly different complexion on the task of biblical criticism. Dibelius holds that we must understand the form of the Gospel accounts as literature before we can properly consider the question of their historicity. He contends that the narratives do not give a biography or a description of the life of Jesus, but consist rather of short, self-contained paragraphs or pericopae that were used in preaching to various groups, including the unconverted, believers, and catechumens.[52] Dibelius divides the narrative materials in the Gospels into paradigms, tales, legends, and myths, and then assigns varying degrees of historical reliability to each of these forms.

As far as the Resurrection accounts are concerned, Dibelius considers only the empty tomb tradition to belong to the earliest oral and written stratum. He thinks that the appearance accounts in the Gospels differ too much from one another to belong to this stratum. He does concede that something happened to the disciples that reversed their despondent attitude and caused them to establish a Christian community. He then adds: "This 'something' is the historical kernel of the Easter faith. How it evolved is nowhere described. Only a few hints and echoes enable us to say anything at all about it. It is clear that Peter, first of all, then the other disciples of Jesus, and then still other followers, including even his hitherto unbelieving brother James, had visions in which they saw their departed Master alive and exalted to heavenly glory."[53] Dibelius maintains that the story of the appearance to Peter evolved over time so that it appears in the Emmaus story in Luke, in the Lake of Galilee appearance in John, and finally in another form in the apocryphal *Gospel of Peter.* Dibelius considers Paul to have supplemented this oldest Petrine tradition with appearances to the five hundred, to James, to all the apostles, and finally to himself, to get his list of six in I Corinthians 15. Dibelius then adds: "The mention of his own conversion experience shows that Paul does not think in terms of a return of Jesus to an earthly kind of existence, however glorified, but of a Lord who is exalted to heaven and who has—for a moment—become visible. He clearly knows nothing about the story of Jesus's tomb being found empty."[54] Dibelius feels that the variety of the appearance stories and the fact that the Gospels locate the appearances at various places indicate that there was no uniform controlling tradition for the appearances, but rather various traditions of uncertain character.

Dibelius emphasizes that his primary objective is not to evaluate the historicity of the appearance stories, but to analyze their form. He concedes some historical basis for the conversion of Paul, but insists that the purpose of the narrative was not to record a historical event but to preserve its superhistorical significance for the faith. Dibelius says that this purpose is best served by telling the story as a miraculous one, a legend.[55] A similar explanation is given for the appearance stories in the Gospels. These stories were illustrations used by preachers, teachers and missionaries who advanced the Christian message. The content of the early preaching (the kerygma) of the Christian itinerants is given to us in the kerygmatic formula found in I Corinthians 15:3f: "that Christ died for our sins in accordance with the scriptures, that he was buried, that he was raised on the third day in accordance with the scriptures, and that he appeared . . . " The appearance stories in the Gospels formed the stories that these preachers and teachers used to illustrate their preaching of Resurrection. Dibelius claims that a purely historical study of the Gospels shows only a pure life that ends in death.[56]

This analysis has proved influential among those who are unsure about the value of approaching the NT literature historically. John Alsup notes that the position of Dibelius on the nature of the gospel accounts has not been challenged much since its influence was first felt,[57] although Alsup himself questions the claim that the gospel stories are dependent on the summary of central dogmas found in I Corinthians 15. Pierre Benoit sums up the theses central to form criticism as follows: (1) the primitive tradition was transmitted in short, self-contained descriptions or sayings known as pericopae, (2) the pericopae were later placed into an editorial framework, such as a chronological or geographical framework, which has no particular value in providing insight into historical events, (3) the early church needed no history of events, for its needs were met by the primitive tradition, and (4) the real authors of the traditions were the members of the primitive community who circulated the stories about and the sayings of Jesus.[58] He considers Bultmann and Dibelius to be heirs to David Strauss because the idea of form criticism is "to withdraw all historical value from the gospel tradition in so far as it enshrines the supernatural."[59]

The effect of critics like Bultmann and Dibelius has been to deflect attention away from the supposed events that the traditional position insisted were reported in the texts, and onto the textual materials themselves. Moderates in the current debate acknowledge that the primitive traditions preserved various stories about Jesus and his sayings in the form of pericopae, that editors and compilers later combined materials together in more or less cohesive writings, and that a critical analysis of the historicity of this material must consider the literary influences and religious expectations and traditions of the time. But not all critics are convinced that no genuinely extraordinary or miraculous events are associated with the relevant narratives. Raymond Brown observed already in 1973 that the followers of Bultmann were no longer insisting that the miraculous constitutes a category that contemporary criticism automatically rejects. He notes, for instance, that Ernst Kasemann, one of Bultmann's foremost pupils, accepted the historicity of the tradition that Jesus was an exorcist, and, by implication, at least some of the world view that Bultmann sought to demythologize.[60]

Although we have no direct way of establishing that the NT stories that tell of post-Resurrection appearances of Jesus were in fact intended as reports of events, several factors militate against Dibelius's view. The early church fathers, who lived much closer than we do to the time of these stories' compilation, regarded them as reports. The discussions of Ignatius, Justin, and Tertullian in the first three centuries,[61] for instance, treat the NT narratives as reports. Even the questionable comparison of the resurrection of Jesus with the resurrection of the phoenix by Clement of Rome, in the first century, supposes that references to the Resurrection of Jesus are reports.[62]

Another important piece of evidence is the tensions created for a reading of Luke-Acts by interpreting the appearance reports in Luke as merely a compilation of fictional stories illustrative of the kerygma. In introducing the narratives of Acts Luke says, "Jesus presented himself alive after his passion by many proofs, appearing to them during forty days, and speaking of the kingdom of God." If the appearance stories in Luke's Gospel are a collection of fictions, how is this remark to be interpreted? Why does Luke say that the appearances were proofs of Jesus's being alive? Why did he not say something that implied that the appearance "accounts" were fictional illustrations of what was being preached?

Similar interpretative problems arise in the sermons of Peter and Paul that Luke summarizes. Luke seems to "quote" them as saying that various people were witnesses to the Resurrection,[63] although it is reasonable to assume that the form in which we have these sermons is that determined by Luke. In Acts 10 Peter is reported as saying: "But God raised him on the third day and made him manifest; not to all the people but to us who were chosen by God as witnesses, who ate and drank with him after he rose from the dead." Luke here presents Peter as taking the appearances as events, and there is nothing to indicate that Luke thought Peter was misrepresenting the character of the appearances by treating them as events rather than as illustrations. One of Paul's sermons in Acts includes a similar remark: "But God raised him from the dead; and for many days he appeared to those who came up with him from Galilee to Jerusalem, who are now his witnesses to the people."[64] Again Luke offers no corrective comment, which one might expect if Paul had represented fictional illustrations as events—a significant misrepresentation. These and other narratives in Luke's gospel seem to purport to report, and it strains credulity to interpret the other two synoptic Gospels differently.

Additional evidence for the claim that at least some of the gospel narratives were intended as reports arises from the fact that there is a continuing tradition of what seem to be *reports* of Christic visionary experiences. The persons I interviewed gave *reports* of their experiences, and the accounts of such visionaries as Teresa of Avila and Julian of Norwich are not open to serious doubt on this point either. Nor is there significant basis for doubt about the examples adduced by Walsh, Brewer, and others that reach back to the early days of the Christian church. Who can read St. Gregory's account of the Christic vision experienced by his aunt, for instance (presented in Chapter 1), without recognizing it as an attempt to report? This chain of evidence supports the claim that at least some of the NT appearance (and vision) accounts were intended as reports. The "no-report" view is not very plausible, and it seems to be losing ground among biblical critics. Its elimination still leaves open various interpretations of these narratives, however.

Karl Barth's "Non-historical" Interpretation

Karl Barth developed a view in the early part of the twentieth century that sought to rise above the uncertainties that inevitably accompany attempts to establish events in the life of Jesus. Barth's position changed during his career, for he grants in his *Church Dogmatics* that a "tiny historical margin" exists in the Easter event, but in *The Epistle to the Romans*, written two decades earlier, he describes the Resurrection as the *non-historical* relating of all of the historical life of Jesus to its origin in God.[65] My interest here is primarily in the position found in *Church Dogmatics*, since it represents his mature work.

Peter Carnley describes Barth as asserting that the Resurrection is not only an event that occurred in time and so was historical, but also an event that can be grasped only in the category of divine revelation, and as such is unlike anything else in history, and so is nonhistorical.[66] Barth's position on the historicity of biblical events resembles that of Martin Kähler, which was expressed several decades earlier and absorbed into German theological scholarship. Kähler held that we can find accounts with historical content in the NT documents, "but certainly not the kind which can be demonstrated to have the value of historical documents in the strict sense of the term. . . . What we do have is simply recollections, which are always at the same time confessional in nature since in presupposition and intention they always witness to something which lies beyond mere historical factuality—something which we call revelation or salvation."[67] Salvation history (*Heilsgeschichte*) is thus differentiated from ordinary history (*Historie*).

Barth describes the Easter event as one that is in the sphere of history and time, no less than the words and acts and death of Jesus.[68] On the one hand, the Resurrection of Jesus was physical,[69] and his body was seen and touched,[70] but on the other hand, it was the resurrection of God, and so the evidence for it can only be fragmentary and contradictory.[71] But Barth also says that no nucleus of genuine history can be extracted from the NT writings apart from the Resurrection itself. For instance, the reference in the Gospels to Jesus appearing for forty days does not give us precise chronological information regarding the appearances, and should therefore be interpreted symbolically or typologically, rather than literally. The appearance narratives themselves are said to be vague, for no clear dividing line between one event and the other is given in them. These narratives, Barth says, are not "history" in our sense of the word, but stories written in the poetical style of historical saga, therefore dealing with an event beyond historical criticism.[72] The term *saga* is used by Barth to refer to narratives that have a typological function. They are intuitive or poetic pictures of a prehistoric reality that became enacted once and for all in time and space in the revelation of God. The object in reading these narratives, or any parts of Scripture, for that matter, is to open oneself to their capacity to bring the Word of God into one's life so that one might become a participant in salvation; the object is not to peer behind them so as to determine the course of historical events to which they are assumed by traditionalists to attest.

Because the Resurrection is unique and singular, and because it belongs to salvation history primarily, rather than human history, knowledge of it is also said to be singular. This knowledge cannot be derived from human life but only from God, and the event cannot be exhausted in any dimension at all, certainly not in an understanding of humanity's temporal past (*Historie*). Knowledge in this eternal domain is described as "a genuine and fruitful knowledge of love for the God who reveals himself in it," but Barth acknowledges that "neutral and objective—'historical'— knowledge is its presupposition."[73]

One might expect Barth to indicate at this point that the neutral and objective knowledge that is the presupposition of the unique kind of religious knowledge appropriate for divine self-disclosure would be knowledge of the events that lie behind the biblical texts, including the appearances so inextricably linked to the Resurrection, but this is not so. He explicitly denies that the object of such knowledge is the historical facts behind the text; rather, it is the text itself. To try to go to the facts behind the text "can only mean the leading away into a Babylonian captivity in which there is no attestation of this event, and can have nothing to do with the knowledge of this event."[74] Barth accordingly refuses to use the critical method to discern later from earlier traditions. But his insistence upon a historical margin is evident from a critique of Bultmann, of whom he complained: "Bultmann does, indeed, insist that the resurrection of Jesus Christ is the act of God. But apparently this does not mean that men beheld the glory of God in the Word made flesh and put to death in the flesh, or that they beheld him raised from the dead in space and time as the outcome of his precious earthly life. They apparently behold his glory only in kerygma, only when he was preached and believed in."[75] These remarks clearly show that Barth considered the life, death, resurrection, and appearances of Jesus to have a historical foundation, and commentators generally concur.[76] But he severely restricted the extent to which these texts should be subjected to criticism.

One of the difficulties with Barth is that his seeming assertions about what would normally be considered events are not clearly meant to be such. Barth repeatedly speaks, for instance, of Jesus appearing for forty days, and one gets the impression that he is referring to an actual period of time during which Jesus was seen by various people. But then he says that this period of time might be legendary rather than literal, and that one should not try to go behind the text to find the facts. We need only stop at the texts.

Barth's view, if generalized, creates considerable difficulties in maintaining that the whole Christ event is an *event*. The point can be conceded that God's self-disclosure (centered in Christ) requires a larger and different framework than that which normally accompanies the historical analysis of events. The question inevitably arises, however, concerning the historical margin present in this event. To concede that there is some margin, but disallow the use of critical techniques leaves one wondering if there is any margin at all. Barth grants that there may be no margin as far as the forty days are concerned, and perhaps none in the appearance stories either, but this makes one wonder why we should concede a margin in the Christ event itself. Barth makes statements that sound as though they belong to *Historie*, but when these are scrutinized he protects them by assigning them to the domain of *Heilsgeschichte*.

D. F. Ford says that Barth was not interested in developing either a natural theology or an apologetic for Christian faith, and was thus content to interpret the Bible primarily using literary and typological categories.[77] Yet, the factuality of the Resurrection is important for Barth, Ford notes, and Barth deals with it by treating the Bible like a realistic novel. While there is "history-likeness" in its narratives, they should not be confused with narratives that have primarily a referential purpose, as disclosed by critical reconstruction.[78] So the Gospels are not biographies of the life of Jesus, but they are not devoid of historical reference either. They adopt a middle distance toward the events mentioned, which means that they are not so exact that they can be harmonized into a completely coherent account, but they are not so vague that no relationship between description and event can be found. Ford remarks that such a position still leaves Barth with the problem of reconciling his insistence that a central revelatory event takes place in time and space with his refusal to employ methods of historical criticism.[79]

Barth's fideism, that is, his insistence on proclaiming the biblical message without seriously addressing questions of historical authenticity, is evidently intended to protect the theology from the vagaries of criticism by making its content independent of history. But it is difficult to sustain *Christian* theological views without endorsing the historicity of at least some of the features of the life of Jesus, whether it is acts he is said to have performed or sayings attributed to him. A defender of Christian theology would certainly not have to maintain the historicity of all the biblical events, as traditionalists insist, but a certain minimum would need to be affirmed. The Judaeo-Christian conception of God is firmly rooted in the conviction that are unique events in history that are acts of God. In this respect the Judaeo-Christian faith is unlike some other religious traditions, such as Buddhism and Hinduism, which are not so dependent on historical claims. G. Ernest Wright suggests that *biblical* faith depends upon whether central events actually occurred:

Biblical skepticism might doubt whether God was the Director of the events, but there was no doubt that there was an Exodus, that the nation was established at Mount Sinai, that it did obtain the land, that it did lose it subsequently, that Jesus did live, that he did die on a cross, and that he did appear subsequently to a large number of independent witnesses. These to the Biblical men are facts: the question is, What do they mean? To assume that it makes no difference whether they are facts or not is simply to destroy the whole basis of the faith.[80]

Ernest Wright's position came into prominence midway into the twentieth century as a response to fideism. N. T. Wright has recently observed that this approach did not succeed in identifying all the events that are to count as revelatory, and did not satisfy the Protestants who insisted that the text itself is divine revelation.[81] But it represents a more reasonable position on the historical content of the biblical narratives than that found in fideism.[82] In rejecting the plausibility of fideism, I am not discounting the place of faith in the life of a religious believer. I am only insisting that uniquely Christian faith must be combined with evidence about the life of Jesus.[83]

Response: The Peculiar "Historical" Character of the Narratives

A number of curious features of the NT documents support the contention that they do not have as much historical "concreteness" as traditionalists have assigned to them. Because the Resurrection belief is both extraordinary and crucial for Christianity, one might expect numerous and detailed accounts defending its authenticity. Moreover, in view of early opposition toward Christians and skepticism of Christianity, writers of documents that began to appear some twenty-five or more years after the alleged events took place might be expected to have gone to considerable lengths to reply to those who rejected the claim that the Resurrection occurred. But this is not what we see. The authors content themselves with several brief stories, or one or two slightly more detailed accounts, or with a list of appearances (such as Paul's) so sketchy that its evidential value is almost negligible. The authors intimate that they knew that they were dealing with a unique phenomenon needing authenticating evidence, for they make a point of describing events in which the risen Jesus was touched, or was seen to eat food, or was seen by many at once, and so on. One would think that they would have tried to provide more details of these events, to make them more convincing. The fact that their accounts lack this effort raises questions about their attitude toward the matters at hand, including the possibility that establishing the historicity of the event was not a very high priority. When one compares the kind of detail that can be obtained from someone reporting a contemporary vision or apparition with that available concerning the NT appearances, it is obvious that the NT presents very little information.

Paul's encounter at his conversion is illustrative of this, for even though the three accounts of it in Acts makes it one of the better attested Christic encounters,[84] none of the accounts explicitly describes what Paul saw. The account in Acts 9 says that he saw a light flash around him and heard someone speak to him identifying himself as Jesus; it also says that the men traveling with him heard a voice but saw no one. The accounts in

Acts 22 and 26 are no more explicit about what was in Paul's visual field. The possibility remains that the bright light combined with the voice and its message were interpreted as an experience in which Jesus appeared. I do not think we can unhesitatingly infer from any of the accounts that Paul saw someone in human form. Luke also says that Paul was blinded by the experience, and it is not clear whether this might have interfered with his sense of sight. C. F. Evans says of Paul's experience, "There was no 'seeing' except of a light which blinds," and he suggests that "the meaning [of 'seeing the Lord'] may be 'to reveal his Son through me to the Gentiles,'" rather than a reference to an ocular experience.[85] Luke does not provide enough details to reject Evans's suggestion outright. If this experience is in fact the model for all the other "appearances," as a number of critics suggest, the traditional view is on uncertain ground.

Another striking feature of the NT accounts is that references to doubts of one kind or another are mentioned in all of the Gospels. Matthew makes reference to a doubt of some kind among the eleven disciples when Jesus commissioned them in Galilee. I. P. Ellis has argued that the reference to doubt here means that a person cannot make up his mind whether or not to believe, rather than that the claim is rejected outright,[86] but the point about doubt still stands. Although the long ending of Mark is not generally taken to be authentic, it is of interest that it too makes reference to some of the eleven being hard of heart and unwilling to believe those who reported that they had seen Jesus. The account of the walk to Emmaus in Luke describes how Jesus scolded his two companions for being slow to believe, and John, finally, mentions the unbelief of Thomas. Various explanations for these doubts could be offered, but one explanation that must be considered is that the appearances may not have been as "historically concrete" as are those that form the normal experience of public objects and events. Doubts by themselves do not establish that the appearance phenomena were "peculiar" events, but they do contribute to such a conjecture.

A third fascinating feature of the post-Resurrection gospel narratives is that they do not describe the physical appearance of Jesus. We rely so heavily upon similarity of physical appearance to support ordinary claims about continuing personal identity that we can hardly be faulted for expecting a similar criterion to be used in claiming that identity has been preserved over death and resurrection. If someone were to report having seen an apparition of a well-known figure such as Napoleon Bonaparte or Abraham Lincoln, we would automatically want an exact description of the content of the percipient's visual field. A significant degree of similarity between the known appearance of the historical figure and the appearance of the apparition figure would be demanded, in order to give the claim any credence. A similar demand is typically made of a person living today who reports a Christic apparition. So it is natural to expect detailed physical descriptions in the NT accounts of what Jesus looked like before his death and after the Resurrection in order to help make credible the claim that he came back to life. But no such descriptions are offered. The author of Revelation gives a description of Jesus, but this is never considered to be similar to the post-Resurrection appearances described in the Gospels. In addition, there are curious references to a lack of recognition on the part of people who could be expected to recognize him immediately: The two disciples who walked to Emmaus did not recognize Jesus, Mary Magdalene did not recognize him just outside his tomb, and the disciples who fished in the Sea of Galilee did not recognize Jesus standing on the shore.[87]

The problem of identity is complicated further by the statement in the controversial ending to Mark, which says that Jesus appeared *in another form* to two of them as they were walking into the country.[88] Many commentators do not discuss this statement because of its questionable authenticity, although some consider it to have some value in revealing something of the early oral traditions.[89] Luke's description of the walk to Emmaus also suggests that the form of Jesus varied. It is a provocative account, for if the post-Resurrection identification of Jesus was generally made on the basis of physical form, and if the resurrected body of Jesus as he appeared always bore a close similarity to the condition of his body at death, one wonders why the two disciples who walked with him did not consider the possibility that they were talking to Jesus. Luke says that they discussed his death on this walk, and spoke about women of their acquaintance who had reported earlier that day that they had seen him alive. They were thinking about him, but they did not recognize him. Were the hands (or wrists?) of Jesus so well concealed by the cloak he wore, his feet so well covered up by his cloak or his sandals, his face and forehead (which must have given evidence of injury from the crown of thorns) so hidden from view, that no marks of wounds were visible suggesting that they were talking to Jesus? The account in Luke leaves us with a host of questions, making the comment in Mark's inauthentic ending more attractive than ever. Elaine Pagels has discussed the question of varying form in connection with the disagreements between Gnostics and orthodox Christians over the Resurrection. She considers Mark's statement and Luke's account of the walk to Emmaus as implying that the form varied.[90] Pheme Perkins remarks that the point of varying appearance was supported by Origen, and also by the Gnostics, who thought of Jesus as a luminous polymorphic being.[91] There are no indisputably authentic NT references to the form of Jesus varying, but the varying form could explain why no reference to physical characteristics is given. Perhaps the appearances varied enough that NT writers saw no point in offering a physical description of what Jesus looked like in order to defend the claim before skeptics that a resurrection had taken place. C. F. Evans suggests that "the resurrection form of Jesus was a temporary state and not one in which he exercises his permanent lordship," and so might have accommodated a varying form.[92]

Some of the appearances did, of course, resemble a crucified person. Thomas wanted to see the marks of nails in Jesus's hands and of a spear in his side, and was evidently satisfied. The crucified form is also implied when John says that Jesus showed his disciples his hands and his side, and when Luke says he showed them his hands and feet. Many Christians consider the body of the resurrected Jesus to have been unvarying in form, a virtual replica of his earthly form at his death, with *all* the marks of scourging, crucifixion, and other tortures, and recognizable by virtue of these physical characteristics. But these beliefs do not have an explicit basis in the canonical NT writings.

These beliefs about a fixed form enter into discussions of contemporary Christic phenomena, including visions, in an interesting way. I mentioned in Chapter 2 that John White described the figure that he saw as having the marks of nails in his hands (palms), not his wrists. He concludes from this that it was not really Jesus that appeared to him, for Jesus would have had the nails driven into his wrists. White evidently thinks that the resurrected body bears a close correspondence to the form of the dead body of Jesus. The discussion of the location of stigmata in the hands of stigmatics also brings up this question of correspondence. Many stigmatics have had wounds appear in their hands rather than their wrists, but, according to Ian Wilson, a present-day stigmatic, Brother Gino Burresi from Rome, is said to exhibit the stigmata on his wrists "in conformity with the location now most favoured from medical experiments, from archaeological discoveries, and from the Turin Shroud."[93] The variety of shapes and locations of stigmatic wounds is such that not all of them could resemble the shape and location of the wounds of the crucified Jesus. Nothing definite can be established at present about the location of the nail marks on the body of Jesus or about the form of his resurrection body. The incompleteness of the NT accounts on the matter of form also suggest that the appearances and visions were peculiar events. The fact that the accounts are incomplete comes into sharper focus when we compare them with the detailed descriptions often available of contemporary Christic apparitions.

One of the questions posed by contemporary experiences is whether immediate recognition, without significant use of other criteria such as physical form, might have occurred in NT times. The account that comes closest to suggesting this is the one in Luke which says that the eyes of the disciples were prevented from recognizing him until he became known to them in the breaking of the bread. But if immediate recognition did take place, it appears not to have occurred all of the time. Jesus evidently needed to reveal his identity to Paul, and he defended his identity to Thomas using physical criteria. But then he reprimanded Thomas for not believing without seeing. Could the reprimand of Thomas stem from the expectation that the preferred method for making an identification was not reliance on physical criteria but something much more nebulous, such as immediate recognition of his identity in whatever physical form he might appear? I present this only as a conjecture. Some critics think that the questions concerning the nature of the Resurrection body that interest us today were not of interest to most of the NT writers.[94] This could explain some of the loose ends left by the NT accounts.

The phenomenon of immediate recognition widely mentioned by contemporary visionaries may not shed light on the NT accounts, but other features of contemporary experiences do illuminate the NT accounts. The phenomenon of varying form in contemporary experiences, for instance, renders the statement in Mark about varying form more plausible than it would otherwise be. But the most striking contribution that contemporary experiences make is to highlight the paucity of detail in the NT accounts, as well as the peculiar sense of history that seems to be behind them. These accounts do not embody well-developed arguments from personal experience. Even Paul, widely considered the best educated and most intelligent of the NT writers, leaves a residue of uncertainty in his list of witnesses. Why he includes private experiences alongside group experiences without a comment, for instance, as though they were comparable in evidential force, is a mystery.

Barth is right to suggest that something is peculiar about the NT accounts, but wrong to see this as a sign we should not delve into the events that lie behind the texts. The detailed truth behind these enigmatic NT statements and stories is unlikely to ever be fully known, but the fact that we do not have answers to our questions does not mean that there are no substantial events to which these documents point. The descriptions of those events may even have been deliberately designed to leave them shrouded in some mystery, to conceal as much as they reveal. Why they might have been so constructed is a speculative question that lies beyond the scope of this book.

Pannenberg on Historical Reconstruction

Wolfhart Pannenberg accepts that the Resurrection is a claim that can be subjected to historical analysis, and endorses the view commonly held among critics that two different early traditions exist, and each needs to be investigated independently: the tradition reflected in Mark that reports only an empty tomb, and the tradition reflected in Paul (I Corinthians 15) that reports only appearances. Pannenberg says: "The historical question of the appearances of the resurrected Lord is concentrated completely in the Pauline report," and adds that the appearances mentioned in the Gospels, but not in Paul, have such a strong legendary character that one can hardly find a historical kernel in them.[95] Pannenberg considers even those gospel accounts that correspond to Paul's list to have legendary elements, particularly those that stress the corporeality of the resurrected body of Jesus. Again the objective is said to be to combat docetism.[96] So Pannenberg assigns a reporting function to only some of the appearance stories and references in the NT, notably those mentioned by Paul in I Corinthians 15.

The historicity of Paul's report is endorsed by Pannenberg, first because of the authority of Paul himself, but second because of the close proximity in time of Paul's writing to the Resurrection event. Pannenberg accepts the view that Paul was converted some three years after the Crucifixion, and probably learned firsthand about the relevant events within three to five years of his conversion. So Paul's knowledge of these events was acquired only six to eight years after they happened. Moreover, Paul likely received formulations of beliefs already in place.[97] All of these conditions are taken to point to the historical reliability of the I Corinthians list of appearances.

Pannenberg also takes his cue from Paul's account in interpreting the appearance tradition. Because Paul classified his own experience at his conversion with the appearances to the other people mentioned in his list, Pannenberg thinks it appropriate to consider all the appearances as having been similar to Paul's. Five elements are found in Paul's account: (1) Paul saw Jesus, (2) Paul saw a spiritual body, not a person with an earthly body, (3) the appearance was from heaven, and was not an encounter that took place on earth, (4) the appearance could have happened as a light phenomenon (*Lichtglanz* in German), since Paul describes a light as having shone upon him from above, and (5) the Christophanic appearance was accompanied by an audition.[98] In light of this model, the corporeal accounts in the Gospels are said to appear nonhistorical. All of the other appearances are considered by Pannenberg to exhibit at least four of these elements (all but the fourth), and would have been interpreted in relation to the general apocalyptic expectation of the Jews concerning the resurrection of all the dead. Pannenberg further views the appearance experiences as visionary in character, and by "vision" he means that "someone sees something that others present are not able to see."[99] Pannenberg wants to avoid conceding that the events in question were imaginary, however; he allows for the possibility that this kind of experience might "lay hold of extrasubjective reality."[100] Pannenberg therefore rejects the *subjective* vision hypothesis, repudiates the impossibility of miracle, and advances the historicity of the Resurrection as reasonable, although he acknowledges the limitations of speaking about this unique event. He interprets the appearances as *objective* visions—visions because only selected people were capable of seeing Jesus (as he chose to reveal himself), and objective because there is some kind of extrasubjective reality to which they correspond. Pannenberg cautiously refers to various parapsychological phenomena such as telepathy and clairvoyance to give additional credence to the notion of objective vision. He does not explain, however, how Paul's reference to the groups who are said to have seen Jesus, including the five hundred brethren, fits in with the vision hypothesis.

Pannenberg observes that the Christian community today experiences the reality of Christ in the sacrament, in worship, and in hearing the Word. He says that members of the community today can be certain that this experience is not delusory because of the reliability of the report of Jesus's Resurrection and exaltation. Pannenberg then remarks: "No one now has an experience of him as risen and exalted, at least not an experience that could be distinguished with certainty from illusion."[101] Perhaps the emphasis is meant to rest on the phrase "with certainty," but I do not know why he is so sure that experiences of Jesus as risen and exalted could not be repeated today. Some of the reports of contemporary visionaries seem to point to experiences similar to those suggested by the biblical narratives, including ones that sound like the corporeal accounts in the Gospels.

Response: Historical Reconstruction of Appearances

Pannenberg's approach to interpreting the NT documents by considering the documents in strict chronological order is characteristic of many critics. Paul's statement of the kerygma in I Corinthians is accorded a primary place in trying to reconstruct the events (which puts Paul's post-Ascension experience on a par with pre-Ascension appearances), and then the Gospels are considered in the likely order of composition: Mark (which has no appearances), Matthew (in which the legendary accretions begin), Luke, and then John. This strategy has led to the position that claims about the corporeality of the body of Jesus are largely devoid of a historical kernel, particularly in view of the prominence given to Mark. However, there is a problem in proceeding with the reconstruction of events in this way, for material from the Gospels is needed in asserting the identity between the

Jesus who was crucified and buried, and the Jesus said to have been resurrected. This claim of continuing identity is more complex than it is usually thought to be, and the problem of establishing identity is exacerbated by features of the appearances mentioned above, such as lack of recognition, doubts, the possibility that the form varied, and the uniqueness of the resurrection body. In addressing this topic of continuing identity I shall also show that critical reflection on apparitions makes an important contribution to the discussion, but first I need to make some comments about criteria for determining the continuing identity of a person.

Philosophers have extensively debated the criteria we conventionally use in identifying someone as the same person over time. The examples they consider include identity claims in ordinary contexts in which references are made to "the same person," as well as imaginary cases designed to test intuitions about proposed criteria. The Resurrection is a real and unique allegation. It is unique, for it is neither the kind of identity at issue in ordinary life, nor exactly the kind of identity conjectured by dualists to exist between persons and their post-mortem selves. It is an allegation of a real occurrence, moreover, not an imaginary one such as philosophers might consider, and as such needs to be discussed with respect to the apparent evidence at hand, however plentiful or meager. Imaginary cases allow one the luxury of including as much detail as one pleases, thus determining the outcome in advance. This luxury is not appropriate in the case of Jesus, given the fact that he is a genuine historical figure and his Resurrection an actual allegation.

The first question that must be considered is what criteria might have been used by early Christians to make the identification of the resurrected person as Jesus. The answer is speculative, but we might conjecture that identity could have been approached on the basis of the following criteria, taken singly or in combination: (1) spatio-temporal continuity between the buried body and the resurrected one, (2) continuity of memory between the person known as Jesus before his Crucifixion, and the person encountered after his (supposed) Resurrection, (3) similarity of personality, (4) similarity of physical form, and (5) similarity of emergent structural properties. Philosophers now sometimes speculate that identity is determined by yet another criterion—identical atomic structures—but to suggest this here would be fanciful. Even if Jesus was resurrected, as this is understood by tradition, we have no obvious way of knowing whether his body was constituted atomically or, if it was so constituted, whether the atoms in the new body were the same kinds of atoms that formed the earlier body. This approach to identity seems inadequate, moreover, for it ignores the structural properties of a being that emerge out of being an organized and living structure, which are more relevant than mere physical components in determining the identity of a person over time. Such structural properties—for example, intellectual or athletic abilities—might not play a significant role in establishing identity, but they could have a minor place, especially if other criteria were lacking.

The criteria of continuity of memory and/or similarity of personality are commonly identified by philosophers as the criteria used in ordinary experience for establishing personal identity. These criteria are supplemented, it seems, when people's personalities change or they lose their memories because of serious physical injury, disease, or the normal aging process. The NT texts do not go out of their way to establish continuity of memory by citing many instances where Jesus remembered previous events, although they include some. Luke reports, for instance, that Jesus made a reference to John the Baptist, who was executed before Jesus's own death. But few references of this kind occur. Continuity of personality is not concretely presented in the gospel narratives, in part because there is so little textual material pertaining to the post-Resurrection state capable of serving this objective. This criterion for personal identity is perhaps of minor significance, for we generally countenance significant changes in personality traits without seriously questioning identity. One could say that the gospel narratives treat the identity of Jesus as though it presented no particular difficulty.

The criterion of spatio-temporal continuity is particularly important in the gospel accounts. The gospel narratives tell a story of a resurrected body appearing in just the place where Jesus was buried. They combine this allegation with claims that the tomb was carefully guarded so that the body could not be stolen, and that the tomb was covered with a stone that was difficult for one person to move, implying that no exchange of bodies occurred. Moreover, they include details suggesting that the old body disappeared, for they speak about grave clothes being found in the tomb, as though the body that had been wrapped in them just vanished into thin air. The claim that it was *Jesus* who was resurrected might have been even more strongly established if someone had observed the resurrected body somehow taking shape out of the remains of the dead body, but that is not reported. No one is privileged to see the Resurrection in such detail, not even in the apocryphal Gospels. It is of interest that the accounts of the first appearance to Mary in Matthew, John, and (late) Mark locate it near the tomb. These narratives thus imply spatio-temporal continuity between the crucified Jesus and the resurrected Jesus, which could be seen as compensating for the limited evidence of continuity of memory. This is how the empty tomb enters the problem of defending the identity claim. The empty tomb suggests that it is *Jesus* that was resurrected, and the empty tomb discredits the disembodied spirit hypothesis to explain the appearances. Spatio-temporal continuity by itself would not establish identity beyond a reasonable doubt, however, for if the being who was thought to have been the resurrected Jesus had been unable to remember anything of his earlier life, or did not recognize even his closest followers, the identity claim would be questionable.[102]

The spatio-temporal continuity just described, combined with continuity of memory, would make quite a convincing case for an identity claim, even if the physical appearance were variable. The texts make it clear, however, that spatio-temporal continuity was present only in the moments after the Resurrection. The accounts go on to describe how Jesus subsequently appeared in locked rooms and disappeared just as quickly. The lack of spatio-temporal continuity in such cases creates a problem for identity, although perhaps not an overwhelming one. The experiences we have in ordinary life are ones in which people are found to exist continuously, not intermittently, and to occupy the space-time positions between which they move, not disappear at one point and then reappear at another.[103] We do not know what we would say about continuing personal identity if ordinary people were to exhibit this strange power. Continuity of memory, and similarity in physical form or personality, would presumably become extraordinarily important.

We surround our identity claims in ordinary life, it seems, with findings (or assumptions) about most of the five elements mentioned above. We obviously experience continuity of existence in space-time, as well as continuity of memory; moreover we find similarity of structural properties, personality, and physical form from moment to moment. Although ordinary thought has not given much attention in the past to atomic structure, now that we know about it we allow for substantial changes in molecular composition, especially in the case of living beings, without considering those changes to threaten personal identity. It is fascinating to observe how the NT accounts of Jesus trifle with criteria of personal identity: Very few incidents exhibiting continuity of memory are included, personality traits are not described in detail, spatio-temporal continuity is maintained in the area of the tomb only for a short time after the Resurrection, and the implication is left that the physical form varied. But enough is said in the NT narratives to have convinced many people in the last two millennia that a corpse disappeared and that a being somehow identical (or continuous) with the dead man mysteriously took its place.

These remarks about identity indicate that the Gospels are more important than is sometimes supposed in discussing the Resurrection of Jesus. If the only writings that are authoritative in forming views on the NT events are I Corinthians 15 (and the Acts accounts that describe Paul's experience), as many expositors, including Pannenberg, now suggest, we are left with very uncertain material concerning *who* was encountered in the appearances and visions.[104] It is common for exegetes to assert that Mark contributes only to the empty tomb tradition, since it has no appearance accounts, and that the appearance accounts in the other gospels have a substantial amount of fictional material in them. But without the Gospels there is no particularly good reason to think that the being who was encountered was *Jesus*, for continuity of memory and/or spatio-temporal continuity of the bodies is needed to make the identity claim, and the material for making this claim is present only in the Gospels. I do not think this point is changed if we adopt the view that all we find in the NT accounts are subjective visions, never appearances (as traditionally understood). The problem that remains concerns the identity of the one who appears in the subjective visions. The information presented in the Gospels is more important than seems to be thought by exegetes who relegate it to a secondary place. Perhaps they smuggle it in when they reconstruct the historical events using primarily I Corinthians. Being thoroughly familiar with all the NT literature, including the Gospels, they might rely on this literature unconsciously.

The point I am making here about the importance of the gospel narratives in asserting identity can be illustrated by considering an apparition experience in which someone reports how a person widely and reasonably thought to have died was subsequently seen by six individuals or groups, including the reporter. This is analogous to providing a historical reconstruction of the Resurrection beginning with Paul's list found in I Corinthians, and then relying on the accounts of Paul's conversion in Acts to give substance to his claim that Jesus appeared to him. In order to avoid developing an example too remote from actual experience, consider Benvenuta Bojani's claim to have seen St. Dominic after his death.[105] Suppose St. Dominic identified himself to Benvenuta (as Jesus did to Paul), and suppose further that Benvenuta supplements her claim with the bare remark that five other individuals or groups also saw St. Dominic after his death (comparable to Paul). Would we count Benvenuta's unadorned remarks as compelling evidence that St. Dominic was *resurrected*? I think not, for we would want some account of what happened to the dead body. Would we count Benvenuta's remarks as compelling evidence that *St. Dominic* was seen in a vision? I again think we would not. We would want some physical description of St. Dominic, or a uniquely identifying property of him, before conceding that it was truly St. Dominic who appeared. Critical reflection on visionary experiences casts light, unexpectedly perhaps, on an important exegetical problem. I conclude that the Gospels cannot be relegated to a secondary place in discussing the resurrection of Jesus.

These remarks show that the approach to historical reconstruction of events that depends upon strict chronological order among documents, and insists that later ones be interpreted in the light of former ones, is implausible. They also show that identity claims about the resurrected Jesus in the NT documents are complex and mysterious. We have to grant that if such an air of mystery surrounds the original claims about Jesus appearing after his death, an even greater air of mystery surrounds claims made two thousand years later that the same person somehow still appears.

Brown's Conservative Approach

Raymond Brown is a Catholic scholar whose views on the virginal conception and bodily resurrection of Jesus have been given the Roman Catholic imprimatur. He writes with respect for the church's ancient understanding of these two central Christological events, and at the same time endorses the modern methods of biblical criticism. He does not consider the Gospels to be simple factual reports of what happened in Jesus's ministry, but "documents of faith written to show the significance of those events as seen with hindsight."[106] He accepts that the Bible can be fallible with respect to historical details, but views this as compatible with the view that the Bible contains no error concerning matters of salvation. He does not think that past formulations of divine truth should be identified as *the* truth, for historical developments can (and do) produce more adequate formulations. Brown charges fundamentalists with having been unable to distinguish between a truth and its formulation.[107] An illustration of how a divine truth has been reformulated is provided by the Catholic teaching on evolution, for theologians now routinely embrace the theory of evolution while continuing to affirm the ancient biblical view that God created humankind. He describes his position as conservative, but not fundamentalist.[108]

Brown rejects the view that the only possibilities open to a biblical interpreter are either that the Resurrection was so corporeal and physical that Jesus was just as tangible as he was during his lifetime, or that a corporeal resurrection did not occur, and the appearances represent only an internal awareness of Jesus's spiritual victory. He stakes out a middle ground, according to which a corporeal resurrection took place, causing the risen body of Jesus to be translated into an eschatological sphere, so that it was no longer bound by space and time, and no longer marked by the physical properties characterizing its temporal existence.[109] The fact that the Resurrection is eschatological in character, that is, it belongs to the end of history, does not mean that it is nonhistorical in the sense that it never happened. The Resurrection is historical, at the very least in the sense that he who was outside the bounds of space and time touched the lives of people who were in history. Brown accepts the view that the tomb Jesus was buried in was known to the disciples and was found to be empty.[110] The faith of the early disciples was evoked by the appearances, he says, and the belief in the glorified Lord allowed them, in turn, to interpret the empty tomb. Brown thinks that just as Christians in antiquity confessed a Jesus who was raised and also appeared, Christians should continue to speak about a bodily resurrection, although it should be nuanced to reflect eschatological realities as well.[111]

Brown rejects an approach to the gospel narratives that requires that all of the stories be harmonized, and considers the three different gospel accounts of appearances to the closest disciples, for instance, as narrating the same appearance.[112] He hypothesizes that, discouraged by the arrest and execution of Jesus, the disciples fled Jerusalem and made their way back to Galilee. When Peter returned to the shore of the Sea of Galilee to fish, Jesus appeared to him "and resurrection faith was born."[113] Jesus then appeared to the Twelve, pouring out his Spirit upon them and commissioning them to proclaim the rule of God on earth. When they returned to Jerusalem some weeks later to celebrate the Jewish Feast of Weeks, a charismatic manifestation of the Spirit they had received from the risen Jesus took place, and the early church was born. Brown does not rule out the possibility of an early appearance to Magdalene, and concedes that Paul's mention of Peter as the first to see the risen Lord may be due to Peter's prominence in preaching the Resurrection faith. Brown offers a speculation, rare among biblical critics as far as I can tell, about the nature of the communication between the risen Jesus and his disciples. He wonders whether it was communication with words, or whether it might have been some type of intuitive communication,[114] since the accounts of what Jesus said to his disciples vary considerably. This speculation is of interest because of frequent reports among modern visionaries about the "intuitive" character of the communications they experience.

Brown's general position on the appearance phenomena (and Resurrection) is a reasonable one. It gives close consideration to the gospel narratives in attempting to determine the probable order of events, but it also gives place to conclusions of biblical criticism. He allows, therefore, for the possibility that various conflicting accounts are the result of differing theological outlooks, or the attempt to present a consecutive narrative, or the result of editorial restructuring. Like other critics who suggest that the Resurrection is a genuine reality but one that transcends the capacity of humans to know or grasp adequately,[115] Brown endorses the historicity of the key appearances, and with that the position of historic Christianity on the Resurrection. He does not rule out collective appearances, or ones involving both sight and touch.

Again, contemporary Christic visions seem to confirm some of the claims of NT accounts. That people now attest to experiences in which Jesus is perceived by both sight and touch, or is seen by groups, or leaves some intersubjectively observed effects, lends credence to claims that similar experiences occurred in NT times and are not merely legendary accretions. This is not a "knock-down" argument, to be sure, but it warrants careful (and further) consideration. The capacity of contemporary experiences to interpret and confirm NT allegations might be small, but it is not without significance. It seems reasonable to me to employ *all* relevant information in addressing a problem as complex as the NT Christic appearances and visions.

Linguistic Issues

A number of authors have commented extensively on the language that is used to describe the NT phenomena. Reginald Fuller's interpretation of the Resurrection narratives is shaped by possible meanings of the Greek term *ophthe* meaning "to see." He takes the irreducible historical minimum behind the narratives to consist of claims of certain disciples to have had visions of Jesus after his death as raised from the dead, and an unverified claim of one or more women that they discovered the tomb of Jesus empty.[116] Fuller believes that the earliest church proclaimed the Resurrection, not the appearances, which were added by Paul to this proclamation.[117] He notes that the appearances mentioned by Paul in I Corinthians 15 are described using *ophthe*, which can be legitimately interpreted as only understanding a message: The appearances "designate not necessarily physical seeing, not necessarily visions in a subjective sense (involving, for example, ecstasy or dreams), but a revelatory self-disclosure or disclosure by God of the eschatologically resurrected Christos."[118] These appearances are not considered experiences to be analyzed for their own sake, but as acts of self-disclosure that accentuate the revelatory action of Christ. Fuller considers even the language of mysticism to be impotent for disclosing the eschatological within history, and contends that all language was made to describe events in this age. He continues: "The farthest we can get perhaps is to say that the *events through which* the Easter revelations were conveyed were visionary, but to describe them as visions, even as 'objective visions,' is not entirely felicitous. The word vision, at best, denotes the this-worldly event through which the eschatological event is mediated."[119] He says further that "[t]heir outward, historically definable form is a vision (perhaps a vision of 'light'), accompanied by an audition (i.e., a communication of meaning)."[120]

W. Michaelis's comments in *The Theological Dictionary of the New Testament* on the use of *ophthe* support Fuller's position. He notes that none of the appearances is said to have taken place in sleep, in a dream, or even at night, and they are never described as visions (*horamata* in Greek). The appearances are always connected with some revelation by word, and the visual aspect is never stressed. He suggests that Paul classifies his experience with the others in I Corinthians 15 because they are all similar, and considers their character to be determinable from Paul's own experience: It reveals the presence of the exalted Lord from heaven "in non-visionary reality; no category of human seeing is wholly adequate for it. . . . On this ground, too, the appearances are to be described as manifestations in the sense of revelation rather than making visible."[121] Michaelis's view is that when *ophthe* is used of the Resurrection appearances, "there is no primary emphasis on seeing as sensual or mental perception. The dominant thought is that the appearances are revelations, encounters with the risen Lord who herein reveals Himself, or is revealed."[122]

Raymond Brown agrees that *ophthe* can have a wide range of meanings, but he does not think its use in I Corinthians 15 favors a purely internal experience. He notes that this list includes a reference to an appearance of Jesus to more than five hundred at once, and remarks that this can hardly be a case of "synchronized ecstasy."[123] Peter Carnley also disagrees with Michaelis and other critics who think that *ophthe* is a technical term for a revelation of God, rather than a term possibly denoting natural ocular experience. Carnley believes that it denotes something between ocular seeing and intellectual seeing, something more than the intellectual grasp of propositional truths and less than the clarity of normal visual seeing.[124] He thinks that there were enough resemblances to ordinary seeing in the appearances to call them "seeing," but enough differences to prevent easy conflation of this experience with ordinary experience.[125] The reality of the raised Christ need not be doubted, Carnley says, and yet the nature of the seeing was not ordinary, especially since the apparent object of this experience was a unique object, namely, the body of Jesus.

Carnley raises the possibility that the appearances can be understood two ways, and adopts the distinction between Christepiphanies and Christophanies, introduced by J. Lindblom some decades earlier, to clarify his meaning. The former term suggests appearances that were ocular experiences, as though Jesus were walking on earth again, while the latter suggests appearances "from heaven," that is, religious and revelatory and something like ordinary ocular seeing, but also different.[126] Carnley suggests that the original appearances were heavenly in character (Christophanies), and that Luke developed the heavenly vision tradition into Christepiphanies: "From a temporal distance and without exact information he imagined what originally took place."[127] Carnley considers this to be a more satisfactory interpretation than one that seeks to harmonize all the Christepiphanies and Christophanies, or regards the gospel narratives as only "visual aids in teaching," as suggested by Dibelius, or as developments of heavenly radiance experiences involving light. The original Easter experiences are "of the raised Christ as one who appeared 'from heaven'" and "the seeing appropriate to Easter faith is to be understood as a 'knowing by acquaintance' rather than just an intellectual seeing of the truth of a proposition about the historical Jesus' true identity."[128] These remarks are intriguing because he identifies features found in both NT and contemporary experiences, namely, that some experiences seem to be ones in which people "see into" or "enter into" heaven (Christophanies), while others seem to be ones in which Jesus enters the sphere of space-time (Christepiphanies).

The remarks of various critics on possible meanings of *ophthe* do not appear to be capable of easy resolution. The ambiguities of the texts, and the resulting competing interpretations of them, are disheartening, and suggest that little headway can be made by confining one's attention to the NT materials. It is questionable whether other literature of that era, such as Jewish writings or the more recently discovered Dead Sea scrolls, could shed might light on the problem, for the uniqueness of the Christic encounters implies that language developed in other experiential contexts would be of limited value. What is needed now is not further scrutiny of ancient *texts*, but deeper understanding of visionary experience, for this is the domain in which relevant concepts are forged. Knowledge of this domain still seems embryonic.

An Objection

It might be objected that I am taking for granted the similarity between contemporary Christic visions and NT experiences. This is an important objection, and I will not claim to be able to give a definitive reply to it. One of the reasons any reply would be incomplete is that there are so many obscure elements in the NT accounts. At the risk of glossing over some of the difficulties in NT interpretation, I shall list some characteristics that contemporary and NT phenomena seem to share, thus supporting the claim that these phenomena might be all of one piece.

The NT accounts suggest that the appearances and visions were not subject to control by percipients. Explicit remarks about lack of control are not made, but the strong impression is left that this was the case. Percipients evidently could not determine when their experiences took place, how long they lasted, what they saw, and so on. The account of Jesus revealing himself to the two disciples at Emmaus, as well as the accounts of his entering and leaving locked rooms at will, for instance, give this impression. Accounts of post-Ascension experiences similarly suggest that these experiences were not self-induced, although it must be acknowledged that nothing is said about whether Paul or Ananias or Stephen sought to bring about their visions by fasting, oxygen deprivation, ingestion of hallucinatory foods, self-flagellation, or other means.[129] The experiences are consistently presented as though an external agent produced them. The Christic experiences I have investigated also seem to have been controlled by something apart from the percipients.

Moreover, some contemporary Christic visions occurred in the ordinary physical environment, and others in a "changed place," as I have already mentioned. Although the settings for most of the immediate post-Resurrection appearances seem to be the normal environment, Luke says that one of Paul's Christic encounters occurred in a trance, and Paul himself says that he was *caught up* into the third heaven. Neither Luke nor Paul elaborate on these experiences, but both might have included a sense of an altered locale. The account in Revelation of seeing Jesus in the heavenly court also suggests a "change of place."

A third similarity can be found in the radiance surrounding or upon Jesus, mentioned in several NT accounts. Revelation describes the face of Jesus as shining like the sun, and Paul's conversion involves a light phenomenon. The transfiguration account is notable for its mention of the face of Jesus being too bright to look at. It is understandable, on the basis of this feature alone, why some might speculate that this story is a displaced post-Resurrection appearance account. I have already drawn ample attention to the radiance that sometimes accompanies contemporary vision and apparition phenomena.

Other similarities can be mentioned briefly: the doubts that occasionally accompany the experiences, the relative insignificance of physical criteria in making the identification, the intimations of varying form, and Jesus's exhibition of remarkable powers. Finally, percipients in both NT and contemporary experiences seem to feel a similar range of psychological effects, including changed lives and feelings of love, awe, joy, fear, and comfort. But establishing definite similarities is hampered by the sketchiness of the NT accounts. Doubts on this point might be settled by canvassing the items in Appendix II on which contemporary percipients were quizzed.[130] We do not know, for example, whether the percipients of the

NT appearances always had their eyes open, ever experienced an altered environment, had unusual kinesthetic sensations, experienced the auditory elements in a normal way, saw a transparent rather than a solid figure, always saw a complete humanoid form, always saw the face of Jesus distinctly, or always saw a being of normal size. Such lacunae indicate that speculation about their character will never end.

The Distinction Between Appearances and Visions

The last point I want to discuss is the sharp distinction that is often drawn between the appearances immediately after the Resurrection and the post-Ascension visions, and its corollary that the appearances were objective experiences whereas the visions were subjective. Luke seems to endorse this position, as C. F. Evans has noted: "In the scheme of Luke-Acts the Lord ceases to appear as the Risen Lord once the Ascension has taken place, and any subsequent 'appearance' (e.g. to Stephen, Acts 7.55, or to Paul) cannot be a 'substantial' appearance, but only a vision."[131] That Luke made a distinction between seeing a vision and "seeing something real" is clear from his comments concerning the story of Peter's release from prison by an angel. Luke says, "He [Peter] did not know that what was done by the angel was real, but thought he was seeing a vision (*horama*)."[132] But critics are also at odds with one another on the timing of the Ascension and the nature of the "appearance" to Paul.

W. O. Walker, for instance, agrees with the position of Evans that Luke-Acts portrays appearances as not occurring after the Ascension, but Walker suggests that Paul disagrees with Luke about the ending of appearances.[133] In Acts Luke presents the appearances as ending with the Ascension, but Paul considers his Christic encounter at his conversion some years later as an appearance. This is how William Craig understands the texts, on the basis of Paul's statement in I Corinthians 15 that he was the last to whom Jesus appeared.[134] But L. Sabourin questions this understanding of Paul's statement, and suggests that Paul might not have meant it literally but might only have meant that there was a privileged period of appearances.[135] Adding to the confusion, Xavier Dufour does not consider Paul's experience an Easter appearance at all but rather a theophany.[136] Wolfhart Pannenberg, however, considers Paul's Damascus experience to be similar to the appearances described in the Gospels.[137] Finally, Eduard Schweizer suggests that the Ascension took place on Easter morning, so that all the appearances, including Paul's, are on the same footing.[138] This small sampling of opposing positions among recent critics demonstrates that the texts forming the basis for the supposed distinction between appearances and visions are too sketchy to allow for definite interpretation.

The apparent conflict in Luke's two accounts of the Ascension is most puzzling. Luke's statement in Acts provides the basis for the traditional belief that the Ascension took place forty days after the Resurrection. He writes: "He [Jesus] presented himself alive after his passion by many proofs, appearing to them during forty days."[139] But Luke's account of the Ascension in his gospel *seems* to put the Ascension on the day after the Resurrection. After he describes how Jesus appeared on the day of his Resurrection to the two disciples who walked to Emmaus, and then made himself known that same night in Jerusalem to the rest of the disciples, Luke immediately adds: "Then he led them out as far as Bethany . . . and was parted from them."[140] Some manuscripts, reflected only in the footnotes of the Revised Standard Version, say explicitly that he ascended, but even the text just quoted implies this. This account would put the end of the appearances much earlier than Luke implies in Acts.

This apparent conflict in Luke-Acts is hard to explain. One explanation might be that Luke is the compilation of pericopae that are poorly connected at certain points. But such an interpretation would further contribute to uncertainty about the character of the "history" in this gospel. Another possibility is that the early Christian church had almost as many conflicting theological tendencies as we see in the church today. Perhaps there were those with "a visionary tendency," for instance, who emphasized the importance of direct encounters with "the resurrected One," while others did not.[141] Maybe this preoccupation with heavenly encounters became so unbalanced (in Luke's mind) by the time Acts came to be written that he decided to introduce a cutoff point of forty days in order to quell this preoccupation: Every encounter within the forty days became an appearance, every encounter after that became "just a vision," and Paul's experience was left ambiguous. But this is just a speculation, and I leave to scholars in the field how these documents should best be interpreted.[142] I say again that the texts shroud events in mystery as much as they illuminate them. The fact that their authors or editors did not remove all the conflicts is noteworthy—perhaps they preserved the oral traditions as they knew them.

I do not challenge the obvious legitimacy of the distinction between experiences whose sources are ultimately external to a percipient and experiences whose sources are internal, although this distinction is a little too simple, as I shall explain in Chapter 7. But I challenge the common belief that the distinction between these experiences is easy to draw. Paul's conversion experience is a case in point. It is often considered to have been a subjective experience, primarily because Paul seems to have been the only one to whom Jesus appeared. But the references in the accounts to observable causal effects make such a classification problematic. The case for objectivity is not helped by the failure of the three accounts to agree on what the effect was, but if there was such an effect, it is implausible to classify the experience as subjective. If categorizing experiences as appearances or visions implies nothing more than that appearances are objective and visions subjective, then I have no objection to their use. But if their use is accompanied by the suggestion that the distinction between appearances and visions is easy to draw, which I suspect is often the case, such use obfuscates rather than clarifies discussion of the phenomena in question. The distinction between external and internal causes of experiences should not be confused with the distinction between knowing (or having reasonable grounds to assert) when the causes are external and when they are internal.

In the experiences I have investigated, visionary and apparition phenomena vary significantly in kind, and defy easy classification. Their variety is apparent from surveying the descriptions and classifications provided in Chapter 2. A similar variety is apparent in the NT literature, for there are references to trancelike experiences, visionary experiences that only selected percipients in a larger group seem to have had, appearances to individuals, appearances involving several perceptual modalities, appearances with observable causal effects, and collective appearances. The inadequacy of the distinction between appearances and visions should be apparent from the NT texts themselves, but if it is not, studies of contemporary visions certainly make it apparent. The variety found in contemporary experience casts doubt on the claim advanced by reductionists that the only one kind of experience in the NT era was the *Lichtglanz* (flash of light). Contemporary Christic visions and apparitions suggest that the appearance phenomena in first-century Christian experience were probably quite varied, and provide modest evidence for the claim there was an objective source for them.

Conclusion

The arguments in this chapter are intended to show that contemporary visionary phenomena add an important perspective for reading the NT documents and assessing interpretative traditions. NT criticism that confines its attention to the documentary evidence of the first century alone (biblical and extra-biblical), as though ongoing phenomena could have no relevance to understanding and testing claims coming to us from antiquity, deprives itself of a vital tool. Claims about what happened in antiquity cannot be divorced from research that outlines the apparent range of empirical possibilities. Paul explains in I Corinthians that Jesus was resurrected to live a new life as an immortal and life-giving spirit. The confidence among Christians that this claim is plausible will always rest primarily upon the documents giving it its initial formulation, but contemporary Christic apparitions also help to corroborate it.

It is clear that many variables are at work in interpreting the NT documents, particularly the narrative material in the Gospels. The traditional view that these documents have a transparent form, that they can be harmonized in a straightforward way, that they cannot benefit from evidence beyond the NT documents, that they were not subject to significant editorial shaping, that the form seen in the appearances (so-called) was unvarying, and that a distinction between appearances and visions can be maintained, is doubtful. But the view that significant events lie behind the NT texts, that experiences in that era might have been more than merely subjective ones, and that both Paul's epistle and the Gospel narratives are important for interpretation, remains intact.

5 | Supernaturalistic Explanations

Many explanations have been offered for visions and apparitions. Some have been developed specifically for Christic encounters, while others have been proposed for similar experiences of all kinds. These explanations can be roughly divided into three main categories: supernaturalistic, mentalistic, and physicalistic.

Supernaturalism asserts that certain events in the world are brought about by entities or forces that transcend the natural order. John Hick remarks that the term *supernatural* is no longer in vogue, and that *supra-natural* and *non-natural* are also inadequate for expressing the concepts relevant to a discussion of transcendentalism.[1] Because *supernatural* has long been used for that purpose, I shall use it despite its supposed defects. Though the salient characteristics of the beings that supernaturalism posits cannot be identified with precision, clearly it ascribes to them certain humanlike qualities, and other qualities that make them quite different from us. They have the familiar human capacities for choice, knowledge, feeling, and acting on the physical world, for instance, but also the capacity to disappear at will, inflict death or disease without direct contact, determine or know certain future events, and so on.

Mentalistic explanations are too diverse to describe succinctly, largely because of the evolution that such theories have undergone in Western culture. The human soul was once considered similar to the beings of supernaturalism, but developments in physical and biological sciences have changed the understanding of mentalism. The dualism persuasively articulated by Plato in antiquity survived well into the modern era, and in Descartes's time it was still customary to speak about the *soul*, and to speculate on the relationship between soul and body. With time the focus came to be placed on *mind* rather than soul—a terminological (and conceptual) change that helped to remove the discussion from the context of religion. William James observed a century ago that the focus had shifted to *consciousness* or *mental events*—terms that have the advantage of sounding much less "thingish" than *soul* or even *mind*. Consciousness and mental events are considered susceptible to scientific scrutiny in a way that soul is not. The term *mentalism* has been used to identify an evolving series of theories, with so much change that the things posited in its latest formulations bear hardly any resemblance to those in its earliest ones. Early forms of mentalism suggested that the spatially extended and disembodied souls (or spirits) of people might account for the experience of seeing apparitions. Current forms of mentalism, however, are apt to suggest that apparitions are brought on by mental states such as stress, or wishing, or a state of expectancy. Unconscious mental states are sometimes considered as well.

Physicalism is an explanatory strategy that employs the conceptual devices of only the "hard" sciences such as physics, chemistry, biochemistry, or computer technology. It seeks to avoid invoking the mental states, processes, or events posited by mentalism, either because the explanatory power of mentalism is considered too meager, or because its ontology is considered false. Physicalists have proposed various reductionistic explanations for mental events in recent years, with behaviorism dominating the discussion in the early part of this century. Psychological behaviorists such as B. F. Skinner thought that human behavior could be described and explained without reference to mental events.[2] The behaviorists evidently hoped that references to observable stimuli and responses would have sufficient explanatory power. Philosophical behaviorists such as Rudolf Carnap[3] and Gilbert Ryle[4] claimed that apparent references to mental events were really references to human behavior or to dispositions to act, and that careful analyses would make that apparent. Other forms of reduction, generally described as materialistic, have replaced these in recent decades.

Identity theorists assert that every single mental event just *is* an event of the central nervous system, much as lightning *is* an electrical discharge.[5] Functionalist materialists, however, advance a less strict relationship between mental events and physical events, claiming only that the causal roles now played by broadly mental functions such as wishing, believing, and so on will be reduced to neurophysiological functions of the human organism.[6] Eliminative materialists, on the other hand, reject the ontology of mentalism as either so inadequate that it is not worth reducing in any of the above forms, or as plainly false. Paul and Patricia Churchland have been among the most influential defenders of eliminative materialism.[7] The eliminative thesis is often stated in a form that refuses even a modest explanatory value to "folk psychology," which Paul Churchland defines as "an integrated body of [folk] lore concerning the lawlike relations holding among external circumstances, internal states, and overt behavior."[8] Patricia Churchland says that it is "overwhelmingly evident" that the human capacity for knowledge, consciousness, free will, representation of the world, and intelligence are "phenomena of the physical brain," and identifies the revolutionary developments that have made this understanding possible to be neuroscientific techniques that allow for detailed descriptions of brain mechanisms, sophisticated studies in experimental psychology and ethology, and computer simulations of neural networks that allow discoveries of how synapse-like connections and parallel organizations can accomplish complex tasks.[9] She maintains that the venerable belief that consciousness is not a state of the physical brain, but a state of a nonphysical soul, as was maintained by Descartes and, more recently, Richard Swinburne and neurophysiologist John Eccles, is inconsistent with biology and physics.[10]

Much of the philosophical discussion now is directed to materialistic alternatives, and substance-dualism is not often considered a significant competitor, although Paul Churchland considers it a theoretical possibility.[11] Recent research into near-death experiences could change this, for it appears to be reviving interest in the ancient theory that the soul is capable of existing in a disembodied form. But no significant change has yet been registered in most philosophical discussions. Philosophers continue to routinely cite the ancient tenets of supernaturalism without argument as examples of false or mistaken ontological posits. Richard Rorty's early defense of the view that folk psychology should be abandoned completely, for instance, used the demon hypothesis to illustrate a theory that had been completely abandoned.[12] Similarly, Paul and Patricia Churchland imply that Satan and the Storm god are supernaturalistic posits whose existence would only be endorsed by Puritans and Neanderthals, respectively.[13] There appears to be little scholarly opposition to these views. Some isolated academic domains still exist in which the posits of supernaturalism are employed for description and explanation, however. Peter Wagner, professor at Fuller Theological Seminary, for instance, recently endorsed the existence of spirits in just the way that Rorty reports to have been abandoned. Wagner describes an incident in which friends were initially prevented from entering his home by "some invisible force" possessing a distinctly unpleasant odor. He goes on to narrate: "They found spirits in three of the rooms, the strongest, predictably, in the master bedroom. In the livingroom they sensed that a spirit had attached itself to a stone puma we had brought as a souvenir from our missionary work in Bolivia."[14]

Freud predicted in 1900 that such remnants of the supernatural would be swept away by scientific explanation. He observed in his own time that besides mystics and priests, there were "intelligent persons, who in other respects are averse from anything of a romantic nature," who continued to embrace the existence of superhuman spiritual powers.[15] Science has not yet made a clean sweep of supernaturalism, and whether it will ever succeed in doing so is questionable. The current intellectual climate is such that physicalism is often thought to be the most promising domain in which to look for explanations. Mentalism is under strong attack, and supernaturalism is widely considered to be devoid of value as an explanatory scheme because of its inability to meet many of the strictures on rational thought that have accompanied the rise of science. I now wish to say more about the inclusion of supernaturalism as one of the possible categories in which explanations for Christic apparitions might be sought, in view of its being such a "poor cousin."

Supernaturalism as Theory

Although my interest is directed toward Christian thought, supernaturalism is a category that extends to all religious belief systems that posit spiritual agencies in explanations. So the gods of Greek and Norse mythology, as well as those of contemporary Hindu thought, are implied in the term. Supernaturalism naturally includes traditional monotheism, the familiar view that there is exactly one God, possessing various powers to superlative or infinite degrees, as well as Christian trinitarianism. Philosophy of religion directs its attention almost exclusively to the problems of monotheism, usually in a form acceptable to the Jewish, Christian, and Muslim faiths. The lesser posits of supernaturalism, such as evil spirits or angels, are often ignored, evidently because they are considered of little interest. This is understandable: The existence of God is of greater significance than the question of whether other spirits might exist. But the subject under discussion does not afford us the luxury of restricting our attention to the supreme Deity. The first question that needs to be addressed is whether supernaturalistic theories should be seriously considered.

Earlier this century logical positivists criticized the use of terms such as *God* and *spirit* on the grounds that they were devoid of meaning. Adherents of this influential school of philosophy argued that the supposed referents of such terms could not be identified in an empirical operation. But recent developments in philosophy of science have convinced many philosophers that this criticism misrepresented the nature of normal scientific theorizing. Many theorists, particularly those known as scientific realists,[16] recognize that normal theorizing proposes explanations in which imperceptible entities are postulated for observable phenomena. Atomistic physics is one of the best-known theories of this kind, but there are others. The biologist Mendel posited the existence of "invisible factors" to account for the transmission of physical characteristics such as eye color from parents to children. These factors have turned out to be molecular structures (genes), which only recently became observable. Geologists have posited the existence of unobserved tectonic plates on which continents rest to account for such phenomena as continental drift and earthquakes. Freudian psychology posits ego, id, and superego, and psychological processes such as cathexis, repression, and sublimation to explain normal and abnormal behavior patterns. Mentalism has come to be understood as a theory that posits unobservable mental states such as reasoning, believing, willing, desiring, and feeling, to explain human behavior. This theory is taken to be embedded in the thought and speech of ordinary language users.[17] Ordinary thought and language are now widely considered to presuppose a theory about human nature—a theory as subject to criticism as any scientific theory might be.

The theories just mentioned take a similar approach to "fixing the reference" of the terms for the newly posited entities. These entities are given a causal role in a specific theory. A mental state such as stress, for instance, does not need to be observable in order to serve as an explanation for some observable behavior pattern, such as an act of violence. It is sufficient that stress can be postulated as the cause of that behavior. Moreover, stress itself might be proposed as the effect of a different observable event, such as nagging or harassment. In a complex network of such causes and effects, stress becomes conceptually grounded, and therefore capable of being proposed as an explanation for some other syndrome. This theory of how terms for unobservables come to refer is known as the causal theory of reference. Although it raises philosophical questions of its own, the theory is widely seen as providing an explanation of how terms for unobservables acquire meaning and possible reference.

The change in outlook, reflected in the causal theory of reference, means that the unique posits of religious belief systems, namely, God, angels, and spirits, should not be thought of as having no meaning. W. V. O. Quine was one of the first among Anglo-American philosophers to approach supposed references to the gods as attempts to posit entities.[18] He did not consider the attempts successful, but he repudiated the position of the logical positivists who maintained that such religious claims were meaningless. It should be noted that theistic language is not interpreted realistically by all philosophers of religion. Some interpret God as the imaginary personification of our spiritual ideals,[19] and others, following Ludwig Wittgenstein, view God as a concept central to a certain kind of language-game whose referential role is not questioned.[20] But a realistic interpretation of theistic language is now the rule, not the exception.

Janet Soskice has explained how the causal theory of reference allows the unique expressions found in theological discourse to have reference.[21] She observes that when a term such as *God* is used, it does not have to be given an exhaustive or unrevisable definition in terms of essential properties; it is sufficient that the supposed referent is placed in causal relationships with phenomena whose status is not in doubt, such as observable events.[22] We can introduce a term such as *gold* in physical science, for instance, before knowing anything about its essential properties. We simply use it to stand for the thing typically causing certain observable effects and typically caused by some other observable phenomena.[23] Religious experience in general serves as a referential mechanism for introducing *God*, according to Soskice. God in the Judaeo-Christian tradition would be that being who is responsible for various events, such as Moses's experience on Mount Sinai, supposing the account in Exodus to be factual, the empty tomb and subsequent appearances of Jesus, again supposing these are factual, and so on.[24] Soskice notes that theories developed along these lines might not give us privileged access to the world as it actually is, but might only afford us *epistemic* access to important causal features of the world.[25] Soskice describes this stance on meaning and reference as one in which "[t]he world informs our theory, although our theory can never adequately describe the world."[26] Soskice says that her position on theological discourse should be described as *realism*, for theistic language is interpreted as purporting to refer, but it can also be described as critical realism, for it makes no claim to definitive knowledge of the referent. This critical theological realism has obvious affinities to critical realism about ordinary perception, which insists that a real world is presented to us in the ordinary experiences of seeing, hearing, and touching, but that ordinary perception does not give us definitive and exhaustive knowledge of our world. Critical theological realism is a natural ally of classical mysticism, which suggests that God is directly encountered in religious experience, but not known in an exhaustive way.

Soskice plausibly sketches the value of the causal theory of reference for supernaturalistic theories in general.[27] This approach to understanding theological theories attempts to put them more or less on a par with other theories, including scientific theories. It carries some risks, for the entities postulated by scientific theories have often been found to be misconstrued or nonexistent, leading to the substantial alteration or complete abandonment of those theories. Altering or abandoning a theory is generally described as reduction, and can take many forms.[28] One could view attempts to ignore the presence of supernaturalistic beliefs in a culture as an attempt to "reduce" supernaturalism by eliminating it. This is comparable to B. F. Skinner's refusal to use mentalistic predicates in descriptions, with the apparent hope that the temptation to use mentalistic language might disappear—and, along with it, the mind/body problem.

Aldous Huxley suggests a different kind of reductive strategy for the posits of trinitarian Christian theology in *The Devils of Loudun*. The effect of Huxley's proposed reduction would be to *replace* theological language with the language of psychology. Huxley examines the common human desire for self-transcendence—the desire to be someone else, or the longing to get out of oneself, or the need to pass beyond the limits of the tiny universe within which one is confined, or to "go beyond the insulated ego."[29] He suggests that trinitarian theology is an attempt to give expression to this psychological insight, and that comparable expressions can be found in other major religions. When we achieve self-transcendence, we have obtained what is described in Christian terms as union with the Father, the Son, and the Holy Spirit, "union with the source and Ground of all being, union with the manifestation of that Ground in a human consciousness and union with the spirit which links the Unknowable to the known."[30]

Huxley is offering us a reduction of traditional Christian trinitarian thought into concepts found in psychological theory. It is an indirect and subtle reduction, however, for we cannot correlate the Father, Son, and Holy Spirit with their psychological counterparts using a series of definitions, as described in classical reduction.[31] Huxley's proposed reduction is of interest, for it suggests that the conceptual resources of traditional religions can be used to express fundamental insights into human experience, although it suggests at the same time that these traditional ways of expressing such insights are neither the final nor the lasting nor the most perspicacious forms.

Biblical interpreters have also proposed reductions for the references to supernatural beings found in Scripture. Rudolf Bultmann rejects the mythological conception of the world embedded in the NT, because it conflicts with the scientific understanding of the world. He observes, "Modern science does not believe that the course of nature can be interrupted or, so to speak, perforated, by supernatural powers. The same is true of the modern study of history, which does not take into account any intervention of God or of the devil or of demons in the course of history."[32] Bultmann demythologizes those ancient views he deems worth preserving by presenting their insights in a form that contemporary people might accept. So the statement that Satan is ruler over the world, for instance, could be understood as a deep insight into the fact that "all particular evils make up one single power which in the last analysis grows from the very actions of men, which form an atmosphere, a spiritual tradition, which overwhelms every man."[33] In this way some of the descriptive value of the ancient ways of speaking about supernatural powers or beings is preserved, using the thought forms (and ontological commitments) that are currently acceptable. Carl Jung offers a similar reduction when he construes the phenomenon of being possessed by spirits, or haunted by a demon, as "a correct rendition of his [the schizophrenic's] psychical condition, for he is invaded by autonomous figures and thought-forms" deriving from the unconscious.[34]

Much more could be said about the status of religious and theological systems as theories, and their susceptibility to reduction. Theories that cannot be reduced presumably posit entities in a final and definitive way, and whether theism does so is a topic of continued discussion.

Traditional Monotheism

In the discussion of various supernaturalistic theories, I will not include traditional monotheism. *Monotheism* strictly interpreted means that only one deity exists, and its traditional formulation ascribes to God a finite number of defining attributes, many of them infinite in character. Richard Swinburne describes God in the following terms: "a person without a body (i.e. a spirit), present everywhere, the creator and sustainer of the universe, a free agent, able to do anything (i.e. omnipotent), knowing all things, perfectly good, a source of moral obligation, immutable, eternal, a necessary being, holy, and worthy of worship."[35] It is curious that monotheism by itself is seldom considered an adequate explanation for specific events, including Christic apparitions.

One of the best-known, though peculiar, characteristics of monotheism is that it can be combined with naturalistic explanations, or even with supernaturalistic explanations using "lesser" beings, to provide explanations at several levels. God plays an overarching "explanatory" role, so to speak, while another explanation identifies the specific causal mechanism(s) involved. Theistic evolutionists, for instance, consider the theory of evolution to identify the specific mechanisms by which flora and fauna have evolved, while simultaneously affirming that the whole process is somehow superintended by God. Similarly, some "big bang" theorists consider God to be the cause of the universe as we know it, but see appropriate laws as best explaining how specific phenomena have unfolded. A monotheist, whether Muslim, Christian, or Jewish, could consider the sciences to provide explanations for all specific phenomena, and might assign God only a general explanatory role in superintending the whole process. A Christian monotheist could even consider Christic apparitions (biblical and post-biblical) to be capable of explanation using the resources of only the natural or social sciences, and might not think we need to advert for an explanation to any kind of "lesser" supernaturalistic being, whether angel, Jesus in a resurrected form, or whatever. Of course Christian theists more commonly propose a supernaturalistic explanation using "lesser" beings, all the while assigning God an all-embracing explanatory role. The fact that monotheists usually supplement their theory with some specific causal mechanism suggests that they view monotheism as incomplete.

Traditional monotheism has other difficulties, some of them arising from the recent suggestion that God might be introduced into a theory by the causal theory of reference. The first difficulty arises from the fact that God is defined in traditional monotheism as having certain well-known attributes such as omnipotence, omniscience, and freedom. Assigning properties to an entity by definition is contrary to the way in which theoretical entities are generally introduced, according to the causal theory of reference. These entities do not have their properties fixed in advance of the empirical inquiry that determines which properties should be tentatively assigned to them. Consider the circumstances in which certain subatomic particles are posited and certain properties are assigned to them. Evidence is often obtained for the existence of new particles from photographic plates that record collisions between known particles. Tracks or gaps on these plates provide the basis for such posits, and a short gap in an otherwise well-defined track indicates that a particle having no electrical charge exists for a short time. Using principles of conservation of mass and energy, physicists can tentatively assign to it various properties such as mass, charge, and life-span. These properties are subject to revision as more information becomes available about the newly posited entity.

What is important here is the empirical openness that is exhibited toward the posited entity in question. It "comes into being" primarily by its causal relationships with known objects or events, but its properties are not determined in advance. They are filled in as empirical information becomes available. Traditional monotheism, by contrast, posits a being with a definition of many of its properties already in place. Instead of allowing properties to evolve as phenomena unfold, traditional monotheism begins with a conception of what it insists on finding. Proposing the causal theory of reference as a methodological device for introducing God as an explanation is incompatible with defining God in advance. Process theology, in contrast with traditional monotheism, adopts a stance in keeping with the methodological principle at work here in theory construction. William James expressed the value of an empirical approach to theology a century ago, urging his fellow philosophers to "leave abstract thinness behind them, and seek together, as scientific men seek, by using all the analogies and data within reach, to build up the most probable approximate idea of what the divine consciousness concretely may be like."[36] Traditional monotheism does not exhibit sufficient empirical openness to explain Christic apparitions plausibly.

Another difficulty with traditional monotheism arises from the attributes such as omnipotence, omniscience, and omnipresence that have been traditionally ascribed to God. Because these attributes are infinite, it is not clear what criteria for them there could be. We could suggest that God is the best explanation for a phenomenon for which we have no other explanation at present, such as the origin of the visible universe, but we have no way of determining that a Being with infinite properties has acted in this or any other event. No matter how extraordinary an event might be that suggests we are witnessing an act of a Being with suprahuman attributes, nothing about that event can indicate that the attribute is infinite. An example might make this clearer. Suppose that with the aid of powerful telescopes we could watch a planet form before our eyes, going through all the evolutionary changes thought to be part of our planet's history, only collapsed into a few years, say, rather than occurring over billions of years. Even if we were to grant that some suprahuman agency is the best explanation for this event, nothing about this phenomenon allows us to construe its source as having omnipotence, say, rather than having some power falling short of omnipotence. Moreover, ascribing omnipotence to it is not desirable, for no criterion for omnipotence can be offered. Theories that introduce new entities are of further explanatory value only if they assign attributes for which we can supply criteria. If the posited entity is given an infinite attribute, we will be unable to offer a criterion for the claim that this entity is present in a particular causal context, much less for the assertion that the same entity is present in some other causal context as well.

Austin Farrer drew attention to this problem of supplying a criterion for the infinite, in one place putting it as follows: "It is not evident by any simple criteria when we are ever up against signs of his [God's] personal communication or self-manifestation, and when we are not. . . . [N]ot all apparent revelation is really such; and how can we ever be sure that we are not the dupes of a counterfeit? We have not the clue in ourselves, for we are not divine, nor do we possess the recipe for acting divinely."[37] Determining that something with infinite attributes is acting is as impossible as determining that the smallest entity in the universe is before us. The problem immediately disappears when we change the description to "the smallest *known* entity." The fact that criteria for infinite attributes cannot be given raises further questions about exactly what kind of theory monotheism is, and about its place in a genuinely empirical study. These questions, however, are beyond the scope of this book.[38]

The claim that infinite attributes lack criteria is superficially similar to a claim that is sometimes made in connection with arguments for the existence of God. David Hume once argued that there is no good reason to postulate a Being with infinite attributes, rather than one with extraordinary attributes falling just short of infinity, to account for otherwise unexplained phenomena. But the point I am making above has to do with criteria for infinite attributes, not with the question of which theory among a set of close competitors might have the greatest plausibility. Hume's problem, as we might call it, introduces another difficulty for monotheism, although it may be capable of resolution.[39]

Two supernaturalistic theories have already been introduced as possible explanations for Christic visions and apparitions, namely, the angelic mediation theory, and the theory that explains them in terms of the activity of the resurrected Jesus, constituted by a new and strange body. These theories are open to empirical information shaping their specific content, and are therefore quite different from traditional monotheism. In the discussion that follows I shall sketch a third supernaturalistic theory for Christic apparitions. This is the theory that attributes such phenomena to the activity of the Holy Spirit.

The "Holy Spirit" Theory

It is curious that Christianity developed the concept of the Holy Spirit in the unique way that it did. The concept was present in the thought and writings of Judaism, of course, but the Holy Spirit came to be considered by Christianity as one of the component beings of God in triune form. One might have thought that a binitarian understanding of God, supplemented with a claim about a unique incarnation of God in Jesus, would have sufficed for the new theology. Theophany was familiar in Judaism, so one might have expected this notion, perhaps suitably modified to do justice to the known facts about Jesus, to have satisfied those who gave Christianity its first formulation. Tertullian remarks that some early critics accused Christians of preaching two gods, while others accused them of preaching three.[40] This fact suggests that trinitarianism emerged out of a flux of competing views. We can only speculate now on how the concept of a Holy Spirit came to assume such a place of importance. Rudolf Bultmann suggests, following Hermann Gunkel, that the origin of the concept of the Holy Spirit in the NT is to be found in surprising psychological phenomena that were experienced by the early followers of Jesus.[41] This suggestion contains the essential idea which I shall explore.

The NT alleges two broad groups of events that evidently influenced the early Christian development of a trinitarian theology. The first pertains to the life and work of Jesus, whom the NT narratives portray as a miracle worker and a teacher who made unusual claims about his origins, his mission, and his authority. That he came to be thought of as God incarnated is understandable, given what is found in the narratives (reflecting early oral traditions). The second group consists of events in the early apostolic era, primarily described by Luke in Acts. Various paranormal events began to occur after the feast of Pentecost that came to be associated with the Holy Spirit. Luke describes how Jesus's disciples heard the sound of a mighty rushing wind, and saw tongues of fire resting upon their heads; this was followed with the strange ability to speak the languages of the visitors to Jerusalem from Parthia, Mesopotamia, Egypt, Libya, Rome, Crete, Arabia, and other places.[42] Luke explains it by saying that they were filled with the Holy Spirit, and presents Peter's explanation of it as having used much the same terminology. We do not know whether this was the first occasion on which the Holy Spirit was posited to account for strange phenomena, but it seems to have become standard.

Luke describes further incidents in which the Holy Spirit was assigned a crucial causal role: Ananias and his wife, Sapphira, were struck dead for lying to the Holy Spirit;[43] Stephen performed wonders and signs by the power of this Spirit, and disputed so effectively he could not be rebutted;[44] the apostles transmitted the Holy Spirit to others by laying their hands on them, in such an impressive way that Simon offered to buy this power;[45] the Spirit instructed Philip to join the chariot of an Ethiopian official, and later "caught him up," apparently transporting him to another place.[46] Luke recounts incidents in which the disciples of Jesus healed the sick, exorcised the "demonized," and brought the dead back to life. He does not always say explicitly that the Holy Spirit was the cause of these alleged events, but he leaves that distinct impression. Many of the puzzling phenomena might have been psychological, as Bultmann suggests, although it seems doubtful that Christianity would have developed in a trinitarian rather than a binitarian direction if the puzzling events had been only psychological. It seems that the conceptual resources of Judaism, perhaps Hellenized, would have been sufficient to account for psychological phenomena alone. The fact that the concept of God already present with Judaism was expanded to allow God to be thought of as a triune being suggests that there were two clusters of extraordinary allegations for which explanations were needed. The emergence of a trinitarian conception of God as the norm for Christian theology, especially in a religious and political climate that made holding such a view life-threatening, is mute witness to these supposed events.

The Holy Spirit, like most ontological posits, could initially have been "a something we know not what," for its essential attributes would not need to be specified, only its causal relationships to things not in doubt. Perhaps a fluid theoretical framework initially was used to provide descriptions and explanations of the extraordinary phenomena that eventually became associated with the Holy Spirit. Converts from non-Jewish religions may well have posited many more beings than necessary to explain puzzling phenomena, given the history of polytheism in that part of the world. Those with more parsimonious tastes may have posited the Holy Spirit as one member of a triune Deity, while still others, being even more parsimonious, may have attributed everything to a single Being, monotheistically understood. What induced theorists to construe the Holy Spirit as the single cause of so many events is lost to us, but some non-empirical factor such as a penchant for simplicity might also have been at work. Any account of how the Holy Spirit came to be introduced is conjectural and reconstructive now, given the scant information available to us, but a conceptual grounding of it is possible using the causal theory of reference in relation to observable phenomena thought to have occurred.[47]

Reflecting on typical theological discussions today of the Holy Spirit, in the light of these conjectural remarks, is instructive. These discussions often focus on puzzles that arise from dogmatic claims about the relationships among the "persons" in the Trinity, about the meaning of such claims as that the Son is *begotten* by the Father but the Spirit *proceeds* from the Father and the Son (or from the Father alone), about the plausibility of describing the Spirit as a person, about the meaning of the claim that the three persons are of one substance, about the feasibility of assigning all the essential properties of God to the Holy Spirit, and so on.[48] Such abstract discussion does not pay attention to the empirical phenomena that seem to have suggested the theory in the first place, but to theoretical elements arising out of subsequent developments in Christian theology. This kind of discussion is comparable to a discussion of the concepts and theoretical postulates of atomism, such as the properties of spin and charm found in electrons, or the nature of the orbitals that electrons occupy, without mentioning the fascinating observable phenomena for which atomism was introduced in the first place. Contemporary theological discussion often restricts its focus so narrowly to theoretical issues that the reasons for proposing the theory have been forgotten. Systematic theologians often seem to overlook the possibility that the theory was initially advanced as an incomplete and approximate explanation, because it had its roots in empirical phenomena too puzzling to handle in anything but an approximate way. It is not uncommon for untrained theorists, which I suppose the early Christian writers to have been, to cast about in a tentative fashion in constructing explanations for novel and compelling phenomena. Later commentators are irresponsible to ignore these phenomena and focus primarily upon the abstract elements of the theory.

The theory that the visual phenomena associated with Jesus since his death are generated by the Holy Spirit seems to have some support in Paul's thought.[49] In I Corinthians 15 he writes:

So it is with the resurrection of the dead. What is sown is perishable, what is raised is imperishable. It is sown in dishonor, it is raised in glory. It is sown in weakness, it is raised in power. It is sown a physical body, *it is raised a spiritual body*. If there is a physical body, there is also a spiritual body. Thus it is written, "The first man Adam became a living being"; *the last Adam became a life-giving spirit*. But it is not the spiritual which is first but the physical, and then the spiritual. The first man was from the earth, a man of dust; the second man is from heaven.

This text could be interpreted to mean that Jesus became the Holy Spirit in the Resurrection. An implication would be that all of the appearance accounts in the NT were experiences caused by the Holy Spirit. Theologian Hans Küng comes close to saying that this is how Paul could be interpreted:

Paul . . . understands the Spirit quite definitely in the light of that great turning point of time which for him is constituted by Jesus' death and resurrection. Since it became evident at that point that God himself acted in Jesus, the *Spirit of God* can now be *understood also as the Spirit of Jesus as exalted to God*. God's Spirit therefore can no longer be misinterpreted as an obscure, nameless, divine power as understood by Hellenistic Gnosticism, but is completely unequivocally the Spirit of Jesus Christ, of the Son. . . . God's power, force, spirit, have become so much his [Jesus's] own as exalted Lord that he not only possesses and controls the Spirit, but, as a result of the resurrection, can himself be understood as Spirit; Jesus has become a life-giving spirit. Indeed, Paul even says "the Lord is the Spirit." Just what does this enigmatic statement mean? As we have already indicated, not a straightforward identity of two personal factors. It means that *the Lord raised up to God is in the Spirit's mode of existence and operation*. He appears as identical with the Spirit as soon as he is considered not in himself, but in his action on community and individual."[50]

Christian theologians often wrestle with the constraints placed upon them by centuries of interpretation, and so are apt to present puzzling, and even paradoxical statements. No theological topic appears to have generated more paradox than the doctrine of the Trinity, concerning which theologians may seem to advance some proposition in one breath, and take it away in the next. So Küng nearly advances the theory that the resurrected Jesus is the Holy Spirit, but distances himself from it in the last three sentences of the quotation.

Perhaps the differences between "the Holy Spirit theory" and "the resurrected body of Jesus theory" would be appreciated only by those inclined to accept much of Christian theology to begin with. But some of these differences are as follows: The immediate post-Resurrection appearances are not generally attributed to the Holy Spirit, but rather to the resurrected body; the Holy Spirit is not considered to have come into being at the Resurrection, although the resurrected Jesus is generally considered to have done so;[51] and the resurrected body is not thought to have produced the extraordinary events in the early Christian church, but the Holy Spirit is thought to have done so. The differences between the Holy Spirit theory and the angelic mediation theory may seem slight in view of the fact that in Christian thought angels are spirits and so share some fundamental similarities with the Holy Spirit. The main differences arise from the fact that the Holy Spirit is a single being and is generally ascribed infinite powers, while the angelic mediation theory posits many limited spirits as the mediating causes of Christic phenomena. It is clear that we are now comparing the obscure with the just-as-obscure, and that strong interest in these competing theories is likely to be found primarily among theorists having theological tastes comparable to those of the scholastics.

The Swedenborg–Van Dusen Theory

Wilson Van Dusen, a clinical psychologist who works with patients in mental hospitals in the United States, advances a theory of hallucinations that fits into the supernaturalistic tradition. After dealing with hundreds of patients who hallucinated, he discovered that he was able to "speak to their hallucinations."[52] He isolated patients who could distinguish between their own thoughts and the things they saw and heard in the hallucinated "world," and then addressed the hallucinated persons directly, instructing patients to give word-for-word accounts of what the voices answered. Most of the information he gathered was verbal, but some was also visual. He discovered through extensive interactions that the independent reports showed great consistency. He was startled to discover that a "world" was described that bore striking resemblance to the "world" of spirits described two centuries earlier by Emanuel Swedenborg.

The hallucinations among Van Dusen's patients generally came on suddenly. One woman, for instance, was working in her garden when an unseen man addressed her. Another person said his hallucinations began with loud noises and voices he heard while riding a bus. Patients said that the voices they heard had the quality of normal human voices, and the things they saw appeared fully real.[53] One patient told how he was awakened by Air Force officers who called him to serve his country. He was dressing when he noticed that their insignia were not quite right. Then their faces altered, and he knew they were from "the other order." Van Dusen says that patients did not refer to their experiences as hallucinations, objecting to this term because it suggested that the hallucinated beings were not real.

Van Dusen discovered two orders or levels of experience, orders that the voices themselves described as higher and lower: "Lower-order voices are as though one is dealing with drunken bums at a bar who like to tease and torment just for the fun of it. They will suggest lewd acts and then scold the patient for considering them. . . . They call the patient every conceivable name, suggest every lewd act, steal memories or ideas right out of consciousness, threaten death, and work on the patient's credibility in every way."[54] These "voices" try to control parts of a person's body, such as an eye; they threaten pain and cause it; they invade every area of personal privacy; they assume no personal identity, though they accept most names and identities given to them; they either conceal or have no awareness of personal memories; they change the quality of their voices so that patients will not know who is speaking, although their vocabulary and range of ideas is limited; they lie, make promises, and have a persistent will to destroy; they are irreligious or antireligious, and occasionally refer to themselves as coming from hell.[55] One female patient argued with a male voice about leaving the hospital. Van Dusen adds: "Like many, this particular hallucination claimed to be Jesus Christ, but his bragging and argumentativeness rather gave him away as of the lower order."[56]

Van Dusen says that the higher-order hallucinations were much rarer, constituting perhaps less than 20 percent of the experiences he documented. He describes a case in which a man heard the lower order arguing for a long while about how they would murder him, but then a light like the sun came to him at night. Van Dusen continues: "He knew it was a different order because the light respected his freedom and would withdraw if it frightened him. . . . This rarer higher order seldom speaks, whereas the lower order can talk endlessly. The higher order is much more likely to be symbolic, religious, supportive, genuinely instructive and communicate directly with the inner feelings of the patient."[57] This man "found himself" in a long corridor with doors at the end, behind which raged "the powers of hell." He was about to release these powers when a powerful and impressive Christlike figure appeared and by direct mind-to-mind communication counseled him to leave the doors closed and follow him into other experiences that were therapeutic. In another case the higher order appeared to a man in the form of a lovely woman who showed him thousands of symbols. Van Dusen says that the patient had only the high school education of a gas-pipe fitter, but this "woman" showed a knowledge of religion and myth far beyond the patient's comprehension.[58] Van Dusen's conversations were with "her"; the patient served only as a relay. Van Dusen concludes his account with remarks that indicate his openness to the possibility that spirits capable of generating auditory and visual perceptions exist, but he also allows that a Jungian interpretation might be adequate. He remarks that the beings of the higher order resemble Carl Jung's archetypes, while those of the lower order resemble Freud's id.[59]

Van Dusen's account does not specifically discuss Christic apparitions, so one can only speculate about the Christ figure mentioned above. Van Dusen's work is of interest because of the detail it provides concerning apparition experiences of those with psychopathologies, and because of his willingness to entertain the possibility of a theory broadly in the supernaturalistic tradition.

Swedenborg described the universe as having a hierarchy of beings belonging to different orders, and yet acting in correspondence with each other. He held that three levels of good spirits exist between God and humans,[60] that three orders of evil spirits exist below humans, and that humans provide the meeting ground.[61] These spirits flow into the feelings of people and seek to express themselves through them. The evil powers seek to destroy humans by whatever opportunities present themselves, and the good powers influence them toward various good ends, including love and knowledge. Swedenborg said he obtained his "information" from conversations with spirits who became visible to him while conscious. They began one evening as his room mysteriously became dim, and the floor was covered with horrid-looking reptiles.[62] The darkness increased, then disappeared, and in the corner of the room sat a man with whom he could converse. This man later revealed himself again, and told Swedenborg he was "the Lord God, the Creator of the world, and the Redeemer." Swedenborg had been accomplished in many domains of physical science to that point in his life, but from then on gave himself to the study of spiritual things, so that he "could see into the other world, and in a state of perfect wakefulness converse with angels and spirits."[63]

Swedenborg seems to have embraced supernaturalism in a literal form. We can only speculate how he would explain contemporary Christic visions, but he might regard some of them as direct encounters with Jesus as God. Van Dusen and Swedenborg both indicate openness to the classical view of Catholic theology that allows also for deceptive visions.

Assessing Supernaturalistic Theories

A fourth theory should be mentioned at this point. The belief that all living persons, including the historical Jesus, have a soul capable of existing apart from the mortal body and appearing to selected individuals seems to be different from any of the supernaturalistic theories mentioned thus far. It is perhaps extraordinary enough at this point in history to be classified as a supernaturalistic explanation, for its implicit metaphysical dualism is increasingly seen as supernaturalistic in character. I shall consider it in the category of mentalistic explanations, however. It is perhaps less "orthodox," from a Christian theological standpoint, than any of the three preceding theories, for it ignores the NT emphasis upon the uniqueness of the body of the resurrected Jesus. It also makes the postmortem Jesus quite ordinary, since billions of people have presumably experienced the same transformation simply by dying.

I will offer some final comments on these three theories: that Christic apparitions are produced by the resurrected body of Jesus appearing to percipients; that they are caused by angelic mediation; and that the Holy Spirit produces them.

A. The Resurrected Jesus

The theory that Christic encounters might be caused by the resurrected Jesus is one that the Christian laity might quite widely embrace. The Huyssens seem to do so, in view of some of their comments in the introduction to their book on visions, and even in their choice of the title, *I Saw the Lord*. This being is unlike the supernaturalistic beings that have figured in many religious systems, for the resurrected Jesus is continuous with (or identical to) a *historical person*, which spirits such as Satan and angels are seldom supposed to be, although theorists such as Origen and Swedenborg claim that people become angels,[64] and Jewish mystical spirituality allows for heroes being transformed into angels.[65] The resurrected Jesus therefore has a link to the public world that very few other supernaturalistic beings have.

The characteristics of Jesus are obtained from the NT texts, which we have already seen to be incomplete and problematic in various ways. Tradition seems to regard the immediate post-Resurrection appearances as having been caused by the resurrected Jesus positioning himself before percipients in such a way that they could use their normal powers of sight, touch, and hearing to obtain the kind of information obtained in ordinary perception. So visual perception occurs as a result of ambient light falling upon the resurrected body and being reflected in various wavelengths to enter the eye, stimulate the retina, and so on, although it must be admitted that defenders of traditional views do not often discuss these details.

Although the resurrected body is considered to have extraordinary powers, such as the ability to disappear instantly, or to move through solid structures, the way percipients learn about him might not be at all extraordinary (although some might allow for telepathic knowing). One could consider variations of this theory, such as one in which the resurrected Jesus stimulates perceptual mechanisms located inside a percipient, rather than on its surface. A defender of such a view might point to Luke's account of the two disciples whose eyes were kept from recognizing him until they had eaten together. Here Luke implies that the resurrected Jesus interfered with a higher cognitive process, such as the capacity to recognize who was talking with them, not with a lower-level process such as stimulation of retinal cells, optic nerves, or the lateral geniculate nuclei.

Raising the possibility of interference in perceptual and cognitive processes suggests several variations of the resurrected body theory. These variations are reminiscent of the theory of angelic mediation, apart from the fact that it is not angels who are bypassing or interfering with usual perceptual or interpretative powers of percipients, but the resurrected Jesus. As we have seen, traditionalists about the post-Resurrection appearances seem to construe the body of the resurrected Jesus as unvarying in form. This must be at least part of the basis for Rahner's remarks that when percipients "encounter" Jesus as child or as crucified they are not seeing him the way he really is. Of course, the dogmatic view holds that the body of Jesus is in heaven and has not been available for visual observation since his Ascension and subsequent apparition to Paul;[66] hence the angelic mediation theory.

Even if we set aside the dogmatic view and assume that this body does not vary in form and might be accessible to normal visual perception, this theory cannot plausibly account for all five kinds of apparition experiences described in Chapter 2.[67] There is just too much variation in the apparent features and even in the size of the figure. One might overlook the variations in dress, perhaps, but the other variations are too significant. Sometimes the body is seen with wounds, for example, but at other times it is not; sometimes it is seen with radiance, but at other times it is not. Moreover, this theory cannot plausibly account for the variations between those apparitions in which the physical environment changes (Group II), and those in which it remains normal (Group III). This theory cannot account for those experiences in which something less than the whole body appears, for example, only the face or a cameo appearance. So only a small number of visionary experiences as reported can be accounted for on this theory.

If the form of the resurrected body is allowed to vary, and if this being is given powers that allow it to determine exactly how it will appear, then all five kinds of apparition experiences can be explained. But now the theory is so flexible that virtually any phenomenon its defenders wish to explain can be explained. This characteristic is usually seen as a defect in a theory, although it must be admitted that in certain very general and overarching theories, such as evolutionary theory and atomism, this "defect" is widely considered to be a virtue. We have to conclude that this first theory is not a very satisfying explanation for the whole set of Christic visions, apparitions, and alleged appearances, even for those who tolerate supernaturalistic theories.

B. The "Angelic Mediation" Theory

The angelic mediation theory appears to be able to account for four of the five groups of experiences quite handily, but not those in which groups experience the same apparition or where the spatio-temporal-causal framework is altered (Group IV). In order for groups to experience the same apparition by angelic mediation, not only would simultaneous stimulation of the perceptual powers of percipients need to occur, but small changes would need to be included to account for slight differences in perspective. This theory could presumably be modified to allow angels to produce the "right" variations, so that percipients all had the impression that they were seeing a real figure. But this again produces a theory that fits any problematic situation. If group apparitions can be accounted for by modification, so could images on photographic film. There does not seem to be much difference between projecting images onto the emulsion of a film, and projecting images onto the cell bodies forming the surface of the retina, or stimulating other perceptual mechanisms internal to a percipient. The theory of angelic mediation advanced by Augustine and refined by subsequent Catholic thought does not appear to have made provision for such alterations, but I suppose that an obdurate proponent of it might want to modify it as required.

C. The Holy Spirit Theory

The Holy Spirit theory, like the angelic mediation theory, appears to be so malleable that nothing prevents it from explaining all of the five kinds of apparition phenomena. This could be viewed as a virtue or a defect, depending on one's point of view. One problem for this theory is providing a criterion for asserting that the being that produces Christic apparitions at the present time is the same being that produced the post-Ascension events described in Acts. It seems impossible to offer some individuating property that would allow one to assert, for instance, that the being who produced the tongues of fire at Pentecost also produced the post-Resurrection appearances, and continues to produce similar apparitions. This problem is exacerbated if the Holy Spirit is considered not to have a body, which is the position advanced in traditional Christian theology, for discovering an individuating property by observation would appear impossible. The biblical writings are ambiguous on whether spirits, and even God, might have a body.[68] The problem of determining whether the Holy Spirit causes Christic apparitions is further exacerbated if the acts of the Holy spirit are capable of being replicated by diabolic spirits. These problems render this theory too problematic to warrant further attention.

We seem forced to conclude that supernaturalistic theories can offer only sketchy explanations of the phenomena in question. We cannot rule out their explanatory power completely, for they exhibit some of the characteristics found in theories of the physical sciences that postulate unobservables to account for observable phenomena. Perhaps the sketchiness of supernaturalistic theories stems from insufficient research into the paranormal phenomena that suggest them in the first place.

Because of the problems posed by supernaturalistic theories, including their imprecise formulations, the lack of specification of the conditions under which they should be considered refuted, and the unlimited powers their agents are often assigned, one might be tempted to discount such theories completely. If physicalistic or mentalistic alternatives should prove to be incapable of providing explanations, however, supernaturalistic theories might be deemed worthy of consideration.

No single supernaturalistic theory is the obvious choice among explanations for Christic apparitions, for each is problematic in its own way. Besides the difficulties already mentioned, there is the formidable problem of determining whether the beings of supernaturalism are *required*. Physicalists are convinced that the conceptual resources now available and still being developed by the sciences will be able to explain everything, and those who do not embrace a pure form of physicalism often expect that some mentalistic theory will complete the list of necessary theories. The fact that supernaturalism conflicts so sharply with the impressive array of theories and data collections presented by physicalists, all woven together in an integrated "web of belief," makes supernaturalism difficult for many to embrace.

6 Mentalistic and Psychological Explanations

Various explanations using mentalistic concepts have been proposed for apparitions of all kinds. Gardner Murphy's suggestion that apparitions might be brought on by wishing,[1] and Julian Jaynes's explanation of hallucinations as arising from stress[2] are examples from psychologists of theories positing mental events. Popular explanations of apparitions in terms of mental events include the theories that they are brought by expecting them to occur, or by vigorous efforts to produce them, or by mental depression.

These explanations are not particularly controversial in the general public, but would be readily questioned by the psychologists, philosophers, and neuroscientists who doubt the value of mentalism as an explanatory scheme. Eliminative materialists expect that this kind of "folk psychology" will ultimately be abandoned, and they might well be correct, but for the time being the general public uses mentalistic explanations extensively. The scientific community does so as well, however reluctantly, for it has no alternative that uses only the constructs of a completed neuroscience. No current theory of apparitions is wholly devoid of mentalistic concepts or assumptions. Every one either relies upon information obtained by introspection, or makes use of such notions as perception, belief, memory, desire, or volition.

The Disembodied Soul Theory

Although orthodox Christians do not consider Jesus to be either dead or disembodied, dualists unable to embrace orthodoxy might think that Christic apparitions are appearances of the post-mortem soul of Jesus. The theory that human beings have souls (or spirits) capable of disembodied existence, either during this life or posthumously, is an integral part of human history. Virtually every culture has embraced some form of it. The earliest version of this theory in Greek culture, according to Jan Bremmer,[3] is to be found in the writings of Homer and Pindar. These writers advanced a dual conception of soul. The "body soul" (*thymos*) is active when a person is conscious, and is responsible for the psychological characteristics common to humans: emotions (*thymos*), intellect (*noos*), and concentrated energy (*menos*).[4] The "free soul" (*psyche*) is inactive during normal consciousness, but becomes active during a dream or a swoon, and represents the individual after death.[5] According to Pindar, "The body of every man follows the call of mighty death; yet there is left alive a phantom or image (*eidolon*) from his time of life, which alone stems from the gods. It sleeps while his limbs are active; but while he sleeps it often announces in dreams their [the gods'] decision of coming joy or sorrow."[6] Greeks considered the free soul to lack the psychological functions found in normal humans such as emotion, intellect, and other normal human capacities. The souls of the dead were considered unable to speak, laugh, feel emotions, or walk; the sounds they made resembled humming or squeaking, and their movements were described as "flitting."[7]

In subsequent Greek literature the two conceptions of soul merged, so that by Plato's time the soul was a unitary thing serving both psychological and postmortem purposes. Socrates has been credited with having bequeathed to Western thought the notion that the *psyche* could reason, choose, and feel emotions.[8] This unitary conception of soul has been at the core of substance dualism in Western thought since Platonic times, penetrating Christian thought soon after the rise of the church and persisting virtually unquestioned until the middle of the nineteenth century.[9] Variations have of course been proposed, for disembodied souls have often been considered to have powers comparable to those of living humans, rather than those of the pathetic shades of Greek antiquity. Triadic accounts of human nature, rather than strictly dualistic ones, have also been advanced. One such account construed the human spirit to be the intermediary object (the *tertium quid*) that allows the soul to act upon the body. In the words of C. S. Lewis: "The spirits were supposed to be just sufficiently material for them to act upon the body, but so very fine and attenuated that they could be acted upon by the wholly immaterial soul."[10]

Philosophers do not now give extensive consideration to the theory of the disembodied soul. Early in the twentieth century Carl Jung observed that to grant "the substantiality of the soul or psyche is repugnant to the spirit of the age,"[11] and William Lycan notes that substance-dualism was the frequent object of mockery among behaviorists.[12] Richard Swinburne has recently defended a form of substance-dualism,[13] but it entails neither the survival nor the immortality of the soul. His position is that human beings have evolved so that they have both body and soul, the body being that thing to which physical properties such as weight and height belong, and the soul being that thing which has mental properties such as beliefs and desires.[14] It is not just humans that have souls; animals that have a mental life of sensation, thought, and purpose also have souls.[15] Human souls just have more complexity and greater powers, such as the capacity for free will. Swinburne maintains that the brain gives a person his or her characteristic mental life: If the heart or liver is replaced, or if a leg is cut off, the person remains intact, but if one's brain were to be transplanted, the mental life (and hence the soul) would go with the brain.[16] Swinburne accepts the possibility that a person's mental life could continue without a brain, but he says that "evidence suggests that the soul functions only when the brain has rhythms of certain kinds, and at death the brain ceases to function altogether."[17]

Swinburne contends that his view of soul is biblical, and that the common but erroneous idea that the soul has a natural immortality of its own is due to Plato's influence upon Christian thought. Swinburne affirms the Christian view that the souls of people who die will exist again when their bodies are resurrected by God at some future time.[18] This particular form of dualism could not be expected to explain the Christic apparition phenomenon.

Some theologians and psychical researchers, however, have proposed that Christic apparitions might be produced by the soul that survives the death of a person. E. J. Payne, Anglican minister, writes "Spiritualism gives ample proof that people do survive death and can sometimes 'materialise' and 'appear' to human sight from out of the after-life. That is what happened in the case of Jesus. He 'appeared' several times to His Disciples after his death by crucifixion."[19] Leslie Weatherhead considers the post-Resurrection body of Jesus to have been an "apparitional form" in a special sense. He supposes that the old body disappeared—became gaseous and escaped through chinks in the cave—and that then Jesus began a spiritual or etheric existence having the same effect on the physical senses of observers as the old one.[20] Weatherhead wonders, however, whether this body affected percipients through usual sensory organs, such as the eardrum and retina.[21] He considers the new body of Jesus to have been a new kind of substance, but just as real as a material body.

In *The Easter Enigma,* Michael Perry also explores the possibility that the post-Resurrection appearances of Jesus might have been an instance of, or similar to, an apparition of the dead. Perry's theory of survival has five main propositions: (1) that some meaning can be attached to the concept of mind divorced from the physical body, (2) after the death of the body this conscious mind, or some part of it, survives, and so we can still speak of a "self" existing after death, (3) this self retains some of its normal memory and psychical characteristics, (4) this self can be aware of what embodied selves are doing, and (5) this self is able to communicate with embodied selves.[22] Perry's view could be described as a limited disembodied soul theory; other views can be found in which many more properties are ascribed to the soul. G.N.M. Tyrrell, for instance, develops an account of the "perfect" or complete apparition, characterized by a total of nineteen properties. Among these are: appearing solid, obscuring the background, capable of being seen from various angles, capable of speaking, giving a cold tactile sensation, capable of picking up material objects, acting as though aware of the observer, incapable of being photographed or leaving footprints, and not offering resistance to a hand that tries to take hold of it.[23] Other psychical researchers advance views on apparitions that coincide with Tyrrell's on various points. For example, G. Bolton says that the "materialized bodies" he touched had the consistency of heavy dough, and felt cold and clammy,[24] and A. T. Baird describes the semimaterialized forms as feeling like cold jellylike matter.[25]

The views of psychical researchers such as Tyrrell and Baird are still very controversial, but recent research into near-death experiences suggests an account of the disembodied soul that is quite similar. Raymond Moody's work on "the spiritual body" in *Life After Life* summarizes the phenomenological descriptions of more than one hundred subjects. Public dissemination of such accounts of NDEs in the last two decades has been so extensive that I need not dwell long on them here. Moody says that although some subjects did not have the sense of being in another body after "death," most thought they were, although describing it was difficult. The following features of this body were commonly mentioned by Moody's subjects:[26] It is invisible and inaudible to people, but it can see and hear them; it lacks solidity; it is weightless; it is spatially located but lacks a sense of moving; it generally has form or shape, although it sometimes is amorphous; it has a top and a bottom; it experiences events in a timeless way; it is capable of thought and perception, although some perception is altered (for example, it can't sense temperature, but vision is enhanced); it does not hear in the normal way, but seems capable of reading the thoughts of others; it is whole, even though the physical body to which it was once "joined" might not be, for example, one's physical body could be missing a leg, but the spiritual body will not; and it is capable of meeting other spiritual bodies.[27] An extensive literature has emerged that disputes the interpretations of the NDE,[28] but our interest here is only in the conception of disembodied soul deriving from it. The question is whether the disembodied soul of Jesus, however this is to be understood, could account for such experiences as those described in Chapter 2.

None of these conceptions of the disembodied soul, whether Perry's, Moody's, or Tyrrell's, can provide an adequate explanation for all five groups of visionary experiences. No version of this theory adequately explains, for instance, those experiences in which the physical location of the percipient seemed to change. Nor does this theory account for the capacity of some percipients to grasp hold of the figure that appeared to them. Moreover, neither those experiences involving groups or observable changes (Group IV) nor those in which Jesus is seen as a child or as crucified (Group V) appear to be adequately explained by any of the versions outlined. Finally, the theory in question seems to suppose that the disembodied soul of a person retains a fixed appearance, and on this supposition it cannot explain the variety of Christic figures reported by percipients.

Whether other evidence attests to the existence of disembodied souls is another question. The general opinion among academics is negative, but a few hold a contrary view. Carl Becker has recently examined the survival hypothesis, surveying evidence coming from reports of spontaneous memories of former lives, possession, apparitions, out-of-body experiences, and NDEs.[29] He suggests that the best evidence for the survival of "discarnate bodies," as he calls them, has emerged in the last decade or so, and he concludes that there is enough evidence to justify belief in survival.[30] Becker mentions a number of theories that suggest ways of reconciling survival with materialism. One theory suggests that discarnate bodies might be "yet inadequately studied particle or wave-like stuff," another that the surviving "body" is a force field, and a third treats surviving bodies as entities belonging to another spatial dimension.[31] The evidence that Becker adduces, and the conclusion he draws, are controversial, but even if his view on survival should happen to be correct, this theory is inadequate for explaining Christic apparitions.

The "Persona" Theory

Hornell Hart advances a theory to explain apparitions based upon phenomena reported by psychical researchers, and in response to several other theories discussed extensively by psychical researchers. The phenomena he considers include apparitions of both dead and living people, apparitions of people seen with animals or inanimate objects such as walking sticks and handbags, apparitions seen via a mirror and seen by groups of observers.[32] Phenomena reported by mediums are also considered. Hart finds the evidence collected on apparitions to be sufficiently impressive to regard them as "self-existent structures."

The persona theory is an attempt to reconcile three other theories, each of which is deemed to have some truth but to be incomplete on its own. The *possession theory* supposes that the surviving spirits of the dead take possession of mediums and speak through them, or that these spirits become embodied and enter into real, although temporary, conscious relationships with percipients.[33] This theory is a version of the disembodied soul theory described above. The *telepathic theory* supposes that apparitions are hallucinations known through extrasensory perception, and are generated either by the one who appears to a percipient or by someone else who has access to relevant information.[34] This theory was first advanced by Edmund Gurney, who emphasized the role of the unconscious mind of the hallucinator in creating the apparition, using clues received telepathically. G.N.M. Tyrrell modified it in 1942 by emphasizing the unconscious partnership of the percipient and the person whose apparition form is seen.[35] The third theory is the *ESP interaction theory*, according to which apparitions are hallucinations generated "by the unconscious mind of the percipient, with no assistance or participation from surviving personalities of the dead."[36] On this theory any veridical information that might be transmitted by apparitions would be derived by extrasensory perception from the living, not the dead. Louisa Rhine suggests a basis for it, noting that just as most people are capable of responding sympathetically to others at the level of emotion, some people, but not a great number, are able to respond sympathetically to others at a level of perception, likely because of an unconscious mental cause.[37]

Hart presents the persona theory using concepts found in each of the three theories mentioned. He defines a persona as "The sum-total of what the 'I' calls 'mine.'"[38] The sorts of things the self (the 'I') considers its own include one's body, one's property, one's memories. Hart says that personas are created by living people, such as those who adopt a role in a certain context and then find that the role has a grip on them,[39] and suggests that personalities that survive the death of their bodies might also be able to create personas, perhaps visible ones. He claims that mediums can unconsciously distort the persona of a surviving personality that seeks to communicate a message.[40] Personas are therefore described as personality structures having varying degrees of fictitiousness, depending on the role of unconscious dramatizing capacities of mediums or of those involved in apparitions.[41] Personas are considered capable of extrasensory perception.

Apparitions are described by Hart as visible, audible, and tangible personas projected into a material setting.[42] The apparitions that are caused by attempting to project one's "presence" to another in a perceptible way are explained as a case of a persona being produced by the person represented.[43] Apparitions of oneself are also possible on this theory, for "a persona may . . . be (at a given moment) a vehicle for the observing and operating consciousness."[44] Because a persona consists of the entire and complex structures of a being, including its body, clothing, memories, and ideas, this theory is also able to explain why some apparitions appear with animals, handbags, and so forth—these "extraneous" objects are part of that complex. Hart accepts the claim that personas can materialize (to greater or lesser extent) and so appear to groups of percipients.[45] In these and similar ways the persona theory is adapted to explain many of the unusual phenomena that have been collected by psychical researchers.

The persona theory uses a fascinating combination of conceptual elements deriving from various fields of inquiry, some of them controversial. Not only does it accept mentalistic constructs in an unreduced form, but it also accepts the constructs of substance-dualism. The claims that personalities survive the death of the body and that personas created by these personalities make use of an "etheric body" tie the theory to an old form of dualism. In accepting unconscious mental states it also uses elements of psychological theory deriving broadly from the psychoanalytic tradition. Finally, it employs the constructs of parapsychology in its generous reference to ESP, telepathy, and clairvoyance, although some theorists might look at these as natural concomitants of substance-dualism. Whatever else one might wish to say about this theory, one must say that its conceptual resources are complex and controversial. The phenomena on which this theory is premised are a far cry from the pallid mental states and jejune mental processes that are the staples of much contemporary discussion of mind. The seriousness with which the theory is advanced by Hart reflects the seriousness with which he takes the paranormal phenomena reported in psychical research. It also indicates his belief that other theories advanced by those who accept the genuineness of paranormal phenomena are inadequate.

The persona theory is evidently capable of explaining most, if not all, of the Christic apparitions reported in the five groups. The first group of apparition experiences are sufficiently like dreams to constitute no serious difficulty. Hart uses his theory to explain dreams, saying that in a dream various personas become visible, audible, and tangible.[46] Group II apparitions would presumably consist of apprehending a persona complete with the new physical environment—part of the persona—in which the apparition is experienced. Group II and III apparitions would again involve personas making their appearance, and if the materialization were to be complete enough, those Group IV apparitions involving collective experiences would be explained. Hart does not appear to have addressed cases in which the apparition produces a change in the spatio-temporal domain, so whether his theory can handle all of the Group IV cases is not clear. He reports that when an apparition originally seen with a walking stick disappeared, the walking stick also disappeared. In Chapter 4, I discussed the apocryphal "footprint test" for a Christic apparition, according to which Andrew asked Jesus to leave his footprint in the sand. Hart does not appear to say whether one could predict on the persona theory that the footprint would disappear with Jesus. Group V apparitions and those involving changing physical forms can be explained by the various personas that surviving personalities can create.

The persona theory presents several difficulties. One is the intrinsic implausibility of the idea that one theory can account for the full range of apparition and mediumistic phenomena, assuming their authenticity for a moment, and even dreams. There are too many differences among these experiences to expect one theory to account for them all. The second major difficulty is determining whether there are as many paranormal phenomena requiring explanation as Hart and other psychical researchers think.

The Jungian Archetype Theory

Carl Jung's explanation for visions and apparitions relies upon concepts unique to his psychological theory. Jung accords the psyche a central place in his theory of human nature, although he declines to say what its ultimate nature might be. He considers it to be as much a part of human life as are the biological and behavioral dimensions. Jung accepts the descriptive and explanatory value of the psyche as a postulated entity, but will not rule on its ontological ultimacy or dismiss the possibility of its living on in a realm beyond the body.[47] Like Freud, Jung places great significance upon the unconscious psyche, but unlike Freud, he does not consider the unconscious to come into existence with consciousness and to disappear with it.[48] For Jung the unconscious psyche has "an indeterminable number of subliminal perceptions, [and] an immense fund of accumulated inheritance-factors left by one generation of men after another."[49] Jung contends that it is no more unreasonable to hold that the unconscious psyche inherits knowledge from one's ancestors than to hold that a person inherits biological characteristics from the animals in its evolutionary past. The evidence for this psychic inheritance comes from dream analysis and the study of psychopathologies. This is the general framework within which archetypes are located by Jung.

Archetypes are primordial mental structures that cannot be explained simply in terms of personal experience or the personal unconscious.[50] They are "universal patterns or motifs which come from the collective unconscious, [and] are the basic content of religions, mythologies, legends and fairy tales."[51] Archetypes represent the point at which the collective experience of humanity interacts with personal experience, and although these archetypes appear in an unlimited number of forms within experience, the changing images represent stable and universal motifs. Jung says: "We do not know what an archetype is (i.e., consists of), since the nature of the psyche is inaccessible to us, but we know that archetypes exist and work."[52] Because they derive from the inaccessible psyche, they are not knowable, but symbols give expression to them.

Jung discusses the case of a hermit who reported seeing an apparition of light in the (circular) form of a human face. The hermit interpreted this terrifying encounter as an experience of God, and Jung accepts this interpretation.[53] Jung sees this experience as deriving from the hermit's unconscious, and spilling over into his conscious mind, holding it spellbound.[54] It is symbolically expressed with the help of the circle, a symbol that goes back to Bronze Age sun wheels found in Mexico, India, Tibet, and China, and to the mandalas found in various parts of the world.[55] Jung notes that in an earlier era the experience would have been unhesitatingly described as an encounter with "God" or "a demon," depending upon a person's cultural heritage, but for a twentieth-century person the experience must be described as one that involves the unconscious because "we have become so bashful in matters of religion."[56] Jung is offering an account of religious phenomena using the constructs of his theory.

Apparitions, like dreams, are considered to involve psychic content from the unconscious that is forced into our conscious life. Such psychic complexes escape the control of our consciousness and appear and disappear according to their own laws.[57] Jung says: "The vision comes in much the same way as a dream, only in the waking state. It enters consciousness along with the perception of real objects, since it is an irruption of unconscious ideas into the continuity of consciousness." For Jung the psyche is not an indivisible unity but a totality of separate parts. Some of these psychic elements might never be associated with a percipient's ego, that is, the center of one's individuality, and because they are strange to the ego, they are externalized and appear as visionary objects.[58] Jung explains St. Paul's apparition experience by suggesting that Paul had already been a Christian for some time, only unconsciously. The incident in which he heard the voice speaking from heaven "marks the moment when the unconscious complex of Christianity broke through into consciousness. . . . The complex, being unconscious, was projected by St. Paul upon the external world as if it did not belong to him."[59] Jung characterizes our scientific age as marked by a desire to know if reports of apparitions are true, without taking into account what the nature of proof would have to be and how it could be furnished.

Jung also applies his theory to the Christian belief in the Resurrection of Jesus. The Resurrection is a story that typifies the life of a hero who conquers death and brings back to life his parents or tribal ancestors.[60] This hero is not annihilated by death, but lives on in some other form, becoming a type of the complete or perfect self (a God-man)—an archetype found in various cultures. The story of the Resurrection represents the projection of "an indirect realization of the self that had appeared in the figure of a certain man, Jesus of Nazareth."[61] By identifying with this archetype, the followers of Jesus were able to overcome fear of being annihilated either by Caesar or by physical death itself.[62] Jung doubts the historicity of the Resurrection, but is not surprised that the primitive Christians felt the need to present the Resurrection as "a concrete, materialistic event to be seen by the eyes and touched by the hands."[63]

Jung's theory has enough conceptual resources to explain many Christic apparitions, but there are some that it seems powerless to explain. It appears to have an explanatory framework rich enough to account for many of the phenomenological variations reported by percipients, such as seeing radiance; seeing a human figure, whether partial, complete, or larger than life; experiencing both tactile and visual sensations; experiencing awe or fear; hearing words of comfort; and seeing Jesus as a child or as crucified. Each of these experiences could presumably be connected with appropriate archetypal content. This point is also a drawback, however, for it seems that no way of determining the number or content of archetypes exists apart from having percipients report the phenomenological elements of their experiences. This suggests that an explanation is being invented precisely to suit the inexplicable phenomena, with no fuller understanding of the experience really achieved by describing its cause as an archetype. Jung's theory is another example of unobservable causes being postulated to account for observable events, with all the strengths and weaknesses that such theories generally exhibit.

The apparition experiences that Jung's theory seems incapable of effectively explaining are collective experiences in which the spatio-temporal domain is influenced. Collective apparitions would require the simultaneous emergence into consciousness of identical archetypes, and this seems highly improbable. Advancing such a position is comparable to asserting that public objects are not really seen by those who think they do so, but are simultaneously hallucinated. Moreover, the claim that archetypes might account for changes in the spatio-temporal domain seems implausible. So until these alleged phenomena can be explained on Jung's theory, it is inadequate. If reports of apparitions of these two important kinds should be found dubious, Jung's theory would be an important competitor. Perhaps it has the importance it is generally given because of the belief that collective apparitions and those that influence the spatio-temporal domain do not exist.

Mental Event Theories

One of the most commonly advanced explanations for apparition experiences is that they occur as a result of some familiar mental state or event, perhaps experienced to an unusually marked degree. Examples of supposed causes include the desire to experience them, or a determined effort of the will intended to bring them about, or anxiety generated by some traumatic event. Sometimes special physical circumstances, combined with mental states, are suggested as an explanation. Self-flagellation, fasts, and sensory deprivation, long associated with mystics and ascetics, are often assigned a concomitant role in producing visions. Religious beliefs and excitement are also frequently included as part of the causal nexus.

Lauretta Bender explains hallucinations in children by reference to their feelings of neglect and loneliness.[64] She observes that young children who hallucinate imaginary companions tend to come from underprivileged or deprived homes, and typically feel neglected and lonely. These feelings are considered to explain why nonpsychotic children hallucinate. When such children mature, or have their social emotional needs met, their hallucinations disappear. She concludes: "At whatever age children's hallucinations occur, they are always a window to the inner life of the child and reveal the child's psychodynamic problems to the observer."[65] One could extend this theory to account for the hallucinations of adults, although Bender does not do so. The psychodynamic concepts employed in it appear to be capable of being extrapolated into the lives of adults, because some adults, too, feel neglected, lonely, and socially vulnerable.

Another popular theory is that stress may cause individuals to experience apparitions. I shall examine it in more detail below. Many other mental states are also popularly suggested as possible explanations for apparitions. This is not surprising because mental states are not often supplied with criteria that would allow such explanations to be tested.

Mentalistic theories generally identify a specific mental state such as wishes, or stress, or despondency, as precipitating an apparition. Such a mental state is not usually offered as the sole cause, however. Other mental and physical states are held to be conducive to producing apparition experiences, but some special mental state triggers them. Moreover, because many of the mental states assigned this causal role are normally present in modest degrees, but do not precipitate apparitions under normal circumstances, some special combination of circumstances or the presence of this mental state to an extreme degree is thought necessary to produce apparitions. Normal wishing, normal stress, or mild despondency, which may be found in almost anyone, are not thought to precipitate visions, but extreme forms of these states can do so. Other mental states that do not occur in degrees, such as intending and knowing, are not often suggested as causing apparitions. Beliefs are commonly assigned some causal role by mentalists; whether these occur in degrees is a matter of dispute.

Establishing the plausibility of the causal claim central to a mentalistic explanation is difficult. If wishing to have an apparition experience is its cause, one would expect, at the very least, that apparitions would regularly occur in conjunction with wishes. But everyday life presents little or no evidence that wishes and Christic apparitions tend to occur together. Many Christians who wish to have a vision of Jesus never do. Now another problem presents itself—the problem of showing that such wishes are really present in oneself or others. Philosophers have discussed this problem extensively. The standard response they gave before Wittgenstein was that one could always determine the presence in oneself of such mental states as wishes by introspection. Moreover, one could conclude that others have wishes by inductively inferring these states from similarities in their behavior to one's own when one wishes. Wittgenstein challenged this, questioning that a person knows his or her mental states by introspection, and the claim that an inductive argument is involved in asserting that others have particular mental states. He ushered in a debate that focusses on the meaning of linguistic expressions that refer to mental states, and on the role of linguistic communities, as opposed to individual speakers, in establishing the criteria for "correctly" using a specific expression.

Even if we grant that no difficulty arises in determining that we or others do have wishes, we still have the problem of determining whether this mental state is present to a degree sufficient to cause its supposed effects. This is not easy to solve. Mentalistic explanations are often complicated further by suggestions that unconscious mental states, such as unconscious wishes or unconscious beliefs, precipitate effects. Such postulated states are of course beyond the capacity of those who experience them to "inspect" directly. These are some of the difficulties facing most mentalistic explanations, to which we must add one more—a problem that seems to be fatal.

Let us suppose that all of the difficulties enumerated above have been addressed by a proponent of the view that wishes cause Christic apparitions. Let us suppose that wishes are assigned only a precipitating cause, so that an explanation with enough subtlety to serve as a plausible candidate for an adequate explanation is under scrutiny. Let us suppose a close correlation between wishing and apparitions is found, or more precisely, that a close correlation between wishes of a certain degree and the occurrence of apparitions is established—a supposition that requires that a measure for the "strength" of a wish be in place. Let us suppose that wishes can readily be detected, and let us suppose that all the difficulties with respect to unconscious wishes have been circumvented. The question that remains is this: What it is about *wishes* that make them especially efficacious in producing Christic apparitions? Why do wishes, rather than states of anxiety or expectancy or sexual frustration, for instance, not have that same causal efficacy? This seems to be an appropriate question to ask. The defender of a mentalistic explanation has nothing to say in response to this question, except perhaps to say that in some future study the answer will become clear. *But this future study would not be in mentalism, but in neurophysiology.* Only something like a more complete theory of neural mechanisms could illuminate why wishes produce apparitions. The capacity of *mentalism* to "explain" apparitions would be exhausted in finding that the requisite correlations between wishes (to appropriate degrees) and apparitions are present, but merely finding correlations between mental states and supposed effects is not really to explain those effects.

This criticism of mentalism touches on a controversial issue in philosophy of science, namely, the question of whether a Humean approach to causation and explanation is adequate. David Hume's analysis of causation focuses on the presence of constant correlation and temporal order between two kinds of events said to be causally related, allowing for a causal connection to be established merely on the basis of correlation and temporal order. Hume explicitly rejects an analysis of causation that depends upon the existence of causal powers exerted by the cause upon its effect, saying that there is no basis in experience for the concept of causal power. He, with his usual succinctness, puts it thus: "All ideas are deriv'd from, and represent impressions. We never have any impression, that contains any power or efficacy. We never therefore have any idea of power."[66] Empiricist philosophers, such as the logical positivists who dominated Anglo-American philosophy during the first half of this century, have generally embraced Hume's approach to causation. In contrast, scientific realists have argued that to establish a causal connection requires showing something of the causal powers that are found in the entities that comprise the cause, where these entities might be unobservable.[67] Because empiricists have been loath to allow for the reality of unobservable entities, they have rejected this approach. This topic is important for the philosophy of science, and in advancing the above objection I have indicated my own predilection for scientific realism over empiricism. This objection would of course be ineffective if the Humean analysis of causation were to be completely adequate, but I do not think it is.

Here is another of those far-reaching methodological assumptions that shape attitudes toward philosophic and scientific inquiry.[68] Its import for Christic apparitions is that mentalistic explanations that attempt to account for them by merely finding correlations with mental states have not really explained them. Such correlations do not exhibit what it is about these mental states, that is, what causal powers these mental states exhibit, that make them uniquely efficacious for producing apparitions. This criticism has the effect of either eliminating mental states from the field of plausible explanations or pushing mentalism in the direction of neurophysiology, for it demands that mental states either be eliminated from explanations (eliminative materialism) or be grounded in neurophysiological phenomena (functional materialism). My sympathies are with functionalist materialism rather than eliminative materialism. This means that I consider the value of folk psychology to lie in its capacity to provide a general outline of the causal connections to be searched out in neurophysiological research. Eliminative materialists of course believe that mentalism will disappear, while functionalists maintain that the neural sciences will greatly illuminate the causal relationships now obscurely expressed using the constructs of mentalism. Even dualists such as Swinburne and Eccles, who reject any assertion of an identity between mental and neural phenomena, generally consider neural phenomena to undergird mental ones.[69]

There is a fascinating empirical issue having to do with the "direction" of causal processes that has implications for this last view. Its outcome could further undermine the cogency of mentalistic explanations. States such as wishing and believing are higher-level cognitive processes, and to suppose that these produce apparitions, which are perceptual and therefore involve some lower-level neural activities, is to suppose that certain kinds of "top-down" neural causal processes are in place. Some theorists believe that the dominant causal direction is "bottom-up" rather than "top-down," that is, from perceptual modules to cognitive processes,[70] but others believe that "top-down" effects are equally important. Paul Churchland argues against the dominance of bottom-up effects, adducing several kinds of evidence for top-down effects. There is neurophysiological evidence for top-down effects in the fact that there are descending neural pathways from the "highest" cortical areas of the brain to the "lowest" processing mechanisms in perceptual systems, for example, in the descending neural fibers from the visual cortex to the lateral geniculate nucleus and on to the retina.[71] This feedback mechanism partially controls what a person sees. Further evidence of top-down effects is supplied by the fact that we are able to control the visual effects of various illusions such as the duck/rabbit figure, the vase/face figure, and the Necker cube by learning to flip the figures back and forth, or by changing assumptions about the object.[72] Even the familiar fact that a person's general knowledge is capable of shaping perceptions is evidence for top-down causal processes, according to Churchland.[73] As an aside, I would point out that it is ironic that Churchland, a defender of eliminative materialism, would adduce evidence for a neural causal process from interactions among the kind of mental states whose ontology he takes to be radically mistaken. These claims are consistent with functionalist materialism, however.

It is instructive to reflect on what would have to be shown, from a neurophysiological standpoint, in order to claim that a higher-level cognitive process such as wishing could cause an apparition, which involves lower-level perceptual modules. We might consider an apparition experience in which the basic orienting, visual, and tactile perceptual systems are simultaneously activated and are functioning in a well-integrated fashion. Pauline Langlois's account (Case 24) is a good example, for she reported that she saw the figure that stood beside her, and then felt its solidity. If wish fulfillment was the cause of this experience, some top-down effect from higher cortical areas (undergirding or identical with wishing) would need to be the cause of the simultaneous and well-integrated lower-level neural phenomena (undergirding or identical with the relevant visual and tactile elements). Moreover, Pauline's situation would have to be one allowing no stimulation of the visual or tactile "areas" at the level of the first transducing systems, in order to eliminate the possibility of "bottom-up" effects. There could be no stimulation of the retinal cells that respond to colors, edges, and contours, or of the nerve endings in the hands that respond to contact with surfaces.

Opponents of the efficacy of top-down causes would naturally take a different view of the matter, perhaps searching for causes in noncortical areas. The conflicting views presented here about the role of top-down and bottom-up effects appear to be capable of being resolved by advancing neurophysiology. Top-down effects may be found to be negligible, for example, if there is stimulation of the retinal cells that cannot be accounted for by reference to the neural activity descending from cells involved in higher-level neural processing. In that case the kind of mentalistic explanation under scrutiny here will have been effectively refuted. Cognitive scientists such as Fodor, who emphasize the relative importance of bottom-up over top-down effects, have already signaled their resistance to the idea that high-level cortical areas can cause perceptual experience, and thus their rejection of the causal efficacy of various mental states (or the neurophysiological correlates of such states).

Jaynes's Theory of Stress

Julian Jaynes supplements the bare concept of stress, as conventionally understood, with the conceptual resources of neurophysiology in order to explain apparitions, or hallucinations, to use his terminology. Jaynes provocatively suggests that human nature at one time was split into two nonconscious parts, one functioning in an executive capacity, and the other in a subordinate capacity.[74] The input from the executive part of the bicameral mind was interpreted by the other part as the voice of a god. This hallucinatory phenomenon was a fundamental source of religious belief in antiquity. Although the mind is now conscious, and hallucination is much rarer than it used to be, Jaynes notes that vestiges of the experience and the supernaturalistic interpretation of it can still be found. Jaynes takes stress to be the trigger for the hallucinatory experience,[75] and he defines stress by specifying empirical operations that allow one to determine its presence or absence. He says that stress can be *observed* in lower mammals, such as in rats who develop ulcers from being forced to cross an electric grid to reach food and water. Such an experimental basis for attributing stress to a living creature is in sharp contrast with the conventional way that stress is "observed." Jaynes thus gives the central concept in his theory a more substantial basis than usually provided for mentalistic concepts.

Jaynes draws upon further empirical findings to account for hallucinations. For instance, the fact that some deaf schizophrenics do not have auditory hallucinations, but have visual ones of sign language, shows that hallucinations have some innate structure in the nervous system underlying them.[76] Wilder Penfield's data about the effects of electrical stimulation of the brain are further evidence. When Penfield stimulated a portion of the right hemisphere (the nondominant side, so-called) that corresponds to Wernicke's area (a major speech area) of the left hemisphere, patients relived past events. Though many of these relived experiences were only auditory in character, like most hallucinations, some were visual as well.[77] Jaynes considers the threshold for the occurrence of hallucinations in normal people to be very high, so they hardly ever experience them. But in psychosis-prone people, the threshold is somewhat lower, probably caused "by the buildup in the blood of breakdown products of stress-produced adrenalin which the individual is, for genetical reasons, unable to pass through the kidneys as fast as a normal person."[78]

Jaynes discusses a few apparitions from classical literature to show how his theory would interpret them. He understands St. Paul's conversion experience as one in which a hallucinated voice was interpreted as the voice of Jesus, and remarks that such visual hallucinations as Yahweh coming to Moses, or Thetis to Achilles, are usually only a shining light or a cloudy fog.[79] None of the other Christic post-Resurrection appearances or visions mentioned in NT literature are discussed by Jaynes, but I think it is safe to say the Jaynes would view his theory as capable of accounting for these phenomena.

Like Jung, Jaynes does not address the alleged intersubjectively observable effects of Paul's conversion experience. This raises a familiar methodological problem. Jaynes seems willing enough to acknowledge that Paul had an extraordinary auditory experience, based upon the accounts in Acts, but he glosses over the intersubjectively observable effect(s) alleged to have been part of the experience. These intersubjectively observable effects would cast doubt on the adequacy of his theory, and one might reasonably wonder how Jaynes can accept that portion that accords with his theory, but gloss over another portion that conflicts with it.

Jaynes's theory belongs to a group that refers to key mental states as causes of apparitions, but it is an improvement over many of the popular theories because of its attempt to define these mental states empirically. But one is still left wondering if stress can be plausibly identified as the key mechanism producing apparitions, particularly Christic ones. It seems that stress could be attributed to any person reporting a Christic vision, no matter how little of it they seemed to exhibit. If Jaynes has not really identified a convincing cause of Christic visions, he has at least opened up the importance of exploring the neurophysiology behind vision experiences, which will be the topic of the next chapter.

The examination of mentalistic explanations to this point has shown that they locate the cause within events, mental or physical, that form part of the life of the percipient. Wishing, expectancy, or stress are events internal to a percipient, although their causal origins, in part at least, may be outside a person. Most of the apparitions in Groups I, II, and V seem to be susceptible to such an explanation, for little or nothing about them requires causes outside a percipient. But mental events cannot explain the kind of alterations to the spatio-temporal order associated with some Group IV apparitions. One cannot explain images left on photographic film or a patch of melted snow by mental states. Perhaps one could concede that physical healings are somehow caused by mental events, but this does not seem feasible in every case either. Of course, the status of Group

IV apparition reports is in some doubt anyway because they are so few in number, so the inability to explain them is perhaps not a serious deficiency.

Mentalistic explanations also seem inadequate for another kind of apparition, however. Some percipients in my sample reported that they were able to look away from the apparition figure to view the ordinary objects around them, and could look back to find that the apparition figure was still visible. What is remarkable is that the apparition figure appeared in just the place it was last seen before looking away, and that it looked just as it did the first time. The whole set of facts in such cases, including the spatial and temporal facts just noted, is hard to explain by means of the class of mentalistic explanations under consideration. One is hard-pressed to explain how stress or wishing would produce these carefully timed events. Was the appropriate degree of stress experienced when their heads faced forward, say, so that an apparition experience occurred? Was this stress so reduced when they turned their heads away that the apparition stopped? And did turning their heads to face forward again trigger enough additional stress so that the apparition—the same one—was experienced again, and in just the same place? It strains credulity to think that the operative triggering mechanism in such a case was stress—or wishing or expectancy, for that matter. One can perhaps comprehend how mental states might produce a whole set of visual phenomena completely different from the physical environment that a percipient is in, such as the cases collected in Group II, but a series of identical apparitions presents much greater difficulties. On the basis of all the preceding remarks about the deficiencies of mentalism, I conclude that this kind of explanation is less persuasive than its popularity would lead one to think.

Psychoanalytic Explanations

Freudian theory is one of the staples in Western culture for explaining psychological phenomena, including experiential aberrations. Freud described hallucinations as experiences "corresponding to regressions, i.e., to thoughts transformed into images," adding that "only such thoughts undergo this transformation as are in intimate connection with suppressed memories, or with memories which have remained unconscious."[80] An interesting application of Freud's theory can be found in Michael Carroll's book on Marian apparitions.[81] Marian apparitions seem similar enough to Christic apparitions, given their religious significance and general phenomenological character, to make Carroll's study of more than passing interest. His explanation of Marian apparitions provides an overview of the leading ideas in the psychoanalytic tradition. It might seem peculiar that I examine Freud's theory, which uses mental states, given what I have just written about mentalism. There is some evidence, however, that Freud thought the unique constructs central to his psychoanalytic theory would be replaced by constructs deriving from the neural sciences.[82] Freud's theory will serve nicely, then, as a bridge to neurophysiological explanations.

Carroll describes hallucinations as mechanisms for discharging excess energy, and advances the Freudian view that the content of the hallucination is shaped by the percipient's desire to gratify an unconscious wish.[83] Neuroses stem from sexual or aggressive impulses that become blocked during the Oedipal period of development, and when the dammed-up libido finally does find discharge through the repressed unconscious, it does so with the help of a regression to an infantile fixation. Carroll's explanation of Marian apparitions is given in terms of repressed sexual impulses. He concentrates on the visual apparition, although of course both auditory and visual experiences of Mary have been reported. Among the fifty percipients selected for examination in Carroll's study,[84] 80 percent were sexually mature individuals who apparently lacked regular sexual partners, because they either were unmarried or belonged to celibate religious orders.[85] In keeping with Freud's view that repressed sexual impulses would activate infantile fixations, Carroll suggests that "for males, Marian devotion derives from a son's repressed sexual desire for the mother, whereas for females, such devotion derives from a daughter's desire for sexual intercourse with, and a child from, her father."[86] The male's sexual desire is not simply to have sexual access to his mother, according to this theory, but to have *exclusive* access to her, thus generating hostility to the father. For female percipients, however, "the whole point of the apparition is to provide the young girl with a way of identifying with Mary and thus vicariously enjoying her own Oedipal fantasy, which is to have sexual intercourse with the father."[87] Carroll predicted, on the basis of this theory, that a father figure would tend to be present (along with Mary) in Marian apparitions for female percipients, but not for males. Carroll takes "father figure" to denote any adult male, such as Jesus as an adult (but not as a child), St. Francis, or St. Dominic. He notes that in the Marian apparitions sampled, 50 percent of the females saw an adult male, while only 7 percent of the male percipients did so. Other factors besides blocked sexual outlets are included in Carroll's explanation of these apparitions, and include "the organic factors that predispose individuals to experience hallucinations in general, the presence of a religious world view that legitimates the belief that the Virgin Mary often makes earthly appearances, and the tendency to imitate previous [known] Marian apparitions."[88] Carroll expands upon these ideas in discussing specific apparition experiences. He suggests, for instance, that Catherine Laboure's Marian apparition in 1830 reflected her unconscious infantile wish "to reestablish the presence of a warm and loving mother who had been lost when Catherine was quite young."[89]

Although the focus of Carroll's attention is on Marian apparitions, he mentions several Christic apparitions, including those reported by Teresa of Avila and some mentioned by Walsh. He remarks, "We quite often come across an associated description of a female seer's encounter with Jesus that is rife with sexual imagery. It is difficult not to think of sexual sublimation when a female seer, in addition to her Marian apparition, reports one in which Christ inserts a phallic-shaped object directly into her body."[90] Examples include the experiences of Ossana, into whom Jesus plunged a "long and terrible nail," of Catherine of Raconigi, into whom Jesus plunged his arm so that he could grasp her heart and wash it, and of Teresa, into whose heart and entrails a male angel plunged a dagger. Carroll would no doubt be inclined to offer explanations from a psychoanalytic perspective for the Christic apparitions I am examining as well.

Various philosophers have given psychoanalytic theory extensive scrutiny, and I shall not venture into the complex issues generated by it. There certainly seems to be merit in supposing that unconscious states have significant causal effects in the experience of people, especially if these states are identified with neural structures. And who can doubt the significance of childhood experiences, including ones involving our sexuality, in shaping subsequent behavior? But this approach, too, is inadequate to explain Christic visions.

Freud's theory cannot account for collective Christic visions or for ones with intersubjectively observable effects. Nor does the theory seem to be particularly effective in explaining Group II apparitions in which percipients have the sense that the whole physical environment has changed. It also invites questions about why sexual abstinence or sexual activity is particularly conducive to producing or inhibiting apparitions. The claim that repressed sexual impulses find their expression in apparitions is evidently an attempt to identify the key causal element, but one is left wondering why it is that repressed impulses are expressed as *apparitions*. Freud's theory seems unable to supply the mechanism by which this occurs. It exhibits the same deficiencies as did the mentalistic theories on which I commented earlier.

This explanation also leaves other questions unanswered, such as the extent to which sexual abstinence can be correlated with the onset of apparitions in a particular percipient's experience, and the extent to which sexual activity can be correlated with their coming to an end. *Close* correlations in both temporal and nontemporal ways would need to be found to give this theory plausibility, for it is not reasonable to suggest that sexual repression is the cause of apparitions simply by discovering that a person experienced sexual repression at one time in his or her life, and had an apparition sometime later. It is interesting to note that Carroll's study focuses on percipients now dead, who can be questioned neither about the correlation of sexual repression with their apparitions, nor the number of instances in which the correlation was observed. I also find it interesting that because the percipients in his study are dead, they cannot be embarrassed by questions about their sexual activities, especially if they were unmarried or members of celibate orders. I do not doubt that delicate methods of investigation could be employed with living percipients to determine whether or not there is a high correlation between sexual abstinence and Christic apparitions, but it would have to be done with consideration for the special states of mind that percipients who have had Christic apparition experiences exhibit. Percipients typically regard these peak religious experiences as among the most significant of their lives. They often consider them to have a transcendent source, and characteristically treat them with such reverence and awe that they divulge them on condition that neither they nor the experiences be subjected to ridicule or humiliation. I have not attempted to discover in the percipients I studied whether any significant correlation between sexual abstinence and the occurrence of Christic apparitions exists. I note only that in the small and self-selected sample of experiences I examined, two-thirds occurred when percipients were married (See Appendix II). This percentage is in sharp contrast to that reported by Carroll, but I concede that my sample is not as large as his.

Like other mentalistic theories, in any case, the psychoanalytical approach to explaining Christic apparitions is not adequate in its present form. It is, at best, a sketch for an explanation of a neurophysiological kind.

7 | Neurophysiological Explanations

Western culture has increasingly come to rely on specialized sciences to give us explanations, and the sorts of unusual phenomena that constitute (or once did) central elements in religious life are widely expected to be explained by sciences already in existence and developing rapidly. Human consciousness is considered by many in the scientific and philosophic communities to be susceptible to scientific explanation, and peak religious experiences, of which Christic apparitions would be one kind, are no exception.

The important question raised by the neural sciences is whether mechanisms internal to a percipient can explain all features of apparitions. Neurophysiological mechanisms are unquestionably *involved* in perceptual experiences of all kinds, including apparitions. Even substance-dualists hold that mental events *depend* upon, or are somehow linked with, those mechanisms, although dualists do not consider neurophysiology capable of exhausting the accounts of human experience. A person experiencing an apparition is thought to have central nervous system (CNS) activity in those areas of the brain associated with perception, belief formation, affective states, and so forth—similar to the CNS activity present in ordinary perception. The question is whether that CNS activity has its causal origins wholly within the percipient experiencing the apparition. This is not so in normal perception, where the stimulation of the cells that produce the CNS events constituting perception occurs from without. In normal perception the neurophysiological story takes over from the rest of the physical story at the point at which external stimuli impinge upon the surface of the body and produce the events that will be experienced as perceptions, whether visual, auditory, or somaesthetic. It seems natural to speculate that the causal origins of what are widely considered aberrant perceptual experiences might be found within an organism, rather than outside.

Experimental work and clinical observation have suggested various neurophysiological explanations for apparition experiences, but a survey of them shows that theorists generally use the conceptual resources of folk psychology and psychoanalysis as well. The complexity of human experience, as well as the practical demands of psychological diagnosis and treatment, leaves theorists and practitioners with no option currently but to combine conceptual frameworks. This mixing of frameworks makes for some fairly sketchy theorizing, and undoubtedly displeases theoretical purists such as eliminative materialists. Weston La Barre is illustrative of those who are confident that the developing sciences will be capable of providing explanations of mysterious religious phenomena. He writes:

We are confident there is no "supernatural" psychic event in tribal life anywhere that may not be better understood as a dissociated state—whether endogenous dream, vision, trance, REM state, sensory deprivation, hysteric "possession"—or as an hallucinatory activity of the brain, under the influence of exogenous psychotropic substances. Supposedly "divine revelation" of some spirit land is merely tapping the id-stream of primary process thinking, and should be approached not as a cosmological but as a psychiatric phenomenon. . . . Technically, supernatural information is misapprehended information about the mind itself. The Mystery is in fact only our own brains and minds, often in an altered state of consciousness; experiencing the "supernatural" is only a functionally differing *state of mind*. Only for the naive and psychologically nonself-perceptive person does hallucination appear to embody an epistemological problem. . . . Revelation, vision, divination are mere "supernormal" functions of the *sub*conscious, when the critical threshold of the more canny conscious mind is lowered in dissociative states.[1]

La Barre here exhibits tolerance for every conceptual framework except supernaturalism and perhaps substance-dualism. But accepting all these conceptual frameworks is not devoid of difficulties. Some philosophers would balk at the "category mistake" in his use of *mind*, as though mind were an object in the sense in which a brain is;[2] behaviorists would reject the explanatory value of such psychoanalytic concepts as id, ego, subconscious, and repression; eliminative materialists would reject the explanatory value of concepts deriving from folk psychology; psychiatrist L. J. West, well-known for his work on hallucinations, would question the lucidity of the concept of dissociative states (traditionally defined as representing the breakup of the stream of consciousness into diverse elements), unless his information-processing model were used to explicate it.[3] Eliminative materialists are to be given credit for insisting that a single set of well-integrated physicalistic concepts should be sought in order to describe and explain "the mental life," although it is questionable if their confidence will ever be rewarded. The following discussion of explanatory possibilities deriving from neurophysiological research will not be devoid of mentalistic concepts. Since *hallucination* is the operative term in this literature, I shall first comment on some of the linguistic and conceptual issues evoked by it.

Hallucination

The Oxford English Dictionary defines *hallucination* as "The apparent perception (usually by sight or by hearing) of an external object when no such object is actually present." It is an Anglicized form of the Latin *alucinari*, meaning "to wander in mind" or "to talk idly," and its first English use occurred in 1572 to refer to "ghostes and spirites walking by nyght."[4] Jean Esquirol introduced it to psychology and medicine as a technical term in 1838, defining it as "ascribing a body and actuality to images," with the implication that to hallucinate was to be "out of touch with reality" or to be insane.[5]

Sarbin and Juhasz remark that its use in medical contexts requires that a person other than the percipient make a judgment on a perceptual experience, and because the person passing judgment is usually in a position of greater status, "hallucination" places a negative evaluation on the experiences of another: "In the most typical case, the degraded status is that of a mental patient, an individual whose choice of metaphysical heterodoxy has been rejected by those who have the power—legitimate, coercive, or expert—to declare a negative valuation on the reported imagining and, by extension, on the imaginer."[6] They contend that the phenomenon has not been given adequate study, primarily because "the behaviors of therapists often function to freeze patients in the nonhuman role of mental patient. This follows from the unwillingness of conservative professionals to grant legitimacy to the fantasies of their patients."[7] They suggest that the scientist who wishes to encounter the phenomena as they occur must be willing to hold in abeyance the conventional categories of reality and scientific method.[8]

Hallucination is a theory-laden expression. It might appear to be straightforwardly descriptive, but in its conventional use it conceals many assumptions about what is real and what humans are capable of knowing. If we assert, for instance, that the person in *delirium tremens* who sees pink rats run across the floor is hallucinating, we imply that there are no external objects that causally produce these experiences. However, if this person should report a sensation of being bitten on the foot at the point where the pink rat is "seen," and become unsure about the pink rats' being hallucinatory, the claim that the experience is hallucinatory might become uncertain, particularly if simultaneous hallucinations in two sensory modalities is thought implausible. If blood were to be drawn (visible to all) at the point where the bite was felt, even though the experient would still be the only one to "see" the rat, or if cheese were to be nibbled, an external source would be indicated. Perhaps *delirium tremens* as it actually occurs does not (ever?) present the numerous complicating features just suggested. Reports of Christic apparitions contain much more complex elements, however. In maintaining that the experiences have their causal sources wholly within a percipient, apart from those contributing elements that result from previous sensory experience of external objects, we are making an implicit commitment to a reasonably large body of beliefs. Erwin Straus suggests this point about theory-ladenness when he remarks: "All statements about the illusory character of the sensory qualities and the reality of neural mechanisms are metaphysical propositions to be evaluated as parts of the whole metaphysical system to which they belong."[9]

The theory-laden character of hallucination reports is rarely mentioned in philosophical discussions. *Hallucination* is often treated as a straightforward descriptive term, with the accompanying suggestion that the hallucinatory phenomenon is easy to spot in real life. The examples used to illustrate it often have a disarming air of simplicity about them. *Delirium tremens* is a typical example, which is virtually stipulated to be hallucinatory: the possible complexities mentioned above, such as feeling bites, drawing blood, and finding cheese nibbled, are hardly ever discussed. Other typical examples are drawn from literature, such as the apparition of a dagger mentioned in Shakespeare's *Macbeth*. Because these examples are fictionalized or drawn from fiction, their hallucinatory character is in effect stipulated. Their value for illuminating the structure of the world of actual experience is limited.

Roland Fischer raises objections to the usual definition of hallucination, on the grounds that pulsed microwaves that induce clicking sounds, or magnetic fields that provoke phosphenes, or the flashes of light (produced by cosmic rays) reported by the Apollo astronauts in translunar flight are perceptions without objects, but the experience of these would not normally be counted as hallucination. So he proposes that the distinction between exteroceptive (externally derived) and interoceptive (internally derived) sensory experiences be made on the basis of a perception's capacity to be verified through "voluntary motor activity."[10] He does not elaborate on the precise test involving motor skills that might verify that perceptions are externally derived, but he might be thinking of attempts by percipients to grasp the objects that appear to them, or of attempts to test reality by looking away and then back again to see if the object still appears. But the first test would not be conclusive, for hallucinating in several sensory modalities at once is widely thought possible. The second test is more impressive, as I already indicated in the previous chapter.

Hallucination has come to be used in connection with a wide variety of phenomena, although the idea expressed in the dictionary definition remains central. G. Sedman subdivides hallucinations into the categories of imagery, pseudo-hallucinations (hallucinations that the percipient recognizes as such), and true hallucinations (hallucinations that the percipient does not recognize), subdividing each of these again based on the percipient having clear consciousness, being in a half-waking state, or having clouded consciousness.[11] But this group of categories does not elucidate the concept very much. Some sense of how broadly it is interpreted can be seen from the fact that the term is used of dreams,[12] the experiences of animals,[13] phantom limb experiences and vertigo,[14] anesthesia and erroneous evaluations of room temperature,[15] delusions of persecution, and sensory peculiarities such as buzzing sounds in one's ear, flashes of light, and impressions of darting movements at the periphery of one's vision.[16]

K. W. M. Fulford recently offered the following classification, to bring some order into the numerous phenomena said to be hallucinatory: (1) normal illusions, such as the bent appearance of a stick in water, (2) disruptions of perceptions caused by some physical cause, for example, "seeing stars" from a blow to the head, (3) physical symptoms, such as double vision, (4) distortion of perceptions caused by psychological factors, for example, the depressive who perceives an innocent remark as critical, (5) type-I pseudo-hallucinations: perceptions without a stimulus that are experienced as real, yet are located as originating inside one's head rather that in outside space, for example, a voice located as coming from inside one's left inner ear, (6) type-II pseudo-hallucinations: perceptions located as originating in outside space, yet not experienced as real, for example, the alcoholic with *delirium tremens* who sees snakes, yet knows they are not there, (7) normal hallucinations: brief hallucinatory perceptions in the absence of a stimulus, experienced as outside and as real at the time, as when a tired doctor, nearly asleep, hears a telephone ring, only to be assured by the hospital switchboard that she "must have imagined it," and (8) normal imagery: images so vivid as to be experienced in outside space and differing from other hallucinations inasmuch as one can change them by effort of will, (9) hysterical hallucinations and (10) visions.[17] Negative hallucinations—failing to see things that are present—are also occasionally mentioned by theorists.[18] It is apparent from this list that the concept is far from simple, and it seems doubtful that a single explanation could account for all of them. The fact that *hallucination* is used by researchers to refer to such a variety of experiences casts uncertainty on the relevance of their investigations to the limited phenomena under scrutiny in this book.

Many theorists openly embrace the idea that delusions and hallucinations may occur in degrees, and therefore suggest that a continuum be introduced for describing them. C. W. Savage observes that a continuity hypothesis has been part of general scientific and philosophic wisdom for a long time. This hypothesis asserts roughly that sensations, perceptions, hallucinations, dreams, fantasies, thoughts, and so on, differ not in kind but in degree—degree of vivacity, coherence, voluntariness, creativeness, concreteness, and veridicality.[19] This position has not been developed further, to my knowledge.

Roland Fischer has attempted a "cartography of inner space" in which various conscious states are mapped onto two perception-hallucination continua. These continua both begin with ordinary perception, but one identifies increasing levels of arousal, whereas the other describes decreasing levels. Both continua end with different hallucinatory states.[20] The first of Fischer's continua is marked by increased activity of the sympathetic nervous system. The state of arousal found in ordinary perception marks the low end of this continuum, and other states along it are sensitivity, creativity, anxiety, and, at the high end, mystical rapture. In the second continuum the states of arousal include the parasympathetic (involuntary) nervous system and result in behavior that reflects decreasing sensitivity to external stimuli. Here the arousal found in ordinary perception is at the high end of the spectrum, while the points along the continuum include states of increasing tranquillity identified in Sanskrit as *zazen* and ending with *nirvichar samadhi*. The aim of the state of *zazen* is to experience everything "on the same low level of subcortical arousal but nevertheless to be receptive and appreciating," whereas the aim of the state of deep meditation in *nirvichar samadhi* is to achieve an emptiness where there is "no form, no perception, no name, no concepts, no knowledge, [n]o eye, no ear, no nose, no tongue, no body, no mind . . . no sound, no smell, no taste, no touch, no objects . . . no knowledge, no ignorance, no decay nor death. It is the Self."[21] The meditative states along the second continuum are correlated by Fischer with beta, alpha, and theta EEG waves measured in hertz frequencies from twenty-six to four. Fischer describes the end points of the two continua, namely, mystical rapture and *nirvichar samadhi*, as "the two most hallucinatory states" known in human experience.[22]

In keeping with the belief that hallucinations occur in degrees, G. Launay and P. Slade developed a scale to measure the predisposition to hallucinate. The Launay-Slade Hallucination Scale was first developed based on research with male and female prisoners,[23] and was later tested using 150 male undergraduate students at a British university.[24] The scale requires responses to such statements as: "No matter how hard I concentrate, unrelated thoughts always creep into my mind," "Sometimes my thoughts seem as real as actual events in my life," "I often hear a voice speaking my thoughts aloud," "I have heard the voice of the devil," and "On occasion I have seen a person's face in front of me when no one was in fact there."[25] Numerical responses allow the predisposition to be given a quantitative value. Because persons without apparent psychopathologies were tested using this scale, Bentall considers the results of this work to be evidence that "hallucinations need not always be considered indicative of pathology."[26] The possibility that hallucinations might occur in degrees complicates the analysis of it considerably, both for theorizing and psychiatric practice. This issue does not admit of clear resolution at present, however, and I shall not take it further.

I shall work with the notion that experiences have either external or internal sources, even though this way of describing it is imprecise. The imprecision arises from the fact that an inner state could have external sources, such as sources in the early history of a percipient. Someone might hallucinate his parents after their deaths, for instance, and although the source of that hallucination at the time of its occurrence might be within the percipient, the memory of them originated from ordinary exteroceptive experiences earlier in life in which the parents were seen, touched, heard, and so on. Neurophysiologist V. B. Montcastle describes the role of previous sensory experience as follows: "At the level of sensation, your images and my images are virtually the same. . . . Beyond that, each image is conjoined with genetic and stored experiential information that makes each of us uniquely private. From that complex integral each of us constructs at a higher level of perceptual experience his own, very personal, view from within."[27]

Clinical observations link some hallucinations directly to physical conditions. Tumors and lesions of the temporal lobe seem to be the cause of some visual hallucinations, and gentle electrical stimulation of this lobe can also produce them.[28] Baldwin describes a case in which such stimulation of a seventeen-year-old male patient resulted in his having images of building a jet racer and hunting with his father, both experiences that he had had several years earlier. Baldwin explains: "As the stimulating electrode activated the depth of his left temporal lobe, he remembered these experiences with a striking sense of familiarity. . . . The scenes were in color and vividly portrayed, and he described them as if he were looking at a cinematic projection in color. Yet, during the description he was oriented to the reality of the environment and he recognized that the recollected scenes were somehow apart from it."[29] Baldwin also reports that some of his patients hallucinated in various sensory modalities, "with the scene before them often described as 'more real than real.' However, the patient is immediately aware of the unreality of the scene."[30] Other researchers report that hallucinations have been induced by sensory deprivation,[31] sleep deprivation,[32] and hypnosis.[33]

Some of the explanations for hallucinations developed in response to perceptual aberrations of various kinds, including the auditory, visual, and tactile. Others developed from examination of special groups, for example, people diagnosed with schizophrenia, and experimental subjects who ingest hallucinogenic drugs or undergo sensory deprivation. We should not assume that explanations for hallucinations arising from sensory deprivation, fasting, brain disease and lesions, obvious psychopathology, and neurological disorders, will be similar to explanations for hallucinations that are apparently spontaneous and unconnected with psychopathology. The value of explanations that arise from psychiatric and pharmacological studies might therefore be questioned; on the other hand, we would be myopic to ignore them in view of the insights they might provide.

Apparition experiences present many features, both aberrant and normal, that require explanation. Some of the aberrant elements found in Chapter 2 include features of the figure in the percipient's visual field, such as radiance, abnormal size, transparency, being motionless, producing auditions without moving the lips, and being an incomplete figure. Other aberrations include feelings of weightlessness and spatial anomalies, such as seeing an altered environment. Normal features of perceptual experience also require explanation, although familiarity with normal perception can obscure this fact. The accounts in Chapter 2 indicate that apparition experiences can seem quite normal in a number of respects. Many percipients indicated that the figure that appeared seemed to be of normal size and appearance for a man, that he obscured other objects and was obscured by them, that he moved and spoke in a normal way, that he communicated meaningful messages, that he seemed to fit in with the spatio-temporal world of the percipient, and that he occasionally seemed to interact with that world. Clearly, the individual facts of each experience need explanation, which is a challenge for any theory to meet.

When Alfred Heilbrun and Nancy Blum classified neurophysiological and psychological explanations a decade ago, they noted that there was little agreement among theorists about their respective merits.[34] The kinds of explanations they identified were are follows: (1) proposals based on psychoanalytic postulates, (2) psychodynamic theories, that is, theories that make reference to a complex set of psychological states, (3) hypotheses that stress the effects of deviant or ambiguous sensory input,[35] (4) theories positing defective cognitive attributes,[36] and (5) theories referring to heightened physiological arousal.[37] Since I have already discussed Freud's theory, which belongs to the first category, and Lauretta Bender's, which belongs to the second, I shall discuss representative explanations that broadly fall into the three remaining groups.

The Perceptual Release Theory

One of the basic ideas many neurophysiologists use to explain hallucinations is that information obtained through sensory perception is stored, altered, and then "released into consciousness" at a later time and experienced as a hallucination. This mechanism has been thought to be the basis for both dreams and hallucinations. Jean Esquirol proposed it in 1838, noting the significant similarity between the content of dreams and hallucinations.[38] Hughlings Jackson, a prominent late-nineteenth-century British neurologist, also advanced this position,[39] as did Freud.[40] Madge and Arnold Scheibel, in their work on the brain stem reticular core, assume that the mechanisms underlying hallucinations are the same as, or overlap with, those that produce dreams, eidetic images, and intense memory images.[41] L. J. West concurs, and calls this explanation for hallucinations the *perceptual release theory*. I shall present it in the form developed by Ernest Hartmann, who bases it on the work of various other theorists, including West.

Hartmann says that hallucinations are so ubiquitous that the marvel is that we do not hallucinate all of the time. He defines the term in the usual way, and notes that hallucinations therefore include dreams, the sensations that a person has when one's eyes are closed, hypnagogic sensations (images that sometimes precede falling asleep), the sensations brought on by chemical stimuli including hallucinogens and alcohol, and the disorders accompanying various psychiatric illnesses. He sees these phenomena as occasions in which "the balance between positive forces tending to produce hallucinations and negative (inhibitory) forces is appropriately shifted—in the direction of greater positive forces and/or less inhibition."[42] The positive forces that tend to produce them are overwhelming wishes or needs, such as a wish to eliminate conflict. Someone in a conflict situation might "externalize" the internal reality, and so begin to feel better. Hartmann suggests that the dream is the prototype of the hallucination. This implies that an understanding of hallucinations can be obtained by considering the distinctive features of dreams, especially when compared to states of wakefulness.

Hartmann notes some obvious similarities between dreams and states of wakefulness: In both dreams and wakeful states we are able to have sensory experience in all modalities, and also emotional states of various kinds.[43] But differences are also obvious: In dreams we find primarily simple and primitive emotions such as anger, joy, and anxiety, whereas wakeful states include many complex emotions; dreams do not exhibit the subtle and modulated emotions that depend on feedback and interaction with others, and the shifts in emotion in a dream can be more abrupt than similar shifts experienced in waking life; the sense of being free, so much a feature of waking life, is generally missing in dreams, as is the ability to shift attention among several objects.[44] Another striking feature of dream experience is the inability to engage in reality testing, which also depends on feedback and interaction. Hartmann notes that the person with an acute drug-induced hallucinatory delirium cannot engage in reality testing at all, and remarks that the chronic paranoid schizophrenic might be capable of fairly good reality testing apart from one encapsulated area of experience in which the patient may have delusions and hear voices.[45]

Hartmann suggests that the essential mechanism in hallucinations consists of "releasing into consciousness" various pieces of information, originally derived from sensory experience, that have been stored and altered. The neurophysiological activities thought to be involved are those in the brain stem, including some originating in the pontine brain stem that bombard the cerebral cortex, possibly the visual area.[46] Hartmann further speculates that defects in the norepinephrine systems involved in neurotransmission could account for some forms of hallucination, and believes that the chemical substructure of such functions as reality testing might be found in the ascending norepinephrine systems that extend to the cerebral cortex. Though the *perceptual release theory* on its own is considered by some theorists to provide an explanation of hallucinations, the ideas central to this theory have found their way into more complex theories, such as the information processing theory.

The Information Processing Theory

Mardi Horowitz suggests four main determinants in understanding how and why hallucinations occur. The first fact that must be recognized about hallucinations is that they are a form of image representation.[47] An image is information that remains after a perceptual event has taken place, capable of being combined with other information derived from memory, thinking, and fantasy. Horowitz contrasts image representation with representation of enactive and lexical kinds.[48] Enactive representation is a remembered motor response to a specific kind of stimulus situation, for example, withdrawing from a painful stimulus. Lexical representation consists of forming concepts that have neither associated actions nor images, such as concepts involving high levels of abstraction. Image representation, however, is the important category for understanding hallucinatory experience. All of the major sensory systems produce image subsystems that are capable of being activated by electrical, mechanical, or chemical stimulation. This can be done, for instance, by stimulating the neural tract between the eyes and the cortex. Subcortical stimulation might not only reactivate particular memories but stimulate a sudden increase in image thinking. But images can be generated by psychological stimuli as well. Horowitz notes that Freud used to place his hand on a patient's forehead, "commanding" the patient to have and report visual pictures when he released the pressure.[49]

The second determinant in image formation is the capacity of the image-forming systems to obtain information from both internal and external origins. Horowitz describes this as *a dual-input model of image formation*. Experimental evidence shows that normal subjects can confuse internal and external signals when the latter are vague or dim. Some subjects who were shown a red circle, for instance, could be induced to report it as the New York skyline at dusk or as a tomato plant, depending on what suggestions were made by the experimenter.[50] Horowitz takes this to imply that image formation and perception share some of the same neural processes. He says that upon entering a hallucinatory state, a percipient blends information coming from internal and external origins. When the images that derive from the fantasy or from memory become intrusive, the percipient may attempt to "stabilize a sense of reality through the use of checking manoeuvres, including changes in perception (looking "harder," closing the eyes, looking away) and in thought (trying to suppress the image, trying to think of something else, evaluating the probability of such events being real)."[51] As the intensity of these images increases, the person might try to label the experience as nonperceptual, with the reassuring thought, "I know it can't be so." In the most advanced stage of hallucination, the percipient reacts to the intense images as if they were real.

Horowitz uses West's perceptual release theory to explain the mechanism involved: Hallucinations occur because of "an intensification or 'release' of images of internal origin when external image formation decreases but the representational system is still 'on.'"[52]According to this theory a sustained level of sensory experience is normally required to inhibit the emergence of percepts and memory traces from within the brain itself. When external stimulation falls below a certain threshold, but cortical arousal remains constant, previously recorded perceptions are released into awareness and are experienced there as hallucinations. West notes, for instance, that when a mystic reduces sensory input by deliberately withdrawing from the outside world, this allows visions to emerge into awareness.[53] West identifies two prerequisites for released perceptions to become conscious with hallucinatory vividness: "First there must be a sufficient general level of arousal for awareness to occur. Second, the particular perception-bearing circuits must reverberate sufficiently to command awareness."[54] The first prerequisite refers to the degree to which the representational system is active. This system allows a percipient to experience perceptions that (normally) represent objects. If it is relatively inactive, the stored perceptions released into consciousness will be experienced only as fantasies or illusions; if it is active, these perceptions will be experienced as dreams or hallucinations: "The greater the level of arousal, the more vivid the hallucination will be."[55] West's second prerequisite is enigmatic as it stands, but he means by it that the neural mechanisms responsible for perceptual experiences of particular kinds must be sufficiently active to attract the attention of the percipient. While the brain is always active, those systems associated with perception must be particularly active. Penfield brought this about experimentally by stimulating the temporal lobe of patients so vivid scenario-like imagery was created. But other circumstances can change the forces that ordinarily dominate consciousness so that the emergence of previously recorded percepts is no longer inhibited.

Ronald Siegel and Murray Jarvik propose mechanisms similar to those identified by West and Horowitz in their account of hallucinations, which they call *the experiential projector theory*. According to this theory, sensory input obtained in normal ways is "transformed, reduced, elaborated, stored, retrieved, and used," with the result that the output becomes projected in experience in the form of images, dreams, and hallucinations.[56] When the level of cortical arousal is low, this result is weak thought images. But higher levels of arousal can yield information that appears to the percipient to be projected on a sensory field outside the body, especially if other sensory inputs are reduced, for example, by being in dim light, or having one's eyes closed, or having recently experienced sensory deprivation. Images are retrieved from memory and are then altered to conform to cultural determinants.[57] Siegel and Jarvik suggest that because their theory refers to CNS mechanisms found in all people, it might explain the archetypes that Carl Jung said were part of humanity's collective unconscious.

The third factor in Horowitz's theory is the susceptibility of the information processing system to becoming impaired. When images are formed, several stages of information processing are automatically engaged. For example, when visual sensation takes place, the percipient assesses the image to determine whether it is real or has been seen before, evaluates the object that is imaged as dangerous, gratifying, and so on, and also establishes the spatial characteristics of the image.[58] Experiments show that percipients who have never experienced a certain image will be more likely to label the experience hallucinatory than those who have already experienced it.[59] Moreover, the brevity and the ambiguity of an image experience can also contribute to its being considered hallucinatory. Horowitz observes: "When the episode is brief, there is insufficient time for appraisal, in addition to poor memory encoding. These conditions foster misinterpretation, especially during states of cognitive impairment or high conflict."[60] Heilbrun and Blum note that everyone occasionally experiences some disorder that could increase the risk of hallucination. For instance, the mechanism that assigns meaning to ambiguous stimuli can be deficient, or one might be forced to use a weak sensory modality, for example, when the hearing impaired find that their only source of vital information is auditory.[61]

The fourth factor that contributes to the emergence of intrusive images is impairment of cognitive functions.[62] Horowitz notes that much clinical evidence supports the claim that shocking visual perceptions can be repeated in waking life long after the initial experience is over. For example, combat veterans often relive their terrifying experiences, skiers sometimes report kinaesthetic images of lifting and turning long after they have stopped skiing, and drivers report visual images of headlights after night driving. These episodes often enter awareness without intention, and resist conscious efforts to prevent their recurrence. Horowitz suggests that hallucinations may also represent emotional states, directly or symbolically. For example, a person who is fearful of others may hallucinate monsters, a person fearful of herself may "give concreteness to vague ideas of disintegration as fragmented or diseased body images," an angry person may hallucinate destructive scenes, and a despairing person will try to relieve sadness by hallucinating replicas of lost objects.[63] These all represent instances in which cognitive abilities are impaired, thus contributing to image formation.

Horowitz considers the mechanisms related to image formation and interpretation to be varied enough to explain many kinds of hallucinatory experiences, but he considers hallucinations too complex for a single model or a succinct explanation.

The Overactive Reticular System Theory

The reticular system is a tight, complex network of fibers at a point where the spinal cord ends and the brain begins. A site of vital brain activity, it is causally related to sleep and arousal, reflexes and muscle tone, and with the organization of the brain as a whole.[64] This portion of the brain is always active, contributing to the homeostasis that is essential to the continuation of life itself.[65] The theory of hallucinations developed by Frank Fish is based upon his observation of schizophrenics, whose reticular systems are overactive. This overactivity causes abnormal events in cell assemblies that are experienced as hallucinations.

A cell assembly is a diffuse structure made up of cells that can briefly act as a closed structure.[66] According to Fish's theory, various cell assemblies are causally linked to one another and to sensory events to produce the organized sequence of events that constitutes the waking life of a normal person. When a person is asleep, another organization among cell assemblies occurs. The cell assemblies are normally well-organized, but disorganization is possible. Fish says that the hallucinations of schizophrenics occur as a result of overactivity of the reticular system, resulting in certain cell assemblies being closer than usual to their firing threshold. When a sensory event occurs, the cell assemblies that are activated acquire greater significance than they normally would, and produce a new set of cell assemblies capable of later becoming active independently of the sensory input that led to their development in the first place. Because this new set of cell assemblies is not well-integrated into the central processes that are part of normal experience, it is not associated with the sense of self that is part of the central processes. So when the new set of cell assemblies is later triggered, producing a hallucination, it is experienced as foreign.[67] Fish describes these new cell assemblies as forming a parallel and interfering process, but one that need not be permanent. Moreover, this interfering process could be active on its own, or occur at the same time as the normal central process. In this way Fish attempts to account for various kinds of hallucinatory experiences, including ones in which the whole sensory domain is abnormal, as in Group II visions, and others in which only portions of it are, as in Group III visions.

Fish says that research has shown that when the reticular system is stimulated, visual clues are better perceived, and the visual cortex becomes more responsive to sensory stimulation. He concludes from this that sensory events would assume much greater significance under reticular stimulation, and that such stimulation would tend to produce a disorganization in the normal sequence of cell assemblies. Fish considers reticular overactivity to be the cause of schizophrenia because the ingestion of amphetamine, which is known to stimulate the reticular system, can produce a psychosis in normal people that "is clinically indistinguishable from paranoid schizophrenia," and because this drug also worsens the symptoms in schizophrenia.[68]

This theory offers some interesting suggestions for the mechanisms that might be involved in hallucinations of various kinds. The observations about the effects of drugs naturally raise important questions about the relationship between drugs and hallucinations, and with this topic I shall conclude my survey of various neurophysiological mechanisms thought to be involved in the hallucinatory experience.

Pharmacology and Hallucinations

The capacity of pharmaceuticals to produce hallucinations suggests that spontaneous hallucinations might be caused by natural hallucinogens. Moreover, the fact that the hallucinations of schizophrenics can be reduced by medications that block neural receptors[69] suggests a neurochemical base to the experience. A generation ago Aldous Huxley attracted public attention to the hallucinatory effects of mescaline in his account of his own experience in *The Doors of Perception* and *Heaven and Hell*. He suggests links between visions and biochemical changes, conjecturing, for instance, that excess carbon dioxide through suppressed breathing or prolonged singing, and insufficient vitamins, due to dietary imbalances or fasting, might have been the sources of many medieval visionary experiences.[70]

Irwin Feinberg conducted a study of the effects of mescaline and LSD on schizophrenic patients in order to determine whether drug-induced visual phenomena were similar to their other hallucinatory experiences.[71] The visual aberrations that frequently follow the ingestion of these drugs were present, such as lattices, cobwebs, tunnels, alleys, vessels, spirals, and "geometricized" objects.[72] Other common visual effects were alterations in color, fluctuation in the size and shape of the perceived objects, and synaesthesia, that is, the "mixing" of perceptual experiences so that grass is "heard" to grow, colors have smells, and so forth. But the visual hallucinations of these patients were rather different when they were not influenced by drugs. The lattice and cobweb forms were almost invariably absent, as was distortion of color. Synaesthesia was not found, and distortion of movement was rare. Feinberg found that the phenomenological content of the spontaneous hallucinations was also quite different: Patients saw a wall waver, or saw people undulate as though they were snakes; they sometimes had brief, reassuring glimpses of familiar people; and they saw "creatures of their own imagination" that satisfied their need for companionship.[73] Feinberg notes that the percipient's environment was sometimes found to be distorted, or it remained unchanged but something was added to it, such as an angel in one case. In some spontaneous hallucinations the normal environment was obliterated, and only the hallucinated objects were seen.

Feinberg grants that drug-induced hallucinations might resemble those typical of schizophrenia in important respects, but he notes four general differences. First, visual hallucinations of schizophrenia appear suddenly, but those of LSD and mescaline "are heralded by unformed visual sensations, simple geometric figures, and alterations of color, size, shape, movement and number."[74] Also, in schizophrenia, hallucinations occur in a psychic setting of intense emotional need or delusional preoccupation, but drug-induced hallucinations develop independently of such emotional needs, or produce their own affective changes. Third, schizophrenic hallucinations are generally seen with open eyes, but those of mescaline and LSD are more readily seen with eyes closed or in darkened surroundings. And last, schizophrenic hallucinations may be superimposed on a normal visual environment, or, more rarely, may appear with the remainder of the environment excluded, but drugs produce distortions of the existing world. Feinberg notes that research shows that LSD interferes with the transmission of neural impulses through the lateral geniculate.[75] This could explain why those who ingest it see distortions of the existing world. Similar differences between the drug-induced hallucinations of normal persons and the hallucinations of schizophrenics have also been confirmed in the experimental work of Eugene Bliss and Lincoln Clark. But Bliss and Clark found that schizophrenics have visual hallucinations infrequently, and when they occur they are almost always monochromatic, rather than richly colored.[76]

One other interesting finding that Feinberg reports shows the poor integration of auditory and visual features in spontaneous hallucinations: "When an hallucinated person appeared to speak, his lips would not be seen to move as in ordinary conversation, and, at best, the voice would appear to emanate from the direction of the hallucination."[77] Other sensory modalities besides hearing and seeing demonstrated a similar lack of genuine integration, although Feinberg mentions a case in which a patient's visual and tactile sensations of spiders crawling on his arm were well-integrated.[78] Baldwin also mentions that sound and color rarely blended in the hallucinatory experiences of his patients with neurological diseases.[79]

Extensive research is being conducted on the neurochemical basis of human experience. The complexity of human neurophysiology, and the puzzling character of hallucinations, given the broad use of this term, allows only some tentative observations and comments.

Neurophysiology and Christic Apparitions

All of the proposals or suggestions coming from neurophysiology are sketches of yet-to-be-completed explanations. None purports to give a complete account, especially not of those aberrant experiences that involve various sensory domains at once. Eccles observed in 1977 that no full understanding had been acquired of the mechanisms at work in the combined experience of hearing, seeing, and somaesthetic sensation. He remarks that because interaction obviously takes place, it must occur in cortical areas to which the areas responsible for these sensations project.[80] Of course other levels of integration are involved when memory and motor activity also occur. Most of the Christic apparition experiences described in Chapter 2 involved a rich interplay of sensory perception, motor activity, and cognitive thought, so an explanation wholly internal to a percipient, if it was adequate, would be very complex. H. B. Barlow remarks that the mechanisms that neurophysiologists know about are largely local in scope, and that the main gap is explaining what "gives unity to our perceptions and prevents them [from] consisting of many small, isolated fragments."[81] Neurophysiological mechanisms will be at work in all of the sensory experiences of visionaries, for the appropriate cortical areas can be expected to be active as percipients see, hear, feel, and experience emotions. But the central question is whether the primary source of the experience is from within the percipient or from without. I say "primary source" in order to take account of the place that internal mechanisms have in all experience. The question whether the external senses are stimulated in an apparition experience is one that seems capable, in principle, of being answered. I drew attention at the end of Chapter 1 to the kind of scientific scrutiny that would be required.

Christic apparitions apparently are rather different from drug-induced hallucinations. The latter tend to consist of seeing geometric figures, or distortions of the existing world, rather than seeing conventional forms, perhaps in settings that do not appear conventional. Christic apparitions exhibit some of the characteristics of the experiences of those diagnosed with schizophrenia, for auditory elements are not often accompanied by movement of the lips of the Christic figure, and the normal background is occasionally obliterated completely. But they often differ from the hallucinations of schizophrenia in a number of significant ways. Christic apparitions are often colored,[82] they integrate various senses quite well, and they do not always occur in a context marked by intense emotional need or delusional preoccupation. Moreover, the percipients that I interviewed did not fit the profile of people diagnosed with schizophrenia, for they were well integrated into society, often held down responsible positions, and so on. They fit the profile of normal people who have aberrant perceptions. The large study of hallucinations carried out in Great Britain at the turn of the last century showed that 9.9 percent of the 17,000 normal persons questioned reported visual, auditory, or tactile hallucinations, or some combination of these.[83] D. J. West's similar study some fifty years later reported that 14.3 percent of a sample group of 1,519 normal persons had experienced a hallucination.[84] That normal people hallucinate is also the assessment of R. P. Bentall and collaborators.[85]

Neither the perceptual release theory nor the other explanatory strategies developed by neurosciences seem capable now of accounting for those Christic apparitions in which percipients repeatedly see the apparition figure in one place after turning their eyes away. It is doubtful, for instance, that perceptual releases of exactly the same kind, or an experience of cognitive impairment would consistently coincide with the orientation of the percipient's head.

Group apparition experiences also seem incapable of being adequately explained in neurophysiological terms, although we might *just* be able to imagine that two or more might hallucinate the same object at the same time. A group apparition of Mary recently was reported from Medjugorje, and a team of French doctors is said to have "documented a simultaneous fixing of the gaze in an identical point, with eye movement ending at the same time."[86] They offered no explanation for this unusual phenomenon, which surely cannot be traceable to the simultaneous experience of perceptual releases, cognitive impairment, or some mental state such as stress. Group hallucinations are conceivable, but do not provide a plausible explanation for a collective perceptual experience. Such an explanation would call into question conventional views about ordinary perception, because shared perceptual experience is basic to our judgment of what is real. Group apparitions provide strong evidence for an external source, as do apparitions that penetrate the spatio-temporal order.

Neurophysiology holds out some promise for explaining a number of apparition experiences, however. It appears to be a strong contender for experiences falling into the first three groups identified in Chapter 2, apart from those cases in which percipients could look away from and back to the apparition figure. It also appears to be capable of handling cases falling into Group V. I suspect that many Christians of a scientific bent would welcome neurophysiological explanations for visionary experiences. The value of these experiences would then not lie in the transcendent realities to which they might point, but in their symbolic value. The symbolic value of a vision of Jesus would perhaps lie in its confirmation of the values with which he is associated, or its capacity to bring a sense of loving comfort, or the belief that life has meaning. These are values that enhance human life, and even if the visionary experience served no other purpose, they would be important.

Neurophysiology will doubtless continue to shed light on the aberrant perceptions that are part of human life, including religious life. But so far, no single idea within neurophysiology provides an explanatory principle for these experiences.

8 | Interpreting Christic Visions and Apparitions

The Christian faith, like its Judaic progenitor, has its source in mysterious experiences interpreted as encounters with a transcendent domain. The Hebrew Bible recounts no fewer than a dozen incidents in the lives of Abraham, Isaac, Jacob, and Moses, the first patriarchs of Judaism, in which God was allegedly encountered in a dream, a vision, or in something even more concrete.[1] These constitute some of the central events in what Jews and Christians interpret as God's covenant with "his people." The New Testament purports to represent a covenant with all humanity. Central to it is the person of Jesus, understood in relation to his remarkable life and mission, as well as his supposed Resurrection evidenced in post-Resurrection encounters. Just as the history of Judaism has been marked with further theophanies to selected individuals, so the history of Christianity has described various Christic visions and apparitions. Several tentative conclusions can be drawn about them.

Christic visions are evidently more common than is ordinarily believed, although a lack of documentation currently makes this conclusion unprovable. The numerous accounts of recent experiences in the books by Sparrow and the Huyssens indicate that they may happen quite often, and the fact that so many of the percipients I interviewed were in British Columbia, a province with fewer than four million inhabitants, suggests that they are quite ubiquitous.[2] Christic visions seem to occur to people who are unlikely to be classified as "saints," and who would resist being described in that way. The visions often occur quite spontaneously, rather than being generated by deliberate efforts to produce them through fasting, oxygen deprivation, focused meditation, or other similar techniques. These experiences likely have significant religious import for those who have them, though this conclusion must be qualified in view of the possibility that only those persons who attached religious significance to their visions would respond to an attempt such as ours to inquire further into them. This goes contrary to received views about the significance of Christic visions, however, and I personally think that they generally have great import for those who experience them.

These experiences vary considerably in phenomenological character, ranging from "encounters" that exhibit the fleeting and tenuous features of dreams to experiences that are virtually indistinguishable from those that mark the ordinary perception of public objects. A rich variety falls between these extremes. The content of percipients' experiences is probably influenced by their background religious beliefs, such as how Jesus should look and what he would wear, but the variety is interesting despite this. Claims about some of the groupings or categories must remain tentative, in view of the small number of cases available for critical reflection. This is particularly significant with respect to cases classified previously as Group IV experiences, whose relevance for reflection on ontological questions is of great importance.

The relationship between contemporary Christic visions and the phenomena that appear to lie behind the NT writings is unclear. However, the sharp distinction between NT appearances and visions commonly made by Christian theologians is questionable. Moreover, the experiences that continue to be reported seem to resemble appearances, so-called, as much as they do visions. Contemporary experiences illuminate elements of the NT documents, but they also accentuate difficulties in them, such as the peculiar character of the narratives as history, and the unwillingness of their authors to provide much phenomenological detail. The phenomena occurring today may feasibly be seen as part of a continuous history of similar experiences that began with what Christians describe as the post-Resurrection appearances of Jesus, however these are to be understood.

Various theorists endorse the cautious exploration of transcendent possibilities. Gardner Murphy has observed that science is quite good at explaining phenomena in "the time-space-motion-energy domain," but is challenged when something is encountered that is not part of this domain and appears to transcend it. He recommends that we tie that which we are forced to describe as "unknown" to that which is known, as best we can, but he also says that we should also be prepared to consider "whether *new principles*—utterly and genuinely new principles—may be necessary in order to give a rounded interpretation."[3] Nevill Drury says that visionary experiences remind us that the universe has dimensions that are less tangible than the world known by ordinary perception: "There are many planes of reality available to human perception; . . . our normal consciousness restricts us to but a small range within the spectrum of experiential possibilities."[4] Philosopher of science Paul Feyerabend has recently suggested that we might reasonably reject the demand that the world views implicit in such ancient writings as the Bible or the *Iliad* be demythologized; rather, we might consider them as possible alternatives to scientific cosmologies.[5] I wish to take up this suggestion, further outlining the reasons for giving transcendentalism serious attention, and stressing the value of an empirical approach.

Intimations of Transcendence

One obvious reason for considering a transcendent source as the cause of Christic visions is that such a source is widely considered a possible explanation for many other phenomena. A transcendent being is widely thought to be the ultimate source of the cosmos and its design, as well as of elements of human life, such as the occurrence of the concept of God itself, the capacity for morality, and the occurrence of religious experience. Philosophers have defended theism on the basis of such phenomena as the conversion experiences described by William James, the numinous phenomena studied by Rudolf Otto, and mystical experiences described by such authors as Evelyn Underhill, W. T. Stace, and R. C. Zaehner. The diverse phenomena collected by the Alister Hardy Research Center at Oxford University could be adduced,[6] and perhaps also some of the phenomena investigated in psychical research, although many of these studies have been construed as supporting the survival hypothesis, not the existence of a transcendent being in another sense. Numerous phenomena have been thought to be incapable of explanation in physicalistic terms.

Sociologist Peter Berger claims that many signals of transcendence exist in the "natural" domain. These are phenomena that "are to be found within the domain of our 'natural' reality but that appear to point beyond that reality."[7] His list includes a sense that there is order in the universe; a sense evoked by joyful play that one has stepped from time into eternity; the hope that there might be another world, kindled by courageous acts in desperate situations; the belief that there is another world in which justice is meted out to those who commit the most heinous moral outrages; and a sense that human finitude will ultimately be overcome. Berger emphasizes that he is reflecting on human experiences that are common, rather than those that are exceptional, such as mystical experience. But he does not exclude the evidential significance of such special experiences.

The claim that the transcendent is encountered in common experiences seems to me plausible primarily because of *uncommon* phenomena suggestive of transcendence, such as the numinous and mystical phenomena studied by Otto and James. It is very questionable whether the common experiences cited by Berger would by themselves provide a plausible basis for maintaining the reality of a transcendent "domain," for many of them seem to be explicable on other grounds.

What is particularly attractive about Berger's approach is his insistence that the starting point for the investigation of religion should be an empirical anthropology. He shares James's attitude toward the study of religious experience, which Robert McDermott summarizes in the following principles: (1) a commitment to reconcile science and religion, (2) a radically empirical approach, (3) a belief that both science and religion give provisional conclusions to ultimate questions, and (4) a belief that knowledge has a personal and subjective character.[8] James's own words on the matter are as follows: "Let empiricism once become associated with religion, as hitherto, through some strange misunderstanding, it has been associated with irreligion, and I believe that a new era of religion as well as of philosophy will be ready to begin."[9]

Hans Küng mentions other common experiences that are "signals of transcendence," including experiences of distress and loneliness, silence, absolute responsibility, unconditional love, unpardonable guilt, and seeing oppressed people liberated.[10] He speaks about his own experience of encountering the transcendent in art, especially music, remarking that there is "only the thinnest of dividing lines between music, the most spiritual of all the arts, and religion, which has always had a close relationship with music."[11] He remarks that religious ecstasy and mystical experience can also be legitimate encounters with the transcendent—with God—although he cautions against interpreting such experiences as providing direct knowledge of God's nature.

Alister Hardy takes up the issue about an evidential basis for transcendence in the words: "Perhaps the greatest question from the psychology of religion is whether the power that may be called God is entirely within the individual—deep in the subconscious—or is, at least in part, transcendent."[12] He thinks that telepathy shows that our minds might be in touch with some larger mental field "possibly like that of the shared subconscious suggested by Jung, beyond our individual selves, or perhaps with something inconceivably greater," such as "a non-material world in which perhaps the numinous . . . might be thought to lie."[13]

Tentative Transcendence

If consideration is given to a transcendental explanation for phenomena that are otherwise inexplicable, I suggest that it be viewed as *supplementing* theories provided by the existing sciences, rather than simply providing an overarching structure for describing and explaining all phenomena. In Chapter 5, I explained how monotheism often serves such an overarching function, but this is not the way in which I would approach a transcendent cause. I would interpret it as a hypothesis designed to account for a limited class of phenomena for which current physicalistic explanations are inadequate. Such tentativeness is required by an empirical approach to the study of religious experience. William James was right to insist that experience is primary, and that religion is an interpretation of that,[14] and Alister Hardy makes much the same point when he writes: "Any authority declaring the nature of God in the sacred writings of the various religions of the world is derived from the experience of the holy men of each of these particular faiths. All such authority is based upon original experience."[15] Both were right to call for a more systematic study of the experience that gives intimations of a divine or transcendent source.

If perceptual religious experiences such as visions have a transcendent cause, it is still unreasonable to suppose that such experiences would give us "the whole truth" about that transcendent cause. For instance, even if we suppose that the post-Resurrection appearances of Jesus took place as traditionalists think, using the normal perceptual abilities of sight, touch, and hearing, it is unreasonable to suppose that these perceptual experiences informed percipients about the "real character" of the resurrected body. Physics and physiology show us that our perceptual capacities select only a narrow band of the information that is reaching us, and shape it in uniquely human ways. We have known for a long time, for instance, that colors are not features of objects the way which shapes are. A critical realist can speak about real objects being blue, for instance, but knows that this way of speaking conceals numerous complexities of what it is about light sources (photons), surface properties of objects (refractive properties of electron shells), retinal cells, and central nervous system events, that causes in normal perceivers the experience of what is commonly called "seeing blue." If we cautiously advance the possibility that there might be some form of transcendent being that significantly impinges upon human life, we will be forced to say that it is "a something we know not quite what." The belief that perception mirrors reality in some straightforward way is evidently mistaken, if our insights into ordinary perception are trustworthy here.

John White describes his Christic visions as symbols of a transcendent reality that involve the normal workings of his brain. This remark embodies a reasonable stance on their interpretation, particularly if *symbol* is taken to imply that one thing stands for something else, not by exact resemblance, but by vague suggestion.[16] Referring to Christic visions as *symbols* avoids asserting that the experiences "mirror" reality, but it simultaneously implies that there is a reality that they represent. At the same time, this position allows full consideration to be given to the neurophysiological mechanisms implicated in the visionary experience.

An empirical investigation of a phenomenon is compatible with proposing a transcendent explanation for it. Even the NT figures and writers implied the legitimacy of this approach by presenting the post-Resurrection appearances as perceptual events, and trying to show their place in the space-time continuum. For instance, the theory that Christic visions occur because "Jesus has become a life-giving spirit," to quote St. Paul once more, could be interpreted empirically, providing that this posit were causally linked to objects in space-time and given properties that evolve with observation. The concept of observation is complex and changing, as philosophers of science have come to recognize, so it is possible that it could be coherently used of this unique posit. Philosopher Dudley Shapere reports that physicists now routinely speak of "observing" the center of the sun, based upon the information obtained from neutrinos collected in carbon tetrachloride vats.[17] J. C. Yates's discussion of the space Jesus might exist in exemplifies the kind of empirical approach I am advocating. Yates opts for the view that Jesus might exist in our own space-time continuum, not in another space, as some philosophers have proposed, since the latter view has not been characterized adequately.[18] This discussion brings physics into theological debate, and allows ever-expanding knowledge of the space-time order to influence religious beliefs. This posited being would have continuity with a "normal" historical being by being linked to the historical Jesus, whatever the content of that history is determined by historians to be. While Christian theists would naturally want to interpret this posit within their historical trinitarian tradition, this part of the interpretation could be bracketed for purposes of exploring its empirical character. Christic "encounters" could be interpreted independently of trinitarianism, perhaps even monotheism, although I am not advocating such interpretations. I suggest that such a transcendent theory forms a plausible competitor to the proposals coming out of the neural sciences.

Jung's theory also suggests that Christic visions are symbolic of a transcendent realm, although its superiority to the transcendental theory just sketched would be cast into doubt by the occurrence of phenomena that penetrate the space–time order. Jung's theory does not appear to do justice to these phenomena. But his theory leans toward giving credence to a transcendent interpretation of the unusual, powerful, and universal experiences that form elements in religious belief systems.

The possibility of deceptive visions requires some comment. Two basic kinds of deception need to be recognized. The first is physical deception, inferred from experiences like those of St. Martin in which Jesus appeared without stigmata.[19] These experiences are taken to be deceptive because the image supposedly fails to reflect adequately the reality that is there. But if visions are symbols of a transcendent reality, and are not expected to mirror that reality because the requirement of mirroring reality is too stringent, variations of this kind are not really problematic. A vision of Jesus that is larger than life, say, or without distinct facial features or marks of crucifixion, can be a symbol of a transcendent reality provided a percipient interprets it that way. St. Martin's insistence that to be Jesus the one who appeared to him had to display stigmata puts undue emphasis on the physical form. It seems that the Dominican theologians who scrutinized the visions of Teresa of Avila were also unduly preoccupied with the physical form in which Jesus was seen.[20] But deception of another kind seems possible. Van Dusen described an incident in which the being encountered in a vision claimed to be Jesus, but exhibited character traits, such as bragging and argumentativeness, implying that it belonged to "the lower order." This kind of deception has also been the object of the Christian church's worry, perhaps its overriding one. It is significant that Van Dusen's evaluation of the vision was made on the basis of the moral characteristics exhibited. This suggests that the important kind of deception belongs to the domain of values and ethics, and is consistent with the common belief among Christians that visions can be evaluated by their effects, especially their effects upon percipients. His reference to "the lower order" implies a kind of "transcendence" that is evil in character, rather than good. Clearly, the notion of deceptive vision involves one both in ontological questions and in value judgments of the most complex kinds. It requires establishing plausible standards of moral goodness, and an evaluation of the evidence for the existence of diabolical forces in the universe. I shall not explore these important topics here, but note only that they would require an examination of an extensive world view at variance with physicalism, as well as an evaluation of controversial kinds of evidence.

A comment is needed, finally, on the curious phenomenon of percipients "knowing instantly" who it was that appeared to them. This is quite inexplicable, suggesting a kind of experience that is self-disclosing or revelatory. The existence of *God* has long been regarded by theorists in the antievidentialist school of theological thought as having that character. Philosopher Alvin Plantinga is best-known among its most recent advocates, but earlier proponents include John Calvin, Soren Kierkegaard, and Karl Barth.[21] Plantinga says that reading the Bible could give one the sense that God is speaking, and that unethical conduct could similarly evoke the belief that there is a God who disapproves, so in these kinds of ways the belief that God exists could arise and also be justified.[22] William Alston has also argued that the experience or perception of God is epistemically similar to perception of physical objects. For example, just as I am justified in claiming that my dog is wagging his tail because something is occurring that looks as if my dog is wagging his tail, so I am justified in claiming that I am experiencing God because that is how the experience presents itself.[23] It must be acknowledged, however, that "knowing instantly" that Jesus (or perhaps an incarnation of God whose conventional name is not known) has appeared is different from "knowing instantly" that God exists and has been encountered, although it is imaginable that certain Christian theists might want to minimize such differences in view of the claims about incarnation that have been a part of historical Christianity.[24]

Other theorists have explored the possibility that some forms of knowledge transcend the knowledge obtained through ordinary sense perception. Michael Polanyi has argued that one form of human understanding is far beyond what "strict empiricism regards as the domain of legitimate knowledge."[25] The constructive (as opposed to deconstructive) postmodern philosophers generally affirm the inadequacy of the approach to knowledge embodied in empiricism, whether it is knowledge of the external world, the past, other minds, or personal identity.[26] William James is prominent among these postmodern thinkers, but their number also includes C. S. Pierce, Henri Bergson, A. N. Whitehead, and Charles Hartshorne. Though this approach to knowledge cannot do justice to the instant recognition claimed by those who experience Christic apparitions, it does challenge the traditional view, established by empiricism, that ordinary sense perception is the only foundation for knowledge claims.

These alternative views on the nature of knowledge, however, do not explain how percipients make the identification or why they generally exhibit so much confidence in it. Though one might argue that general beliefs that are part of the culture can adequately explain the identification, they are unlikely to explain the confidence percipients feel. One cannot legitimately assert that percipients *know* who appears to them, for knowledge claims involve being able to supply a justification for a belief, and justifications are notoriously lacking when it comes to Christic apparitions. I consider the general problem of identifying an experience as Christic—

whether it is visual, auditory, a sense of presence, a conversion experience, or whatever—to be incapable of satisfactory resolution. Something evidently convinces percipients that the experience is Christic, but the claim does not appear to admit of justification in a public sense.

Further Study

Christic visions and apparitions present a number of intriguing and difficult challenges. That any visions at all are interpreted as Christic is intriguing, given the controversy surrounding Jesus and the fact that there is no account of his physical appearance. One of the greatest challenges of Christic apparitions is that their study touches on many disciplines. Biblical exegesis and interpretation, as well as Christian history and theology, come into play simply by describing an experience as Christic; psychology, parapsychology, and neurophysiology are included by virtue of the fact that visions are the objects of scrutiny; epistemology and metaphysics are implicated because reports have to be assessed for credibility, and competing explanations, some of them possessing controversial ontologies, need to be evaluated. The extensive bodies of literature belonging to the disciplinary domains just mentioned makes the task of interpreting these experiences difficult.

Christic visions and apparitions could be approached in many ways, and many questions could be posed about the study I have undertaken. One could question, for instance, the decision to select *Christic* visions as the focal point of a study, and suggest that visions in general should be examined at the same time. One might question the decision to ignore Christic experiences of other kinds, such as OBEs and NDEs in which Jesus is thought to be encountered, conversion experiences, or dreams. Andrew MacKenzie thinks that concentrating on apparitions (in general) alone is a mistake, maintaining that the whole of psychic research needs to be surveyed, with apparitions forming only one class within this broader field.[27] These probing questions and comments suggest that the current study is either too broad or too narrow. Perhaps some think that visionary experiences should not be critically examined at all but rather, as peak religious experiences, ought to be left at the periphery of knowledge, so that their mysterious dimensions are not disturbed. These criticisms are worth pondering, for how to best approach the phenomena under scrutiny is not clear. But fears that critical scrutiny will penetrate so far into their character that their symbolic value will be destroyed appear unfounded. Even if a neurophysiological account for all of the trustworthy reports should be found, for example, the experience is likely to retain its symbolic significance for many percipients.

From his study of religious experience, William James concluded that such experiences have authority primarily for those who have them, that others have no duty to accept their insights, and that religious experience limits the authority of the "rationalist consciousness" by showing that another consciousness is available. The transcendent quality of Christic visions is certainly present for the percipients I interviewed, but one can safely generalize this presence, based on textual evidence from such authors as Julian of Norwich and Teresa of Avila. The visionary experience also dramatically exhibits the presence of a kind of consciousness at variance with the ordinary one.

The greatest obstacle to developing more definite conclusions about Christic visions is the paucity of information available about them. More extensive studies are obviously required in order to support, or lay to rest, the lingering suspicion that the Christic visionary experience forms one kind of interaction with a transcendent realm. Many more Christic visions and apparitions need to be examined to determine whether the categories that have been tentatively put forward are adequate, whether important phenomenological elements have been overlooked, whether feelings or emotions of one particular kind are more prevalent than another, whether these experiences resemble those of persons who have been diagnosed with psychological disorders, whether a single explanation is likely to prove adequate, and so on. Determining the prevalence of these experiences is crucial, for my own small sample does not allow any significant statistical conclusions to be drawn. Another investigation could explore the plausibility of assigning degrees of "hallucinatoriness" to apparition experiences in general, and to Christic apparitions in particular. A smaller degree of hallucinatoriness might apply, for example, to experiences that involve several sensory modalities rather than one, that are independent of volition rather than dependent on active choice, or that are collective rather than private. These and other items could be weighted to reflect their relative importance, and a rough measure could perhaps be devised. Studying Christic apparitions in cross-cultural contexts would help determine the extent to which prior beliefs appear to shape its content and interpretation.

One could study the Christic visionary experience as one kind of Christic experience, one kind of religious experience, one kind of mystical experience (in one sense of the term), one kind of hallucination, one kind of apparition experience, one kind of state of altered consciousness, one kind of psychic phenomenon—and to suggest this is to identify seven broad categories of experience already identified in religious, psychical, and psychological research. Each of these categories is large, and has the capacity to shape assessments of the Christic apparition experience, just as the latter has the capacity to influence the former.

We have yet to fully understand the profound and mysterious religious experiences of humans everywhere, experiences that shape attitudes toward life and arouse hopes for transcendence and personal immortality. The Christic visionary experience is among these, and deserves closer examination.

Appendixes, Notes, Bibliography, and Index

Appendix I

The information on religious background reflects the descriptions that percipients gave of themselves at the time of their vision experience, or of their first experience, if they had several. Many percipients indicated that their religious involvement had undergone changes, and many resisted close identification with any particular Christian denomination. The identification of vocation reflects the most recent information I obtained, or the work in which percipients have been primarily engaged.

NAME	SEX	ETHNICITY	EDUCATION	RELGION AT EXP.	VOCATION
H Bezanson	F	French-Irish Can.	high school	Anglican	homemaker
E Chilvers	F	British Canadian	nursing & theol.	Evangelical	retired nurse
S Dalrymple	F	Scottish-Irish Can.	some university	United Church of Can.	homemaker
B Dyck	M	Dutch-German Can.	near BA & theol.	Evangelical	stockbroker
R Fairs	F	Ukrainian Canadian	high school	Greek Orthodox	homemaker
M Galiffe	F	Anglo-Irish	high school	Pentecostal	dressmaker
F Haskett	F	Scottish Canadian	high school	United Church of Can.	ret. insurance agent
M Hason	F	English Canadian	teach. ed. & near BA	Anglican	homemaker
M Hathaway	F	Welsh	high school	None	library assistant
H Hinn	M	Jewish Canadian	high school	Evangelical	minister
E Hollands	M	British Canadian	some high school	None	prison ministry
H Huizinga	F	Dutch Canadian	some college	Chr. Reform/Baptist	library technician
P Isaac	M	Dutch-German Can.	BA & B. Relig. Ed.	Mennonite	retired teacher
J Kinsey	F	Swed.-Scot. Amer.	some high school	Pentecostal	homemaker
P Langlois	F	French Canadian	some high school	Roman Catholic	homemaker
R Lindsay	M	British Canadian	high school & theol.	Catholic/Pentecostal	evangelist
J Link	M	Brit.-German Can.	technical & theol.	Evangelical	minister
K Logie	M	Norwegian Amer.	high school & theol.	Pentecostal	minister
C M	M	German American	near BA	Roman Catholic	sales
M Martinez	F	Cuban American	some college	Roman Catholic	homemaker & bus.
M Moyse	F	Brit.-Fren. Aust.	high school	None	artist & homemaker
K Nelson	F	English Australian	high school & Sect.	Charismatic	homemaker & sect.
J Occipinti	M	Italian American	high school & Theol.	Evangelical	minister
E Sabo	F	German Canadian	some university	Evangelical	homemaker & student
D Stamm-Loya	F	German American	BA, MA	None	minister
J Vasse	M	Hungarian American	BA	None	ret. computer analyst
R Wheeler	M	Brit.-Hung. Can.	high school & theol.	Greek Orthodox	laborer
E Zelle	F	Greek American	BS	Greek Orthodox	office manager

Appendix II

The information in this table supplements that contained in the detailed descriptions of Chapter 2. Some entries call for explanation:

1. The 'Y' stands for 'Yes,' the 'N' for 'No,' and question marks indicate either that percipients were unsure about the appropriate answer, or that they did not report on the experience in sufficient detail to provide an answer.

2. The 'O/C' under the first column beside "Marian Hathaway' indicates that her eyes were open for part of the vision, and closed during another part.

3. I count John Occhipinti's experience to be a private one (Column 3), but I add the question mark because of the simultaneous tactile sensation reported by his friend.

4. The column that records the distance away from the percipient that the apparition figure seemed to be located gives approximate values, and does not always reflect all the details of the experience(s). When percipients indicated that they touched the figure that appeared to them, I enter 0 as the distance. The 'V' that is occasionally entered signifies that the distance varied.

	Eyes open (O) or closed (C)	Altered (A) or norm.(N) envir.	Private (P) or group (G)	Haptic Sensation	Kinesthetic sensation	Auditory sensation	Intersubjective effect	Distance of figure (in feet)	Movement of figure	Traditional appearance	Solid (S) or transparent (T)	Distinct (D) or vague (V) face	Radiance	Complete humanoid form	Normal size	Marital status: Sing., Mar., Div.	Age at experience	Year of experience
H Bezanson	O	A	P	Y	N	N	N	9	Y	Y	S	D	Y	Y	Y	M	21	1955
	O	N	P	N	N	N	N	?	Y	?	S	D	N	Y	Y	M	51	1985
E Chilvers	O	N	P	N	N	N	N	7	N	Y	S	D	N	N	Y	S	91	1987
S Dalrymple	O	N	P	N	N	Y	N	20	Y	Y	Y	D	N	Y	Y	M	36	1982
B Dyck	O	N	P	Y	N	N	Y	0	Y	Y	S	V	Y	Y	Y	S	18	1974
R Fairs	O	N	P	N	N	N	N	7	Y	Y	S	D	N	N	Y	M	25	1953
	O	N	P	N	N	N	N	7	N	Y	S	D	N	Y	Y	M	60	1988
M Galiffe	?	A	P	N	N	Y	N	10	Y	Y	T	V	Y	Y	Y	M	39	1991
F Haskett	O	N	P	N	N	N	N	7	Y	Y	S	V	Y	Y	Y	M	30	1950
M Hason	O	N	P	N	N	N	N	4	Y	Y	S	D	N	N	Y	M	29	1982
	O	N	P	N	N	Y	N	3	Y	Y	S	D	N	?	Y	M	32?	1985?
M Hathaway	O/C	N	P	Y	N	N	N	0	Y	Y	S	D	Y	N	N	M	30	1969
H Hinn	O	N	P	N	N	?	Y	8	Y	Y	T	D	N	Y	Y	S	19	1976
E Hollands	O	A	P	Y	N	Y	N	0	Y	Y	S	D	N	Y	Y	S	44	1975
H Huizinga	O	N	P	N	N	Y	N	15	N	Y	S	V	Y	Y	N	M	40	1969
P Isaac	O	N	P	N	N	N	N	6	Y	?	S	D	N	Y	Y	M	44	1964
	O	A	P	Y	Y	N	N	V	Y	N	S	Y	N	Y	Y	M	70	1990
J Kinsey	C	A	P	N	N	Y	Y	13	Y	Y	S	D	N	Y	Y	M	24	1957
P Langlois	O	N	P	Y	N	N	N	0	Y	N	S	?	N	Y	Y	S	23	1980
	O	N	P	N	N	N	N	?	?	?	?	?	?	Y	N	N	M	32	1989
R Lindsay	O	N	P	N	N	Y	N	30	Y	Y	S	D	Y	N	Y	S	21	1965
J Link	O	A	P	N	N	N	N	18	Y	Y	S	V	N	Y	Y	M	27	1962
	O	A	P	N	Y	Y	N	3	?	Y	S	D	Y	N	?	M	42	1977
K Logie	O	N	G	Y	Y	Y	Y	0	Y	Y	S	D	?	Y	Y	M	26	1954
	O	N	G	N	N	N	Y	V	Y	Y	S	D	Y	Y	Y	M	31	1959
C M	O	N	P	N	N	Y	N	2	Y	N	S	D	N	Y	Y	S	27	1980
M Martinez	O	N	P	N	N	Y	N	7	Y	Y	T	D	N	Y	Y	S	8	1964
M Moyse	O	N	P	N	N	N	N	8	N	Y	S	D	N	Y	Y	M	26	1952
K Nelson	O	N	P	N	N	N	N	9	Y	Y	S	D	Y	N	?	M	36	1992
J Occipinti	O	N	P?	N	N	N	Y	8	Y	Y	S	D	N	Y	Y	S	19	1958
E Sabo	O	N	P	N	N	N	N	15	Y	Y	S	D	N	Y	Y	S	14	1975
D Stamm-Loya	O	A	P	N	N	Y	N	5	Y	Y	S	D	Y	Y	Y	D	22	1972
J Vasse	?	N	P	N	Y	N	N	?	Y	Y	?	V	Y	?	?	M	41	1984
R Wheeler	O	A	P	Y	N	N	Y	0	Y	Y	S	?	N	Y	Y	M	38	1984
E Zelle	O	A	P	Y	N	N	N	0	Y	?	S	D	N	Y	Y	D	45	1988
	O	A	P	N	N	N	N	8	Y	Y	S	D	N	Y	Y	D	46	1989

Appendix III

The position that the Resurrection of Jesus is highly probable on the NT evidence alone and that this belief cannot receive confirmation (expressed using the probability calculus) from additional evidence, including contemporary Christic apparitions, can be shown to be implausible. It requires an argument for the position that the probability of the Resurrection, given both the reports of appearances in the NT era *and* reports of contemporary apparitions, is greater than the probability of the Resurrection given only the NT appearance reports. This statement can be abbreviated as follows, using the usual symbols for probability statements:

$$\text{T: } P(R,N \ \& \ C) > P(R,N).$$

"R" stands for "the claim that Jesus was resurrected" (interpreted in close keeping with the traditional understanding of this), "N" stands for "the reports of appearances in the NT era," and "C" stands for "the reports of contemporary Christic apparitions." Some traditionalists disagree with T, maintaining that the probability of the Resurrection on the NT evidence alone is very high, and that other supposed evidence is neutral. In formal terms, this means that $P(R,N)$ has a value close to 1, and that $P(R,N \ \& \ C)$ equals $P(R,N)$, which contradicts T.

The crucial probability value in T on which the debate turns is $P(R,N \ \& \ C)$. According to Bayes's Theorem, which is a formal implication of the probability calculus, the following equation can be advanced:

$$P(R,N \ \& \ C) = P(N,R \ \& \ C) \times P(R,C) / P(N,C).$$

When the value on the righthand side of this equation is substituted for "$P(R,N \ \& \ C)$" in T above, the following inequality results:

$$T': P(N,R \ \& \ C) \times P(R,C) > P(R,N) \times P(N,C).$$

Traditionalists who think NT reports are decisive naturally hold this inequality to be an equality, and therein lies the point of contention.

It is reasonable to assign a very high value to $P(N,R \ \& \ C)$, the probability that the NT appearance reports were advanced, on the supposition that the Resurrection occurred and that there are reports of contemporary Christic apparitions. In fact, the probability that the NT appearance reports were advanced, simply given that the Resurrection occurred, is very high without any reference to reports of contemporary Christic apparitions. This is because it is reasonable to assert that if the Resurrection took place much as traditionalists believe, then the probability of appearances occurring is high. So the first probability function in T', namely $P(N,R \ \& \ C)$, can be effectively ignored because it is so close to 1. Moreover, $P(R,N)$ in T' is high, perhaps close to 1 (by assumption in the traditional position), so it effectively cancels out $P(N,R \ \& \ C)$. The question then reduces to whether $P(R,C) > P(N,C)$ or whether $P(R,C) = P(N,C)$ (or approximately so), with the traditional defenders in effect asserting the latter. An example of these values where $P(N,R \ \& \ C)$ and $P(R,N)$ are both high but not quite equal is as follows: $P(N,R \ \& \ C) = 1$, $P(R,C) = .1$, $P(R,N) = .9$, and $P(N,C) = .11$; the difference between $P(N,C)$ and $P(R,C)$ is quite small.

The crux of the issue reduces to evaluating the probability of the NT appearance reports being advanced, given the contemporary reports of Christic apparitions, $P(N,C)$, compared with the probability of the Resurrection, given the contemporary reports of Christic apparitions, $P(R,C)$. The position that traditionalists are forced into—namely, that these probability functions are pretty much equal—is counterintuitive. It seems plausible to consider the probability of the NT appearance reports being advanced, given the reports of contemporary Christic apparitions (which have some interesting similarities to the NT appearance reports) to be considerably higher than the probability of the Resurrection given only the reports of contemporary Christic apparitions. The earlier probability function, $P(N,C)$, could be a significant value, for instance, if a similar explanation for the NT appearance reports and the contemporary reports of Christic apparitions were to be advanced—an explanation that did not appeal to the Resurrection. The subjective vision hypothesis offered by some critics for the NT appearance reports, for instance, might be suggested also for the contemporary Christic apparitions reported. But the other probability function, namely, the probability that the Resurrection occurred, given only contemporary Christic apparitions, can realistically be assigned a low value—surely it is primarily the NT appearance reports, not contemporary apparitions experiences, that give the Resurrection belief any of its initial credibility, even if it is not as high as some Christian apologists think. I conclude, then, that the contention that the probability of the Resurrection claim is high, and cannot be significantly enhanced by evidence additional to that coming from the NT appearance stories, is suspect.

Notes

Introduction

1. When I interviewed Jim in 1988 he worked in Toronto as a supply manager for an electrical company, and also did some lay preaching. Since that time he has gone into pastoral work.

2. *Visions and Prophecies*, p. 9.

3. Janice Connell includes an extensive bibliography of religious studies of Marian apparitions in *The Visions of the Children: The Apparitions of the Blessed Mother at Medjugorje*. Recent examples of sociological studies of the phenomenon are Michael Carroll's *The Cult of the Virgin Mary: Psychological Origins* and Sandra Zimdars-Swartz's *Encountering Mary: From La Salette to Medjugorje*.

4. *I Am With You Always: True Stories of Encounters with Jesus*, p. 11.

5. Thus R. C. Zaehner on the essence of religion, in *Concordant Discord*, p. 3.

6. *Gold in the Crucible*, p. 67f.

7. Ithamar Gruenwald, "Major Issues in the Study and Understanding of Jewish Mysticism," p. 7; cf. p. 23.

8. See, for example, W. T. Stace, *Mysticism and Philosophy*; W. Wainwright, *Mysticism: A Study of its Nature, Cognitive Value and Moral Implications*; and R. H. Jones, *Mysticism Examined: Philosophical Inquiries into Mysticism*.

9. *Otherworld Journeys*, p. 7.

10. *The Existence of God*.

11. *The Evidential Force of Religious Experience*.

12. *The Visions of the Children*, p. xii.

13. "Anthropological perspectives on hallucination and hallucinogens," p. 40.

14. *Putting the Soul Back in Psychology*, p. 87.

15. See W. Christian, *Apparitions in Late Medieval and Renaissance Spain* and *Moving Crucifixes in Modern Spain*.

16. Sparrow includes a large group of experiences in *I Am With You Always*, including physical and emotional healings, dreams, and encounters in which percipients are instructed, confronted, or awakened to spiritual realities (p. 3).

17. Braude, *The Limits of Influence: Psychokinesis and the Philosophy of Science*, p. 14.

18. "Do we need a new word to supplement 'hallucination'?"

19. See the Revised Standard Version. This version will be used throughout.

20. *Essays in Psychical Research*, ed. Robert McDermott, p. 73.

21. *Gold in the Crucible*, p. 37; see Gruenwald, "Major Issues in the Study and Understanding of Jewish Mysticism," p. 11, for similar comments.

22. *Visions and Prophecies.*

1. Christic Apparitions in Christian History

1. *A Dictionary of Miracles.*

2. *The Apparitions and Shrines of Heaven's Bright Queen.*

3. Walsh, *Apparitions and Shrines*, vol. 3, p. 288.

4. Paul M. Hanson, *Jesus Christ among the Ancient Americans*, p. 159f.

5. Walsh, *Apparitions and Shrines*, vol. 1, p. 37.

6. Described in John 11.

7. Brewer, *Dictionary*, p. 482.

8. *Ibid.*, p. 325.

9. *Ibid.*, p. 20.

10. *The Revelations of Divine Love*, chap. 4.

11. See Paul Molinari, *Julian of Norwich: The Teaching of a 14th Century English Mystic*, p. 63; Grace Jantzen, *Julian of Norwich: Mystic and Theologian*, p. 76; Brant Pelfrey, *Christ our Mother: Julian of Norwich*, p. 78f; Frances Beer, *Women and Mystical Experience in the Middle Ages*, p. 138f; and Ritamary Bradley, *Julian's Way: A Practical Commentary on Julian of Norwich*, p. 4.

12. See Allison Peers, *Mother of Carmel: A Portrait of St. Teresa of Avila*; Stephen Clissold, *St. Teresa of Avila*; Victoria Sackville-West, *The Eagle and the Dove*; Deirdre Green, *Gold in the Crucible*, p. 52; and Rowan Williams, *Teresa of Avila*.

13. Brewer, *Dictionary*, p. 62.

14. *Ibid.*, p. 63.

15. *Ibid.*, p. 61.

16. *Ibid.*, p. 62.

17. *Dialogues*, vol. 2, p. 1.

18. Brewer, *Dictionary*, p. 367.

19. *Ibid.*, p. 323.

20. *Ibid.*, p. 368.

21. Walsh, *Apparitions and Shrines*, vol. 2, p. 281f.

22. Brewer, *Dictionary*, p. 297.

23. *Ibid.*, p. 19.

24. *Ibid.*, p. 323.

25. Walsh, *Apparitions and Shrines*, vol. 3, p. 61.

26. *Ibid.*, p. 149.

27. *Ibid.*, vol. 2, p. 167.

28. *Ibid.*, p. 172.

29. Brewer, *Dictionary*, p. 416.
30. *Ibid.*, pp. 20–21.
31. *Dialogues*, vol. 4, p. 17.
32. Brewer, *Dictionary*, p. 19.
33. *Ibid.*, p. 20.
34. *Ibid.*, p. 19.
35. Walsh, *Apparitions and Shrines*, vol. 3, p. 211f.
36. Brewer, *Dictionary*, p. 481.
37. Walsh, *Apparitions and Shrines*, vol. 1, p. 249.
38. *Ibid.*, vol. 2, p. 27.
39. *Ibid.*, p. 138.
40. *Ibid.*, p. 291.
41. Brewer, *Dictionary*, p. 325.
42. Walsh, *Apparitions and Shrines*, vol. 2, p. 34.
43. *Ibid.*, p. 286.
44. Brewer, *Dictionary*, p. 59.
45. *Ibid.*, p. 20.
46. Walsh, *Apparitions and Shrines*, vol. 1, p. 126.
47. *Ibid.*, p. 313.
48. *Ibid.*, vol. 3, p. 126f.
49. *Ibid.*, vol. 2, p. 321.
50. *Ibid.*, vol. 3, p. 197f.
51. *Ibid.*, p. 204f.
52. *Holy Women of Russia: The Lives of Five Orthodox Women Offer Spiritual Guidance for Today*, p. 126.
53. *Ibid.*, p. 99.
54. See Cyril J. Davey, *Sadhu Sundar Singh*.
55. Huyssen, *Visions of Jesus*, p. 34.
56. *I Am With You Always*, p. 11.
57. *Genesis*, vol. 12, sec. 6, chap. 15.
58. *Mysticism: A Study in the Nature and Development of Man's Spiritual Consciousness*, p. 283.
59. *Genesis*, 12.3.4.
60. *Julian of Norwich*, p. 62; italics in original.
61. *Mysticism*, p. 281.
62. *Genesis*, 12.17.35.
63. *Ibid.*, 12.12.25.
64. *Ibid.*, 12.14.29. The translator says that the Latin *spiritus* in this passage could be rendered *imagination* (n. 13, p. 301).
65. Chap. 10.
66. *Ibid.*, chap. 17; italics added.
67. *On The Trinity*, chap. 11.
68. *Ibid.*, 4.21.31.
69. "Paul and the Beginning of Jewish Mysticism," p. 97.
70. Article on Visions, vol. 14, p. 717.
71. *Genesis*, 12.36.69.
72. *Summa Theologica*, vol. 2, ques. 174, art. 2.
73. *Ibid.*, 1.111.3.
74. *Ibid.*, 2.172.2.
75. *Ibid.*, 3.30.2; cf. 2.174.2.

76. *Ibid.*, 1.111.3.
77. "Vision," *The Catholic Encyclopedia* (1912).
78. For example, J. C. Yates, "Disembodied Existence in an Objective World."
79. *Visions and Prophecies*, p. 40.
80. *Ibid.*, p. 38.
81. *Ibid.*, p. 32.
82. *Commentary on The Acts of the Apostles*, 7:56.
83. *Visions and Prophecies*, p. 41.
84. *Ibid.*, p. 41f.
85. *Ibid.*, p. 49.
86. *Ibid.*, pp. 50–51.
87. *The Mystical Theology of the Eastern Church*, p. 211, quoting Evagrius, a fourth-century Christian mystic.
88. *Encyclopedia of Theology: A Concise Sacramentum Mundi*, p. 1806.
89. *Ibid.*, p. 1807; cf. W. Christian's discussion of the criteria used to evaluate the visions of Jeanne d'Arc in *Apparitions in Late Medieval and Renaissance Spain*, p. 188f.
90. *Luther's Works*, vol. 6, p. 329.
91. "Visions," *New Catholic Encyclopedia* (1967).
92. *The Life of Antony and the Letter to Marcellinus*, p. 43.
93. *Ibid.*, pp. 35–36.
94. *Dialogues*, 4.51.
95. *Ascent of Mount Carmel*, chap. 11, para. 3.
96. *Ibid.*, 17.4.
97. *Ibid.*, 11.2.
98. *Ibid.*, 11.7 and 11.12.
99. *Ibid.*, 12.6.
100. *Visions and Prophecies*, p. 58.
101. *Gold in the Crucible.*
102. See the discussions of Elizabeth Minnich, *Transforming Knowledge*, p. 159f; and Eve Cole, *Philosophy and Feminist Criticism: An Introduction*, p. 73f.
103. "Vision," *Encyclopedia of the Lutheran Church* (1965).
104. *Works*, vol. 6, p. 329.
105. *Ibid.*, 3.10.
106. *Ibid.*, 3.12.
107. *Ibid.*, 3.330.
108. Genesis 32.
109. *Works*, 6:144.
110. See the comment in Pomerius, *The Contemplative Life*, p. 179.
111. *Commentary on Acts* 16:10.
112. *Commentary on Acts* 9:10.
113. *Commentary on Acts* 27:23.
114. *Commentary on Acts* 23:11.
115. *Commentary on Acts* 7:31.
116. In *Spiritual and Anabaptist Writers: Documents Illustrative of the Radical Reformation,* ed. G. H. Williams.
117. "Theology," *Mennonite Encyclopedia*, 1990 ed.; italics in original.
118. *Miscellaneous Letters and Writings of Thomas Cranmer*, p.66.
119. Thus Christian psychiatrist John White, *Putting the Soul Back in Psychology*, p. 87f.

120. *Apparitions and Shrines*, vol. 1, preface.
121. See Ian E. Gordon, *Theories of Visual Perception* for a discussion of various visual perceptual theories.
122. *Visions and Prophecies*, p. 49.
123. *Ibid.*, pp. 50–51.
124. Gordon, *Theories of Visual Perception*, p. 101.
125. *Ibid.*, p. 118f.
126. Rahner mentions in *Visions and Prophecies*, p. 36, that this was noted by Duret in 1929.
127. See Gordon, *Theories of Visual Perception*, chap. 8.

2. Contemporary Christic Visions and Apparitions

1. The term *anointing* is used by some to refer to a special bestowal of divine favor.
2. This is known as glossolalia or speaking in tongues.
3. *Apparitions and Ghosts: A Modern Study*, p. 7.
4. *Ibid.*, p. 273.
5. Ernie Hollands (with Doug Brendel), *Hooked*. Ernie passed away in October, 1996.
6. The United Church of Canada is a union of Methodist, Presbyterian, and Congregationalist churches.
7. Luke 24:45.
8. This is the same church in which Joy Kinsey reported the experience described in Case 1.
9. *On Prophesying by Dreams*, in *The Basic Works of Aristotle*, 462b1–3.
10. *The Bleeding Mind: An Investigation into the Mysterious Phenomenon of Stigmata*.
11. *The Life of St. Francis*. In *Bonaventure*.
12. 23.8 in *A Select Library of the Nicene and Post-Nicene Fathers of the Christian Church*, vol. 2.
13. For example, G.N.M. Tyrrell, *Apparitions*, p. 8f.
14. Richard Cavendish, ed., vol. 8, pp. 1093–1101.
15. *Putting the Soul Back in Psychology*, p. 87.
16. *The Orthodox Church*, p. 128.
17. *Praise Records* FRS1026.
18. Esther, *The Torn Veil: The Story of Sister Gulshan Esther*.
19. May 16, 1994.
20. *Stigmata: A Medieval Mystery in a Modern Age*, p. 109.
21. H. A. Baker, *Visions Beyond the Veil*.
22. P. 47f.
23. J. Z. Young, *Philosophy and the Brain*, p. 107f.

3. Evaluation of the Evidence

1. See Berger's *A Rumor of Angels: Modern Society and the Rediscovery of the Supernatural*, p. 38f.
2. *Theism in an Age of Science*.

3. See John Austin's taxonomy of performative functions of language in *How to Do Things with Words*.

4. *The Limits of Influence*, p. 1f.

5. The report of the virgin birth of Jesus in the NT is an example of anecdotal evidence, since it is not presented as a kind of event occurring repeatedly.

6. *Ibid.*, p. 55.

7. *Ibid.*, p. 51.

8. *Ibid.*, p. 17f.

9. *Ibid.*, p. 19.

10. *Contextual Realism: A Meta-physical Framework for Modern Science*, p. 250ff.

11. *Ibid.*, p. 252.

12. Reported on *Turning Point*, ABC Network, June 8, 1994.

13. *Ibid.*

14. From Hume's "Of the Authenticity of Ossian's Poems," quoted in C. A. J. Coady, *Testimony: A Philosophical Study*, p. 182.

15. *The Existence of God*, p. 260.

16. *Ibid.*, p. 254.

17. *The Evidential Force of Religious Experience*, p. 96.

18. *Ibid.*, p. 115.

19. *Ibid.*, pp. 37–54.

20. *Testimony*, p. 32f.

21. *Ibid.*, p. 82.

22. For examples see Gary Habermas in Habermas and Antony Flew, *Did Jesus Rise From the Dead: The Resurrection Debate*, and C. A. Evans, "Authenticity Criteria in Life of Jesus Research."

23. See Habermas, *ibid.*, p. 58; F. F. Bruce, *The New Testament Documents: Are They Reliable?*, p. 62; and John W. Montgomery, *History and Christianity*, p. 40.

24. First Epistle to the Corinthians, chap. 25.

25. "Life-of-Jesus Research and the Eclipse of Mythology," p. 13ff.

26. See the cover story in *Time* magazine for April 10, 1995, titled "The Meaning of Miracles," for a report on changing popular attitudes.

27. *Paranormal Experience and Survival of Death*, p. 145.

28. *The Limits of Influence*, preface.

29. *Founders of Constructive Postmodern Philosophy: Peirce, James, Bergson, Whitehead and Hartshorne*, p. 16.

30. I Corinthians 9:1.

31. *The Biology of God: A Scientist's Study of Man the Religious Animal*, p. 121f.

32. *A Sense of Presence: The phenomenology of certain kinds of visionary and ecstatic experience, based on a thousand contemporary first-hand accounts*, p. 1.

33. *The Biology of God*, p. 216f.

34. *Ibid.*, p. 220.

35. See John Macbeath, *The Face of Christ*, p. 14, and Denis Thomas, *The Face of Christ*, p. 12, for representative expressions of this belief.

36. *The Likeness of Christ: Being an Inquiry into the Verisimilitude of the Received Likeness of Our Blessed Lord*, p. 15f.

37. *Ibid.*, p. 23.

38. *Rex Regum: A Painter's Study of the Likeness of Christ from the Time of the Apostles to the Present Day.*

39. *The Face of Christ: Earliest Likenesses from the Catacombs*, pp. 4–5.
40. *Holy Faces, Secret Places: An Amazing Quest for the Face of Jesus*, p. 90.
41. *Ibid.*, p. 88.
42. For expressions of this view, see Stephen Katz, *Mysticism and Religious Traditions*, p. 4; John Smith, "William James's Account of Mysticism: A Critical Appraisal," in Katz, *ibid.*, p. 248; and Carol Zaleski, *Otherworld Journeys*, p. 195f. Joy Kinsey told me that Kenneth Logie often told his congregation that if they had a vision of Jesus, he would appear as they expected him to look.
43. *Rex Regum*, p. 82.
44. *How Did Christ Look?*
45. *Ibid.*, p. 18.
46. *Ibid.*, p. 22.
47. *Ibid.*, p. 10.
48. *Ecclesiastical History*, 7.18.
49. See *The Mysterious Shroud* and *Holy Faces, Secret Places*.
50. Lucille Huyssen and Chester Huyssen, *I Saw the Lord*, p. 137.
51. *The Link*, 1 (1981): 101.

4. Christic Appearances and Visions in the New Testament

1. John Dominic Crossan, in *The Cross that Spoke: The Origins of the Passion Narratives*, is an exception to this general rule.
2. I Corinthians 15:42–4.
3. Mark 16:8.
4. Matthew 28:1ff.
5. Matthew 28:19.
6. Luke 24:30–1.
7. Luke 24:36.
8. John 20:25.
9. All of John 21 is devoted to this encounter.
10. Luke 9:29.
11. These are discussed by Reginald Fuller in *The Formation of the Resurrection Narratives*, p. 160ff, and by John Dominic Crossan in *The Historical Jesus: The Life of a Mediterranean Jewish Peasant*, p. 395ff.
12. See accounts in Acts 9, 22 and 26.
13. Slight discrepancies make reconciliation of these accounts difficult. In Acts 9:7, for instance, Luke relates that the men who traveled with Paul heard the voice but saw no one, but in Acts 22:9, Luke gives Paul's version of the event, according to which the men did not hear the voice. It is possible, of course, that Luke faithfully preserved Paul's erroneous version of the event.
14. Acts 22:17f.
15. II Corinthians 12:1–2.
16. Christopher Rowland suggests this in *The Open Heaven: A Study of Apocalyptic in Judaism and Early Christianity*, p. 380f.
17. Acts 9:10.
18. Acts 9:12. The phrase *in a vision* (*en horamati*) is in the Greek text, but the *RSV* does not translate it.
19. Acts 7:8.

20. J. M. Robinson draws attention to this in "Jesus: From Easter to Valentinus (or to the Apostle's Creed)."

21. Revelation 1:14–16.

22. *The Open Heaven*, p. 414.

23. Pheme Perkins discusses these extensively in *Resurrection: The New Testament Witness and Contemporary Reflection*, p. 338ff.

24. In Wilhelm Schneemelcher, *New Testament Apocrypha*, vol. 1, p. 391f.

25. C. S. Lewis discusses this in *The Discarded Image: An Introduction to Medieval and Renaissance Literature*, p. 167.

26. Schneemelcher, *New Testament Apocrypha*, vol. 1, p. 285f.

27. *Ibid.*, p. 249ff.

28. Chapter 11, in the Ethiopic version.

29. In Hennecke, *New Testament Apocrypha*, vol. 2, pp. 442f and 448f.

30. Schneemelcher, *New Testament Apocrypha*, vol. 1, p. 348.

31. In E. Hennecke, *New Testament Apocrypha*, vol. 2, pp. 279f, 284, and 297.

32. *The Other Bible*, p. xviii.

33. "The Historicity of the Resurrection," pp. 133–44.

34. *Ibid.*, p. 140.

35. *I believe in the resurrection of Jesus*, p. 91f.

36. *Ibid.*, p. 99.

37. *Ibid.*, p. 128.

38. *Assessing the New Testament Evidence for the Historicity of the Resurrection of Jesus*.

39. *Fragments: Concerning the Intention of Jesus and His Teaching*.

40. *A New Life of Jesus*, vol. 1, p. xii.

41. *Ibid.*, p. 421.

42. In "Emmaus Revisited (Luke 24,13–35 and Acts 8,26–40)," p. 465.

43. I. Epstein describes the Midrashic literary form as adapting a text to a new situation not provided for in the text, in Freedman and Simon, *Midrash Rabbah: Genesis*, vol. 1, pp. x–xiii.

44. P. 261ff.

45. "The Resurrection: A Confusing Paradigm-Shift," p. 257.

46. William James, *Essays in Psychical Research*, p. 28; F.W.H. Myers, *Human Personality and Its Survival of Bodily Death*, p. 297; and Michael Perry, *The Easter Enigma: An Essay on the Resurrection with Specific Reference to the Data of Psychical Research*.

47. See John Hick, *Disputed Questions in Theology and the Philosophy of Religion*, p. 42f, for a discussion of resurrections alleged in Hindu sources of the last century.

48. "New Testament and Mythology," p. 15.

49. *Jesus Christ and Mythology*, p. 52.

50. "New Testament and Mythology," p. 39.

51. *Ibid.*, p. 42.

52. *Gospel Criticism and Christology*, p. 29. In *From Tradition to Gospel*, p. 288, he describes the function of the narratives in general as providing propaganda for those who preach, teach, and proselytize.

53. *Jesus*, p. 131.

54. *Ibid.*, p. 132.

55. *Gospel Criticism and Christology*, p. 92.

56. *Ibid.*, p. 101.

57. *The Post-Resurrection Appearance Stories of the Gospel Tradition*, p. 22.

58. *Jesus and the Gospel I*, p. 16.

59. *Ibid.*, p. 38.

60. *The Virginal Conception and Bodily Resurrection of Jesus*, p. 30.

61. See Ignatius's *The Epistle to the Trallians*, chap. 24, and his *The Epistle to the Philadelphians*, chap. 7, in *The Fathers of the Church: A New Translation*, vol. 1; Justin's *The First Apology*, chap. 21; and Tertullian's *On the Resurrection of the Flesh* in *The Ante-Nicene Fathers: Translations of the Writings of the Fathers down to A.D. 325*, vol. 3.

62. See Clement of Rome, *The First Letter to the Corinthians*, chap. 25, in *The Fathers of the Church*. The editors remark that this fable was related by Pliny, Ovid, and Tacitus (p. 30), but we do not know from whom Clement took it.

63. See Acts 2:32, 3:15, 5:32, and 10:41f as examples.

64. Acts 13:30–31.

65. Thus W. Pannenberg, *Jesus—Man and God*, p. 111.

66. *The Structure of Resurrection Belief*, p. 100.

67. *The So-called Historical Jesus and the Historic Biblical Christ*, pp. 125–26.

68. *Church Dogmatics*, vol. 3, pt. 2, p. 442.

69. *Ibid.*, p. 451.

70. *Ibid.*, pt. 3, p. 507.

71. *Ibid.*, pt. 2, p. 452.

72. *Ibid.*

73. *Ibid.*, vol. IV, pt. 2, p. 149.

74. *Ibid.*, pp. 149–50.

75. "Rudolf Bultmann—An Attempt to Understand Him," p. 101.

76. See T. F. Torrance, *Karl Barth: An Introduction to His Early Theology, 1910–1931*, p. 81; G. W. Bromiley, *An Introduction to the Theology of Karl Barth*, p. 248; and D. F. Ford, "Barth's Interpretation of the Bible," p. 72.

77. "Barth's Interpretation," p. 68f.

78. *Ibid.*, p. 77.

79. *Ibid.*, p. 80.

80. *God Who Acts: Biblical Theology as Recital*, pp. 126–27.

81. *The New Testament and the People of God*, p. 21.

82. The relationship between salvation history and mundane history continues to be debated. N. T. Wright's survey in *The New Testament and the People of God*, p. 468f, of the contemporary debate is moderate on issues of historicity.

83. The emphasis upon evidence within the NT documents themselves is fascinating. For instance, Paul appeals to sense experience to defend the genuineness of the resurrection of Jesus, and Jesus himself is described by Luke as encouraging his disciples to touch his resurrected body in order to falsify the speculation that he might be a disembodied spirit. These documents are much more sympathetic to empirical evidence than fideists often acknowledge.

84. See Xavier L. Dufour, *Resurrection and the Message of Easter* for a detailed parallel analysis.

85. *Resurrection and the New Testament*, pp. 66 and 56, respectively.

86. "'But Some Doubted,'" pp. 574–80.

87. See Luke 24, John 20, and John 21.

88. Mark 16:12.

89. Raymond Orlett, "An Influence of the Early Liturgy upon the Emmaus

Account," considers it to be a late summary of the Emmaus tradition but influenced by the early liturgy (p. 213); Ulrich Wilckens, *Resurrection: Biblical Testimony to the Resurrection: An Historical Examination and Explanation*, considers it the latest phase in the transmission of the call-to-vocation tradition (p. 65); and J.I.H. McDonald, *The Resurrection: Narrative and Belief* considers it to give a bare summary of the Emmaus tradition.

90. *The Gnostic Gospels*, p. 5.

91. *Resurrection*, p. 373.

92. *Resurrection and the New Testament*, p. 66.

93. *The Bleeding Mind*, p. 64. Wilson's footnotes indicate that only one person's body killed by crucifixion in antiquity (crucifixion is still practiced in some parts of the world) is known to have been recovered by archaeologists. This body exhibits a pronounced scratch at the wrist-end of the radius bone. His reference to the Shroud of Turin is of course controversial, since its dating is in dispute.

94. See, for example, W. Marxsen, *The Resurrection of Jesus of Nazareth*, p. 68.

95. *Jesus—Man and God*, p. 89.

96. Thus also Gerd Ludemann, *The Resurrection of Jesus: History, Experience, Theology*, p. 147. However, R. H. Fuller suggests in *Resurrection Narratives*, p. 79, that the desire to narrate the appearances as objective events required that they be modeled on the stories of encounters with Jesus during his earthly ministry.

97. *Jesus—Man and God*, p. 90.

98. *Ibid.*, pp. 92–93.

99. *Ibid.*, p. 93.

100. *Ibid.*, p. 95.

101. *Ibid.*, p. 28.

102. Persons skeptical of the historicity of the whole scheme of alleged events would look askance at the NT accounts, and if their skepticism were to be justified, we would be left with a collection of "accounts" that pieced together bits of "information" that created a reasonably convincing and quite subtle Resurrection story. The marvel then would be not that a complex of subtle facts created a remarkable event, but that writers were able to put pieces in place so that when the puzzle was complete, it resulted in a fairly well-integrated fiction.

103. This is suggested with respect to the resurrected Jesus, and also in the strange "teleportation" event that Luke tells about Philip in Acts 8:39f.

104. The Acts material has to be included to give substance to Paul's claim in I Corinthians that he, like others, saw Jesus after the Resurrection.

105. William J. Walsh, *The Apparitions and Shrines of Heaven's Bright Queen*, vol. 2, p. 148.

106. *The Virginal Conception*, p. 17.

107. *Ibid.*, p. 71.

108. *Ibid.*, p. 2.

109. *Ibid.*, p. 85.

110. *Ibid.*, p. 126.

111. *Ibid.*, p. 128.

112. *Ibid.*, p. 106.

113. *Ibid.*, p. 109. Brown considers this not to have been written by John but added by a later editor (p. 99).

114. *Ibid.*, p. 107

115. See, for example, McDonald, *The Resurrection*, p. 45.

116. *Resurrection Narratives*, p. 182.

117. *Ibid.*, p. 66.

118. *Ibid.*, p. 31.

119. *Ibid.*, p. 33, italics in original.

120. *Ibid.*, p. 49.

121. *Theological Dictionary of the New Testament*, p. 359.

122. *Ibid.*, p. 358.

123. *The Virginal Conception*, p. 91.

124. *The Structure of Resurrection Belief*, p. 227.

125. *Ibid.*, p. 243. Carnley invokes the idea of family resemblance as propounded by Ludwig Wittgenstein in *Philosophical Investigations* to shed light on different ways in which *ophthe* can be used.

126. *Ibid.*, p. 234.

127. *Ibid.*, p. 240.

128. *Ibid.*, pp. 242–43.

129. These are popularly thought to produce visions; cf. Aldous Huxley, *The Doors of Perception* and *Heaven and Hell*, Appendices 1 and 2.

130. I am not intimating that my list in Appendix 2 exhausts the interesting phenomenological details.

131. *Resurrection and the New Testament*, p. 55.

132. Acts 12:9.

133. "Postcrucifixion Appearances and Christian Origins," p. 162.

134. *Assessing the New Testament Evidence*, p. 82.

135. "The Resurrection of Jesus," p. 278.

136. *Resurrection and the Message of Easter*, p. 75.

137. *Jesus—Man and God*, p. 92f, but Evans does not agree, in *Resurrection and the New Testament*, p. 66.

138. *Lordship and Discipleship*, p. 38.

139. Acts 1:3.

140. Luke 24:50.

141. See Christopher Rowland, *The Open Heaven*, p. 370f, for a discussion of attitudes within the early church toward visions.

142. Gerald O'Collins, in *The Easter Jesus*, notes that Luke is vague about the reference to forty days, and comments on significant Jewish parallels, such as Moses on Mt. Sinai. He observes that the Ascension after forty days serves Luke's theology well, including closing the regular appearances, portraying Jesus's body as having physical reality, providing a climax to the story of Jesus's earthly ministry, and ushering in a new era of the Spirit. See p. 87.

5. Supernaturalistic Explanations

1. *Disputed Questions in Theology*, p. 15.

2. In "Behaviorism at Fifty," p. 90, Skinner observes that students watching a pigeon learn to turn in a clockwise direction described its behavior using such terms as *hoping, expecting, feeling, observing*. He repudiates the value of such mentalistic terms in psychology, however, remarking (p. 106) that his radical behaviorism found no place for the formulation of anything that is mental.

3. "Psychology in physical language," pp. 23–28.

4. *The Concept of Mind*.

5. Its early proponents were U. T. Place, "Is Consciousness a Brain Process?" pp. 44–50; J. J. C. Smart, "Sensations and Brain Processes," pp. 141–56; and Herbert Feigl, *The "Mental" and the "Physical": The Essay and a Postscript*.

6. Its proponents include Jerry Fodor, *Psychological Explanation*; Hilary Putnam, "The Nature of Mental States," pp. 47–56; and William Lycan, *Consciousness*.

7. See Paul Churchland, "Eliminative Materialism and the Propositional Attitudes," and *A Neurocomputational Perspective: The Nature of Mind and the Structure of Science*; Patricia Churchland, *Neurophilosophy*; and Patricia Churchland and Terrence J. Sejnowski, "Neural Representation and Neural Computation," pp. 15–48. Earlier proponents of eliminativism include Richard Rorty, "Mind-Body Identity, Privacy, and Categories," pp. 24–54, and Paul Feyerabend, "Mental Events and the Brain," pp. 295–296.

8. Paul Churchland, *A Neurocomputational Perspective*, p. 2.

9. "Is Neuroscience Relevant to Philosophy?" p. 324f.

10. *Ibid.*, p. 331.

11. *A Neurocomputational Perspective*, p. 71.

12. "Mind-body identity, privacy, and categories." This is a classic example of an eliminativist position. Theorists of this persuasion often cite phlogiston theory of the late eighteenth century as another example of a theory that has been completely abandoned. This theory attempted to account for burning, rusting, calcification, and other instances of chemical change. It was completely abandoned when fundamental elements such as oxygen, hydrogen, carbon, and so on, were identified, and no attempt to reduce phlogiston to these elements was made.

13. "Stalking the Wild Epistemic Machine."

14. *Warfare Prayer*, p. 82. Wagner seems to be making an ontological commitment in these statements, but they could perhaps be interpreted another way. Morton Kelsey, in *Discernment: A Study in Ecstasy and Evil* speaks about the value of interpreting Christian statements about spiritual realities as myths. He understands myth to be story that uses images and symbols to convey descriptions of psychic or nonphysical reality (p. 94). The same reality could expressed in historical facts, so a sharp distinction between myth and history cannot be maintained (p. 95).

15. *Interpretation of Dreams*, p. 138.

16. See the accounts of scientific realism in Richard Boyd, "On the Current Status of Scientific Realism," pp. 195–222; and Larry Laudan, "A Confutation of Convergent Realism," pp. 19–48.

17. Functionalists understand such mental states and processes to be conceptually grounded by being causally linked to observable events, such as overt acts and behavior patterns. See David Lewis, "Psychophysical and Theoretical Identifications," p. 250f for an account.

18. *From a Logical Point of View*, p. 44.

19. See, for example, Don Cupitt in *Taking Leave of God* and *The World to Come*.

20. See D. Z. Phillips, *Religion without Explanation*; cf. W. W. Bartley, *Wittgenstein*, p. 150ff.

21. *Metaphor and Religious Language*.

22. This strategy was developed by Saul Kripke in "Naming and Necessity," pp. 253–355, and by Hilary Putnam, "The Meaning of 'Meaning'," pp. 131–93.

23. Soskice, *Metaphor*, p. 129.
24. *Ibid.*, p. 140.
25. *Ibid.*, p. 131.
26. *Ibid.*, pp. 131–32.
27. The only minor qualification I would add to this general account of how theoretical terms acquire reference is that relations other than causality could help to fix the reference of a term. We might also help to fix the reference of *gold*, for instance, by identifying it as the thing bearing other relations to other things, for example, relations of similarity, of class inclusion or exclusion, and spatial and temporal relations. I am not minimizing the importance of causal relationships in fixing the reference of terms for unobservables, however.
28. For an overview, see C. Hooker, "Towards a General Theory of Reduction."
29. *The Devils of Loudun*, p. 72f.
30. *Ibid.*, pp. 74–5.
31. See Ernest Nagel, *The Structure of Science*, chap. 11.
32. *Jesus Christ and Mythology*, p. 15.
33. *Ibid.*, p. 21.
34. "On the Psychogenesis of Schizophrenia," p. 134.
35. *The Coherence of Theism*, p. 2.
36. *A Pluralistic Universe*, p. 312.
37. *Interpretation and Belief*, pp. 40–41.
38. Christian theologian V. Chakkarai, who also sought to bring insights from Hinduism to bear on issues arising in Christian theology, writes in *Jesus the Avatar*: "The Lord God does not write in letters of fire across the heavens that He exists so that the atheist and agnostic may be convinced. The existence of God and His attributes are in the first place matters of spiritual perception or faith, and secondarily of intellectual reasonings which may not amount to more than strong probability" (p. 27).
39. In *The Coherence of Theism* Swinburne argues that an infinite property makes for a simpler hypothesis, therefore a preferable one (p. 94f). But Michael Banner, in *The Justification of Science and the Rationality of Religious Belief*, questioned Swinburne's appeal to simplicity on the grounds that a simpler theory might only provide a basis for *preferring* it to a rival, not provide a basis for *believing* it. He also raises a query about the simplicity of Christian theism, given its trinitarian character (p. 153).
40. *Against Praxeas*, chap. 3.
41. *Jesus Christ and Mythology*, p. 47.
42. Acts 2.
43. Acts 5.
44. Acts 6.
45. Acts 8.
46. Acts 8.
47. See Gary Colwell, "Speaking of the Holy Spirit: Two Misconceptions," for similar remarks.
48. For a discussion, see Jaroslav Pelikan, *The Christian Tradition: A History of the Development of Doctrine, Vol. 1: The Emergence of the Catholic Tradition*, p. 211.
49. Fran Haskett (Case 20, chap. 2) mentioned that a minister offered this as an explanation of her vision.

50. *On Being a Christian*, p. 470, orig. ital.; cf. *Does God Exist? An Answer for Today*, p. 700f.

51. Barth evidently does not, for he says that in the Resurrection Jesus's eternal nature was revealed.

52. "Hallucinations as the World of Spirits," p. 55.

53. *Ibid.*, p. 57.

54. *Ibid.*

55. *Ibid.*, p. 58f.

56. *Ibid.*, p. 59.

57. *Ibid.*

58. *Ibid.*, p. 60.

59. *Ibid.*

60. *Heaven and Its Wonders and Hell from Things Heard and Seen (Heaven and Hell)*, sec. 5, para. 29f.

61. *Ibid.*, sec. 56, para. 542.

62. This account is given by Benjamin Worcester, *The Life and Mission of Emanuel Swedenborg*, p. 203.

63. *Ibid.*, p. 204, quoting Swedenborg.

64. Origin says, in *De Principiis*, 1.8.4, that some people become angels. Swedenborg says, in *Heaven and Hell*, para. 329, that some children become angels.

65. Alan F. Segal, "Paul and the Beginning of Jewish Mysticism," p. 101f.

66. Rahner, *Visions and Prophecies*, p. 32.

67. The five groups are: trancelike experiences (Group I); experiences in which the physical environment seems to change (Group II); private experiences that involved no change to the physical environment (Group III); experiences that occur to groups or involve some intersubjectively observable change (Group IV); and experiences in which Jesus is experienced as a child or as crucified (Group V).

68. For a discussion of this issue, see Grace Jantzen (Dyck), *Incorporeal Identity*, p. 216ff.

6. Mentalistic and Psychological Explanations

1. "An Outline of Survival Evidence," pp. 2–34.

2. *The Origins of Consciousness in the Breakdown of the Bicameral Mind*.

3. *The Early Greek Concept of the Soul*, p. 9.

4. *Ibid.*, p. 53f.

5. *Ibid.*, p. 21.

6. Quoted in Karl R. Popper and John C. Eccles, *The Self and Its Brain*, p. 159.

7. Bremmer, *The Early Greek Concept of the Soul*, p. 84f.

8. See John Burnet, "The Socratic Doctrine of the Soul," pp. 235–59; A. E. Taylor, *Socrates: The Man and His Thought*, p. 132; and M. Cornford, *Before and After Socrates*, p. 50.

9. Carl Jung, "The Basic Postulates of Analytical Psychology," p. 200.

10. *The Discarded Image*, p. 167.

11. "The Basic Postulates of Analytical Psychology," p. 203.

12. *Mind and Cognition*, p. 5.

13. *The Evolution of the Soul*.

14. *Ibid.*, p. 145.
15. *Ibid.*, p. 203.
16. *Ibid.*, p. 147.
17. *Ibid.*, p. 298.
18. *Ibid*, p. 311.
19. *Orthodox Religion and Spiritualism*, p. 7. A similar view was expressed by medical doctor Abraham Wallace several decades earlier in *Jesus of Nazareth and Modern Scientific Investigation from the Spiritualist Standpoint*, p. 30.
20. *The Resurrection of Christ*, p. 49f.
21. *Ibid.*, p. 83.
22. *The Easter Enigma*, p. 155.
23. *Apparitions*, p. 85f.
24. *Ghosts in Solid Form: An Experimental Investigation of Certain Little-Known Phenomena (Materialisations)*, p. 28.
25. *A Casebook for Survival*, p. 264.
26. *Life After Life*, pp. 42–54.
27. Moody considers the general conception of the spiritual body that he found among his subject group to be similar to the concept of disembodied soul found in Plato's writings, especially *Phaedo, Gorgias* and *The Republic* (p. 116).
28. See Carol Zaleski's review in *Otherworld Journeys*, chap. 10.
29. *Paranormal Experience and Survival of Death*.
30. *Ibid.*, p. 187.
31. *Ibid.*, pp. 170–73.
32. *The Enigma of Survival*, p. 159f.
33. *Ibid.*, p. 189.
34. *Ibid.*, p. 190.
35. *Ibid.*, p. 165.
36. *Ibid.*, p. 190.
37. *ESP in Life and Lab: Tracing Hidden Channels*, p. 217.
38. *The Enigma of Survival*, p. 192.
39. *Ibid.*, p. 195.
40. *Ibid.*, p. 192.
41. *Ibid.*, p. 201.
42. *Ibid.*, p. 196.
43. *Ibid.*, p. 204.
44. *Ibid.*
45. *Ibid.*, p. 201.
46. *Ibid.*, p. 196.
47. "The Basic Postulates of Analytical Psychology," p. 213. Grosso says that the deep unconscious contained genuine intimations of immortality for Jung, in "Jung, Parapsychology, and the Near-Death Experience: Towards a Transpersonal Paradigm," p. 211.
48. *Ibid.*, p. 216. Consciousness is considered by Jung to be a derivative of the unconscious, rather than the other way around.
49. *Ibid.*, p. 215.
50. Grosso, "Jung, Parapsychology, and the Near-Death Experience," p. 179.
51. Daryl Sharp, *C. G. Jung Lexicon: A Primer of Terms and Concepts*, p. 29.
52. "On Resurrection," p. 249.
53. "Brother Klaus," p. 227f.

54. *Ibid.*, p. 229.
55. *Ibid.*, p. 231.
56. *Ibid.*, p. 229.
57. "The Psychological Foundations of Belief in Spirits," p. 256.
58. *Ibid.*, p. 257f.
59. *Ibid.*, p. 257.
60. "On Resurrection," p. 249.
61. *Ibid.*
62. *Ibid.*, p. 250.
63. *Ibid.*, p. 251.
64. "The maturation process and hallucinations in children," pp. 95–101.
65. *Ibid.*, p. 100.
66. *A Treatise of Human Nature*, bk. 1, pt. 3, sec. 14.
67. See Wesley Salmon, *Scientific Explanation and the Causal Structure of the World* for extensive discussion of this question.
68. Cf. Chapter 3.
69. See Swinburne, *The Evolution of the Soul*, p. 174f.
70. See the extensive discussion of this issue in Jerry Fodor, *The Modularity of Mind: An Essay on Faculty Psychology*; cf. J. Z. Young, *Philosophy and the Brain*, p. 141f.
71. *A Neurocomputational Perspective*, p. 266.
72. *Ibid.*, p. 260. Illustrations of these illusions can be found in any introductory textbook on psychology.
73. An example of this is interpreting a circular red disk in an experimental set-up as a tomato or an apple, even though nothing in the figure warrants it.
74. *The Origins of Consciousness*, p. 84.
75. *Ibid.*, p. 93.
76. *Ibid.*, p. 91.
77. *Ibid.*, p. 104f.
78. *Ibid.*, p. 93.
79. *Ibid.*, p. 96.
80. *Interpretation of Dreams*, sec. 7, pt. B.
81. *The Cult of the Virgin Mary*.
82. Robert Solomon, "Freud's Neurological Theory of Mind," p. 26f.
83. *The Cult of the Virgin Mary*, p. 141.
84. He uses information derived largely from Walsh, *Apparitions and Shrines*, whose work was mentioned in Chapter 1.
85. *Ibid.*, p. 143. Carroll grants that neither of these conditions guarantees celibacy.
86. *Ibid.*, p. 144.
87. *Ibid.*
88. *Ibid.*, p. 146.
89. *Ibid.*, p. 169.
90. *Ibid.*, p. 142.

7. Neurophysiological Explanations

1. "Anthropological perspectives on hallucination and hallucinogens," pp. 40–41; orig. ital.

2. Gilbert Ryle is famous for having introduced this notion in *The Concept of Mind*.

3. "A general theory of hallucinations and dreams," p. 305.

4. Thomas Sarbin and Joseph Juhasz, "The social context of hallucinations," p. 242.

5. *Ibid.*

6. *Ibid.*, p. 244.

7. *Ibid.*, p. 254.

8. Van Dusen has attempted to enter the world of the hallucinator in a sympathetic manner, as I remarked in Chapter 6.

9. "Hallucinations in neurologic syndromes," p. 221.

10. "Cartography of inner space," p. 203.

11. "A comparative study of pseudo-hallucinations, imagery and true hallucinations," pp. 9–17.

12. E. Hartmann, "Dreams and other hallucinations: An approach to the underlying mechanism," pp. 71–79.

13. R. K. Siegel and M. E. Jarvik, "Drug-induced hallucinations in animals and man," pp. 81–161.

14. F. K. Taylor, "On pseudo-hallucinations," pp. 265–71.

15. M. T. Orne, "Hypnotically induced hallucinations," p. 216.

16. L. J. West, "A clinical and theoretical overview of hallucinatory phenomena," p. 307.

17. *Moral Theory and Medical Practice*, pp. 230–31. Fulford adds the qualifier "having 'supernatural external stimuli?'" to the category of visions, indicating his own uncertainty about their place.

18. Including L. J. West in "A clinical and theoretical overview of hallucinatory phenomena," p. 305.

19. "The continuity of perceptual and cognitive experiences," pp. 257–86; cf. J. S. Strauss, "Hallucinations and delusions as points on continua functions," pp. 581–86, for a similar view.

20. "Cartography of inner space," pp. 197–239.

21. *Ibid.*, p. 209. The Sanskrit terms used to identify the states of increasing tranquillity reflect the cultural traditions in which these have been most closely observed.

22. *Ibid.*, p. 205.

23. "The Measurement of Hallucinatory Predisposition in Male and Female Prisoners," pp. 221–34.

24. R. P. Bentall and P. D. Slade, "Reliability of a scale measuring disposition towards hallucination: a brief report," pp. 527–529.

25. *Ibid.*, p. 528.

26. "The Illusion of Reality: A Review and Integration of Psychological Research on Hallucinations," p. 83.

27. Quoted in Popper and Eccles, *The Self and Its Brain*, p. 274.

28. M. Baldwin, "Hallucinations in neurologic syndromes," p. 78f.

29. *Ibid.*, p. 82.

30. *Ibid.*, p. 83.

31. P. Solomon and J. Mendelson, "Hallucinations in sensory deprivation," pp. 135–45.

32. H. L. Williams et. al., "Illusions, hallucinations and sleep loss," pp. 158–65.

33. Orne, "Hypnotically induced hallucinations," pp. 211–19.

34. "Cognitive Vulnerability to Auditory Hallucination: Impaired Perception of Meaning," p. 508.

35. For example, see *Hallucinations*, specifically L. J. West, "A general theory of hallucinations and dreams," pp. 275–91; E. V. Evarts, "Neurophysiologic theory of hallucinations," pp. 1–14; and I. Feinberg, "A comparison of the visual hallucinations in schizophrenia with those induced by mescaline and LSD-25," pp. 64–76.

36. For example, Alfred Heilbrun, "Impaired recognition of self-expressed thought in patients with auditory hallucinations," pp. 728–36.

37. See Frank J. Fish, "A neurophysiological theory of schizophrenia," pp. 828–39.

38. L. J. West, "A clinical and theoretical overview of hallucinatory phenomena," p. 287.

39. L. J. West, "A general theory of hallucinations and dreams," p. 277.

40. *The Interpretation of Dreams*, lect. 7, pt. B.

41. "Hallucinations and the brain stem reticular core," p. 16.

42. "Dreams and other hallucinations," p. 72.

43. *Ibid.*, p. 74.

44. *Ibid.*

45. *Ibid.*, p. 75.

46. *Ibid.*, p. 76; cf. Fischer, "Cartography of inner space," p. 201.

47. "Hallucinations: an information-processing approach," p. 168.

48. *Ibid.*, p. 168f.

49. *Ibid.*, p. 172; cf. Freud, *The Origin and Development of Psycho-Analysis*, lect. 2.

50. *Ibid.*, p. 174.

51. *Ibid.*, p. 175.

52. *Ibid.*, p. 176.

53. West, "A general theory of hallucinations and dreams," p. 289.

54. West, "A clinical and theoretical overview of hallucinatory phenomena," p. 301.

55. *Ibid.*

56. "Drug-induced hallucinations in animals and man," p. 148.

57. *Ibid.*, p. 136f; cf. Edwin Weinstein, "Social aspects of hallucinations," for observations about differences in the content of hallucinations among different ethnic groups.

58. *Ibid.*, p. 184.

59. Cf. Heilbrun and Blum, "Cognitive Vulnerability to Auditory Hallucination," p. 508.

60. "Hallucinations: an information-processing approach," p. 185.

61. "Cognitive Vulnerability to Auditory Hallucination," p. 508.

62. "Hallucinations: an information-processing approach," p. 188.

63. *Ibid.*, p. 190.

64. B. Wallace and L. E. Fisher, *Consciousness and Behavior*, p. 25.

65. J. Z. Young, "What's in a brain," p. 3.

66. Fish, "A neurophysiological theory of schizophrenia," p. 832.

67. *Ibid.*, p. 834.

68. *Ibid.*, p. 836f.

69. George Fink, "Homeostasis and hormonal regulation (neuroendocrine reflections of the brain)," pp. 130–59.

70. Huxley, *The Doors of Perception* and *Heaven and Hell*, Appendices 1 & 2.

71. "A comparison of the visual hallucinations in schizophrenia with those induced by mescaline and LSD-25," pp. 64–76.

72. *Ibid.*, p. 65; see Siegel and Jarvik, "Drug-induced hallucinations in animals and man," for artistic illustrations.

73. *Ibid.*, p. 68.

74. *Ibid.*, p. 70.

75. *Ibid.*, p. 71.

76. "Visual hallucinations," p. 90.

77. "A comparison of the visual hallucinations in schizophrenia with those induced by mescaline and LSD-25," p. 67.

78. *Ibid.*

79. "Hallucinations in neurologic syndromes," p. 84.

80. In Popper and Eccles, *The Self and Its Brain*, p. 244. Eccles mentions the superior temporal sulcus as a possible cortical area involved in combined sensation.

81. "Perception: what quantitative laws govern the acquisition of knowledge from the senses?" p. 36.

82. Andrew MacKenzie says in *The Seen and the Unseen*, p. 200, that the studies of Celia Green and C. McCreery showed that one-half to two-thirds of visual apparitions are colored.

83. H. A. Sidgewick et. al., "Report on the census of hallucinations," p. 39.

84. "A Mass-Observation Questionnaire on Hallucinations," pp. 187–96.

85. See Bentall and Slade, "Reality testing and auditory hallucinations," Bentall et. al., "The multidimensional nature of schizotypal traits: A factor analytic study with normal subjects," pp. 363–75; and Bentall, "The Illusion of Reality."

86. J. T. Connell, *The Visions of the Children*, p. 34, quoting *Birmingham* (Ala.) *News*, December 2, 1988. I assume the source for this newspaper from Alabama was a wire service.

8. Interpreting Christic Visions and Apparitions

1. Most of Genesis and the first half of Exodus are accounts of these encounters, although their interpretation is the subject of much controversy. Five separate encounters are attributed to Abraham, including one in which the Lord "appeared," accompanied by two other beings (Genesis 18).

2. Specific regions may be anomalous when it comes to religious experiences, for reasons not now apparent. This needs further study.

3. *Challenges of Psychical Research: A Primer of Parapsychology*, p. 290f; orig. ital.

4. *The Visionary Human: Mystical Consciousness and Paranormal Perspectives*, p. 1.

5. *Against Method*, p. 33.

6. Some of the findings of the Alister Hardy Research Center are published in Alister Hardy, *The Spiritual Nature of Man: A Study of Contemporary Religious Experience*; Edward Robinson, *The Original Vision: A Study of the Religious Experience of*

Childhood; Timothy Beardsworth, *A Sense of Presence*; and David Hay, *Exploring Inner Space: Scientists and Religious Experience*.

7. *A Rumor of Angels*, p. 59.

8. Preface to James, *Essays in Psychical Research*.

9. *A Pluralistic Universe*, p. 314.

10. "Rediscovering God," p. 98.

11. *Ibid.*, p. 93.

12. *The Biology of God*, p. 121.

13. *Ibid.*, p. 173.

14. See J. E. Smith, "William James's Account of Mysticism: A Critical Appraisal," p. 247.

15. *The Biology of God*, p. 183.

16. Theologian Paul Tillich makes extensive use of this meaning of *symbol* in his writing, distinguishing symbols from signs by noting that signs bear no relation to that to which they point, while symbols participate in the reality for which they stand. See *Systematic Theology*, vol. 1, p. 239.

17. "The Concept of Observation in Science and Philosophy," pp. 485–526. An implication of this is that the epistemological, ontological, and methodological principles that form a world view undergo evolution as crucial concepts change.

18. "Disembodied Existence in an Objective World," p. 535.

19. Described in Chapter 1.

20. The Dominican theologians endorsed the Augustinian tradition, while Ignatian spirituality allowed contemplation to be "exercised quite concretely with the entire wealth of incarnate mediations: anthropological, christological, and ecclesiological," Antonio Sicari writes in "Teresa of Avila: Mystical experience in defense of dogma," p. 97. He notes that it was a Jesuit who encouraged her to concentrate her thought on the humanity of Jesus, by meditating each day on a passage from the Passion.

21. W. P. Alston, "Plantinga's Epistemology of Religious Belief," p. 293.

22. "Is Belief in God Properly Basic?" *Nous* 15 (1981): 46f.

23. "Perceiving God," p. 656. Alston develops this position in detail in *Perceiving God: The Epistemology of Religious Experience*.

24. The notion of incarnation is itself complex, as Sarah Coakley has indicated in *Christ Without Absolutes: A Study of the Christology of Ernst Troeltsch*. She discusses six separable notions, ranging from one which implies that God is merely involved in human life, to those that assert that Jesus is in a category distinct from all other forms of revelation, or that he is identical in substance to God, as expressed in the statement of the Council of Chalcedon (p. 104f).

25. *The Study of Man*, p. 21.

26. Griffin, *Founders of Constructive Postmodern Philosophy*, p. 23.

27. *The Seen and the Unseen*, p. 275.

Bibliography

Allen, Diogenes. "Resurrection Appearances as Evidence," *Theology Today* 30 (1973): 6–13.

Alston, W. P. *Perceiving God: The Epistemology of Religious Experience.* Ithaca, NY: Cornell University Press, 1991.

——. "Perceiving God," *The Journal of Philosophy* 83 (1986): 655–65.

——. "Plantinga's Epistemology of Religious Belief." In *Alvin Plantinga*, pp. 289–311. Edited by J. E. Tomberlin and P. van Inwagen. Dordrecht, Netherlands: D. Reidel, 1985.

Alsup, John E. *The Post-Resurrection Appearance Stories of the Gospel Tradition.* Stuttgart: Calwer Verlag, 1975.

Aquinas, Thomas. *Summa Theologica.* Translated by Dominican Fathers. New York: Benzinger Brothers, 1948.

Aristotle. *On Prophesying by Dreams.* Translated by J. I. Beare. In *The Basic Works of Aristotle.* Edited by Richard McKeon. New York: Random House, 1966.

Athanasias. *Life of Antony.* In *The Life of Antony and the Letter to Marcellinus.* Translated by R. C. Gregg. New York: Paulist Press, 1980.

Augustine. *The Care to be Taken for the Dead.* Translated by J. A. Lacy. New York: Fathers of the Church, 1955.

——. *The City of God.* Translated by Marcus Dods. In *A Select Library of the Nicene and Post-Nicene Fathers of the Christian Church.* Vol. 2. Edited by Philip Schaff. Grand Rapids, MI: Wm. B. Eerdmans, 1956.

——. *The Literal Meaning of Genesis.* Translated by J. H. Taylor. New York: Newman Press, 1982.

——. *The Trinity.* Translated by A. W. Haddan. In *A Select Library of the Nicene and Post-Nicene Fathers of the Christian Church.* Vol. 3. Edited by Philip Schaff. Grand Rapids, MI: Wm. B. Eerdmans, 1956.

Austin, John. *How to Do Things with Words.* Cambridge, MA: Harvard University Press, 1962.

Baird, A. T. *A Casebook for Survival*. London: Psychic Press, 1949.
———. *Richard Hodgson: The Story of a Psychical Researcher and His Times*. London: Psychic Press, 1949.
Baker, H. A. *Visions Beyond the Veil*. Monroeville, PA: Whitaker Books, 1973.
Baldwin, Maitland. "Hallucinations in neurologic syndromes." In *Hallucinations*, pp. 77–86. Edited by L. J. West. New York: Grune & Stratton, 1962.
Banner, Michael C. *The Justification of Science and the Rationality of Religious Belief*. Oxford: Clarendon Press, 1990.
Barlow, H. B. "Perception: What quantitative laws govern the acquisition of knowledge from the senses?" In *Functions of the Brain*, pp. 11–43. Edited by C. W. Coen. Oxford: Clarendon Press, 1985.
Barnstone, Willis, editor. *The Other Bible*. San Francisco: Harper, 1984.
Barth, Karl. *Church Dogmatics*. Translated by H. Knight et. al. Edinburgh: T & T Clark, 1960.
———. *Dogmatics in Outline*. Translated by G. T. Thomson. New York: Harper & Row, 1959.
———. "Rudolf Bultmann—An Attempt to Understand Him." Translated by R. H. Fuller. In *Kerygma and Myth: A Theological Debate*, Vol. 2, pp. 83–132. Edited by Hans-Werner Bartsch. London: SPCK, 1962.
Bartley III, W. W. *Wittgenstein*. Second edition. Lasalle, IL: Open Court, 1985.
Batson, C. Daniel. "Experimentation in Psychology of Religion: An Impossible Dream," *Journal for the Scientific Study of Religion* 16 (1977): 413–18.
Bayliss, Sir Wyke. *Rex Regum: A Painter's Study of the Likeness of Christ from the Time of the Apostles to the Present Day*. London: George Bell & Sons, 1898.
Beardsworth, Timothy. *A Sense of Presence: The phenomenology of certain kinds of visionary and ecstatic experience, based on a thousand contemporary first-hand accounts*. Manchester College, Oxford: The Religious Experience Research Unit, 1977.
Becker, Carl B. *Paranormal Experience and Survival of Death*. Albany: State University of New York Press, 1993.
de la Bedoyere, Michael. *Francis: A Biography of the Saint of Assisi*. London: Collins Publishers, 1962.
Beer, Frances. *Women and Mystical Experience in the Middle Ages*. Woodbridge, Suffolk, England: Boydell Press, 1992.
Bender, Lauretta. "The maturation process and hallucinations in children." In *Origins and Mechanisms of Hallucinations*, pp. 95–101. Edited by W. Keup. New York: Plenum, 1970.
Bennetts, H.J.T. *Visions of the Unseen: A Chapter in the Communion of Saints*. London: A. R. Mowbray, 1914.
Benoit, Pierre. *Jesus and the Gospel I*. Translated by B. Weatherhead. London: Darton, Longman & Todd, 1973.
Bentall, R. P. "The Illusion of Reality: A Review and Integration of Psychological Research on Hallucinations," *Psychological Bulletin* 107 (1990): 82–95.
———, and P. D. Slade. "Reality testing and auditory hallucinations: A signal detection analysis," *British Journal of Clinical Psychology* 24 (1985): 159–69.
———, and P. D. Slade. "Reliability of a scale measuring disposition toward hallucination: a brief report," *Personality and Individual Differences* 6 (1985): 527–29.
———, G. S. Claridge, and P. D. Slade. "The multidimensional nature of schizotypal traits: A factor analytic study with normal subjects," *British Journal of Clinical Psychology* 28 (1989): 363–75.

Berger, Peter. *A Rumor of Angels: Modern Society and the Rediscovery of the Supernatural*. Second edition. New York: Anchor Books, 1990.

Blanton, Margaret G. *The Miracle of Bernadette*. Englewood Cliffs, NJ: Prentice Hall, 1958. First published as *Bernadette of Lourdes*, 1939.

Bliss, E. L., and L. D. Clark. "Visual hallucinations." In *Hallucinations*, pp. 92–107. Edited by L. J. West. New York: Grune & Stratton, 1962.

Bolton, Gambier. *Ghosts in Solid Form: An Experimental Investigation of Certain Little-Known Phenomena (Materialisations)*. London: William Rider & Son, 1914.

Bonaventure. *The Life of St. Francis*. In *Bonaventure*. Translated by E. Cousins. New York: Paulist Press, 1978.

Boyd, Richard. "On the Current Status of Scientific Realism," *Erkenntnis* 19 (1983). Reprinted with emendations in *The Philosophy of Science*, pp. 195–222. Edited by Richard Boyd et. al. Cambridge, MA: MIT Press, 1991.

——. "Observations, Explanatory Power, and Simplicity: Toward a Non-Humean Account." In *Observation, Experiment, and Hypothesis in Modern Physical Science*. Edited by P. Achinstein and O. Hannaway. Cambridge, MA: MIT Press, 1985. Reprinted with emendations in *The Philosophy of Science*, pp. 349–77. Edited by Richard Boyd et. al. Cambridge, MA: MIT Press, 1991.

Bradley, Ritamary. *Julian's Way: A Practical Commentary on Julian of Norwich*. London: HarperCollins, 1992.

Braude, Stephen. *The Limits of Influence: Psychokinesis and the Philosophy of Science*. London: Routledge & Kegan Paul, 1986.

Bremmer, Jan. *The Early Greek Concept of the Soul*. Princeton, NJ: Princeton University Press, 1983.

Brewer, E. C. *A Dictionary of Miracles*. London: Chatto & Windus, 1884.

Bromiley, G. W. *An Introduction to the Theology of Karl Barth*. Edinburgh: T & T Clark, 1979.

Brown, Raymond E. *The Virginal Conception and Bodily Resurrection of Jesus*. New York: Paulist Press, 1973.

Bruce, F. F. *The New Testament Documents: Are They Reliable?* Revised edition. Downers Grove, IL: Intervarsity Press, 1960.

Bulgakov, Sergius. *The Orthodox Church*. Crestwood, NY: St. Vladimir's Seminary, 1988.

Bultmann, Rudolf. *Faith and Understanding I*. Sixth edition. Translated by L. P. Smith. London: SCM, 1969.

——. *Jesus and the Word*. Translated by L. P. Smith and E. H. Lantero. New York: Charles Scribner's Sons, 1958.

——. *Jesus Christ and Mythology*. New York: Charles Scribner's Sons, 1958.

——. "New Testament and Mythology." In *Kerygma and Myth: A Theological Debate*, pp. 1–44. Edited by Hans W. Bartsch. Translated by R. H. Fuller. New York: Harper & Row, 1961.

Burnet, John. "The Socratic Doctrine of the Soul," *Proceedings of the British Academy* 8 (1915–16): 235–59.

Butler, Samuel. *The Evidence for the Resurrection of Jesus Christ as Given by the Four Evangelists, Critically Examined*. London, 1865.

Byrnes, Joseph F. *The Psychology of Religion*. New York: The Free Press, 1984.

Calvin, John. *Commentary on The Acts of the Apostles*. Translated by J. W. Fraser. Edinburgh: Oliver & Boyd, 1966.

Cameron, N. *Personality Development and Psychopathology: A Dynamic Approach*. Boston: Houghton Mifflin, 1963.

Carnap, Rudolf. *The Logical Foundations of Probability*. Chicago: University of Chicago Press, 1950.

———. "Empiricism, Semantics, and Ontology." In *Meaning and Necessity*, pp. 205–11. Enlarged edition. Chicago: University of Chicago Press, 1956.

———. "Psychology in physical language," *Erkenntnis* 3 (1932). Partially reprinted in *Mind and Cognition: A Reader*, pp. 23–28. Edited by W. G. Lycan. Oxford: Blackwell, 1990.

Carnley, Peter. *The Structure of Resurrection Belief*. Oxford: Clarendon Press, 1987.

Carroll, Michael P. *The Cult of the Virgin Mary: Psychological Origins*. Princeton, NJ: Princeton University Press, 1986.

———. "Visions of the Virgin Mary: The Effect of Family Structures on Marian Apparitions," *Journal for the Scientific Study of Religion* 22 (1983): 205–21.

Castaneda, Carlos. *The Teachings of Don Juan*. New York: Ballantine, 1969.

The Catholic Encyclopedia. Edited by Charles Herbermann et. al. 15 vols. New York: Robert Appleton, 1912.

The Catholic Encyclopedia Dictionary. Edited by Donald Attwater. London: Cassell, 1949.

Cavendish, Richard, ed. *Man, Myth and Magic: An Illustrated Encyclopedia of the Supernatural*. New York: Marshall Cavendish Corp., 1970.

Chakkarai, V. *Jesus the Avatar*. Second edition. Madras, India: Christian Literature Society for India, 1930.

Christian, William A. Jr. *Apparitions in Late Medieval and Renaissance Spain*. Princeton, NJ: Princeton University Press, 1981.

———. *Moving Crucifixes in Modern Spain*. Princeton, NJ: Princeton University Press, 1992.

Churchill, John. "Beliefs, Principles, and Reasonable Doubts," *Religious Studies* 23 (1987): 221–32.

Churchland, Patricia S. *Neurophilosophy: Toward a Unified Science of the Mind-Brain*. Cambridge, MA: MIT Press, 1986.

———, and T. J. Sejnowski. "Neural Representation and Neural Computation." In *Neural Connections, Mental Computations*, pp. 15–48. Edited by L. Nadel et. al. Cambridge, MA: MIT Press, 1989.

———. "Is Neuroscience Relevant to Philosophy?" *Canadian Journal of Philosophy*, supplementary vol. 16 (1990): 323–41.

Churchland, Paul M. *A Neurocomputational Perspective: The Nature of Mind and the Structure of Science*. Cambridge, MA: MIT Press, 1992.

———. "Eliminative Materialism and the Propositional Attitudes," *Journal of Philosophy* 78 (1981). Reprinted in *Mind and Cognition: A Reader*, pp. 206–23. Edited by W. G. Lycan. Oxford: Blackwell, 1990.

———, and Patricia Churchland. "Stalking the Wild Epistemic Machine," *Nous* 17 (1983). Reprinted in *Mind and Cognition: A Reader*, pp. 300–311. Edited by W. G. Lycan. Oxford: Blackwell, 1990.

Clark, W. Royce. "Jesus, Lazarus, and Others: Resuscitation or Resurrection?" *Religion in Life* 49 (1980): 230–41.

Clayton, John. "Religions, Reasons and Gods," *Religious Studies* 23 (1987): 1–17.

Clement of Alexandria. *Exhortation to the Greeks*. Translated by G. W. Butterworth. London: William Heinemann, 1919.

Clement of Rome. *The Letter to the Corinthians*. In *The Fathers of the Church: A New Translation*, Vol. 1, pp. 9–58. Edited by Roy J. Deferrari. Translated by F. X. Glimm et. al. Washington, D.C.: Catholic University of American Press, 1947.

Clissold, Stephen. *St. Teresa of Avila*. London: Sheldon Press, 1979.

Coady, C.A.J. *Testimony: A Philosophical Study*. Oxford: Clarendon Press, 1992.

Coakley, Sarah. *Christ Without Absolutes: A Study of the Christology of Ernst Troeltsch*. Oxford: Clarendon Press, 1988.

—— "Is the Resurrection a 'Historical' Event? Some Muddles and Mysteries." In *The Resurrection of Jesus Christ*, pp. 85–115. Edited by Paul Avis. London: Darton, Longman & Todd, 1993.

Cole, Eve Browning. *Philosophy and Feminist Criticism: An Introduction*. New York: Paragon House, 1993.

Colwell, Gary. "Speaking of the Holy Spirit: Two Misconceptions," *Religious Studies and Theology* 8 (1988): 55–65.

Connell, Janice T. *The Visions of the Children: The Apparitions of the Blessed Mother at Medjugorje*. New York: St. Martin's Press, 1992.

Cornford, F. M. *Before and After Socrates*. Cambridge: Cambridge University Press, 1968.

Craig, W. L. *Assessing the New Testament Evidence for the Historicity of the Resurrection of Jesus*. Lewiston, NY: Edwin Mellen Press, 1989.

Cranmer, Thomas. *Miscellaneous Letters and Writings of Thomas Cranmer*. Edited by J. E. Cox. Cambridge, England: The University Press, 1846.

Crossan, John Dominic. *The Cross That Spoke: The Origins of the Passion Narratives*. San Francisco: Harper & Row, 1988.

——. *The Historical Jesus: The Life of a Mediterranean Jewish Peasant*. Edinburgh: T & T Clark, 1991.

Cupitt, Don. *Christ and the Hiddenness of God*. London: Lutterworth Press, 1971.

——. *Taking Leave of God*. London: SCM Press, 1980.

——. *The World to Come*. London: SCM Press, 1982.

Davey, Cyril J. *Sadhu Sundar Singh*. Bromley, England: STL Press, 1980. First published as *The Yellow Robe*, SCM Press, 1950.

Davis, Caroline Franks. *The Evidential Force of Religious Experience*. Oxford: Clarendon Press, 1989.

Davies, J. G. "Factors Leading to the Emergence of Belief in the Resurrection of the Flesh," *Journal of Theological Studies* 23 (1972): 448–55

Denison, Henry. *Visions of God*. London: Robert Scott, 1914.

Dibelius, Martin. *From Tradition to Gospel*. Translated from the second revised edition by B. L. Woolf. Cambridge: James Clark, 1971.

——. *Gospel Criticism and Christology*. London: Ivor Nicholson & Watson, 1935.

——. *Jesus*. Translated by C. B. Hedrick and F. C. Grant. London: SCM Press, 1963.

Dingwall, E. J. *Ghosts and Spirits in the Ancient World*. London: Kegan Paul, Trench, Truebner & Co., 1930.

Dobson, Cyril C. *The Face of Christ: Earliest Likenesses from the Catacombs*. London: Centenary Press, 1933.

Doede, Robert Paul. "The Body Comes All the Way Up," *International Philosophical Quarterly* 34 (1994): 215–27.

Dresser, Horatio W. *The Open Vision*. London: George G. Harrap, (n.d.).

Drury, Nevill. *The Visionary Human: Mystical Consciousness and Paranormal Perspectives*. Shaftesbury, England: Element, 1991.

Dufour, Xavier L. *Resurrection and the Message of Easter*. London: Geoffrey Chapman, 1974.

Eisenberg, Leon. "Hallucinations in children." In *Hallucinations*, pp. 198–210. Edited by L. J. West. New York: Grune & Stratton, 1962.

Ellis, I. P. "'But Some Doubted'," *New Testament Studies* 14 (1967–68): 574–80.

Enc, Berent. "Reference of Theoretical Terms," *Nous* 10 (1976): 261–82.

The Encyclopedia of the Lutheran Church. Edited by Julius Bodensieck. Minneapolis, MN: Augsburg Publishing House, 1965.

Encyclopedia of Southern Baptists. Edited by C. J. Allen et. al. Nashville, TN: Broadman Press, 1958.

Encyclopedia of Theology: A Concise Sacramentum Mundi. Edited by Karl Rahner. London: Burns & Oates, 1975.

Esther, Gulshan. *The Torn Veil: The Story of Sister Gulshan Esther*, as told to Thelma Sangster. Noble Din, interpreter. London: Marshall Pickering, 1992.

Eusebius, *The Ecclesiastical History*. Translated by Kirsopp Lake. London: William Heinemann, 1938–49.

Evangelical Dictionary of Theology. Edited by W. A. Elwell. Grand Rapids, MI: Baker Book House, 1984.

Evans, C. A. *Jesus*. (*Institute of Biblical Research Bibliographies*, No. 5.) Grand Rapids, MI: Baker Book House, 1992.

——. "Authenticity Criteria in Life of Jesus Research," *Christian Scholars Review* 19 (1989): 6–31.

——. "Life-of-Jesus Research and the Eclipse of Mythology," *Theological Studies* 54 (1993): 3–36.

Evans, C. F. *Resurrection and the New Testament*. London: SCM Press, 1970.

Evarts, E. V. "Neurophysiologic theory of hallucinations." In *Hallucinations*, pp. 1–14. Edited by L. J. West. New York: Grune & Stratton, 1962.

Farrer, Austin. *Interpretation and Belief*. Edited by C. C. Conti. London: SPCK, 1976.

Feigl, Herbert. *The "Mental" and the "Physical": The Essay and a Postscript*. Minneapolis: University of Minnesota Press, 1967.

——. "The "Orthodox" View of Theories." In *Analysis of Theories and Methods of Physics and Psychology* (*Minnesota Studies in the Philosophy of Science*, Vol. 4), pp. 3–16. Edited by M. Radner and S. Winokur. Minneapolis: University of Minnesota Press, 1970.

Feinberg, I. "A comparison of the visual hallucinations in schizophrenia with those induced by mescaline and LSD-25." In *Hallucinations*, pp. 64–76. Edited by L. J. West. New York: Grune & Stratton, 1962.

Feyerabend, Paul. *Against Method*. Revised edition. London: Verso, 1988.

——. "Mental Events and the Brain," *Journal of Philosophy* 60 (1963): 295–296.

Fink, George. "Homeostasis and hormonal regulation (neuroendocrine reflections of the brain)." In *Functions of the Brain*, pp. 130–59. Edited by C. W. Coen. Oxford: Clarendon Press, 1985.

Fischer, R. "Cartography of inner space." In *Hallucinations: Behavior, experience and theory*, pp. 197–239. Edited by R. K. Siegel and L. J. West. New York: Wiley, 1975.

Fish, F. J. "A neurophysiological theory of schizophrenia," *Journal of Mental Science* 107 (1961): 828–39.

Flew, Antony. *Hume's Philosophy of Belief*. New York: Humanist Press, 1961.

Fodor, Jerry A. *Psychological Explanation*. New York: Random House, 1968.

——. *The Modularity of Mind: An Essay on Faculty Psychology*. Cambridge, MA: MIT Press, 1983.

Fogelin, R. J. *Wittgenstein*. Second edition. London: Routledge & Kegan Paul, 1987.

Ford, D. F. "Barth's Interpretation of the Bible." In *Karl Barth: Studies of his Theological Method*, pp. 55–87. Edited by S. W. Sykes. Oxford: Clarendon Press, 1979.

Ford, Lewis S. "The Resurrection as the Emergence of the Body of Christ," *Religion in Life* 42 (1973): 466–77.

Freedman, H., and M. Simon, eds. *Midrash Rabbah*. Third ed. Translated by H. Freeman. London: Soncino Press, 1983.

Freeman, Eileen. *Touched by Angels*. New York: Warner Books, 1993.

Freud, Sigmund. *A General Introduction to Psycho-Analysis*. Chicago: Encyclopaedia Britannica, 1952.

——. *The Interpretation of Dreams*. Chicago: Encyclopaedia Britannica, 1952.

——. *The Origin and Development of Psycho-Analysis*. Chicago: Encyclopaedia Britannica, 1952.

Fulford, K.W.M. *Moral Theory and Medical Practice*. New York: Cambridge University Press, 1991.

Fuller, D. P. *Easter Faith and History*. London: Tyndale Press, 1968.

Fuller, Reginald H. *The Formation of the Resurrection Narratives*. London: SPCK, 1972.

Furst, Jeffrey. *Edgar Cayce's Story of Jesus*. London: Neville Spearman, 1968.

Gibson, James J. *The Senses Considered as Perceptual Systems*. Westcott, CT: Greenwood Press, 1966.

Goldstone, Sanford. "Psychophysics, reality and hallucinations." In *Hallucinations*, pp. 261–74. Edited by L. J. West. New York: Grune & Stratton, 1962.

The Gnostic Scriptures. Translated and annotated by Bentley Layton. London: SCM Press, 1987.

Goodman, Nelson. *Fact, Fiction, and Forecast*. Second edition. Indianapolis, IN: Bobbs-Merrill, 1965.

Gordon, Ian E. *Theories of Visual Perception*. Chichester, England: John Wiley & Sons, 1989.

Grassi, J. A. "Emmaus Revisited (Luke 24,13–35 and Acts 8,26–40)," *The Catholic Biblical Quarterly* 26 (1964): 463–67.

Grayling, A. C. *Wittgenstein*. Oxford: Oxford University Press, 1988.

Greeley, Andrew M. *The Sociology of the Paranormal: A Reconnaissance*. Beverly Hills, CA: Sage Publications, 1975.

Green, C. and C. McCreery. *Apparitions*. Institute of Psychophysical Research. Oxford University, 1989.

Green, Deirdre. *Gold in the Crucible*. Longmead, England: Element Books, 1989.

Gregory the Great. *Dialogues*. Translated by O. J. Zimmerman. New York: Fathers of the Church, 1959.

Grey, E. Howard. *Visions, Previsions and Miracles in Modern Times*. London: L. N. Fowler, 1915.

Greyson, Bruce. "The Near-Death Reliability Scale." In *The Near-Death Experience: Problems, Prospects, Perspectives*, pp. 45–60. Edited by Bruce Greyson and C. P. Flynn. Springfield, IL: Charles C Thomas, 1984.

Griffin, David R., et. al. *Founders of Constructive Postmodern Philosophy: Peirce, James, Bergson, Whitehead and Hartshorne*. Albany: State University of New York Press, 1993.

Grosso, Michael. "Jung, Parapsychology, and the Near-Death Experience: Towards a Transpersonal Paradigm." In *The Near-Death Experience: Problems, Prospects, Perspectives*, pp. 176–214. Edited by Bruce Greyson and C. P. Flynn. Springfield, IL: Charles C Thomas, 1983.

Gruenwald, Ithamar. "Major Issues in the Study and Understanding of Jewish Mysticism." In *Judaism in Late Antiquity (Part Two: Historical Syntheses)*, pp. 1–49. Edited by Jacob Neusner. Leiden, Netherlands: E. J. Brill, 1995.

Guthrie, Stewart Elliott. *Faces in the Clouds: A New Theory of Religion*. New York: Oxford University Press, 1993.

Habermas, Gary and Antony G. N. Flew. *Did Jesus Rise From the Dead: The Resurrection Debate*. Edited by Terry L. Miethe. San Francisco: Harper & Row, 1987.

Hanson, Norwood Russell. *Patterns of Discovery*. Cambridge: Cambridge University Press, 1958.

Hanson, Paul M. *Jesus Christ among the Ancient Americans*. Independence, MO: Herald Publishing House, 1959.

Hardy, Alister. *The Biology of God: A Scientist's Study of Man the Religious Animal*. London: Jonathan Cape, 1975.

——. *The Divine Flame: An Essay Towards a Natural History of Religion*. London: Collins, 1966.

——. *The Spiritual Nature of Man: A Study of Contemporary Religious Experience*. Oxford: Clarendon Press, 1979.

Harrison, Ted. *Stigmata: A Medieval Mystery in a Modern Age*. New York: St. Martin's Press, 1994.

Hart, Hornell. *The Enigma of Survival*. London: Rider and Co., 1959.

Hartmann, Ernest. "Dreams and other hallucinations: An approach to the underlying mechanism." In *Hallucinations: Behavior, experience and theory*, pp. 71–79. Edited by R. K. Siegel and L. J. West. New York: Wiley, 1975.

Haskins, Susan. *Mary Magdalene: Myth and Metaphor*. New York: Harcourt Brace and Co., 1993.

Hay, David. *Exploring Inner Space: Scientists and Religious Experience*. Revised edition. London: A. R. Mowbray & Co., 1987.

——, and Ann Morisy. "Reports of Ecstatic, Paranormal, or Religious Experience in Great Britain and the United States—A Comparison of Trends," *Journal for the Scientific Study of Religion* 17 (1978): 255–68.

Heaphy, Thomas. *The Likeness of Christ: Being an Inquiry into the Verisimilitude of the Received Likeness of Our Blessed Lord*. Edited by Wyke Bayliss. London: David Bogue, 1880.

Hebb, D. O. *The Organization of Behaviour*. London: Chapman & Hall, 1949.

Heilbrun, A. B. "Impaired recognition of self-expressed thought in patients with auditory hallucinations," *Journal of Abnormal Psychology* 89 (1980): 728–36.

——, and N. A. Blum. "Cognitive Vulnerability to Auditory Hallucination: Impaired Perception of Meaning," *British Journal of Psychiatry* 144 (1984): 508–12.

Hempel, Carl G. "Empiricist Criteria of Cognitive Significance: Problems and Changes," *Revue Internationale de Philosophie* 4 (1965). Reprinted with emendations in *The Philosophy of Science*, pp. 71–84. Edited by Richard Boyd et. al. Cambridge, MA: MIT Press, 1991.

——. "On the "Standard Conception" of Scientific Theories." In *Analysis of Theories and Methods of Physics and Psychology (Minnesota Studies in the Philosophy of Science*, Vol. 4), pp. 142–63. Edited by M. Radner and S. Winokur. Minneapolis: University of Minnesota Press, 1970.

——. "Studies in the Logic of Confirmation," *Mind* 54 (1945): 1–26, 97–121.

Hennecke, E. *New Testament Apocrypha*. Two volumes. Translated by R. McL. Wilson. Edited by Wilhelm Schneemelcher. Philadelphia: Westminster Press, 1963, 1965.

Hick, John. *Death and Eternal Life*. Louisville, KY: Westminster/John Knox Press, 1976.

——. *Disputed Questions in Theology and the Philosophy of Religion*. New Haven, CT: Yale University Press, 1993.

——. *The Metaphor of God Incarnate*. London: SCM Press, 1993.

Hill, G. F. *Medallic Portraits of Christ*. Oxford: Clarendon Press, 1920.

Hollands, Ernie (with Doug Brendel). *Hooked*. Toronto: Mainroads Productions, 1983.

Holm, Nils G. "Mysticism and Intense Experiences," *Journal for the Scientific Study of Religion* 21 (1982): 268–76.

Hood, Ralph W. "The Construction and Preliminary Validation of a Measure of Reported Mystical Experience," *Journal for the Scientific Study of Religion* 14 (1975): 29–41.

Hooker, C. "Towards a General Theory of Reduction," *Dialogue: Canadian Philosophical Review* 20 (1981): 38–59, 201–36, 496–529.

Horgan, Terence, and James Woodward. "Folk Psychology Is Here to Stay," *Philosophical Review* 94 (1985). In *Mind and Cognition: A Reader*, pp. 399–420. Edited by W. G. Lycan. Oxford: Blackwell, 1990.

Horowitz, M. J. "Hallucinations: an information-processing approach." In *Hallucinations: Behavior, experience and theory*, pp. 163–95. Edited by R. K. Siegel and L. J. West. New York: Wiley, 1975.

Horton, Robert F. *The Mystical Quest of Christ*. London: George Allen & Unwin, 1923.

Horvath, Tibor. "The Early Markan Tradition on the Resurrection," *Revue de l'Universite d'Ottawa* 43 (1973): 445–48.

Huffman, N. "Emmaus among the Resurrection Narratives," *Journal of Biblical Literature* 64 (1945): 205–26.

Humber, Thomas. *The Sacred Shroud*. New York: Pocket Books, 1977.

Hume, David. *A Treatise of Human Nature*. Edited by L. A. Selby-Bigge. Oxford: Clarendon Press, 1888.

Huxley, Aldous. *The Devils of Loudun*. Harmondsworth, England: Penguin, 1971.

——. *The Doors of Perception* and *Heaven and Hell*. Harmondsworth, England: Penguin, 1959.

Huxley, Julian. *Religion Without Revelation*. New York: Mentor Books, 1957.

Huyssen, Chester and Lucille Huyssen. *I Saw the Lord*. Tarrytown, NY: Fleming H. Revell, 1992. Reissue of *Visions of Jesus*. Plainfield, NJ: Logos International, 1977.

Hyslop, James H. *Psychical Research and the Resurrection*. Boston: Small, Maynard and Co., 1908.

Ignatius, St. *The Epistle to the Trallians.* In *The Fathers of the Church: A New Translation,* vol. 1, pp. 102–106. Edited by Roy J. Deferrari. Translated by F. X. Glimm et. al. Washington, D.C.: Catholic University of American Press, 1947.

Jaffe, Aniela. *Apparitions and Precognition: A Study from the Point of View of C. G. Jung's Analytical Psychology.* New York: University Books, 1963.

James, William. *Essays in Psychical Research.* Edited by Robert McDermott. Cambridge, MA: Harvard University Press, 1986.

———. *A Pluralistic Universe* and *Essays in Radical Empiricism.* Published in one volume. Gloucester, MA: Peter Smith, 1967.

———. *The Principles of Psychology.* Chicago: Encyclopaedia Britannica, 1952.

———. *The Varieties of Religious Experience: A Study in Human Nature.* London: Collins, 1960.

———. "Does 'Consciousness' Exist?" *Journal of Philosophy, Psychology and Scientific Method* 1 (1904). Reprinted in *Essays in Radical Empiricism,* pp. 1–38. Gloucester, MA: Peter Smith, 1967.

Jantzen, Grace. *Incorporeal Identity.* Unpublished doctoral dissertation. The University of Calgary, 1974. Written under name Grace Dyck.

———. *Julian of Norwich: Mystic and Theologian.* London: SPCK, 1987.

Jaynes, Julian. *The Origins of Consciousness in the Breakdown of the Bicameral Mind.* Toronto: University of Toronto Press, 1976.

John of the Cross. *Ascent of Mount Carmel.* Translated by Kieran Kavanaugh. London: SPCK, 1987.

———. *The Dark Night of the Soul.* Translated by Benedict Zimmerman. Cambridge: James Clarke & Co., 1973.

Jones, Richard H. *Mysticism Examined: Philosophical Inquiries into Mysticism.* Albany: State University of New York Press, 1993.

Julian of Norwich. *Revelations of Divine Love.* Translated by J. Walsh. London: Burns & Oates, 1961.

Jung, C. G. "The Psychological Foundations of Belief in Spirits," *Proceedings of the Society for Psychical Research,* 31 (1919). Reprinted in *Contributions to Analytical Psychology,* pp. 250–69. Translated by H. G. and C. F. Baynes. New York: Harcourt, Brace and Co., 1928.

———. "The Basic Postulates of Analytical Psychology." First published in *Europaeische Revue* (1931). Reprinted in *Modern Man in Search of a Soul,* pp. 200–25. Translated by W. S. Dell and C. F. Baynes. New York: Harcourt, Brace and Co., 1936.

———. "Brother Klaus." First published in *Neue Schweizer Rundshau* 4 (1933) (Zurich). Reprinted in *Psychology and Western Religion,* pp. 225–32. Translated by R.F.C. Hull. Princeton, NJ: Princeton University Press, 1984.

———. "On the Psychogenesis of Schizophrenia," *Journal of Mental Science* 85 (1939). Reprinted in *Theories of Psychopathology and Personality: Essays and Critiques,* pp. 128–36. Second edition. Edited by Theodore Millon. Philadelphia: W. B. Saunders Co., 1973.

———. "On Resurrection." First published in *The Symbolic Life, Collected Works,* Vol. 18. Princeton, NJ: Princeton University Press, 1955. Reprinted in *Psychology and Western Religion,* pp. 247–51. Translated by R.F.C. Hull. Princeton, NJ: Princeton University Press, 1984.

———. *Memories, Dreams, Reflections.* Edited by Aniela Jaffe. New York: Vintage Books, 1963.

——. *The Structure and Dynamics of the Psyche. Collected Works*, Vol. 8. London: Routledge and Kegan Paul, 1969.

Justin Martyr. *The First Apology.* In *The Ante-Nicene Fathers: Translations of the Fathers Down to A.D. 325.* Vol. 1. Edited by A. Roberts and J. Donaldson. Reprint of Edinburgh edition. Grand Rapids, MI: Wm. B. Eerdmans, 1953.

Kähler, Martin. *The So-called Historical Jesus and the Historic Biblical Christ.* Translated by C. E. Braaten. Philadelphia: Fortress Press, 1964.

Katz, Jonathan. "The One That Got Away: Leslie's Universes," *Dialogue: Canadian Philosophical Review* 29 (1990): 589–95.

Katz, Steven T., editor. *Mysticism and Religious Traditions.* New York: Oxford University Press, 1983.

Kelsey, Morton. *Discernment: A Study in Ecstasy and Evil.* New York: Paulist Press, 1978.

Kersten, Holger, and Elmar R. Gruber. *The Jesus Conspiracy: The Turin Shroud and the Truth about the Resurrection.* Shaftesbury, England: Element, 1994.

Kress, Robert. "Resurrection Faith: Life or Fuga Mundi?" *Review for Religious* 30 (1973): 97–101.

Kripke, Saul. "Naming and Necessity." In *Semantics of Natural Language*, pp. 253–355. Edited by D. Davidson and G. Harman. Dordrecht, Netherlands: D. Reidel, 1972.

Kuhn, Thomas. *The Structure of Scientific Revolutions.* Chicago: University of Chicago Press, 1962.

Küng, Hans. *Does God Exist? An Answer for Today.* Translated by Edward Quinn. Garden City, NY: Doubleday, 1980.

——. *On Being a Christian.* Translated by Edward Quinn. Garden City, NY: Doubleday, 1976.

——. "Rediscovering God." Translated by F. McDonagh. In *On the Threshold of the Third Millennium.* Edited by Concilium Foundation. Philadelphia: Trinity Press International, 1990.

La Barre, Weston. "Anthropological perspectives on hallucination and hallucinogens." In *Hallucinations: Behavior, experience and theory*, pp. 9–52. Edited by R. K. Siegel and L. J. West. New York: Wiley, 1975.

Ladd, George E. *I believe in the resurrection of Jesus.* London: Hodder & Stoughton, 1975.

Laski, Marghanita. *Ecstasy in Secular and Religious Experiences.* Los Angeles: Jeremy P. Tarcher, 1961.

Laudan, Larry. "A Confutation of Convergent Realism," *Philosophy of Science* 48 (1981): 19–48.

Launay, G., and P. Slade. "The Measurement of Hallucinatory Predisposition in Male and Female Prisoners," *Personality and Individual Differences* 2 (1981): 221–34.

Lewis, C. S. *The Discarded Image: An Introduction to Medieval and Renaissance Literature.* Cambridge: Cambridge University Press, 1964.

Lewis, David K. *On the Plurality of Worlds.* Oxford: Basil Blackwell, 1986.

——. "An Argument for the Identity Theory," *Journal of Philosophy* 63 (1966): 17–25.

——. "How to Define Theoretical Terms," *Journal of Philosophy* 47 (1970): 427–46.

——. "The Paradoxes of Time Travel," *American Philosophical Quarterly* 13 (1976): 145–52.

———. "Psychophysical and Theoretical Identifications," *Australasian Journal of Philosophy* 50 (1972): 249–58.

Locke, John. *Essay Concerning Human Understanding.* Two volumes. London: J. M. Dent, 1961.

Lossky, Vladimir. *The Mystical Theology of the Eastern Church.* Crestwood, NY: St. Vladimir's Seminary Press, 1976.

Ludemann, Gerd. *The Resurrection of Jesus: History, Experience, Theology.* Translated by J. Bowden. London: SCM Press, 1994.

Luther, Martin. *Luther's Works.* Edited by Jaroslav Pelikan. Fifty-five volumes. St. Louis, MO: Concordia Publishing House, 1958–67.

Lycan, William G. *Consciousness.* Cambridge, MA: MIT Press, 1987.

———, ed. *Mind and Cognition: A Reader.* Oxford: Blackwell, 1990.

Macbeath, John. *The Face of Christ.* Fifth edition. London: Marshall, Morgan & Scott, 1954.

Mack, Burton. *The Lost Gospel: The Book of Q and Christian Origins.* San Francisco: HarperCollins, 1993.

MacKenzie, Andrew. *Apparitions and Ghosts: A Modern Study.* London: Arthur Barker, 1971.

———. *The Seen and the Unseen.* London: Weidenfeld & Nicolson, 1987.

Mackie, J. L. *The Miracle of Theism: Arguments For and Against the Existence of God.* Oxford: Clarendon Press, 1982.

Maitland, T. R. "A Place for Religious Assertions?" *American Philosophical Quarterly* 29 (1992): 45–52.

Maloney, G. A. *The Mystics of Fire and Light: St. Symeon the New Theologian.* Denville, NJ: Dimension Books, 1975.

Margolis, Robert D., and Kirk W. Elifson. "A Typology of Religious Experience," *Journal for the Scientific Study of Religion* 18 (1979): 61–67.

Marxsen, W. *The Resurrection of Jesus of Nazareth.* London: SCM Press, 1970.

———. "The Resurrection of Jesus as a Historical and Theological Problem." In *The Significance of the Message of the Resurrection for Faith in Jesus Christ (Studies in Biblical Theology,* Second series, Vol. 8.), pp. 15–50. Edited by C.F.D. Moule. London: SCM Press, 1968.

McDonald, J. I. H. *The Resurrection: Narrative and Belief.* London: SPCK, 1989.

McDougall, William. *Religion and the Sciences of Life and Other Essays on Allied Topics.* London: Methuen, 1934.

Meehan, Brenda. *Holy Women of Russia: The Lives of Five Orthodox Women Offer Spiritual Guidance for Today.* San Francisco: HarperCollins, 1993.

Meille, Giovanni E. *Christ's Likeness in History and Art.* London: Burns, Oates & Washbourne, 1924.

The Mennonite Encyclopedia. Edited by C. J. Dyck and D. D. Martin. Scottdale, PA: Herald Press, 1990.

Merleau-Ponty, M. *Phenomenology of Perception.* Translated by Colin Smith. London: Routledge & Kegan Paul, 1962.

Minnich, Elizabeth K. *Transforming Knowledge.* Philadelphia: Temple University Press, 1990.

Mitchell, Basil. *The Justification of Religious Belief.* New York: Oxford University Press, 1981.

Modell, Arnold H. "Hallucinations in schizophrenic patients and their relation to psychic structure." In *Hallucinations,* pp. 166–75. Edited by L. J. West. New York: Grune & Stratton, 1962.

Molinari, Paul. *Julian of Norwich: The Teaching of a 14th Century English Mystic.* London: Longman, Green & Co., 1958.

Montgomery, John W. *History and Christianity.* Downers Grove, IL: Intervarsity Press, 1964.

Moody, Raymond A. *Life After Life.* Covington, GA: Mockingbird Books, 1975.

———. *Reflections on Life After Life.* New York: Bantam Books, 1977.

———. *Reunions: Visionary Encounters with Departed Loved Ones.* New York: Villard Books, 1993.

Moore, Peter. "Christian Mysticism and Interpretation: Some Philosophical Issues Illustrated in the Study of the Medieval English Mystics." In *The Medieval Mystical Tradition in England,* pp. 154–76. Edited by Marion Glasscoe. Cambridge: D. S. Brewer, 1987.

Moore, Sebastian. "The Resurrection: A Confusing Paradigm-Shift," *The Downside Review* 98 (1980): 257–66.

Moule, C. F. D. "The Post-Resurrection Appearances in the Light of Festival Pilgrimages," *New Testament Studies* 4 (1957–58): 58–61.

Murphy, Gardner. *Challenges of Psychical Research: A Primer of Parapsychology.* New York: Harper & Row, 1961.

———. "An Outline of Survival Evidence," *Journal of the American Society for Psychical Research* 39 (1945): 2–34.

Myers, F. W. H. *Human Personality and Its Survival of Bodily Death.* Abridged edition of the 1903 edition. New York: University Books, 1961.

Nagel, Ernest. *The Structure of Science.* New York: Harcourt Brace Jovanovich, 1961.

New Catholic Encyclopedia. Edited by W. J. McDonald et. al. Eighteen volumes. New York: McGraw-Hill, 1967.

New Dictionary of Theology. Edited by S. F. Ferguson and D. F. Wright. Downers Grove, IL: Intervarsity Press, 1988.

The New International Dictionary of the Christian Church. Second edition. Edited by J. D. Douglas. Grand Rapids, MI: Zondervan, 1978.

Niebuhr, Richard R. *Resurrection and Historical Reason: A Study of Theological Method.* New York: Charles Scribner's Sons, 1957.

Nola, Robert. "Fixing the Reference of Theoretical Terms," *Philosophy of Science* 47 (1980): 505–31.

O'Collins, Gerald. *The Easter Jesus.* Second edition. London: Darton, Longman & Todd, 1980.

———. *Interpreting Jesus.* London: Geoffrey Chapman, 1983.

Origen. *De Principiis.* In *The Ante-Nicene Fathers: Translations of the Writings of the Fathers down to A.D. 325.* Vol. 4. Edited by A. Roberts and J. Donaldson. Reprint of Edinburgh edition. Grand Rapids, MI: Wm. B. Eerdmans, 1956.

Orlett, Raymond. "An Influence of the Early Liturgy upon the Emmaus Account," *The Catholic Biblical Quarterly* 21 (1959): 212–19.

Orne, Martin T. "Hypnotically induced hallucinations." In *Hallucinations,* pp. 211–19. Edited by L. J. West. New York: Grune & Stratton, 1962.

Oster, G. "Phosphenes." *Scientific American* 222 (1970): 83–87.

O'Toole, R. F. "Luke's Understanding of Jesus' Resurrection-Ascension-Exaltation," *Biblical Theology Bulletin* 9 (1979): 106–14.

Otto, Rudolf. *The Idea of the Holy: An inquiry into the non-rational factor in the idea of the divine and its relation to the rational.* Second edition. Translated by John W. Harvey. London: Oxford University Press, 1950.

Oxford English Dictionary. Oxford: Oxford University Press, 1971.

Pagels, Elaine. *The Gnostic Gospels*. New York: Random House, 1979.

Panikkar, R. *The unknown Christ of Hinduism: toward an ecumenical Christophany*. London: Darton, Longman & Todd, 1981.

Pannenberg, W. *Jesus—Man and God*. Translated by L. L. Wilkins and D. A. Priebe. London: SCM Press, 1968.

Payne, E. J. *Orthodox Religion and Spiritualism*. London: Psychic Press, 1946.

Peacocke, Arthur. *Theology for a Scientific Age*. Enlarged edition. Minneapolis, MN: Fortress Press, 1993.

Peers, E. Allison. *Mother of Carmel: A Portrait of St. Teresa of Avila*. London: SCM Press, 1945.

Pelfrey, Brant. *Christ our Mother: Julian of Norwich*. London: Darton, Longman & Todd, 1989.

Pelikan, Jaroslav. *The Christian Tradition: A History of the Development of Doctrine*. Five volumes. Chicago: University of Chicago Press, 1971.

Penelhum, Terence, ed. *Faith*. New York: Macmillan, 1989.

Penfield, Wilder. *The Mystery of the Mind: A Critical Study of Consciousness and the Human Brain*. Princeton, NJ: Princeton University Press, 1975.

Penrose, Roger. *The Emperor's New Mind: Concerning Computers, Minds, and the Laws of Physics*. Oxford: Oxford University Press, 1989.

Perkins, Pheme. *Resurrection: The New Testament Witness and Contemporary Reflection*. London: Geoffrey Chapman, 1984.

——. "The Resurrection of Jesus of Nazareth." In *Studying the Historical Jesus: Evaluations of the State of Current Research*, pp. 423–42. Edited by Bruce Chilton and Craig A. Evans. Leiden, Netherlands: E. J. Brill, 1994.

Perry, Michael C. *The Easter Enigma: An Essay on the Resurrection with Specific Reference to the Data of Psychical Research*. London: Faber & Faber, 1959.

Phillips, D. Z. *Religion without Explanation*. Oxford: Blackwell, 1976.

Place, U. T. "Is Consciousness a Brain Process?" *British Journal of Psychology* 47 (1956): 44–50.

Plantinga, Alvin. *God and Other Minds: A Study of the Rational Justification of Belief in God*. Ithaca, NY: Cornell University Press, 1967.

——. "Is Belief in God Properly Basic?" *Nous* 15 (1981): 41–51.

——. "Is Belief in God Rational?" In *Rationality and Religious Belief*, pp. 7–27. Edited by C. F. Delaney. Notre Dame, IN: University of Notre Dame Press, 1979.

Polanyi, Michael. *The Study of Man*. Chicago: University of Chicago Press, 1959.

Pomerius, Julianus. *The Contemplative Life*. Translated and noted by Mary Josephine Suelzer. Westminster, MD: Newman Press, 1947.

Popper, Karl R. *Conjectures and Refutations*. London: Routledge & Kegan Paul, 1963.

——. *The Logic of Scientific Discovery*. Revised edition. London: Hutchinson, 1968.

——, and John C. Eccles. *The Self and Its Brain*. Berlin: Springer-Verlag, 1977.

Putnam, Hilary. *Reason, Truth and History*. Cambridge: Cambridge University Press, 1981.

——. "The Meaning of 'Meaning.'" In *Language, Mind and Knowledge (Minnesota Studies in the Philosophy of Science*, Vol. 7), pp. 131–93. Edited by K. Gunderson. Minneapolis: University of Minnesota Press, 1975.

——. "Minds and machines." In *Dimensions of Mind*. Edited by S. Hook. New York: Collier Books, 1960.

——. "The Nature of Mental States." First published as "Psychological Predicates" in *Art, Mind and Religion*. Edited by W. H. Capitan and D. D. Merrill. University of Pittsburgh Press, 1967. Republished in *Mind and Cognition: A Reader*, pp. 47–56. Edited by W. G. Lycan. Oxford: Blackwell, 1990.

Quine, W.V.O. *From a Logical Point of View*. Second edition. New York: Harper & Row, 1963.

——. *Ontological Relativity and Other Essays*. New York: Columbia University Press, 1969.

——. *Word and Object*. Cambridge, MA: MIT Press, 1960.

Quinn, Philip L. "Some Problems about Resurrection," *Religious Studies* 14 (1978): 343–59.

Rahner, Karl. *Visions and Prophecies*. (*Questiones Disputatae 10*.) New York: Herder & Herder, 1963.

Randall, John L. *Parapsychology and the Nature of Life*. New York: Harper & Row, 1975.

Rawls, John. *A Theory of Justice*. Cambridge, MA: Harvard University Press, 1971.

Redmond, M. "The Hamann-Hume Connection," *Religious Studies* 23 (1987): 95–107.

Reimarius, H. S. *Fragments: Concerning the Intention of Jesus and His Teaching*. Edited by C. H. Talbert. Translated by R. S. Fraser. Philadelphia: Fortress Press, 1970.

Rhine, J. B. "Research on Spirit Survival Reexamined," *Journal of Parapsychology* 20 (1956): 127.

Rhine, Louisa E. *ESP in Life and Lab: Tracing Hidden Channels*. New York: Macmillan, 1967.

Roberts, R. H. "Karl Barth's Doctrine of Time: Its Nature and Implications." In *Karl Barth: Studies of His Theological Method*, pp. 88–146. Edited by S. W. Sykes. Oxford: Clarendon Press, 1979.

Robinson, Edward. *The Original Vision: A Study of the Religious Experience of Childhood*. New York: Seabury Press, 1983.

Robinson, John A. T. *Honest to God*. London: SCM Press, 1963.

Robinson, J. M. "Jesus: From Easter to Valentinus (or to the Apostle's Creed)," *Journal of Biblical Literature* 101 (1982): 5–37.

Rorty, Richard. *Philosophy and the Mirror of Nature*. Princeton, NJ: Princeton University Press, 1979.

——. "Mind-Body Identity, Privacy, and Categories," *Review of Metaphysics* 19 (1965): 24–54.

Rosenthal, David M. *Materialism and Mind-Body Problem*. Indianapolis, IN: Hackett, 1987.

Rowland, Christopher. *The Open Heaven: A Study of Apocalyptic in Judaism and Early Christianity*. London: SPCK, 1982.

Ryle, Gilbert. *The Concept of Mind*. London: Hutchinson, 1949.

Sabourin, L. "The Resurrection of Jesus," *Biblical Theology Bulletin* 5 (1975): 269–93.

Sackville-West, Victoria. *The Eagle and the Dove*. London: Penguin, 1988.

Salmon, Wesley. *Scientific Explanation and the Causal Structure of the World*. Princeton, NJ: Princeton University Press, 1984.

Sampson, Holden E. *Portraits of Jesus*. London: William Rider & Son, (n.d.).

Sanders, E. P. *The Historical Figure of Jesus*. London: Penguin, 1993.

Sarbin, T. R., and J. B. Juhasz. "The social context of hallucinations." In *Hallucinations: Behavior, experience and theory*, pp. 241–56. Edited by R. K. Siegel and L. J. West. New York: Wiley, 1975.

Savage, C. Wade. "The continuity of perceptual and cognitive experiences." In *Hallucinations: Behavior, experience and theory*, pp. 257–86. Edited by R. K. Siegel and L. J. West. New York: Wiley, 1975.

Scheibel, Madge E., and Arnold B. Scheibel. "Hallucinations and the brain stem reticular core." In *Hallucinations*, pp. 15–35. Edited by L. J. West. New York: Grune & Stratton, 1962.

Schillebeeckx, Edward. *Jesus: An Experiment in Christology*. New York: Crossroad, 1981.

Schlagel, Richard H. *Contextual Realism: A Meta-physical Framework for Modern Science*. New York: Paragon House Publishers, 1986.

Schneemelcher, Wilhelm, ed. *New Testament Apocrypha*. Revised edition. Translated by R. McL. Wilson. Cambridge: James Clarke & Co., 1991.

Schoen, Edward L. *Religious Explanations: A Model from the Sciences*. Durham, NC: Duke University Press, 1985.

Schweizer, Eduard. *Lordship and Discipleship*. London: SCM Press, 1960.

———. "Resurrection—Fact or Illusion," *Horizons in Biblical Theology* I 1979: 137–59.

Sedman, G. "A comparative study of pseudo-hallucinations, imagery and true hallucinations," *British Journal of Psychiatry* 112 (1966): 9–17.

Segal, Alan F. "Paul and the Beginning of Jewish Mysticism." In *Death, Ecstasy, and Other Worldly Journeys*, pp. 95–122. Edited by John J. Collins and Michael Fishbane. Albany: State University of New York Press, 1995.

Sellars, Wilfrid. *Science, Perception and Reality*. London: Routledge & Kegan Paul, 1963.

Seymour, St. John D. *Irish Visions of the Other-World: A Contribution to the Study of Medieval Vision*. London: SPCK, 1930.

Shallice, Tim. *From Neuropsychology to Mental Structure*. Cambridge: Cambridge University Press, 1988.

Shapere, Dudley. "The Concept of Observation in Science and Philosophy," *Philosophy of Science* 49 (1982): 485–526.

Sharp, Daryl. *C. G. Jung Lexicon: A Primer of Terms and Concepts*. Toronto: Inner City Books, 1991.

Shurley, Jay T. "Mental imagery in profound experimental sensory isolation." In *Hallucinations*, pp. 153–57. Edited by L. J. West. New York: Grune & Stratton, 1962.

Sicari, Antonio. "Teresa of Avila: Mystical experience in defense of dogma," *Communio: International Catholic Review* 16 (1989): 89–104.

Sidgewick, H. A., et. al. "Report on the census of hallucinations," *Proceedings of the Society for Psychical Research* 10 (1894): 25–422.

Siegel, Ronald K. "The Psychology of Life After Death." In *The Near-Death Experience: Problems, Prospects, Perspectives*, pp. 71–120. Edited by Bruce Greyson and C. P. Flynn. Springfield, IL: Charles C Thomas, 1984.

———, and M. E. Jarvik. "Drug-induced hallucinations in animals and man." In *Hallucinations: Behavior, experience and theory*, pp. 81–161. Edited by R. K. Siegel and L. J. West. New York: Wiley, 1975.

Singh, Sundar. *Visions of the Spiritual World*. London: Macmillan, 1926.

Skinner, B. F. *Science and Human Behavior*. New York: Macmillan, 1933.

———. "Behaviorism at Fifty." In *Behaviorism and Phenomenology: Contrasting Bases for Modern Psychology*. pp. 79–108. Edited by T. W. Wann. Chicago: University of Chicago Press, 1964.

Slote, Michael. "Religion, science, and the extraordinary," *The American Philosophical Quarterly Monograph Series* 3 (1969): 188–205.

Smart, J.J.C. "Sensations and Brain Processes," *Philosophical Review* 68 (1959): 141–56.

Smith, John E. *Experience and God*. London: Oxford University Press, 1968.

———. "William James's Account of Mysticism: A Critical Appraisal." In *Mysticism and Religious Traditions*, pp. 247–78. Edited by Steven T. Katz. Oxford: Oxford University Press, 1983.

Solomon, Philip, and Jack Mendelson. "Hallucinations in sensory deprivation." In *Hallucinations*, pp. 135–45. Edited by L. J. West. New York: Grune & Stratton, 1962.

Solomon, Robert. "Freud's Neurological Theory of Mind." In *Freud: A Collection of Critical Essays*, pp. 25–52. Edited by R. Wollheim. New York: Anchor Books, 1974.

Soskice, Janet. *Metaphor and Religious Language*. Oxford: Clarendon Press, 1985.

Sparrow, G. Scott. *I Am With You Always: True Stories of Encounters with Jesus*. New York: Bantam Books, 1995.

Spong, John S. *Resurrection: Myth or Reality?* San Francisco: HarperCollins, 1994.

Stace, W. T. *Mysticism and Philosophy*. London: Macmillan, 1960.

Steiner, Rudolf. *From Jesus to Christ*. London: H. Collinson, 1911.

Stevenson, Ian. *Twenty Cases Suggestive of Reincarnation*. Second edition. Charlottesville: University Press of Virginia, 1974.

———. "Do we need a new word to supplement 'hallucination'?" *American Journal of Psychiatry* 140 (1983): 1609–11.

Stich, Stephen. "Autonomous Psychology and the Belief-Desire Thesis," *Monist* 61 (1978): 573–91.

———. "Reflective Equilibrium, Analytic Epistemology, and the Problem of Cognitive Diversity," *Synthese* 74 (1988): 391–413.

Straus, Erwin W. "Phenomenology of hallucinations." In *Hallucinations*, pp. 220–32. Edited by L. J. West. New York: Grune & Stratton, 1962.

Strauss, David F. *The Christ of Faith and the Jesus of History*. Translated by L. E. Keck. Philadelphia: Fortress Press, 1977.

———. *A New Life of Jesus*. Two volumes. London: Williams & Norgate, 1865.

Strauss, John S. "Hallucinations and delusions as points on continua functions," *Archives of General Psychiatry* 21 (1969): 581–86.

Suppe, Frederick, ed. *The Structure of Theories*. Urbana: University of Illinois Press, 1974.

Swedenborg, Emanuel. *Angelic Wisdom Concerning the Divine Love and the Divine Wisdom (The Divine Love and Wisdom)*. Translated by J. C. Ager. New York: Swedenborg Foundation, 1915.

———. *Heaven and Its Wonders and Hell from Things Heard and Seen (Heaven and Hell)*. Translated by J. C. Ager. New York: Swedenborg Foundation, 1952.

Swinburne, Richard. *The Coherence of Theism*. Oxford: Clarendon Press, 1977.

———. *The Evolution of the Soul*. Oxford: Clarendon Press, 1986.

———. *The Existence of God*. Oxford: Clarendon Press, 1979.
———, ed. *Miracles*. New York: Macmillan, 1989.
———. *Revelation*. Oxford: Clarendon Press, 1992.
Taylor, A. E. *Socrates: The Man and His Thought*. New York: Doubleday Anchor Books, 1953.
Taylor, F. Kraeupl. "On pseudo-hallucinations," *Psychological Medicine* 11 (1981): 265–71.
Tenney, Merrill C. *The Reality of the Resurrection*. Chicago: Moody Press, 1963.
———. "The Historicity of the Resurrection." In *Jesus of Nazareth: Saviour and Lord*, pp. 133–44. Edited by C.F.H. Henry. London: Tyndale, 1966.
Teresa of Avila. *The Interior Castle*. Translated by K. Kavanaugh and O. Rodriguez. London: SPCK, 1979.
——— *The Life of the Holy Mother Teresa of Jesus*. Translated by E. Allison Peers. London: Sheed & Ward, 1946.
Tertullian. *On the Resurrection of the Flesh* and *Against Praxeas*. In *The Ante-Nicene Fathers: Translations of the Writings of the Fathers down to A.D. 325*. Vol. 3. Edited by A. Roberts and J. Donaldson. Reprint of Edinburgh edition. Grand Rapids, MI: Wm. B. Eerdmans, 1957.
Theological Dictionary of the New Testament. Edited by G. Friedrich. Translated by G. W. Bromiley. Grand Rapids, MI: Wm. B. Eerdmans, 1967.
Thomas, Denis. *The Face of Christ*. London: Hamlyn, 1979.
Thouless, R. H. *From Anecdote to Experiment in Psychical Research*. London: Routledge & Kegan Paul, 1972.
Tillich, Paul. *Systemic Theology (Three Volumes in One)*. Chicago: University of Chicago Press, 1967.
Thrall, Margaret E. "Resurrection Traditions and Christian Apologetic," *Thomist* 43: 197–216.
Torrance, T. F. *Karl Barth: An Introduction to his Early Theology, 1910–1931*. London: SCM Press, 1962.
Trites, Allison A. *The New Testament Concept of Witness*. Cambridge: Cambridge University Press, 1977.
Turner, Victor, and Edith Turner. "Postindustrial Marian Pilgrimage." In *Mother Worship*, pp. 145–73. Edited by J. J. Preston. Chapel Hill: University of North Carolina, 1982.
Tyrrell, G. N. M. *Apparitions*. London: Gerald Duckworth & Co., 1942.
———. *The Personality of Man: New Facts and Their Significance*. West Drayton, England: Penguin, 1948.
Underhill, Evelyn. *Mysticism: A Study in the Nature and Development of Man's Spiritual Consciousness*. Twelfth revised edition. London: Methuen, 1930.
Van Dusen, Wilson. "Hallucinations as the World of Spirits." In *Frontiers of Consciousness: The Meeting Ground Between Inner and Outer Reality*. Edited by J. White. New York: Julian Press, 1974.
Von Balthasar, Hans Urs. *The Theology of Karl Barth*. Translated by J. Drury. New York: Anchor Books, 1972.
Wagner, Peter. *Warfare Prayer*. Ventura, CA: Regal Books, 1992.
Wainwright, William J. *Mysticism: A Study of Its Nature, Cognitive Value and Moral Implications*. Madison: University of Wisconsin Press, 1981.
Walker, W. O. "Postcrucifixion Appearances and Christian Origins," *Journal of Biblical Literature* 88 (1969): 157–65.

Wallace, Abraham. *Jesus of Nazareth and Modern Scientific Investigation from the Spiritualist Standpoint.* Second edition. Manchester, England: The "Two Worlds" Publishing Co., 1920.

Wallace, Benjamin, and L. E. Fisher. *Consciousness and Behavior.* Second edition. Boston: Allyn & Bacon, 1987.

Walsh, William J. *The Apparitions and Shrines of Heaven's Bright Queen.* Four volumes. New York: Cary-Stafford Co., 1906.

Walsh, William T. *Saints in Action.* New York: Doubleday, 1961.

Weatherhead, Leslie D. *The Resurrection of Christ.* London: Hodder & Stoughton, 1959.

Weinstein, Edwin A. "Social aspects of hallucinations." In *Hallucinations*, pp. 253–88. Edited by L. J. West. New York: Grune & Stratton, 1962.

West, D. J. "A Mass-Observation Questionnaire on Hallucinations," *Journal of the Society for Psychical Research* 34 (1948): 187–96.

West, Louis J. "A clinical and theoretical overview of hallucinatory phenomena." In *Hallucinations: Behavior, experience and theory*, pp. 287–311. Edited by R. K. Siegel and L. J. West. New York: Wiley, 1975.

——. "A general theory of hallucinations and dreams." In *Hallucinations*, pp. 275–91. Edited by L. J. West. New York: Grune & Stratton, 1962.

White, John. *Putting the Soul Back in Psychology.* Downers Grove, IL: Intervarsity Press, 1987.

Wiebe, Phillip H. *Theism in an Age of Science.* Lanham, MD: University Press of America, 1988.

——. "Authenticating Biblical Reports of Miracles," *Journal of Philosophical Research* 18 (1993): 309–25.

Wilckens, Ulrich. *Resurrection: Biblical Testimony to the Resurrection: An Historical Examination and Explanation.* Translated by A. M. Stewart. Edinburgh: St. Andrews Press, 1977.

——. "The Tradition-History of the Resurrection of Jesus." In *The Significance of the Message of the Resurrection for Faith in Jesus Christ (Studies in Biblical Theology*, Second series, Vol. 8), pp. 51–76. Edited by C.F.D. Moule. London: SCM Press, 1968.

Williams, G. H., ed. *Spiritual and Anabaptist Writers: Documents Illustrative of the Radical Reformation.* London: SCM Press, 1957.

Williams, Harold L., et. al. "Illusions, hallucinations and sleep loss." In *Hallucinations*, pp. 158–65. Edited by L. J. West. New York: Grune & Stratton, 1962.

Williams, Rowan. *Teresa of Avila.* London: Geoffrey Chapman, 1991.

Wilson, Ian. *The Bleeding Mind: An Investigation Into the Mysterious Phenomenon of Stigmata.* London: Paladin, Grafton Books, 1991.

——. *Holy Faces, Secret Places: An Amazing Quest for the Face of Jesus.* New York: Doubleday, 1991.

——. *The Mysterious Shroud.* Garden City, NY: Doubleday, 1986.

Wittgenstein, Ludwig. *Philosophical Investigations.* Oxford: Blackwell, 1953.

Wolter, Franz. *How Did Christ Look?* Translated by C.C.H. Drechsel-Lancaster. Munich: Hugo Schmidt, 1930.

Worcester, Benjamin. *The Life and Mission of Emanuel Swedenborg.* Boston: Little, Brown and Co., 1907.

Wright, G. Ernest. *God Who Acts: Biblical Theology as Recital. (Studies in Biblical Theology*, No. 8). London: SCM Press, 1952.

Wright, N. T. *The New Testament and the People of God*. Minneapolis, MN: Fortress Press, 1992.

Yates, J. C. "Disembodied Existence in an Objective World," *Religious Studies* 23 (1987): 531–38.

Yee, Margaret M. *The Validity of Theology as an Academic Discipline: A Study in the Light of the History and Philosophy of Science and with Special Reference to Relevant Aspects of the Thought of Austin Farrer*. Unpublished doctoral dissertation. Oxford University, 1987.

Young, J. Z. *Philosophy and the Brain*. Oxford: Oxford University Press, 1986.

——. "What's in a brain." In *Functions of the Brain*, pp. 1–10. Edited by C. W. Coen. Oxford: Clarendon Press, 1985.

Zaehner, R. C. *Concordant Discord*. Oxford: Clarendon Press, 1970.

Zaleski, Carol. *Otherworld Journeys*. New York: Oxford University Press, 1987.

——. "Religious Experience: Why Does It Embarrass Theologians?" Unpublished essay, 1992.

Zimdars-Swartz, Sandra. *Encountering Mary: From La Salette to Medjugorje*. Princeton, NJ: Princeton University Press, 1991.

Index

Biblical Names Index

Printed in the United States
109767LV00001BA/76/A